# SYMBOLS OF TRANSCENDENCE

LOUVAIN THEOLOGICAL & PASTORAL MONOGRAPHS
22

# SYMBOLS OF TRANSCENDENCE

## RELIGIOUS EXPRESSION IN THE THOUGHT OF LOUIS DUPRÉ

by Paul J. Levesque

PEETERS PRESS
LOUVAIN

W.B. EERDMANS

© Peeters, Bondgenotenlaan 153, B - 3000 Leuven (BELGIUM), 1997

D. 1997/0602/70
ISBN 90-6831-961-2

*for my father and my mother*

who are always
symbols of love for me

# CONTENTS

# FOREWORD

## by Louis DUPRÉ

Having to introduce a study on one's work appears a pleasant enough task. But the pleasure comes not without some discomfort. The critic encompasses in a single vision what for the author was a succession of false starts, renewed attempts, many failures, and occasional insights. Writing from a distance the critic perceives implications and applications of which the author had remained unaware. Reading the present competent study I realize that I must leave the interpretation and assessment of my efforts to others. But regardless of their success or failure, Paul Levesque has, in his own way, grasped the need for a philosophy of symbols for maintaining a central segment of Christian doctrine and practice against the onslaught of modern thought.

Simultaneously with the need of transcendence that modern believers increasingly feel, they have become intensely aware of the difficulty a historical faith encounters in attempting to satisfy it. Lessing's "ugly, broad ditch" between eternal truths and historical events appears to have widened despite the efforts of biblical hermeneutics to fill it. Many long to integrate an existence fractured by distending forces within an all-encompassing transcendent unity. Yet, at least in the West, ever fewer find it in the historical words and events that have given meaning to past generations. Our spiritual quest appears to have moved entirely to an existential *now*, in which the remote Gospel story appears to have lost its meaning. What started in the eighteenth century as the predicament of an intellectual elite has grown into an almost universal problem for the educated of our time.

To a major extent we must blame the loss of symbolic perceptiveness for this state of affairs. Our exclusively objective
conception of truth, so successful in the sciences, has closed off
the symbolic perspective within which alone religious meaning
can become manifest. In recent years resistance to the objectivist view has gained strength. In art and literature symbolic
sensitivity was, of course, never lost, and today it has become
more refined than ever. But with respect to the "truth" of the
foundational words and events of the Christian faith, we still
feel restricted by the strictly literal interpretation, recognizing
no other assessment than the conclusions attained by historical-
critical methods. Thus these paradigmatic words and events
become reduced to the level of mere *facts*. Even believers attach
an exaggerated significance to methods which, however justified in themselves, when applied as exclusive means of interpretation, relegate the origins of faith to the area of historical
memory.

The literalism that has determined the encounter with the founding
deeds of our faith has weakened our capacity for grasping their
sacramental nature. Yet, as the Greek Fathers knew, the historical
report need not exclude symbolic meaning. Events may be situated
in a well-defined historical past and yet function as signs referring to
a transhistorical permanent reality. Only those capable of perceiving
this symbolic reference can convert transient actions into repeatable
rituals, inexhaustible fountains of grace. The issue extends well
beyond the field of sacramentology narrowly defined. If the words
of the Bible contain more than an historical meaning, subject
to philological criticism like any other ancient text, they must
also function as sanctifying symbols that surpass their historical
limitations.

Paul Levesque shows the need for a philosophy of truth as
symbolic disclosure for the justification of that sacramental vision

essential to Christianity. I am gratified that he found some of my ideas useful for this important task.

Louis DUPRÉ
*Yale University*

# PREFACE

While there have been countless hours of private research and work in solitude to produce this work, it has been an endeavor that I would call fundamentally "relational." I would like to thank those who have been an integral part of this experience. Sections of this book originally appeared as part of my doctoral dissertation at the Katholieke Universiteit, Leuven (Louvain, Belgium). In its initial form I took the opportunity of offering my fervent thanks to many people. While echoing these once again, of necessity I must limit my remarks.

First, I offer profound appreciation to my promotor, Prof. Dr. Lambert Leijssen for his professional direction, precision about detail, and constant encouragement. His spirit exemplifies that in the rigorous academic pursuits of scholarship and learning, human compassion and personal sensitivity are never supplemental accessories. I am indebted to Prof. Louis Dupré not only for the dialogue between author and reader, but for allowing this relation to move beyond the written page to a more personal exchange of ideas. I thank him for his generous assistance in compiling the bibliography of his works, his graciousness in meeting with me in Milwaukee and Kortrijk, and his abundant willingness to direct and read my work, while providing innumerable suggestions. I am grateful to him for revealing to me his erudition which is coupled by his human concern and Christian commitment. I thank Profs. Kristiaan Depoortere and Jozef Lamberts for their supportive work as correctors. I am grateful to Profs. Terrence Merrigan, Lambert Leijssen, the board of *LTPM*, and the reviewer for their gracious efforts in bringing this volume to publication.

I thank those who encouraged me during my writing, including Ferdinand Santos, Christopher Fusco, Arul Pragasam, James Zona, William Yip, and especially Michael Frisch. My gratitude to Jocelyn Lacson, Luth Lacson, and particularly Edith Marik for their generosity in offering their time and research skills. I thank Gordon Moreland, S.J. and Pat Philbin, S.M. for welcoming me on many days to the House of Prayer, which for me became the House of Study.

My project has taken me to numerous libraries for research. I offer particular thanks to Patricia Fessier, the Director of St. John's Seminary Edward L. Doheny Library and to Mary DiNielli for their kind assistance in locating copies of certain specialized journals and books.

Finally, I offer my deepest gratitude to those who have stood by me the longest — my mother, father and sister. Of all those who have assisted me in this project, no one has been more attentive at every stage than my father. He labored in both Leuven and California, trekking to numerous libraries, searching for books, photocopying, cataloging, and proofreading. He mastered the systems of more libraries in Leuven than most students even step inside. Thank you for everything.

# ABBREVIATIONS

**Abbreviations of Frequently Cited Works by Louis Dupré**
Numbers in [] refer to entry numbers in the bibliography.

AESTHETIC      "Aesthetic Perception and Its Relation to Ordinary Perception," in *Aisthesis and Aesthetics,* The Fourth Lexington Conference on Pure and Applied Phenomenology 1967, ed. Erwin Straus and Richard Griffith (Pittsburgh: Duquesne University Press; Louvain: Nauwelaerts, 1970), 171-177. [A65]

CL      *The Common Life: The Origins of Trinitarian Mysticism and its Development by Jan Ruusbroec* (New York: Crossroad, 1984). [A179]

DH      *A Dubious Heritage: Studies in the Philosophy of Religion after Kant* (New York: Paulist Press, 1977; New York: Newmann Books, 1979). [A127]

DL      *The Deeper Life: An Introduction to Christian Mysticism* (New York: Crossroad, 1981). [A154]

KT      *Kierkegaard As Theologian: The Dialectic of Christian Existence* (New York: Sheed & Ward, 1963; reprint, London: Sheed & Ward, 1964). [A10]

LL      *Light from Light: An Anthology of Christian Mysticism* (New York: Paulist Press, 1988). [A221]

MC      *Metaphysics and Culture,* The Aquinas Lecture 1994 (Milwaukee: Marquette University Press, 1994). [A280]

MYSTICISM      "Mysticism," in *The Encyclopedia of Religion,* vol. 10, ed. Mircea Eliade (New York: Macmillan, 1987), 245-261. [A213]

NEGATIVE        "Negative Theology and Affirmation of the Finite,"
                in *Experience, Reason and God,* Studies in Philosophy
                and the History of Philosophy 8, ed. Eugene Long
                (Washington, D.C., 1980), 149-157. [A146]

OD              *The Other Dimension: A Search for the Meaning of
                Religious Attitudes* (New York: Doubleday, 1972).
                [A77]

PM              *Passage to Modernity: An Essay in the Hermeneutics
                of Nature and Culture* (New Haven: Yale University
                Press, 1993). [A274]

RITUAL          "Ritual: The Sacralization of Time," *Revue de
                l'Université d'Ottawa* 55 (October-December 1985):
                261-269. [A197]

SH              *De symboliek van het heilige,* trans. Guido Vanhees-
                wijck, intro. Jacques De Visscher (Kampen: Kok
                Agora; Kapellen: DNB/Pelckmans, 1991). [A260]

SPIRITUAL       "Spiritual Life in a Secular Age," *Daedalus* 111
                (Winter 1982): 21-31. [A171]

TS              *Transcendent Selfhood: The Loss and Rediscovery of
                the Inner Life* (New York: Seabury, 1976). [A112]

# INTRODUCTION

Symbol, transcendence, mysticism, self, culture: these are the main themes that are interwoven within the works of Louis Dupré. Never content to enumerate a static exposition of details, he unites philosophy, theology, history, the sciences, and the arts in creating the tapestry of his thought. In doing so, he argues numerous points and proposes an even greater number of questions to ponder. Throughout his writings on philosophy of religion, symbols which manifest the transcendent emerge as the primary expression for the interpretation of religious thought.

Louis Dupré was born in Veerle, Belgium. He received a Licentiate in Philosophy from the Berchmanianum in Nijmegen, The Netherlands in 1950 and a Ph.D. from the Higher Institute of Philosophy in Louvain in 1952. His doctoral dissertation on the starting point of Marxist philosophy was published two years later under a government grant. Emigrating to the United States in 1958, he taught philosophy at Georgetown University until 1972. In 1973 he was appointed T. Lawrason Riggs Professor in Philosophy of Religion at Yale University, a position he continues to hold at the present. He has lectured at universities in the United States, Belgium, The Netherlands, Ireland, and Italy. He is past president of the Hegel Society of America and the American Catholic Philosophical Association and was elected a member of the Royal Belgian Academy of Letters, Arts and Sciences, and of the American Academy of Arts and Sciences. Honorary doctorates have been conferred upon him from Loyola College, Baltimore, Sacred Heart University, Fairfield, and Georgetown University. He received Yale's Phi Beta Kappa medal as Teacher of the Year (1996) and the

Aquinas Medal from the American Catholic Philosophical Association for outstanding work in philosophy (1997). As the bibliography enumerates, Dupré has written over a dozen books and has edited another six. He has published over 150 original articles in a variety of academic and scholarly journals. Some of these books and articles have been translated into Dutch, French, German, Polish, Spanish, Chinese, and Korean. Prof. Dupré's writings often read like a who's who in the humanities which serves to illustrate the breadth of his knowledge and the expanse of his scholarship.

The main objective of this book is to demonstrate that in Louis Dupre's work all religious expression, insofar as it has a transcendent reference, is intrinsically symbolic. Religious language is never purely objective nor purely subjective, but a dialectical relation with a transcendent dimension; as such religion is never detachable from its symbolic expression.

In investigating symbols of transcendence, Chapter One first asserts the necessity of employing symbols in general for religious expression. We begin by taking a look at the meaning of "religious" for Dupré, in order to clarify our field of interest. Then, a twofold justification to speak of symbol as primary is presented. The first is theological and proceeds from Dupré's conception of mysticism as belonging to the essence of religious faith. Mysticism must use the language of symbols, and since Dupré argues that a mystical impulse belongs to the core of religion, religion of necessity must employ symbolic language. The second argument is philosophical, employing Schleiermacher polemically and Hegel in a more positive fashion. In contrast to Schleiermacher, Dupré distinguishes religious experience which requires symbolic expression from a purely aesthetic feeling which does not. In agreement with Hegel, Dupré accepts religion as representation, and interprets this as asserting the necessary use of symbols for religious expression. The justification also extends beyond the question at hand to the larger justification of the methodology that Dupré embraces, which is to some extent both philosophical and theological, phenomenological and ontological.

The second and third chapters study in detail Dupré's appreciation of symbol. Chapter Two investigates Dupré's symbol theory in general. It begins with an outline of certain features of the thought of Cassirer, Hegel, and Langer. These authors are foundational for Dupré's perception of symbol. Next, symbols are discussed in their necessary relationship to Dupré's interest in culture and metaphysical ultimacy. In addition, three general patterns essential to understanding symbols are culled from Dupré's thought. They are form, representation, and language. In investigating these concepts, key elements of Dupré's general regard for symbols are manifested. Chapter Three applies this general knowledge to the specific religious symbols of ritual, sacraments, and religious art. At this point in our presentation we are prepared to single out transcendence as the unique referent that sets symbols which give rise to religious understanding apart from symbols which do not.

Chapter Four examines the modern inability to fully form religious symbols. In the history of Western culture, the shift from premodernity to modernity entails the breakup of the unified concept of nature into its component parts of cosmic, human, and transcendent spheres. This fracturing occurs in the eviction of transcendence to a realm distinct from nature, and in the severing of the human subject from the cosmos. These occurrences created a new situation in which human culture became devoid of a transcendent dimension. This predicament is still operative today as Dupré designates the contemporary scene more properly as "late modernity" than "postmodernity." Without a transcendent referent, religious symbols lose their religious significance. While some suggest solutions such as returning to the past or locating transcendence within secular experiences, Dupré advances an inward turn akin to the mystical practice of past ages. This does not recover a sense of transcendence for culture, however, but it is successful in doing so for one's personal spiritual life. The fourth chapter develops these ideas under three sections detailing first, the move from premodernity to modernity, second, the modern situation and third, hope for the future.

Lastly, I have compiled a complete bibliographical tool of all of the works of Louis Dupré through June 1997. I have also collected an extensive listing of reviews of Dupré's books and other works on his thought.

The main methodology of this project is a synchronic investigation of Dupré's thought. While some historical ordering of his books and articles will be noted, the primary presentation is by way of synthesis. The strategy of this book is not to critique his works, but to provide an elucidation and application of his conception of symbols and the ideas it entails. Note that in his earlier writings Dupré followed the accepted style of his day employing masculine pronouns instead of inclusive terms. We will leave the quotations as originally printed, acknowledging this limitation here and recognizing that in later works he is sensitive to this need.

# CHAPTER ONE

# JUSTIFICATION OF "SYMBOL" AS PRIMARY EXPRESSION OF RELIGIOUS UNDERSTANDING

As we begin this study, we seek to justify both the statement that "symbols in general are primary to the expression of religious understanding" and the method that Dupré uses to make this assertion. Addressing the statement itself, Dupré offers both a theological and a philosophical justification. One should not expect to open his books or articles and find these justifications didactically worked out. Rather, it is the underlying thread which is woven through certain works.

As preparation to help elucidate our justification, we will first examine the meaning of the term "religious" for Dupré. Then, turning to find justification to assert symbol as primary expression for religious understanding in Dupré's thought, we begin the search from a theological perspective. We start with mysticism, since Dupré considers it the purest form of the religious experience. This leads the discussion to the notions of image mysticism, negative theology, and Trinity; these are tied together in their capacity as mystical language. Underneath and essential to this development of mysticism is the concept of symbol. Next, from a philosophical perspective, we single out Dupré's interpretation of Schleiermacher and Hegel. As he identifies a deficiency in the former and a strength in the latter, we uncover a philosophical warrant for asserting symbol as primary in expressing religious understanding. Finally, to complete this initial chapter on justification, we investigate Dupré's own methodology to examine its effectiveness and limitations.

## A. "RELIGIOUS"

Before we can begin to make our theological or philosophical case, we must take a look at the term religious, to help to clarify the meaning of "religious understanding." "Religious" can connote a variety of meanings, from pietistical emotionalism to staunch institutionalism. We will concentrate upon its meaning for Dupré, and for him it implies neither of these two extremes. In clarifying Dupré's view it would be a false distinction to force a separation in his thought between "religious" and "religion." *Religion* develops out of the *religious* attitude. Thus, here we will speak both of "religious" and the religious attitude as embodied in "religion."

### 1. *Neither Purely Objective nor Purely Subjective*

Oftentimes, a definition of the essence of religion is presented, or key universal characteristics are proposed, or it is clarified by opposition to a notion such as faith. But for Dupré such demarcations do not respect the complexities of the term: "religion has no definable 'essence', for religion never *is* — it always becomes."[1] This is to say that the religious attitude is not purely objective, but neither is it purely subjective for Dupré. Instead, religion must be viewed as "a complex dialectical relation of the mind to reality."[2] Dupré further explains:

> [religion is] dialectical because it is both active and passive, but primarily because it continues to negate its acquired positions. In the process it opens up a new dimension in human existence. But it is never an *a priori* definable reality.[3]

---

[1] Louis Dupré, *The Other Dimension: A Search for the Meaning of Religious Attitudes* (New York: Doubleday, 1972), 19-20. [Hereafter *OD*].

[2] *OD*, 2.

[3] *OD*, 2.

Viewed objectively, religion could be the acceptance of a reality as sacred. But objects are not sacred or profane in and of themselves; "every object is potentially religious ... [and] no object is sacred *in itself*."[4] The sacred can be discovered in all domains of life; and for any individual at any given time, anything can be considered sacred since an object is sacred through the attitude which a person brings to it. Dupré does acknowledge that different religions do possess objective qualities that can be categorized, but these characteristics "can never be deduced from an *a priori* form nor can they be reduced to a common denominator."[5] Doing so would deny not only the uniqueness between religions, but also the changes in the religious attitude through history.

There have also been a number of other objectivistic approaches to religion which, in viewing the positive sciences as the only valid strategy, attempt to impose this methodology. In simplified terms, the argument may at its roots be similar to: since only object language is admissible, and religious speech is not object directed, religious assertions are not possible, or at best not meaningful. Dupré argues against these approaches as manifested in materialism, naturalism, logical positivism, neopositivism, and devotes his strongest efforts against those who advocate the principle of falsifiability to demonstrate the meaninglessness of religious assertions.[6] Religious evidence should not be put in the same class with scientific evidence nor be treated as such.

Viewed subjectively, the religious attitude is purely a state of consciousness. This position is equally unacceptable to Dupré.

---

[4] *OD*, 14.
[5] *OD*, 20.
[6] On these various approaches see *OD*, 63-72. Also see *OD*, 207 and below beginning on p. 99.

He disagrees with what he calls an 'empiricist view of religion' which reduces religion to a subjective experience. He argues that the psychological approaches of Carl Jung, Sigmund Freud, and William James provide significant insights into the understanding of religious attitudes, but are inadequate insofar as they purport to explain religion in its entirety.[7] A related philosophical approach would advocate God's existence only as an idea in the human mind. Feuerbach remains a clear expression of this thought, holding that human attributes are projected into an imaginary world above, creating God.[8] Today, this view has taken different forms with Phillips[9] and Cupitt,[10] for example, yet the terminus remains human and could never be a response to transcendent reality.

## 2. *The Religious Attitude is Dialectical*

For Dupré, religion is not constituted by an object that is sacred in and of itself; religion requires a full involvement of the human subject, without being purely subjective. In addition, and of greater consequence, the "religious attitude is *dialectical* insofar as it is a relation (and therefore an opposition) to a transcendent term."[11] This is evidenced within the religious act itself as explained in the introduction to *The Other Dimension*, where Dupré summarizes the basic message of the book:

[7] See *OD*, 82-94.

[8] See Ludwig Feuerbach, *The Essence of Christianity*, trans. George Eliot (New York: Harper & Row, 1957). Also see *OD*, 99-104.

[9] See e.g., Dewi Phillips, "Faith, Scepticism and Religious Understanding," in *Religion and Understanding*, ed. Dewi Phillips (Oxford: Basil Blackwell, 1967), 63-79.

[10] See Don Cupitt, *Taking Leave of God* (London: SCM Press; New York: Crossroad, 1980). For Cupitt, our spiritual ideals are personified into an imaginary God.

[11] *OD*, 15.

The religious act is not a simple experience, but a complex movement by which the mind discovers a new reality which, although lying beyond the phenomenal and contrasting with it, ultimately integrates all reality in a higher synthesis.[12]

When he does hazard a working definition of "religious," it is this transcendent quality which is primary, "As I use the term 'religious' here, it will refer exclusively to the need for, and the presence of, a transcendent dimension in human existence, in whatever form or shape it may be expressed."[13] Similarly, he refers to religion "as a personal relation to the transcendent."[14] The relation to the transcendent term must always include some level of opposition, otherwise the distinction would cease to exist between immanent and transcendent reality. Still, the dialectical tension acknowledges the *attainment of* the transcendent and not merely a *reaching toward*, as the religious act continues to negate its positions.[15]

However, one could raise the objection that a recognition of absolute reality is not necessarily religious. Dupré in fact holds this position: "Yet the distinction between absolute and relative being is not *per se* religious: it also appears in nonreligious metaphysical speculation. A further specification is needed."[16]

---

[12] *OD*, 10.

[13] Louis Dupré, "The Religious Crisis of Our Culture," in *The Crisis of Culture*, Analecta Husserliana 5, ed. Anna-Teresa Tymieniecka (Dordrecht, Holland: D. Reidel, 1976), 205.

[14] Louis Dupré, "Meditations on Secular Theology," *The Christian Century* (November 20, 1968): 1471.

[15] See *OD*, 108: "The religious act does not 'reach' toward an unknown transcendence. It attains it. ... the religious act attains its terminus, but never possess it: it makes its terminus immanent only by constituting it as entirely transcendent. The paradox of the act of faith is that it throws a bridge by declaring the gap unbridgeable."

[16] *OD*, 14.

What makes the religious perception of absolute reality unique is its *dialectical* and *symbolic* nature.

As to its dialectical nature, following what has been said above, without entering into faith a philosophical distinction between transcendence and immanence cannot attain the same dialectical relation found within the religious act. Philosophy may argue to an absolute being, but only the religious act can transform it into an awareness of God. In speaking of "God," the philosopher begins not from philosophy but from religious faith. "For the concept of God originates exclusively in, and is developed solely by, the religious act. It never is a philosophical discovery and no philosophical argument can prove it to be true or false."[17] This does not imply that philosophy cannot add to the discussion on the concept of God. On the contrary, "philosophy provides this key religious concept with a logical structure enabling it to justify the central position which faith claims for it."[18]

In transforming a philosophical awareness of the transcendent into an awareness of God, the religious act provides the basis for a commitment, and in fact requires a commitment. This is not the type of commitment as advocated by secular theologians such as van Buren, who views commitment as a moral attitude without any need of a transcendent term.[19] Dupré maintains that some type of transcendence is necessary for a commitment to the gospel to be understandable or justifiable. There are clearer moral writers and systems to follow than the Bible. The distinguishing factor is its relation to the transcendent. "One thing can make the commitment

---

[17] *OD*, 11. See *OD*, 112: "My thesis is that philosophy alone never reaches the idea of God." On this position of Dupré, see Joseph Donceel, review of *The Other Dimension*, in *International Philosophical Quarterly* 15 (March 1975): 100-105.

[18] *OD*, 11.

[19] See Paul van Buren, *The Secular Meaning of the Gospel* (London: SCM Press, 1963), 193-200.

to Christ different from any other moral commitment: the transcendent authority of the teacher and of the message."[20] As the basis *for* commitment, the religious act of naming the transcendent also compels the believer *to* a commitment by its very nature. The believer commits to a transcendent named "God" and the believer must speak to God and ultimately about God. This immanent language does not and cannot explain the transcendent God, but relies on the symbolic quality of the religious perception.

## 3. *The Religious Attitude is Symbolic*

The symbolic quality also distinguishes the religious perception of the transcendent from a nonreligious one. This is because "religion expresses its meaning in symbols."[21] For example, while the universe is often experienced in its vastness as mysterious, this is not necessarily a religious perception. To a religious perception, the universe in its mystery "conveys, upon reflection, a symbol of an *overwhelming*, transcendent *reality*."[22] At a basic level, science searches for empirical facts, philosophy argues to the way things are, while the religious term is always symbolic in the truth it wishes to convey. Yet, these symbols which express the religious attitude are always viewed as inadequate; they are limited within the dialectic of immanence and transcendence.

There are also two traits of the religious attitude which Dupré designates as essential. They are "[1] dissatisfaction with empirical reality and [2] unlimited hope of ultimate liberation."[23] These two traits are joined in the religious term "salvation." "Religion is

---

[20] Dupré, "Meditations on Secular Theology," 1471.
[21] *OD*, 66.
[22] *OD*, 28.
[23] *OD*, 19.

always directed towards salvation,"[24] beyond the limits and struggles of life. Yet, salvation is always in process, leading one to union with the transcendent, but never fully possessing it, otherwise the distinction would cease to exist. Here, once again, we see the dialectical quality of a religious term. The dialectical tension between immanence and transcendence is operative, leading one from empirical reality and attaining the transcendent, yet prohibiting the completion of ultimate liberation.

### 4. *The Religious Attitude Integrates*

Finally, to complete this overview of the meaning of "religious" for Dupré, we turn to Donald Berry who counts Dupré with Michael Novak, John Dewey and H. Richard Niebuhr as exemplifying an approach to religion that he labels, "hermeneutics as integration."[25] Berry begins by arguing that what is genuinely "religious" is better understood not by referring to various 'states of affairs' in the world, but understanding religion as a 'way of regarding the world'. By religious 'states of affairs' Berry has in mind the outward expression of religion through ritual, practice, organization and the like, as well as inner experiences of depth, consciousness, etc. By a religious 'way of regarding the world', Berry means accepting 'a general point of view' of life which is religious.

Applying Kurt Baier's idea of morality as a point of view, Berry proposes two formal conditions for anything to be a point of view:

---

[24] Gerardus Van der Leeuw, *Religion in Essence and Manifestation: A Study in Phenomenology*, trans. J. Turner (London: Allen & Unwin, 1938; reprint in two vols., with additions of the second German edition by Hans Penner, New York: Harper & Row, 1963), § 108, 3. In *OD*, 19 n. 19, Dupré nuances this passage, "This statement is certainly correct for cultural religion. Whether the term 'salvation' would be appropriate for primitive religion is a matter of dispute."

[25] Donald Berry, "Religion as a Point of View," *Perspectives in Religious Studies* 9 (Fall 1982): 209- 227, especially 221-224.

1) the ambiguity of experience and 2) the creativity of the subject. He identifies the second condition as present in Dupré's thought. Berry further acknowledges five hermeneutical strategies which emphasize in varying degrees these two conditions. He identifies options which he designates as representation, recognition, decipherment, integration, and personalization, which, while not exhaustive, express religion in term of a religious point of view. In the category of integration, where he locates the thought of Dupré, the religious point of view is characterized as having "a transformative outcome for the perceiving subject."[26] It probably was not too difficult for Berry to place Dupré into this category (or build the category around him?) as Berry quotes Dupré, "Religion can change all its conceptual expressions but it must die when it can no longer integrate."[27] Yet, Berry critiques Dupré as not fully employing the first formal condition of ambiguity of experience. Integration may bring about destruction as well as preservation. Still, Berry finds satisfactory recognition of the condition of ambiguity in Dupré's comment that "it is in its integrating function that religion is most apt to degenerate into a power structure."[28] Since these are categories required by Berry, there is no purpose to argue with how he expects their embodiment, (though he was the one who chose Dupré and others as representative of his view in the first place).

We mention Berry's work because it is helpful in highlighting in Dupré's thought both religion as a point of view (religion not as objective) and its integrative quality. We must in fact move beyond Berry's reading, for he fails to even mention what is key to Dupré's perception of integration. While integration is transformative

---

[26] Berry, "Religion," 221.

[27] *OD*, 18. See Berry, "Religion," 221-222.

[28] *OD*, 19. Also see Berry, "Religion," 222, where he adds that these power structures (Berry makes the plural) are "presumably bad."

(the extent of Berry's assessment), it is primarily the "ability to reconcile opposites (including its own opposite) under an ultimate unity."[29] The religious perception discovers the original unity and participates in it by way of myth and ritual; only then does a transformation of the struggles of life begin to take place. This integration is "the ultimate aim of all religious experience."[30] It is completed by the mystical union which is the highest expression of religious meaning. We will therefore turn in our next section to mysticism in developing the theological justification for symbol as primary expression of religious understanding.

5. *Summary Sentence*

In summary (without attempting a definition of "religious," for this would produce a contradiction since it has no definable essence), we offer this sentence: For Dupré, religious understanding is neither purely objective nor purely subjective but in a dialectical relation with the transcendent (attaining it, yet always remaining distinct from it) expressed symbolically, in an attempt to give coherence and a new dimension to empirical life in hope of ultimate liberation. Keeping this in mind, we can now turn to the theological and philosophical justifications for stating that symbols in general are primary to the expression of religious understanding.

B. THEOLOGICAL JUSTIFICATION

While Dupré is primarily a philosopher of religion and does not claim to be a theologian *per se*, his inspiration is theological which

[29] *OD*, 18.
[30] *OD*, 545.

is then explained and developed philosophically. There are two of Dupré's works which are the clearest expression of this theological inspiration, namely, *The Deeper Life: An Introduction to Christian Mysticism*[31] and *The Common Life: The Origins of Trinitarian Mysticism and its Development by Jan Ruusbroec.*[32] Both are illustrations of Dupré's theology, as the first contains edited versions of nine lectures given to the monks of Gethsemani Abbey in Kentucky in 1975 and the second comprises five further lectures given at the abbey in 1982. From these two books and articles related to them, we will assert on the basis of his appreciation of the mystics, particularly their use of negative theology and understanding of the Trinity, that Dupré considers all religious experience essentially symbolic. In addition to these works which are primarily theological in focus, the last chapter of *The Other Dimension* where Dupré philosophically reflects upon the mystical vision is also pertinent to this first section.

## 1. *Introductory Comments on Mysticism*

Our purpose here is not to completely explain what Dupré holds to be mystical experience nor the distinctions he makes within it, but to do so insofar as this acknowledges the role mysticism plays in his theology. To begin to understand Dupré's theology, one must comprehend the primary place given to the mystics. In *The Other Dimension*, Dupré offers a philosophical reflection upon religious experience. The thrust of the book leads to the last chapter proclaiming the need for mystical contemplation for an experience

---

[31] Louis Dupré, *The Deeper Life: An Introduction to Christian Mysticism* (New York: Crossroad, 1981). [Hereafter *DL*].

[32] Louis Dupré, *The Common Life: The Origins of Trinitarian Mysticism and its Development by Jan Ruusbroec* (New York: Crossroad, 1984). [Hereafter *CL*].

of the other dimension.[33] His editorial work and words in *Light From Light*[34] and *Christian Spirituality*[35] as well as *The Deeper Life* and *The Common Life* also extol the ways of the mystics. Why is mysticism so important? "Mysticism in the widest sense, understood as some passively infused experience, belongs to the core of all religious faith, whether communal or private."[36] While this is not a definition of mysticism, it does suggest some key elements.[37] First of all, a mystical experience is passive. Even if the mystic engages in techniques of meditation or prepares himself or herself through practices such as fasting, the experience is given gratuitously and one no longer claims control; it is a grace. It is infused in that it permeates one's entire being. We may speak of soul, body, spirit, mind, and heart, but the experience encompasses all of these and contains both cognitive and emotive qualities. Common estimation often considers the mystical experience to be private, yet, at its root and properly understood, the mystical experience is communal.[38] As such, it belongs to communal faith as well as private.

[33] See Kenneth Schmitz, "Scrutinizing the Inscrutable. Critical Study: *The Other Dimension*, in *Review of Metaphysics* 27 (December 1973): 347: "The chapter on mystical vision does not merely close the book; it completes the author's investigation."

[34] Louis Dupré and James Wiseman, eds., *Light from Light: An Anthology of Christian Mysticism* (New York: Paulist Press, 1988). [Hereafter *LL*].

[35] Louis Dupré and Don Saliers, eds. in collaboration with John Meyendorff, *Christian Spirituality III: Post-Reformation and Modern*, World Spirituality: An Encyclopedic History of the Religious Quest 18 (New York: Crossroad, 1989).

[36] *DL*, 20.

[37] See Louis Dupré, "Mysticism," in *The Encyclopedia of Religion*, ed. Mircea Eliade, vol. 10 (New York: Macmillan, 1987), 245: "No definition could be both meaningful and sufficiently comprehensive to include all experiences that, at some point or other, have been described as 'mystical.' " [Hereafter MYSTICISM].

[38] See *DL*, 19: "Never, in the patristic period, did the term mystical refer to a purely subjective, private experience. Experience it was, but the experience of the entire Christian community. The Eastern Church has preserved this communal sense of the term even today." Also see *OD*, 485.

These key elements generally take into account, and are enhanced by, the four characteristics of mystical experience proposed by William James: ineffability, noetic quality, transiency, and passivity.[39] Dupré suggests that instead of transiency we should speak of the rhythmic quality, since 'transiency' has been correctly challenged on the grounds that some mystic states are rather prolonged. To speak of a rhythmic quality illustrates that there are moments of intense experience within the extended state. Dupré also adds a fifth characteristic of the capacity to integrate all appositions in a transcendent reality. Yet, to maintain the religious character, a sense of transcendence must remain, and therefore a certain tension prohibiting total integration.

Finally, and most importantly for our project, mysticism "belongs to the core of all religious faith."[40] This does not mean that mysticism is the essence of religion. It does mean "that the mystical *belongs* to the very essence of every religion, even though that essence usually contains other elements as well."[41] An objection, that Dupré himself acknowledges, raises the question that if mysticism belongs to the essence of religion, how is it that so few people have a mystical religious experience.[42] Further, if mysticism

[39] See William James, *The Varieties of Religious Experience*, The Gifford Lectures 1901-1902 (London: Longman, Green, 1902; reprint, New York: Collier Books, 1961), 299-301. For an outline of a number of other related lists and approaches see Cheslyn Jones, "Mysticism, Human and Divine," in *The Study of Spirituality*, ed. Cheslyn Jones, Geoffrey Wainwright, and Edward Yarnold (London: SPCK, 1986), 17-24.

[40] *DL*, 20.

[41] *LL*, 6-7. Notice that Dupré remains consistent in his terminology. *LL*, 6-7, quoted; *OD*, 486: "It permeates the entire religious experience"; *DL*, 20: "[It] belongs to the core of all religious faith."

[42] Gilkey is most critical: "I found it surprising that at the end of the book mysticism, again in its Christian forms, was clearly affirmed to represent the highest level of religious existence. ... Such a *descriptive* judgment is impossible because there are too many forms of Christian piety (not to mention other religions)

belongs to the core of faith, how is it that Christianity does not identify holiness with the attainment of mystical states, as do other religions like Vedantic Hinduism? Also related is the basic question, why is mysticism part of the essence of religion?

A twofold answer addresses these questions. First, it is true that the vast majority of people do not attain mystical contemplation. However, every religious person participates, even at the lowest level, in the mystic's experience. For example, prayers of intercession for others, petition, thanksgiving and confession seek communication and thus a type of union with God. At some point or other the religious person experiences the presence of God, perhaps in the joys and sorrows of life, in nature, or in ritual expression. "Without some share of spiritual experience religion withers away in sterile ritualism, arid moralism, or theological intellectualism."[43] Mysticism belongs to the essence of religion because to some degree or other every religious person has some sort of mystical experience. This can be further appreciated by introducing the term 'unio mystica' or 'mystical union'. "All monotheist religion aims at some union with God."[44] But this does not require every religious person to gain full mystical union. Instead,

which to an unbiased mind must be given their own Christian authenticity and yet which are consciously unmystical or even anti-mystical in character." Langdon Gilkey, "The Dimensions of Dupré" review of *The Other Dimension*, in *Commonweal* 97 (October 20, 1972): 66. There are also these searing words of Clark Pinnock, review of *The Other Dimension*, in *Christianity Today* (December 8, 1972): 255: "He is another Catholic author who, with Bultmann's demythologizing of the New Testament for his guide, has begun his pilgrimage to the contentless mysticism of the East. ... This book is yet another sad monument to the move within modern Catholicism toward the theological ambiguity that has been the blight of protestantism." Also see Robert Ayers, review of *The Other Dimension*, in *International Journal for Philosophy of Religion* 6 (Fall 1975): 197.

[43] *LL*, 7.

[44] Louis Dupré, "The Christian Experience of Mystical Union," *The Journal of Religion* 69 (January 1989): 11.

most religious individuals will view mystical union as a spiritual or moral ideal to bring one to perfection. What distinguishes the mystic's perception from the average believer's view is that rather than being a spiritual or moral ideal, mystical union is the full expression of all being. "The mystic ... emerges as the *homo religiosus* par excellence, the one who recognizes that reality remains incomplete until it becomes reunited with its source."[45] While the ordinary believer may never achieve such a notion of union, he or she clearly recognizes the general merit of union with God. Thus, throughout this book when we speak of 'mysticism' it should be understood more in the sense of what we call a 'spiritual experience'.

Second, an inclination toward mysticism is present from the beginning of Christianity through the desire to attain union with God. The term "*unio mystica*" probably appeared as early as the fourth century, with it sources in the New Testament. The words and actions of Jesus as portrayed in the synoptic Gospels "present Jesus as dwelling in the continuous, intimate presence of God."[46] Dupré suggests that in the Gospel of John there is a clear expression of the mystical life of Jesus. There is the union of the Word

---

[45] Dupré, "The Christian Experience of Mystical Union," 11-12. Also see this article for a more complete view of Dupré's understanding of mystical union. For example, pertinent to our discussion is the traditional distinction between *unitas spiritus* (unity of mind) and *unitas indistinctionis* (ontological or substantial unity). Dupré suggests their interdependence.

[46] MYSTICISM, 251. Dupré continues by offering these examples: "His public life begins with a prayer and a vision: 'While Jesus after his baptism was at prayer, heaven opened and the Holy spirit descended on him in bodily shape like a dove' (*Lk.* 3:21-22). It ends with a prayer of total abandonment: 'Father, into your hands I commend my spirit' (*Lk.* 23:46). Jesus initiates all important public acts with a prayer. He often withdraws from the crowd for long periods of solitary prayer. He interprets his entire existence through its reference to God, whom he calls Father. To himself he applies Isaiah's messianic words: 'The Spirit of the Lord is upon me.' The same Spirit he promise to those who pray in his name."

with God and in becoming flesh not only continues this union, but extends it to his followers through the spirit.[47]

At first glance, it may appear that exegetical studies suggest a different interpretation. Raymond Brown writes, "It should be noted that none of these passages [i.e., John 14:17, 21; Matthew 28:20; and others] is concerned with the presence of Jesus encountered by mystics; the presence of Jesus is promised, not to an ascetical elite, but to Christians in general."[48] However, this does not actually refute Dupré's position, for Brown envisions mystical union with Jesus as attainable only by a privileged few. But we have noted above that mysticism belongs to the core of the Christian religion not because most Christians attain a profound mystical state, but because all Christians enter mystical union to some degree or other.

Still, Brown's argument may be understood at a deeper level. Turning to Brown's study of the word μένειν (remain, abide, stay, dwell) he claims that "None of the Johannine passages appears to be a reference to ecstatic experience."[49] Combining this sentence with the one quoted above, we can say that for Brown, "mystics" are those "ascetical elite" who have "ecstatic experience[s]." This is certainly a common view of mystics. But Dupré is not satisfied with an average interpretation. Dupré is aware that even the term "mystic" "was not used as a noun until the sixteenth century."[50] So, in response to Brown's statements, we invoke the following distinction by Dupré: "we should distinguish the general state of

---

[47] See John 14:10-21.

[48] Raymond Brown, *The Gospel According to John*, vol. 2, The Anchor Bible 29A (Garden City, NY: Doubleday, 1966; London: Geoffrey Chapman, 1971), 646.

[49] Raymond Brown, *The Gospel According to John*, vol. 1, The Anchor Bible 29 (Garden City, NY: Doubleday, 1966; London: Geoffrey Chapman 1971), 510.

[50] Dupré, "The Christian Experience of Mystical Union," 2.

[mystical] union, which implies a unified vision of reality, from those ecstatic experiences that occasionally accompany it, but by no means constitute its essence."[51] The ecstatic experience is not to be equated with mystical union *per se*. Dupré notes the continual historical debate over the need and type of union. Brown refutes the idea that later understandings of mystical union are found in the Bible, and Dupré would agree with this. Unfortunately, Brown then jettisons any credence to mystical union in the Bible, which is unacceptable to Dupré. "Despite all deviations and excesses, there rarely was any doubt [through history] about the essential principle, namely, that in a most intimate way the Christian becomes united with God in Christ."[52] Thus, mystical union is not always ecstatic and this is not the type of mystical union that one should expect to locate in the Bible. Dupré speaks of the "mystical impulse"[53] in the Bible, not a fully developed ecstatic experience.

Biblical scholarship further suggests that in John μένειν imparts an obligation toward others. Brown uses this fact as further proof against finding in John an "exalted mysticism"; we quote at length his assertion:

> From xiv 10-11 and xvii 21, 33, there can be no doubt that the intimate indwelling of Father and Son is being transferred through the Son to the Christian. ... The mutual indwelling of the Father and the Son is not a static but a dynamic relation. ... common indwelling, life, and love are but different facets of the basic unity binding Father, Son, and believer (xvii 11, 21, 23). Divine indwelling is an

---

[51] Dupré, "The Christian Experience of Mystical Union," 5. Also see p. 2 note 2 where Dupré acknowledges his affinity with von Balthasar. See Hans Urs von Balthasar, *The Glory of the Lord: A Theological Aesthetics*, vol. 1, *Seeing the Form*, trans. Erasmo Leiva-Merikakis, ed. Joseph Fessio and John Riches (Edinburgh: T. & T. Clark, 1982; San Francisco: Ignatius Press; New York: Crossroad, 1985), 378: "A mysticism of radical union is necessarily alien to the 'spiritual senses', but it is likewise alien to the Christian way as such."

[52] Dupré, "The Christian Experience of Mystical Union," 2.

[53] MYSTICISM, 251.

intimate union that expresses itself in a way of life lived in love. If we understand this truth, we shall avoid the mistaken identification of John's concept of indwelling with an exalted mysticism like that of a Teresa or of a John of the Cross. To remain in Jesus, or in the Father, or in one of the divine attributes or gifts is intimately associated with keeping the commandments in a spirit of love (John xv 10; I John iv 12, 16), with a struggle against the world (I John ii 16-17), and with bearing fruit (John xv 5) — all basic Christian duties.[54]

We have already indicated that Dupré agrees that one cannot prove an exalted mysticism in the Bible. However, the necessity of outward service does not preclude the interpretation of mystical union, in fact it strengthens it. Dupré finds this quality as necessarily operative in Christian mysticism: "No mysticism can claim to be Christian that does not include a spiritual love for the creature."[55] This is probably the most distinctive character of Christian mysticism.[56] The mystic "must combine a contemplative life with one of active service ... the two intimately collaborate and reinforce each other."[57]

[54] Brown, *Gospel According to John*, 1:511-512. Also see Rudolf Schnackenburg, *The Gospel According to St. John*, trans. Kevin Smyth, vol. 1 (New York: Crossroad, 1987), 162: "The Johannine 'mysticism' of fellowship with Christ is inseparable from ethics. 'Bringing forth fruit' is the goal of 'abiding' in the vine, 15:4-8; 'abiding in the love of Christ' presupposes the keeping of his commandments, 15:9f. ... The 'new' commandment of brotherly love, in which moral exhortation is summed up and crowned, is outlined in its novelty and uniqueness in view of Christ: 'that you love one another, as I have loved you' (13:34)."

[55] *DL*, 54.

[56] See *DL*, 53: "What is perhaps the most distinctive and certainly the most admirable quality of Christian mysticism, namely, its capacity to embrace all creatures in the one act of divine love. The Christian mystic loves all life, also deformed, sickly or even dying life, because he or she cherishes that life *for its own sake*, not for its capacity to please or fulfil him or her."

[57] Dupré, "The Christian Experience of Mystical Union," 7-8. See Evelyn Underhill, *Mysticism* (London: Methuen, 1930[12]), 414: "It is the peculiarity of the unitive life that it is often lived, in its highest and most perfect form, in the world; and exhibits its works before the eyes of men." Also see below, p. 29 for a comment on Jan van Ruusbroec on rest and work.

Brown concludes, "Thus, indwelling is not the exclusive experience of chosen souls within the Christian community; it is the essential constitutive principle of all Christian life."[58] This is precisely one of the points Dupré maintains. The life of every Christian is to proceed ever closer to union with the divine life of Christ, as also suggested in 2 Corinthians.[59] Following from these Biblical examples, Dupré concludes that "the presence of a mystical element [is] at the heart of the Christian faith."[60] At its inception, Christianity has an essential mystical element, even though it may not be the mysticism of profound ecstatic experience, it seeks the soul's identity with God.

## 2. *Image Mysticism and Negative Theology*

In addition to the Christian scriptures, Hellenistic Judaism and Neoplatonism shaped the early Christian approach to mysticism. In third century Alexandria the concept of the image emerges from the combination of these three influences.

While Dupré cautions against categorizing mystics into types of mysticism, he admits that it is essential to the task of interpretation.

[58] Brown, *Gospel According to John*, 1:512.

[59] See *New Revised Standard Version Bible* (New York: Oxford University Press, 1989), 2 Corinthians 3:18: "And all of us, with unveiled faces, seeing the glory of the Lord as though reflected in a mirror, are being transformed into the same image from one degree of glory to another; for this comes from the Lord, the Spirit." Dupré recognizes this passage as "the traditional starting point of mystical speculation." *LL*, 7.

[60] *LL*, 7. A further argument is made by Rudolf Bultmann when he asserts that "[A. Schlatter] rightly stresses the fact that the plural ὑμεῖς, makes plain the unmystical nature of the sentence [John 14:20]. 'The mystic always thinks unavoidably of the individual'." Rudolf Bultmann, *The Gospel of John: A Commentary*, trans. G. Beasley-Murray (Oxford: Basil Blackwell, 1971), 620 n. 3. Also see Adolf Schlatter, *Der Evangelist Johannes* (Stuttgart: Calwer, 1930), 300. In response, Dupré maintains the communitarian nature of the mystical experience.

There are the various schools of mysticism that have been identified through the centuries, including English, the Low Countries, German, Spanish and French. Further branches of mysticism must be acknowledged outside of Christianity in Jewish, Buddhist, Hindu and Islamic circles and even outside of religion altogether. There are types of mysticism that have been classified, for example, image, trinitarian, love, monist, and eschatological.

Here we turn to the theology of the image, for it is key to the early Christian approach to mysticism.[61] Origen (*c*. 185 - *c*. 253) is the first to articulate this theology in a developed manner in the first systematic theology of the mystical life in Christ.[62] Dupré offers an outline of the history of image mysticism:

> The Christian theology of the image, implicit in the New Testament, and first speculatively developed by Origen, survived uninterruptedly in the East. It reemerged in the twelfth century Cistercian schools of the West. After the mystical schools of the Rhineland and Flanders it faded away in the fifteenth century, only to reappear with renewed vigor in the twentieth century (Merton, Teilhard de Chardin).[63]

[61] See *LL*, 9-10: "We may regard it a proven fact of history, I believe, that theoretical writing on the elevation of the mind to ecstatic levels ... focused on the soul as image of God and, by the same token, as residence of God's own eternal Image, the Word."

[62] See MYSTICISM, 251-252. Also see Origen, *First Principles*, especially, 3.6.I, in *The Ante-Nicene Fathers*, ed. Alexander Roberts and James Donaldson, vol. 4 (Edinburgh, 1885); id., *In Numeros homiliae*, 27, in *Die Griechischen christlichen Schriftsteller*, vol. 30, *Origenes 7* (Leipzig: Hinrichs'sche Buchhandlung, 1921); id., *Commentary on the Song of Songs*, in *Origen: The Song of Songs Commentary and Homilies*, Ancient Christian Writers 26, trans. R. Lawson (Westminster, MD: The Newman Press, 1957).

[63] *LL*, 10-11. MYSTICISM, 254: "It [theology of the image] survived in the theological theories of uncreated grace (e.g., Lessius, De la Taille, Rahner), in patristic studies (Petavius, de Regnon), and in Cistercian spirituality."

In the conclusion to *The Deeper Life*, Dupré alludes to the concept of image which is later developed in *The Common Life*.[64] Image mysticism begins with the biblical assertion that every person is the image of God. This is interpreted not in a physical or external way, but only in an interior manner. The creature or soul, is not simply a likeness of God. Rather, God's uncreated image dwells in the soul "as a presence of, and, ultimately, as an identity with God."[65] Even the deepest unrepentant sinner is united with God — even if the person does not acknowledge this union. Of course, the goal of the spiritual life is to move ever closer to being the image of God. This is accomplished, for example, by recognizing in love the Logos — which is the divine image of God and dwells in one's soul, making one the image of God (Origen),[66] — or by purifying oneself from all creatures and unruly affections, the image of the divine nature will be seen in

---

[64] See *CL*, 13-37.

[65] Louis Dupré, "Negative Theology and Affirmation of the Finite," in *Experience, Reason and God*, Studies in Philosophy and the History of Philosophy 8, ed. Eugene Long (Washington, D.C.: The Catholic University of America Press, 1980), 152. [Hereafter NEGATIVE].

[66] Origen presents the journey of the interior ascent in *Commentary on the Book of Numbers* 27. The soul separates itself from the world in its confusion and wickedness, and recognizes the transitoriness of the world. Suffering through many types of trials, the soul receives consolation and visions for strength against future trials. [See *Commentary on the Song of Songs* 2, 171. The next step is union of the soul with the Logos. He explains this union through the image of Christ being born in the heart and growing in the soul. [See *Commentary on the Song of Songs*, prol. 85]. But most especially he uses the imagery of a mystical marriage. [See *Commentary on the Song of Songs*, I, 4]. See Johannes Quasten, *Patrology*, vol. 2, *The Ante-Nicene Literature After Irenaeus* (Utrecht: Spectrum, 1950), 94-100. Note that in the version translated by Jerome, the Church is the bride of Christ, while in the version translated by Rufinus, the individual soul is the bride. See Quasten, 2:50; 3:266.

one's own beauty as a union of love (Gregory of Nyssa),[67] or
"living toward the Image" as the center of one's existence
(Ruusbroec, 1293-1381).[68]
How does the mystic articulate this union with God? The answer
is found in mysticism's intimate bond with negative theology.

Negative theology means far more than that we find no adequate
names for God. It means, on a practical-spiritual level, that there
exists no failproof method for reaching God, and hence that my only
hope lies in the humble awareness of my inadequacy.[69]

We can look to Gregory of Nyssa (c. 335-394) for whom a dark
cloud of unknowing surrounds the God of whom the soul is
nevertheless an image.[70] Also, we can turn to the sixth century
Pseudo-Dionysius who had such a profound influence upon
Christianity's understanding and employment of negative theology
(first in the East and later in the West).[71] Characteristic of his

[67] See Gregory of Nyssa, *Sermon on the Beatitudes*, 6, in *Gregory of
Nyssenus*, Ancient Christian Writers 18, trans. Hilda Graef (Westminster, MD:
Newman, 1954), 85-175. On the union of the soul and God as a mystical marriage, see e.g., id., *In Canticum hom.*, 1, in *Gregorii Nysseni In Canticum Commentarius*, Gregorii Nysseni Opera 6, ed. Herman Langerbeck (Leiden: Brill,
1960). Dupré states, *CL*, 16: "More than Origen or Clement [of Alexandria], St.
Gregory of Nyssa emphasizes that this growing toward the Image results in the
*love* of God." Dupré also calls this fourth century Cappadocian "the great spiritual theologian of the image of God." *CL*, 15.

[68] See Jan van Ruusbroec, *The Spiritual Espousals*, English and Latin
translation with Middle Dutch original, in *Corpus Christianorum, Continuatio
Mediaevalis*, vol. 103, ed. J. Alaerts, intro. P. Mommaers, trans. H. Rolfson
(Turnhout: Brepolis; Tielt: Lannoo, 1988).

[69] *DL*, 44-45.

[70] See Gregory of Nyssa, *Homily on the Canticle of Canticles*. Also see
MYSTICISM, 252; NEGATIVE, 153; *OD*, 510.

[71] See Pseudo-Dionysius, *The Divine Names*, in *Pseudo-Dionysius: The Com-
plete Works*, The Classics of Western Spirituality, trans. Colm Luibheid (New York:
Paulist Press, 1987), 47-131; id., *The Mystical Theology*, in *Pseudo-Dionysius: The
Complete Works*, 133-141. Also see MYSTICISM, 252; *DL*, 32; *OD*, 510.

thought is an extreme Platonism along with a negative theology which is coupled with image mysticism. Yet, probably the master at uniting negative theology and image mysticism is Johannes Eckhart (c. 1260-1327/8).[72] He combines the thought of Pseudo-Dionysius with Thomistic terms to which he instilled new meanings. Arguing from the principle that God alone is, for God is Being, Eckhart holds that the creature, then, of itself is not, for it has no being by itself. Without discussing here the process of his thought or its full ramifications, we note that "human understanding ... is in the final analysis the presence of God to the soul — eternal, uncreated, and unintelligible."[73] It is doubtful that much, if anything, ultimately can be said positively of God in Eckhart.

Despite the need for negative theology, there is a further necessity for some type of affirmation in Christianity. To stop with negative theology leaves one in complete silence about God. This is acceptable to mystics of silence in certain Buddhist traditions, but it can never be suitable in Christianity which is a religion of the Logos — of the Word through whom all was created and redeemed. The Christian God "is essentially a *manifest* one"[74] and as manifest we must be able to pass from the unknowing of negation to affirmative speech. The question is how to make this step from negation to affirmation. From a speculative theological approach, Dupré refers to Thomas Aquinas' (c. 1225- 1274) proposal of the *via remotionis* (way of removal) as the process by which a

---

[72] See MYSTICISM, 253: "Johannes Eckhart, possibly the most powerful mystical theologian of the Christian Middle Ages, synthesized the Greek and Augustinian theories of the image with a daring negative theology in one grandiose system. His mystical vision became the basis of an entire theology and, indeed, of a metaphysics of being."

[73] OD, 517. Further interpretation of Eckhart's thought may be found in OD, 511-523; DL, 33-37; CL, 22-26; NEGATIVE, 151-152; MYSTICISM, 253.

[74] NEGATIVE, 150. See DL, 48; OD, 366.

higher affirmation can be made.[75] This is not acceptable to Dupré for Aquinas' solution still does not overcome the "objection of negative theology that no subsequent negation can ever overcome the inherent finitude of names which belong entirely to the human order of expression."[76] From a mystical approach, Dupré proposes his solution.

> Finding the finite incommensurate to God's Being, the mystic ulti-mately abandons even his right to judge the finite on his own (also finite) terms and asserts its divine, immanent reality. He thus reaf-firms the finite, not by qualifying his original affirmation, but by radicalizing its negation so as to include negation itself and by allowing the divine affirmation to shine forth in its own right.[77]

The problem with negative theology is that it stops short of com-pleting the process of negation. Negative theology brings one to the first step of acknowledging all finite determinations as incom-mensurate to the Absolute. Then, in realizing this negative per-spective as itself created, the second radical negation occurs.

---

[75] See Thomas Aquinas, *Scriptum super libros sententiarum magistri Petri Lombardi*, ed. R. Mandonnet, vol. 1 (Paris: P. Lethielleux, 1929), I, d. III; id., *On the Power of God*, vol. 3, trans. The English Dominican Fathers (Westminster, MD: Newman Press, 1952), III, q. 7, art. 5; id., *Summa contra Gentiles*, trans. Anton Pegis, vol. 1 (Notre Dame, IN: University of Notre Dame Press, 1975), I, q. 14.

[76] *OD*, 357. Aquinas, of course, also suggests that there is an analogous relationship between God and humanity. While Dupré recognizes many merits to the theory of analogy, "it cannot serve as a means for defining the Being that is God. By analogy alone man produces a notion of God's Being after the likeness of his own being. A truly transcendent notion of God must combine the affirmation with a genuine negation." *OD*, 332.

[77] NEGATIVE, 150. Dupré approaches negative theology from both the viewpoints of speculative theology and mystical writings. His thought from the direction of speculative theology is found in *OD*, 358-367. For his discussion from the direction of mystical writings, which is our concern here, see *OD*, 506-523 and NEGATIVE, 149-157.

Thus, the solution to breaking out of the darkness of negative theology is to negate the viewpoint of the creature itself. In taking this second step of negation one must acknowledge that it is not within one's own power to reach the presence of the divine. So, this radical negation does not turn in on itself and conclude that the finite does not actually exist as finite. Instead, this radical negation asserts that the finite depends even in its finitude upon the infinite.[78] This negation of negation brings us from darkness into the light of God's self-manifestation.

In other words, in asking "how can I speak of the infinite," the soul then asks "how can I speak of the finite" and answers both questions "I can speak only in negative terms." Precisely in the act of negating finitude, the soul discovers, "as I speak of the finite only in negative terms, I realize the complete dependency of the finite upon the infinite." It is in and through the infinite that the finite is positively affirmed. It is God's viewpoint of the finite that becomes the soul's own.

We speak here in terms of the affirmation of the *finite* and not of the affirmation of the *infinite* as one might expect precisely because it is the transcendent which affirms the finite. The "radical negation of the finite is an attempt to grasp the divine as it is itself."[79] The divine reaffirms the finite and the union is so complete that we cannot even speak of a comparison between creature and creator:

> Divine transcendence ceases to mean negation of the creature, and instead becomes its elevation. Transcendence is no longer found *above* creation, but *in* creation. The creature is *in* God and God is *in*

---

[78] See *OD*, 524, where Dupré follows the thought of John of the Cross, *The Ascent of Mount Carmel*, in *The Complete Works of St. John of the Cross*, trans. E. Allison Peers, vol. 1 (Westminster, MD: Newman, 1933), book II, 8. Also see *DL*, 47-50. In *OD*, 523-545, Dupré identifies the process from negation through second negation to union in the three stages of purgation, illumination, and union in love mysticism.

[79] *OD*, 524.

the creature. It is *as creature* and not only as uncreated essence that the creature manifests transcendence: God is the ultimate dimension of the finite reality, the inaccessible in the accessible.[80]

Here we reach the fullness of what is meant by image mysticism. The image is not a likeness or a similitude, but the actual divine presence. Union with God is accomplished through God's inner presence in the soul, and only from this inner presence is one able to perceive a divine presence in the visible world.

To speak in these terms Dupré is compelled to employ the concept of symbol. In this context, he explicitly asserts that "the reality disclosed by the symbol is not an extrinsic one, but *its own*: the finite *intrinsically* participates in the Infinite."[81] The radical negation moves further than negative theology, and speaks of more than similitude. In this second negation what is signified is presence. "Far from denying religious symbols their significant power, I argue that this significance is one of *presence* rather than of similitude."[82] This recognition of presence points to a fundamental quality of religious symbols. "Symbols are religious mainly because they convey a powerful, extraordinary *presence*."[83]

We will need to investigate Dupré's understanding of religious symbols further in the next two chapters. For now we turn to the immediate questions which remain, namely, if this understanding of the second negation leads to affirmative speech, what is affirmed, and how is this relationship with the transcendent expressed? The mysticism of Eckhart leads to a basic silence of God and does not substantially answer these questions for Dupré. So, he turns to the writings of Jan van Ruusbroec to provide the key to their resolution.

---

[80] *OD*, 524-525 and quoted in NEGATIVE, 150.
[81] NEGATIVE, 155.
[82] NEGATIVE, 156.
[83] NEGATIVE, 157.

## 3. *Trinity*

It is "precisely the mystery of the Trinity [that] transforms negative theology into a mysticism of light and charitable communication."[84] By and large, the theology and spirituality of the Greek Fathers was centered on the Trinity and continues in the Eastern Church into the present.[85] While Western theology identifies God as the transcendent Absolute and then extrapolates to the three persons, mysticism followed Eastern theology in starting from the creator God who speaks his Word. This difference in starting points has profoundly shaped two different approaches to God between East and West. An abstract, theoretical idea of God precedes and stands outside of experience in Western thought and the Trinity becomes exclusively a matter of revelation. However, for the mystics who follow the thought of the East, through the economy of salvation God is discovered as the revealing one as well as the revealed: from the Word to the Father in the Spirit.

The "psychological" explanation of the Trinity by Augustine (354-430), had a definitive impact upon the trinitarian theology of the West and opened its horizons to a slightly more Eastern flavor. He searches for the image of the Trinity in the soul and describes the image in terms of external analogies (such as the trinity of memory, understanding and love of self/God).[86] In the twelfth century when Augustine's thought was read along with the Greek Fathers, his understanding of the image of the Trinity in the soul began to be interpreted less as a psychological external analogy and more profoundly as an immanent presence.

---

[84] *LL*, 13.

[85] For this section see *CL*, 10-12, 20-22; *LL*, 11-13.

[86] See Augustine, *On the Trinity*, Books 9-14, in *A Selected Library of the Nicene and Post-Nicene Fathers of the Christian Church*, First Series, vol. 3, ed. Philip Schaff, trans. Arthur Haddan and revised by William Shedd (New York, 1887).

Dupré suggests that the earliest synthesis of Augustinian and Greek thought is found in Cistercian spirituality, probably first attested to by the writings of William of Saint Thierry (c. 1085-1148).[87] Also worthy of note is the work of the Benedictine Richard of St. Victor (d. 1173) which helped to make the Abbey of St. Victor a main center for trinitarian spiritual theology.

With the Flemish mystic Jan van Ruusbroec (1293-1381), we reach the height and exemplar of trinitarian spirituality.[88] When he was a parish priest in Brussels, before he withdrew to a hermitage in Groenendaal outside the city, he had already completed his masterpiece, *The Spiritual Espousals*, along with four other mystical works. He is in agreement with negative theology insofar as God does exist in darkness and absolute oneness. He writes, "In the abyss of this darkness in which the loving spirit has died to itself, there begin the revelation of God and eternal life."[89] Yet, Ruusbroec goes beyond the *via negativa* and advocates a second movement. Through God's self-manifestation in the image of the Son, the soul is lifted to the light of God's being: "And out of our proper ground, — that is, out of the Father and out of all that is living in Him — there shines an eternal brightness, which is the birth

---

[87] See William of St. Thierry, *The Golden Epistle: A Letter to the Brethren at Mont Dieu*, Cistercian Fathers Series 12, trans. Theodore Berkeley (Kalamazoo, MI: Cistercian Publications, 1980).

[88] See *LL*, 13, 174; *CL*, 26, 29; Louis Dupré, "Preface" to *Jan van Ruusbroec: The Spiritual Espousals and other Works*, The Classics of Western Spirituality, trans. James Wiseman (New York: Paulist Press, 1985), xi-xv. Also see Underhill, *Mysticism*, 148, who calls Ruusbroec "one of the greatest — perhaps the very greatest — of the mystics of the Church." Also see Louis Cognet, *Introduction aux mystiques rhéno-flamands* (Paris: Desclée, 1968), 281. Dupré acknowledges his sources in *CL*, 8: "I have shamelessly exploited the excellent work done by present members of the Antwerp-based Ruusbroecgenootschap; especially by Albert Ampe, Joseph Alaerts, and Paul Mommaers."

[89] Ruusbroec, *Espousals*, 3.1, c55-56.

of the Son."[90] The purpose of the spiritual life is to draw ever
more closely toward, and live in, an increasing awareness of the
divine image: "And thus the contemplative persons are attaining
their eternal image to which they were made, and they contemplate God and all things without distinction in a one-fold seeing,
in divine brightness."[91] As the Trinity is a dynamic relation, so the
soul as image of the triune God must move from rest to action.
"Contemplation" is not simply rest. There is a balance between
the interior life of divine rest and a moving out with the divine
Persons in works of charity; this is the core of his complex notion
of "the common life."[92] The life of action, contemplation and
union is fashioned in the image of the Trinity.

In addition to these witnesses, the importance of the Trinity for
all mysticism cannot be overlooked. "In a sense, all Christian
mysticism has been trinitarian. God's self-expression forms the
center of the mystery that holds the mystic's mind."[93] Evelyn
Underhill also affirms that:

> the dogmas of Christianity ... are necessary to an adequate description
> of mystical experience — at least, of the fully developed dynamic
> mysticism of the West. ... Some form of Trinitarian dogma is found
> to be essential, as a method of describing observed facts, the moment
> that mysticism begins either (a) to analyse its own psychological con-
> ditions, or (b) to philosophize upon its intuitive experience of God.[94]

With trinitarian mysticism, particularly as witnessed in Ruusbroec,
we are lead out of the standstill of a thoroughly negative theology.

[90] Ruusbroec, *Espousals*, 3.1, c137-139.
[91] Ruusbroec, *Espousals*, 3.1, c158-160. Also see *DL*, 87; *CL*, 13-14, 30.
[92] Jan van Ruusbroec, *The Sparkling Stone*, English and Latin translation with
Middle Dutch original, in *Corpus Christianorum, Continuatio Mediaevalis*, vol. 110,
ed. G. de Baere, Th. Mertens and H. Noë, intro. Th. Mertens and P. Mommaers,
trans. A. Lefevere (Turnhout: Brepols; Tielt: Lannoo, 1991), E780.
[93] *LL*, 12.
[94] Underhill, *Mysticism*, 107.

The symbol of the Trinity moves beyond darkness through the Father who begets his Word and the breath of the Holy Spirit which is the bond of love between them. As understood by Dupré, the entire doctrine of the Trinity as espoused by mystical writers is a justification for symbol to be considered primary in the expression of religious understanding.

## 4. Conclusion

In the past pages, we have been weaving our way through main sections of Dupré's theological thought. At the beginning of our project we indicated that religion attains its completion in the mystical union with God. The experience of God can be expressed only in symbolic form. All modes of Christian mysticism, image mysticism, as well as trinitarian mysticism, can speak only in symbols. At least then, at its deepest level, religious meaning is expressed symbolically.

Now, since a mystical impulse belongs to the core of religion (even though it may not constitute its very essence) we seem to be justified in assuming that religion itself, however literally it states its dogmas, never overcomes the symbolic nature of its expression required by its very essence. Therefore, from this theological perspective, we maintain that symbol can be viewed as primary for the interpretation of religious thought in the work of Dupré.[95]

---

[95] While approaches vary, the same point is argued by others. See especially, Karl Rahner, "The Theology of the Symbol," in *Theological Investigations*, vol. 4, *More Recent Writings*, trans. Kevin Smyth (London: Darton, Longman & Todd, 1966), 235-245; 245: "The concept of symbol ... is an essential key-concept in all theological treatises [Trinity, Christology, ecclesiology, sacraments], without which it is impossible to have a correct understanding of the subject-matter of the various treatises in themselves and in relation to other treatises."

## C. PHILOSOPHICAL JUSTIFICATION

After suggesting this theological justification, we must still admit that in his approach Dupré aims to explore the religious phenomenon not as a theologian, but as a philosopher of religion. So it is quite proper to expect that if we are correct in asserting symbol as primary religious expression for Dupré, then we should be able to exact some philosophical justification in his thought. There are indeed many philosophers whose works have influenced and shaped Dupré's thought. A list of the philosophical heritage with which he is invariably in dialogue includes Kant, Marx, Kierkegaard, Hegel, and Husserl, just to name a few. Here we begin to weave Dupré's philosophical justification for stating that symbol is a primary religious expression by turning to Schleiermacher and Hegel. Schleiermacher is chosen because through a critique of his thought Dupré identifies the primacy of symbols in discourse on religion. After this basically polemical approach to Schleiermacher, we turn to a greater acceptance of Hegel's exposition of religion as representation which provides positive justification for the primacy of symbol.

In Chapter Two we shall present the influences of Cassirer and Langer upon Dupré's concept of symbol. They are not treated here because our present focus is to provide a philosophical justification that symbols in general are primary to the expression of religious understanding and not to develop Dupré's concept of symbol *per se*. The second and third chapters will discuss Dupré's general symbol theory and its specific application to religious symbols, respectively. Schleiermacher and Hegel provide the best foils to justify the present concern.

### 1. *Friedrich Schleiermacher*

Without denying that Schleiermacher's thought should be contextualized by the philosophies of Fichte and Schelling, as well as within romanticism, Dupré particularly recognizes the influences imposed on Schleiermacher by Kant's concept of autonomy and the "ideal of humanistic self-sufficiency of German classicism."[96] Kant places religion outside the domain of speculative reason and within the sphere of practical reason. Friedrich Schleiermacher (1768-1834) moves beyond Kant's critique and expels religion entirely from the sphere of reason.

Schleiermacher places religion in a domain he calls "feeling" or "immediate consciousness."[97] Religion is not to be identified with cognition, for the cognitive act considers the meaning of the universe for us, proceeding from finite human nature. In contrast, the religious attitude considers "the infinite nature of the Whole, in the One and the All."[98] Neither is religion to be identified with the moral attitude. The moral attitude is always active, centered on one's own perfection, proceeding from the consciousness of freedom. Morality cannot be the essence of religion, for religion "appears as a surrender, a submission to be moved by the Whole that stands over against man."[99] Finding its identity in neither metaphysics nor praxis, Schleiermacher locates the essence of religion in feeling.

Yet, Schleiermacher does not deny that there is some connection between feeling, knowing and doing. Knowing and doing pertain to feeling "inasmuch as the stirred-up Feeling sometimes comes to rest in a thinking which fixes it, [and] sometimes discharges itself in an action which expresses it."[100] Metaphysical and moral teaching

---

[96] Louis Dupré, *A Dubious Heritage: Studies in the Philosophy of Religion after Kant* (New York: Paulist Press, A Newman Book, 1977), 9. [Hereafter *DH*].

[97] Friedrich Schleiermacher, *On Religion: Speeches to Its Cultured Despisers*, trans. John Oman (London: Routledge & Kegan Paul, 1893), e.g., 45, 101; id., *The Christian Faith*, trans. H. Mackintosh and J. Stewart (Edinburgh: T. & T. Clark, 1928), § 3.

[98] Schleiermacher, *On Religion*, 36.

[99] Schleiermacher, *On Religion*, 37.

[100] Schleiermacher, *The Christian Faith*, § 3.4.

may serve to prepare or help express the religious feeling. The connection between the three can also be viewed from the perspective of how religious feeling serves action and thinking. Schleiermacher rhetorically asks, "What can man accomplish that is worth speaking of, either in life or in art, that does not arise in his own self from the influence of this sense for the Infinite?"[101]

By regarding feeling as the essence of the religious experience, Schleiermacher responds to the problem raised by Kant as to how a religious experience of the transcendent can be reconciled with human autonomy. Human autonomy is reconciled with experience of the transcendent by identifying religion as the feeling of absolute dependence revealing the transcendent. Caution must be exercised in interpreting the meaning of "feeling." Dupré is among those who correctly understand that to speak of religion as "feeling" does not make religion purely subjective. Dupré recognizes, "that although *feeling* has a subjective connotation, strictly speaking, it is not more subjective than objective, since it belongs to a stage of consciousness in which subject and object are still basically identical."[102] Without entering further into the discussion, we note that for Schleiermacher full consciousness is reached in stages. Originally, there is an identity of object and subject. When they break apart, consciousness becomes cognition if the object predominates, and if the subject controls, it leads to consciousness of freedom or activity. Religion for Schleiermacher is not merely a subjective experience; the feeling of dependence is "a revelation of the ultimate ground of reality and consciousness."[103] Far from being a sentimental experience, Schleiermacher recognizes that all feelings are not religious. The essence of religion is feeling, only

---

[101] Schleiermacher, *On Religion*, 39.

[102] *DH*, 11. Feeling is not a "faculty" but a quality of self-consciousness.

[103] *DH*, 22. See Schleiermacher, *The Christian Faith*, § 6.1.

insofar as religious feeling is a feeling of absolute dependence that reveals the transcendent ground of self-consciousness.

Dupré offers a number of nuances and clarifications to Schleiermacher's thought, as well as a primary objection. This primary criticism is explicitly presented in *A Dubious Heritage*, where Dupré argues that "Schleiermacher did not clearly perceive the distinction between the religious experience and aesthetic feeling."[104] While in itself this critique is not our immediate concern, one of the consequences arising from it addresses the core of our interest. In advocating an understanding of religion as feeling and blurring the distinction between aesthetic feeling and religious experience, Schleiermacher is unable to locate the necessary role of symbol in religion.

Dupré summarizes this objection in other writings. We read, "The idea of religion as a purely interior feeling, detachable from its symbolic expression, was first advanced by the young Schleiermacher, who later saw it as a romantic illusion."[105] This separation of symbol from the essence of religion is not acceptable to Dupré. We also find this summary statement:

> Several religious thinkers in the last century have tried to lead philosophy of religion away from self-adoration and back to its religious origin. The exodus started with Schleiermacher. Unfortunately, even though the German philosopher had the vision of faith, his romantic lack of appreciation for the intrinsic necessity of symbols prevented him from ever reaching the promised land.[106]

Simply stated, Dupré's does not deny that there are religious feelings, but he is against leaving out symbol. For Dupré, "the religious act

---

[104] *DH*, 24.

[105] Louis Dupré, "Phenomenology of Religion: Limits and Possibilities," *American Catholic Philosophical Quarterly* 66 (Spring 1992): 178.

[106] Dupré, Preface to *Faith and Reflection*, by Henry Duméry, ed. Louis Dupré, trans. Stephen McNiernery and M. Benedict Murphy (New York: Herder & Herder, 1968), x.

is never exclusively a feeling. In fact, feelings can be called *religious* only to the extent that they are determined by a more outward-oriented act. By themselves they remain self-centered and should not be called religious."[107]

A more complete explanation of Dupré's objections to Schleiermacher is found in *A Dubious Heritage*.[108] We start with Schleiermacher's identification of religion as feeling. We then follow Dupré's assertion that Schleiermacher did not properly differentiate between religious experience and aesthetic feeling. Next, we must understand how Dupré moves beyond the thought of Schleiermacher in distinguishing between aesthetic and religious experiences. In classifying the two, Dupré first advocates the essential role of symbol in each; "the aesthetic and the religious experiences are both essentially symbolic ... [for both are] expression[s] of the mind in its totality, subjective and objective, sensuous and spiritual."[109] Yet, the function of symbol is unique between the two experiences. For aesthetic experiences, idea and image are intimately linked; the aesthetic symbol properly represents the idea. The meaning of the aesthetic image exists in its appearance. In contrast, the function of religious forms is more complex. For religious experiences, there is a distance between idea and image; in religion, in an attempt to be free of all limiting determinations, the image is continuously transcended. This is to say that "the image is there only as a temporary, yet necessary, counterpart of an idea striving to free itself from all limiting determinations."[110] Religious forms "intend something over and above their own intrinsic meaning."[111]

---

[107] *OD*, 35.

[108] See especially, *DH*, 24-28. A similar line of thought is found in *OD*, 34-36.

[109] *DH*, 25.

[110] *DH*, 25.

[111] *DH*, 26. Also see *OD*, 35: "The religious symbol ... never fully symbolizes its transcendent content. It merely *points to* it in a loose connection between symbol and content, unintelligible to the uninitiated, whom it impresses as merely strange."

Granting this distinction, which Schleiermacher does not properly recognize, we can now reach the conclusion implicit in Dupré's text — based on the two explicit summary statements noted above from other works — that to correctly grasp the meaning of religion, the primacy of symbols must be acknowledged.

For completeness, we note in passing that Dupré argues to a further consequence of obscuring religious and aesthetic experiences. Based on the above characteristics of religious symbols, to the uninitiated their meaning may appear variable or arbitrary. Dupré acknowledges that Schleiermacher recognizes this arbitrary quality.[112] Yet, Dupré suggests that this leads to a further step which Schleiermacher does not take. Schleiermacher "fails to see how the very distance between the religious experience and its symbolic expression indicates an intrinsic necessity for reflection."[113] By denying the reflective quality of the religious act, Schleiermacher removes a fundamental action that arises from symbols and once again limits the need for symbols in religious understanding.

Thus, Dupré identifies that Schleiermacher's "great importance consists in having shown that the religious experience is in the very center of human experience, and that a religious determination is therefore essential to human existence."[114] Yet, while Dupré agrees with Schleiermacher's basic insight into the nature of religion, Schleiermacher still "lacked the philosophical equipment to work it out in a satisfactory way."[115] Dupré admits the existence of religious feeling, but as feeling, he places it within the realm of aesthetics

---

[112] See *DH*, 26. Schleiermacher, *The Christian Faith*, § 4.4: "The transference of the idea of God to any perceptible object, unless one is all the time conscious that it is a piece of purely arbitrary symbolism, is always a corruption."

[113] *DH*, 26. Dupré continues an argument on the necessity of the reflective quality of the religious act (which Schleiermacher denies) in *DH*, 26-28.

[114] *DH*, 28.

[115] *DH*, 28.

and not that of religion. By distinguishing between religious and aesthetic experience,[116] and locating feeling as more of an aesthetic than religious quality, Dupré emphasizes the essential symbolic quality of religious experience, in contrast to the thought of Schleiermacher.

## 2. G. W. F. Hegel

In contrast to the polemical approach to Schleiermacher, Dupré finds an agreeable philosophical basis in G. W. F. Hegel (1770-1831) for stating symbol as primary religious expression. Dupré's appreciation of Hegel is quite extensive, not to mention Hegelianism and Neohegelianism. One need only turn to *The Other Dimension* to witness the extent to which Dupré regards the thought of Hegel, even if he rejects certain formulations and even conclusions.[117] We must limit our concern to how Dupré's understanding of Hegel provides a philosophical justification to consider symbol as primary expression of religious understanding.

For his part, Hegel reacts against Schleiermacher's consideration of the religious act exclusively as a feeling of absolute dependence.

---

[116] We will return to the relation of aesthetics and religion below, pp. 157-164.

[117] See e.g., *OD*, 140-146, 149-157, 257-259, 287-292, 345-346, 442-447, (and 202-242 though he does not refer to Hegel by name his influence is apparent; Dupré does mention in *DH*, 72 n. 29 that he develops Hegel's thought on these pages). Certain reviewers of *OD* refer to his Hegelian inspiration. I single out the most articulate representative, Joseph Donceel, review of *The Other Dimension*, in *International Philosophical Quarterly* 15 (March 1975): 100: "Like all philosophers he [Dupré] has been greatly influenced by many great thinkers of the past and of the present, but he always remains himself, and while assimilating the contributions of the masters, he soon spots their weaknesses and tries to carry on where they may have faltered. His treatment of Hegel is most remarkable in this respect." It is no wonder that David Tracy refers to "Louis Dupré's Hegelian phenomenology." *Blessed Rage for Order: The New Pluralism in Theology* (New York: Seabury Press, 1975), 99.

"If we say that religion rests on this feeling of dependence, then animals would have to have religion, too, for they feel this dependence."[118] Hegel's understanding of religion, of course, is characterized not by feeling, but as representation (*Vorstellung*). Aesthetic experience is basically a matter of feeling, whereas religion is an activity of thought. Though this does not deny that art can lead consciousness toward the Absolute, religion is a better candidate precisely because the Absolute is Thought. Yet it is philosophy which reaches the level of pure thought, where religious thought remains pictorial. (The revealed religion, Christianity, is the pictorial representation of philosophy.)

Already, the interconnectedness of Hegel's philosophy should be apparent. We cannot approach Hegel's thought on religion as if it can be separated from the rest of his work. "For Hegel the 'system' of philosophy that begins with *Logic* and ends with the *Philosophy of Spirit* has no other content than religion."[119] Hegel's entire philosophical undertaking is permeated with religious significance. Intertwined are such concepts as Spirit (subjective, objective, Absolute, as well as holy), consciousness, God, representation, Thought, history, myth, and the list continues. Yet the relationship of one concept to another — often the subject of debate among interpreters of Hegel — is a matter of consequence. For example, Dupré maintains the distinction in Hegel between Absolute Spirit and God, which some have blurred or denied. "The Absolute Spirit unites the infinite and the finite *within* itself, while the idea of God, though also immanent in the finite, essentially transcends it."[120]

[118] G. W. F. Hegel, *Lectures on the Philosophy of Religion*, ed. Peter Hodgson, trans. R. Brown, P. Hodgson, J. Stewart, vol. 1, *Introduction and The Concept of Religion* (Berkeley: University of California Press, 1984), 279 (1824 lecture).
[119] *OD*, 143.
[120] Dupré, "Hegel's Absolute Spirit: A Religious Justification of Secular Culture," *Revue de l'Université d'Ottawa* 52 (October-December 1982): 555.

There is also a separation between representation and image which Dupré embraces. This latter distinction is particularly important for our purposes. In religion, while images are necessary, they play a subordinate role in the representation. "Representation [is] the image elevated into its universality."[121]

For Hegel, representation mediates between intuition (*Anschauung*) on the one hand, and conceptual thought (*Denken*) on the other.[122] Representation proper does not require the presence of the represented object nor must it refer to a definite individual; (these *would* hold for intuitions — sensations, perceptions). Conversely, representations do include an image or pictorial element; (these *would not* hold for concepts — thoughts, ideas). proposes three stages within the representation, (moving from intuition to thought), namely, recollection (*Erinnerung*), force of imagination (*Einbildungskraft*), and memory (*Gedächtniß*).

The first stage called recollection is an inward process, taking on its own space and time. There is "at this stage a content which is not only intuitively perceived in its immediacy, but is at the same time recollected, inwardly, posited as *mine*."[123] This content is an image or picture of the object. At this point the image itself is not universal, but it no longer has the complete determinateness of intuition. This is representation in its simplest stage, an involuntary calling forth of an image that is *mine* in a manner in which intuitions and external object are not.

In the second stage of the force of imagination, Hegel distinguishes between the reproductive imagination (which voluntarily recalls an image), the associative imagination (which not only

---

[121] Hegel, *Lectures*, 1:238.

[122] For this section see G. W. F. Hegel, *Hegel's Logic: Part One of the Encyclopedia of the Philosophical Sciences with the Zusätze*, trans. William Wallace (Oxford: Clarendon Press, 1873), §§ 451-464.

[123] Hegel, *Encyclopedia*, § 451 Zusatz.

voluntarily recalls images but relates them to one another, primarily as universals), and the productive phantasy.

The productive phantasy is of particular interest to us. It does not recall an image, but produces its own. Thus, Hegel characterizes Hinduism as the religion of phantasy insofar as he regards it as representing ultimate reality by the fleeting connections presented by phantasy through natural, finite, worldly things (and not by essential connections).[124] Phantasy extends beyond synthesis and reaches a singularity. This is to say, that by abandoning "the order of actual perception in favor of a purely subjective succession of images ... [phantasy is directed by an] overriding representation [which] assembles a number of disparate perceptions into an entirely new structure."[125] As Hegel explains,

> Phantasy is the activity of giving shape either to what is inwardly abstract or to what is external, what is initially an immediate being (for example, thunder or the ocean's roar); it shapes both of these aspects and posits them as something concrete ... the result is that the external being is no longer independent but is downgraded into being just a sign of the indwelling spirit.[126]

In this third type of imagination of productive phantasy, the universal conception, then, is associated with a sign (*Zeichen*).

---

[124] See G. W. F. Hegel, *Lectures on the Philosophy of Religion*, ed. Peter Hodgson, trans. R. Brown, P. Hodgson, J. Stewart, vol. 2, *Determinate Religion* (Berkeley: University of California Press, 1987), 316 (1824 lecture). In the 1827 lecture Hegel no longer refers to Hinduism as the religion of phantasy, but advances two primary characteristics of Hinduism, namely, the unity of substance and the multiplicity of powers; phantasy is operative only in the second. See *Lectures*, 2:579-586 (1827 lecture). In the 1831 lecture, Hinduism is defined as the religion of abstract unity, which highlights the first characteristic. *Lectures*, 2:731-725.

[125] *OD*, 155. Also see *DH*, 59. Dupré is basically commenting on *Encyclopedia*, § 457.

[126] *Lectures*, 2:657. Also see *Encyclopedia*, § 457.

The sign does not present itself but presents a meaning beyond the appearances. With the sign the representation is abstract; the content of the intuition and what is signified need not be related. Hegel contrasts signs to symbols, for with symbols he regards the representation as concrete; the content of the intuition is more or less what is signified. Thus there is a greater depth and creativity that is ascribed to the sign according to Hegel. Dupré does not agree with this exaltation of the sign over symbol, but he concurs with Hegel on the primary necessity of representation. On a related topic, Dupré distrusts Hegel's subordination of the symbol to the form of pure thought. Yet in so doing, Hegel regards symbols as always leading to reflection, an idea with which Dupré agrees.[127]

Also in discussing the productive phantasy, Hegel expresses the primacy of the linguistic sign. It is through language alone that the representations are capable of conveying complete transcendence. Extending Hegel's thought, one can say that the "verbalization is constitutive of the religious representation: without it the representation would never move beyond a very primitive potentiality."[128] Dupré explains that the representation is able to become a symbol of transcendence through language because the system of meaning imposed by language opens the connection between the symbolized content and the symbolizing intuition to new levels of

[127] Recall in his disagreement with Schleiermacher, Dupré asserts that religious symbols necessitate reflection. With regard to Hegel, Dupré comments in *OD*, 157: "[Symbols] invite thinking because they require interpretation. By pointing beyond their appearance, symbols draw attention to something that wants to be discovered but is at least partly concealed. Now it is typical of rationalism [most definitely including Hegel] to understand this to mean that rational thought at a certain stage of reflection must take over and substitute for the symbol. On the contrary, thought remains subordinate to the symbol: that is why we call it 'interpretation.' "

[128] Libert Vander Kerken, "De religieuze beleving als voorstelling," *Tijdschrift voor Philosophie* 34 (March 1972): 14. Translation by Louis Dupré in *DH*, 63-64.

conceptualization.[129] This must be explained further, but we have already crossed the barrier between Hegel's thought and that of Dupré's and so will hold this explanation for Chapter Two where the uniqueness of the symbolism of words for Dupré is further expanded.

Finally, the third stage in representation after recollection and imagination is memory. In fact we have basically made the transition to memory in recognizing the importance of linguistic signs. It is sufficient to further note here that through memory a connection is forged between a given sign and a given conception so that this relationship can be considered a universal representation or word-type. The need for an intuition or even an image becomes superfluous as the name given to the represented suffices. The representation has thus been fully internalized.

The preceding has centered on Hegel's view of representation in the *Encyclopedia* in the division on psychology under the section of the subjective Spirit. In addition to the occasional references to the *Lectures* above, there are certain qualities of religious representation that can summarily be acknowledged from the lectures he offered on religion in 1821, 1824, 1827 and 1831. First, Dupré appropriately observes Hegel's acknowledgement of an objective character of the representation. Granting them some objectivity, religious representations avoid becoming only subjective truth for the individual, or deification of oneself, or religious intolerance or fanaticism.[130]

Next, following Fackenheim we briefly note religious representation's reference to the Infinite.[131] This is an essential quality, as the representation must mediate between the finite human and

[129] See *DH*, 64.

[130] See Hegel, *Lectures*, 1:240. Also see *DH*, 61; and *OD*, 156.

[131] See Emil Fackenheim, *The Religious Dimension in Hegel's Thought* (London: Indiana University Press, 1967), 122, 154-155.

the radically other Infinite, by relating the two and yet respecting the separation. Thus, religious representation refers to the Infinite and not a finite picture (*Bild*). Yet, the representation must refer to the Infinite in a finite way, by way of such means as analogies from natural life, connecting terms ("and" and "also"), and by regarding the Infinite (the represented) as external to the referring finite human.[132] Still, the representation itself is able to acknowledge its own inadequacy in attempting to finitely refer to the Infinite. This points to the dialectical nature of the representation.

Among the many other characteristics of representation worthy of note, we conclude with a final word on the relation of representation and thought; (this can also be viewed as the relation of religion and philosophy). This final remark is made to further suggest the necessary role of symbol in religion. Hegel maintains:

> Humanity does not just exist as pure thinking; instead, thinking itself is manifested as intuiting, as representing. Hence the absolute truth, as revealed to human beings, must also be [present] for them as representational, intuitive beings, as beings engaged in feeling and sensation. This is the form that distinguishes religion in general from philosophy.[133]

While there is clearly a distinction in Hegel between representation and thinking and between religion and philosophy, the representation (the power of symbol) is necessary for religion. "In representing, human beings are also thinking, and the content of truth comes to

---

[132] See Hegel, *Lectures*, 1:400-406; 2:360-361. Also see Fackenheim, *The Religious Dimension*, 155.

[133] Hegel, *Lectures on the Philosophy of Religion*, ed. Peter Hodgson, trans. R. Brown, P. Hodgson, J. Stewart, vol. 3, *The Consummate Religion* (Berkeley: University of California Press, 1985), 357.

them as thinking beings. Only what thinks can have religion, and thinking includes representing."[134] Precisely in developing the concept of representation, Hegel provides the philosophical foundation for religion.

Accordingly, in Hegel's understanding of religion as representation we can locate the primary role of symbol. Fackenheim asserts, "The required aspects of religious representation all unite in the religious *symbol*."[135] This is also Dupré's understanding, "[Philosophy of religion] must be above all a study of symbols, situating the symbolic activity within the totality of consciousness. This, I take it, is what ... Hegel in his theory of representation attempted to accomplish."[136] In reviewing the book of another, Dupré again gives a nod to a foundational principle for his own thought, "Hegel's theory of religion as the absolute in the form of representation also assigns religious symbols to mediate between the sensuous and the spiritual order."[137] While remaining critical, it is precisely his appreciation of Hegel's view of religion as representation that provides the philosophical basis for Dupré to treat symbol as primary religious expression.

---

[134] Hegel, *Lectures*, 3:357. He immediately adds, "but it is only thinking that is the free form of truth." On this point Dupré responds: "Although I had been a student of his [Hegel's] philosophy for a long time, I could not bring myself to take seriously a definition of religion according to which philosophy must 'go beyond' religion even while continuing to need it for its inspiration." *OD*, 9. Also see *OD*, 146.

[135] Fackenheim, *The Religious Dimension*, 122.

[136] *OD*, 140. These sentences are a good 'clue' to Dupré's use of Hegel, and are an addition to Dupré's earlier article "Metaphysics and Religious Faith," in *The Future of Metaphysics*, ed. Robert Wood (Chicago: Quadrangle Books, 1970), 263-273, which becomes part of *OD*, including the paragraphs around this new section (*OD*, 112-113, 130-131, 138-147).

[137] Louis Dupré, review of *The Emergence of Philosophy of Religion*, by James Collins, in *Theological Studies* 29 (March 1968): 104.

## 3. Conclusion

From this limited presentation of Dupré's understanding of Schleiermacher and Hegel, we have sought to elucidate the philosophical ground underlying his works that can justify our claim of symbol as primary expression for religious understanding in his thought.

Regarding Schleiermacher, Dupré takes issue with his use of symbol within his explanation of religion. Dupré basically considers Schleiermacher as having neglected the necessary role of symbol. He credits Schleiermacher with insights into the essential place of religion in human experience, but is disenchanted with Schleiermacher's approach. In commenting upon Schleiermacher, Dupré presents his own philosophical approach for his understanding of religion that accords a primary place to symbol.

Regarding Hegel, Dupré builds upon his understanding of religion as representation. With Hegel, Dupré acknowledges the necessity of representation within religion; in Hegel's own words, "But since religion is of itself the subjective side in the element of self-consciousness, *representation* [*Vorstellung*] is altogether more essential for it — representation [as] distinguished from *image* [*Bild*]."[138] Without the religious representation, the absolute — in which the finite finds its ultimate justification — could not be thought. Among other critiques, Dupré disagrees with Hegel's method of distinguishing between sign and symbol. Yet, through Hegel's concept of representation the power and necessity of symbol is manifested. Thus from his philosophical perspective, we maintain that symbol can be viewed as primary religion expression in the thought of Dupré.

---

[138] Hegel, *Lectures*, 1:238.

## D. JUSTIFICATION OF METHOD

Before completing this introductory chapter on justification, we look for Dupré's justification of his own methodology. As a philosopher of religion, he must assume a certain approach. Yet, preliminary to investigating his philosophical approach, we must answer the more basic question whether he is engaged in philosophy or theology. So far we have assumed Dupré's status as a philosopher of religion but our justification has been both theological and philosophical. We now investigate further Dupré's statements of how he views his work, and we must ask whether he follows the method he has articulated.

### 1. *Philosopher or Theologian?*

*The Deeper Life* and *The Common Life* by Dupré have already been acknowledged as theological works, as well as his introductory remarks in *Light From Light* and *Christian Spirituality*. Of the rest of his works, approximately half are of a philosophical nature not concerned with religion. Of the others that are in some way concerned with religion, it would be a futile exercise to determine the degree to which each is philosophical as opposed to theological. Instead of embarking upon such a venture, we will investigate only *The Other Dimension*. This choice is made for three reasons. First, it has established itself as an important work on religion and is used in a number of different sections of our current project. Second, it is his longest work and segments of it have appeared as various articles. Third, and most important, it is this work which has caused some reviewers to question whether Dupré is engaged in theology more than he admits.

Dupré himself maintains that his approach in *The Other Dimension* is that of a philosopher critically reflecting upon religion. However, some have suggested that this work is more from the viewpoint of a theologian[139] or perhaps a philosophical theologian,[140] engaging not in philosophy but in religious philosophy[141] or 'crypto theology'.[142] These distinctions are reminiscent of the debate of "Christian philosophy," recalling Étienne Gilson, Jacques Maritain, and Maurice Blondel, among others and akin to current methodological questions being raised regarding philosophers of religion.

While it would be an oversimplification to say that there are almost as many ideas of the nature of theology as there are theologians/schools of theology and as many ideas of the nature of philosophy as there are philosophers/schools of philosophy, there is indeed much debate. Instead of becoming entangled in a plethora

[139] See Tyson Anderson, review of *The Other Dimension*, in *National Catholic Reporter* 8 (May 26, 1972): 15; Gilkey, Review, 65; David Tracy, "The Dialectical Nature of Religion," review of *The Other Dimension*, in *The Christian Century* 89 (December 6, 1972): 1252; Bernard Murchland, review of *The Other Dimension*, in *Philosophy and Phenomenological Research* 33 (June 1973): 593; John McCormack, review of *The Other Dimension*, in *Thought* 48 (Summer 1973): 312.

[140] See Eugene Long, review of *The Other Dimension*, in *International Journal for Philosophy of Religion* 5 (Fall 1974): 178: "For while Dupré talks about critical reflection and does say that philosophers must appeal to philosophical criteria, it is at times difficult to distinguish his approach from that of a philosophical theologian who views his task as one of reflecting on faith from within the community of faith with the aim of providing foundations for faith within the universal structures of human experience."

[141] See David Burrell, review of *The Other Dimension*, in *The Thomist* 38 (April 1974): 377: "Dupré allows his predilection for religion to lead him to adopt those philosophical styles which prove sympathetic with it. The result is closer to what has been called religious philosophy than to philosophy of religion ... For Dupré re-states many a religious position in philosophical terms."

[142] See Robert Ayers, Review, 194: "It appears that Dupré has written a defense for a certain type of Christian faith under the guise of an objective analysis and that his work might be characterized as a cryptotheology." On the general ambiguity of Dupré's method, see Jean Galot, Review of *L'autre dimension*, in *Gregorianum* 59 (1978): 416, and Bernard Nachbahr, review of *The Other Dimension*, in *Theological Studies* 33 (June 1972): 348-349.

of differentiations, we turn now to Dupré's own distinctions to assist in categorizing his position.

Dupré accepts the time honored position that philosophy is "the ultimate reflection upon experience."[143] As such, philosophy must rely on other sources for its subject. The philosopher of religion reflects upon anthropological, theological, and religious assertions. The outcome produces a distinct demarcation:

> As a result, theological statements used in a philosophical context change their meaning rather basically. The theologian reflects *within* his faith: he does not question his basic commitment. The philosopher, on the contrary, uses everything but takes nothing for granted. ... My study, then, can never lend support to religious assertions by supplying them with a philosophical foundation. Beyond establishing the *possibility* of meaningful religious assertions, the philosopher can give no assistance.[144]

So the question remains, does Dupré apply this method in his work, or does he actually slip into theology? The most convincing nuance that is suggested to classify Dupré's approach is Long's distinction noted above between a philosopher (of religion) who operates from no particular faith claim and a philosophical theologian who argues from within a particular religion; there is general acceptance of this differentiation.[145] Philosophical theology critically assesses every aspect of religion and is not an apologia in

---

[143] *OD*, 7. See e.g., Aristotle, *Metaphysics*, 1.1, 980ᵃ-980ᵇ, in *Aristotle*, vol. 17, *The Metaphysics I, Books I-IX*, The Loeb Classical Library, ed. T. Page, trans. Hugh Tredennick (London: William Heinemann; Cambridge: Harvard University Press, 1933).

[144] *OD*, 7-8.

[145] See e.g., James Collins, *God in Modern Philosophy* (London: Routledge & Kegan Paul, 1960); Hendrik Vroom, *Religions and the Truth: Philosophical Reflections and Perspective*, trans. J. Rebel (Grand Rapids: MI: Eerdmans, 1989), 387: "By philosophical theology we understand the reflection on the beliefs of a tradition within that tradition, using philosophical methods."

defense of religion or a natural theology which inquires into human knowledge of God through natural reason.

On the one hand, since Dupré is evaluating philosophically the common human experience of religion (as a pervasive feature of culture), if his estimation of the religious experience is different from ours, this is not necessarily a problem with his method, but illustrates the breath of his understanding and marks the uniqueness of his philosophy.[146] On the other hand, there is a fine line between philosophy and theology in discussing such issues as rites, sacraments, salvation and mysticism. Those who suggest that Dupré reflects within faith emphasize the topics he discusses, but one cannot assume that if the topic is theological so the method must be also. His work can be considered as a philosophical reflection upon theological issues.[147]

Still, Dupré's own caveat intimates a resemblance to philosophical theology:

> Of course, this does not mean that the author can be on both sides of the fence at once. A careful reflection requires that at one time or other, the philosopher has been personally exposed to the experience upon which he reflects. Since this experience is always limited, the reflection upon it tends to be somewhat one-sided.[148]

I would maintain that his approach in *The Other Dimension* is indeed closer to that of philosophical theology. He does remain consistent in following his assertion: "The main objective of philosophy of religion is to determine the specific nature of the religious act in and through its various expressions."[149] Yet, even

[146] Contrasted to the views of Robert Ayers, Review, 194, and Gilkey, Review, 65-66.

[147] See Antoine Vergote, review of *The Other Dimension*, in *Revue Philosophique de Louvain* 73 (May 1975): 427, 432. Contrasted to Murchland, Review, 593; Gilkey, Review, 65; and McCormack, Review, 312.

[148] *OD*, 8.

[149] *OD*, 140.

though he demonstrates great agility in investigating the religious expressions of a variety of traditions, his reflection returns to the Judeo-Christian tradition (as he admits it might) and more specifically that of a Catholic Christian tradition. For example, It is not impossible from outside the tradition to find the ultimate expression of religion in mystics such as John of the Cross and Teresa of Avila, as is reached in the last chapter of *The Other Dimension*; however, his argumentation and presentation indicate that he has arrived at this discovery through reflection from within the tradition. True enough he devotes a section to Hindu mysticism, but its overall impact upon the larger discussion is minimal.[150]

This assessment does not weaken any of Dupré's work. In fact, when *The Other Dimension* is read as a work of philosophical theology it is strengthened, for instead of being confronted by the expectations of philosophy of religion, which it is not always able to meet, its merits are evident within the criteria set forth by philosophical theology. Dupré's venture does not solely examine religious ideas in general (which would be the project of philosophy of religion) but he ultimately interweaves his reflection on general religious experience with his understanding of the Christian faith (in accord with a philosophical theology). In his own style, Dupré creates a synthesis with philosophy and theology instead of juxtaposing the two.[151]

[150] See Gilkey, Review, 65-66.

[151] This bears similarities with the unity of philosophy and theology suggested by Rahner and the proposal by Lonergan to return to an integrated systematic theology. See e.g., Karl Rahner, "Philosophy and Theology," in *Theological Investigations*, vol. 6, trans. Karl-H. and Boniface Kruger (London: Darton, Longman & Todd, 1969), 71-81; id., "Philosophy and Philosophising in Theology," in *Theological Investigations*, vol. 9, trans. Graham Harrison (London: Darton, Longman & Todd, 1972), 46-63. Bernard Lonergan, *Method in Theology* (New York: Herder & Herder, 1973²), 335-340.

The true key to understanding *The Other Dimension* as well as his other religious works is through appreciating his use of the phenomenological method. In *The Other Dimension* he writes, "Phenomenological analysis has directly and indirectly been used throughout this work."[152] Yet, "phenomenology alone cannot yield the entire meaning of the act, unless it somehow participates in the faith which establishes the actual connection with the transcendent."[153] Once again we are faced with the question of faith in philosophy. But now it is raised not to question Dupré's authenticity as a philosopher, but it is raised precisely by Dupré the philosopher (philosophical theologian) to search for a justification of his method. So, having briefly viewed some of the objections raised regarding Dupré's approach in *The Other Dimension*, we now turn to other works, not to confront them with the same objection, but — granting the interplay between philosophy and theology — to further understand his phenomenological methodology.

## 2. *Phenomenological Method*

In *The Other Dimension*, Dupré extolls the phenomenological method as providing the proper balance between objectivism and subjectivism: the religious act taken objectively is always interpreted by the subject, yet, "at the same time the intentional orientation prevents the religious act from being reduced to a mere experience [of the subject]."[154] By citing "intentional orientation," Dupré immediately has in mind "an experience which points beyond itself toward a transcendent terminus."[155] Herein lies the root of

---

[152] *OD*, 104.

[153] *OD*, 109.

[154] *OD*, 105.

[155] *OD*, 104; also see 106. At its base, Dupré has in mind Husserl's concept of "intentionality." For comparison and contrast of Brentano and Husserl on intentionality, see e.g., Louis Dupré, "The Concept of Truth in Husserl's *Logical*

what must be justified in order for phenomenology to be a viable methodology to investigate the religious act: its approach to the transcendent. Specifically, Dupré suggests three basic questions to determine the extent to which the phenomenological approach is justifiable for religious inquiry. First, how can the religious object remain transcendent and also be described phenomenologically? Second, can phenomenology conclude to real transcendence? Third, what is the relation between the truth proper to religion and a phenomenological understanding of truth?[156] Our precise interest is to what extent a phenomenological method, according to Dupré's interpretation, can adequately respond to these needs. It is with this intent (and taking as a given a general knowledge of phenomenology) that we briefly inquire into these three questions.

## a. Question of Transcendence

On the one hand, if the primary object of religion is transcendent, then its essence falls beyond description and remains only a matter

Investigations," *Philosophy and Phenomenological Research* 24 (March 1964): 349-354. Also see Herbert Spiegelberg, *The Phenomenological Movement: A Historical Introduction*, Phaenomenologica 5 (The Hague: Martinus Nijhoff, 1982³), 36-38, 97-100, 746-747.

[156] Dupré consistently returns to justification through these three questions; note that the dates range from 1964 to 1992:

Dupré discusses the first two questions from various perspectives with some overlap in id., "Philosophy of Religion and Revelation: Autonomous Reflection vs. Theophany," *International Philosophical Quarterly* 4 (December 1964): 499-513; *OD*, 104-111; and *DH*, 75-91.

The third question appears as id., "The 'Truth' of Religion," in *Morality within the Life — and Social World: Interdisciplinary Phenomenology of the Authentic Life in the "Moral Sense,"* Analecta Husserliana 22, ed. Anna-Teresa Tymieniecka (Dordrecht, Holland: D. Reidel, 1987), 457-463; and in different form as part of id., "Truth in Religion and Truth of Religion," in *Archivio di Filosofia* 56 (1988): 493-494, 502-516.

All three questions are discussed in id., "Phenomenology of Religion: Limits and Possibilities," 175-188.

of faith. On the other hand, the approach of phenomenology claims to attain an intuition of the object of the experience. Thus, if the phenomenological method can justifiably be applied to religion, its ability to investigate the transcendent must be substantiated. In developing an answer to this dilemma, one solution would be to compromise the transcendence of the religious object, (which changes our concept of God and is unacceptable to the believer). A second solution would hold that phenomenology can describe the transcendent terminus (but this would move phenomenology into ontology, or at best an act of faith). A logical third solution would mediate between the two extremes with some distinction or reinterpretation.

In offering a phenomenological explication of religion, Max Scheler insists on the negative and symbolic character of the believer's intuition of God. Yet, Dupré also finds in Scheler "the possibility of a genuine a *Wesensschau* [essential intuition] of the divine."[157] Through God's symbolic revelation in the world, the believer knows God through a direct, non-rational intuition. This solution is not acceptable to Dupré because "such a position jeopardizes the transcendence of the religious terminus or it reduces phenomenological insight to an act of faith."[158] Thus, Dupré critiques Scheler's approach as proposing either of the first two extreme solutions indicated above.

Even though Gerardus Van der Leeuw should not be placed with Scheler's philosophical understanding of phenomenology (and it is only later interpreters of Van der Leeuw who provide the label 'descriptive phenomenology' to his thought),[159] he also proposes a solution to the problem at hand. Van der Leeuw distinguishes

---

[157] *DH*, 77.

[158] *DH*, 77. On questions of interpreting Scheler on religion, particularly his concept of God, see Spiegelberg, *Phenomenological Movement*, 299-300.

[159] See in particular Van der Leeuw's two concluding chapters on phenomenology, *Religion in Essence and Manifestation*, §§ 109, 1 - 110, 2.

between religion-as-experience and religion-as-transcendent. Phenomenology is capable of explaining the former but not the latter. However, even from the perspective of religion-as-experience, religion reaches for, but never attains its transcendent object. It searches for the meaning of life in its totality,

> but this meaning is never understood, this last word is never spoken; always they remain superior, the ultimate meaning being a secret which reveals itself repeatedly, only nevertheless to remain eternally concealed. It implies an advance to the farthest boundary, where only one sole fact is understood: — that all comprehension is 'beyond'; and thus the ultimate meaning is at the same moment the limit of meaning.[160]

Still, this solution is not complete for it must accept a limitation of applying the phenomenological method to religion. Namely, phenomenology is able to describe only the immanent experience of reaching toward the unknown transcendent being. It cannot describe the non-phenomenal religion-as-transcendent.

Additionally, in itself Dupré does not accept Van der Leeuw's description of religion reaching for but never attaining the transcendent. Dupré maintains that "the religious act does not merely *reach* toward an unknown, as may appear to the outsider; it *attains* its transcendent object."[161] Once again we return to the chasm between the religious attitude and phenomenological investigation. Ultimately Dupré concludes,

> no purely phenomenological analysis can adequately describe the religious act, because the object of this act never becomes sufficiently immanent in the experience to allow a complete analysis of the act without recurring to a transcendent and, therefore, trans-phenomenological datum.[162]

---

[160] Van der Leeuw, *Religion in Essence and Manifestation*, § 108, 1.
[161] *DH*, 77.
[162] Dupré, "Philosophy of Religion and Revelation," 504-505.

However, phenomenology may still be a valid methodology to investigate the religious experience, for there remains an immanent quality in religion and its object. "If there is a religious *experience* at all, it must obviously be immanent and, consequently, describable in a purely phenomenological fashion."[163] However, phenomenology of itself will be severely impeded in its efforts, for in religion, there is a connection between the immanent experience and the transcendent object which cannot be removed from the realm of investigation. For this connection to be evident, some type of faith is necessary. "If a transcendent reality can only be an object of faith, it is also true that faith alone renders an object transcendent."[164]

Dupré is not suggesting that the phenomenologist must have personal faith in his investigation. Neither is he advocating that personal faith is a sufficient basis by which to phenomenologically describe religion; the phenomenologist must be conversant with religion of many times and cultures. Dupré suggests that some type of minimum faith is required. "The phenomenologist must in some way enter into the religious act, either through present or past faith, or also through an actual acquaintance with religious acts and experiences analogous with the ones he attempts to analyze."[165]

The solution, then, that Dupré proposes to the dilemma of how phenomenology can investigate the transcendent which is a matter of faith, is for phenomenology to appropriate to itself some degree of faith. This avoids the extremes of denying transcendence or

---

[163] Dupré, "Philosophy of Religion and Revelation," 505.

[164] *DH*, 77.

[165] Dupré, "Phenomenology of Religion," 179. Also see id., "Philosophy and the Religious Perspective of Life," Presidential Address, *Proceedings of the American Catholic Philosophical Association* 45 (1971): 4; and *OD*, 110. Dupré discusses both Scheler and Van der Leeuw on the role of faith and finds both deficient; see particularly *OD*, 109 and id., "Philosophy of Religion and Revelation," 503, 506-507.

reshaping phenomenology into ontology. For a true phenomenological description of the religious act to occur, some degree of
empathy must be present on the part of the philosopher for the
religious subject.

b. Question of Real Existence

Granting the dependence of phenomenology upon faith, this raises
another problem: "How can the phenomenological *epoché* be
maintained when a principle of understanding is involved which is
always committed to the *real* existence of the transcendent object?"[166] In other words, how far can faith effect the method of the
phenomenologist? Through faith the believer is committed to
the real existence of the transcendent religious object. But the
phenomenological *epoché* (the bracketing of all presuppositions
about phenomena, of all existential elements), restricts the move
from the religious act *intending* the real existence of its object to
*actual* real existence of the object.

The only way to make this move is for the phenomenologist to
completely appropriate the believer's faith. However, this is unacceptable, for then the investigation is no longer phenomenological
but purely religious. "The intentional object is present only in its
ideal aspect and the phenomenologist knows nothing of an existence
beyond consciousness."[167] While the phenomenologist can indeed
be a believer, his or her investigation must remain critical and
affirmations of real transcendence cannot play a part in the
phenomenological investigation. Thus, for Dupré the phenomenologist cannot move to an affirmation of real existence of the
religious object.

---

[166] Dupré, "Philosophy of Religion and Revelation," 505.
[167] Dupré, "Philosophy of Religion and Revelation," 506.

In light of this and other concerns, in order to more fully explicate a method for philosophy of religion, Dupré further investigates the approaches of Edmund Husserl, Maurice Blondel and Henry Duméry. Following Duméry he advocates a solution to the problem of acknowledging real existence. The solution at this juncture is not to move to faith, but from phenomenology to an ontological affirmation. "Since faith also is ultimately a matter of being and non-being, a phenomenology of religion must always be complemented by a philosophy in the older, metaphysical sense of the term."[168] Given that religion considers matters of existence and so must ask questions of being and nonbeing, Dupré also includes an ontological study which is more appropriate at this turn than phenomenology.

c. Question of Truth

There still remains another problem. On the one hand, the phenomenologist, as any philosopher, approaches the question of truth from a certain perspective. On the other hand, religion has its own understanding of truth from within the viewpoint of faith. Once again we must attempt to reconcile two divergent positions. Actually, Dupré suggests that instead of a divergence to bridge, phenomenology provides a theory of truth that is particularly receptive to the truth claims of religion.

Dupré discusses the correspondence and coherence theories of truth and acknowledges that each have much to contribute to the understanding of truth proper to religion. However, caught in the modern move to the subject, each has become estranged from the religious understanding of its truth.[169] Dupré also traces the lines

---

[168] *OD*, 111.

[169] Particularly Dupré has in mind the difficulty of accepting revelation when the human subject becomes the sole source of equation or coherence. See Dupré, "Truth in Religion and Truth of Religion," 509-510. The modern subjective turn will be discussed below in the fourth chapter.

of a disclosure model of truth from Parmenides and demonstrates particular interest in Husserl's notion of truth. Disclosure focuses on ontological truth over epistemic truth. It is important to recognize the historical facts of religion (which a disclosure model can accommodate), but key to religious truth is the essential role of revelation, that is, the self-manifestation of the transcendent. And this is precisely contained in a disclosure model, "the real discloses itself — it *appears* with its own evidence."[170] As in the ancient model of illumination, it must accept a religious truth whose fullest revelation cannot be expressed in words. "The paradoxes of mystical knowledge affect religious truth *as such*: it discloses what can never be fully disclosed."[171] Within this phenomenological understanding Dupré locates a philosophical foundation for religious truth.

## 3. *Concluding Comment*

In this modest attempt to elucidate Dupré's justification of his method, we have recognized that he is aware of its limits as well of its strengths and possibilities. He demonstrates that while he is honest in his phenomenological approach by not trying to maneuver it to accomplish what is contradictory to its essence, neither is he blindly tied to it as his sole methodology.

His overall approach finds its justification in the phenomenological method which discovers the meaning of the religious act in the act itself. Thus, he advances the primacy of experience, but he also recognizes that experience alone cannot fully reveal its own foundation. The experience that is described must to some degree be a matter of faith to the investigator, otherwise its transcendent object which is beyond experience cannot be understood. In addition,

---

[170] Dupré, "Phenomenology of Religion," 187.
[171] Dupré, "Truth in Religion and Truth of Religion," 514.

Dupré finds it necessary to move outside the phenomenological method to reach the ontological foundation of the religious experience. Finally, Dupré justifies the possibility of reflecting upon religious truth without jeopardizing what faith understands by its truth. "Phenomenology presents a theory that preserves the specific nature of religious truth: one that envisions reality as entirely symbolic of a higher meaning and yet does not sacrifice such other levels of truth as that of historical facts."[172]

Since for Dupré religious truth recognizes reality as completely symbolic of a higher meaning, and given the theological and philosophical justifications of symbol as primary religious expression in his thought, it is to a closer appraisal of symbol that we must now give our attention.

[172] Dupré, "Phenomenology of Religion," 188.

# CHAPTER TWO

# SYMBOL THEORY IN GENERAL

After weaving our study with rather varied threads which included the mysticism of Ruusbroec and the philosophy of Hegel to produce a pattern which is shaped by the fundamental role of symbol, it is time to inquire directly into symbol as it is appreciated by Dupré. Symbols have been investigated from a variety of approaches. These include literary and psychological understandings, general philosophical investigations and those providing theological insights, as well as studies of religion from other social sciences and humanities including historical and social anthropological approaches. Paul Ricoeur, having himself earlier considered symbols from the fields of psychoanalysis, poetics, and the history of religions, suggests that the issue of symbols is so divided over diverse fields of research that it tends to become lost in the process.[1] It is neither our intent to discuss such views in themselves nor to confront them with Dupré's thought. The latter will be accomplished only to the extent that a particular author has directly influenced Dupré.

To that end, this chapter begins with a look at the foundations for Dupré's thought on symbol through a selected presentation of the works of Ernst Cassirer and Susan Langer, with an additional comment on Hegel. Then, turning directly to Dupré's appreciation of symbol, we discuss his approach to a metaphysics of culture

---

[1] See Paul Ricoeur, *Interpretation Theory* (Forth Worth: Texas Christian University Press, 1976), 53.

which is intimately linked with symbol. Finally, to complete this exposition of Dupré's general symbol theory, a summary of three 'patterns' of symbol as found in Dupré will be enumerated.


## A. FOUNDATIONS

The two people who have influenced Dupré's understanding of symbol the most are first, Cassirer and secondarily, Hegel.[2] Thus, we begin this section by acknowledging a few points in Cassirer which are key for Dupré. Then, without either repeating what has been said above nor attempting to exhaust Hegel's thought, additional notes on Dupré's utilization of Hegel will be given. Similarly, a few general comments on Langer will be sufficient to complete the presentation of foundations. For it is not that Dupré completely appropriates these authors to himself, rather he employs them as a grounding for his development of religious symbols.

### 1. *Ernst Cassirer*

The philosophical thought of Ernst Cassirer (1874-1945) was shaped by his own works on the history of philosophy. His interests included modern philosophy from Nicholas of Cusa to Kant, and from the German idealism of Kant through Hegel and Cassirer's own time. Cassirer the historian of philosophy, was particularly interested in the problem of knowledge. He uncovers the relationship between philosophical theories of knowledge and scientific

---

[2] In *OD*, 148 Dupré acknowledges that he has adopted "for the general discussion of symbolism the basic principles of Kant, Cassirer, and Susanne K. Langer." The thought of Hegel is also influential. Cassirer is placed as primary and Hegel as secondary based on a general analysis of Dupré's works and substantiated by Louis Dupré, interview by the author, 6 June 1994, Kortrijk, Belgium.

approaches, focussing on various periods of history. This style of intertwining historical and theoretical interests was one of the characteristic traits of Neokantianism as embodied in the Marburg school.

## a. Roots

Cassirer asserts that "the term 'neo-Kantianism' must be determined functionally rather than substantially. It is not a matter of the kind of philosophy as dogmatic doctrinal system; rather, it is a matter of a direction taken in question-posing."[3] Though Cassirer is the primary influence upon Dupré's understanding of symbol, it is precisely in Cassirer's Neokantianism that Dupré departs from Cassirer. True, the Neokantianism of Cassirer is not tied to Kant's claim that we cannot know the thing-in-itself (*Ding an sich*); yet with Cassirer we always remain in an image-world:

> True, we still remain in a world of "images" — but these are not images which reproduce a self-subsistent world of "things"; they are image-worlds whose principle and origin are to be sought in an autonomous creation of the spirit. Through them alone we see what we call "reality," and in them alone we possess it: for the highest objective truth that is accessible to the spirit is ultimately the form of its own activity. ... True, the question of what, apart from these spiritual functions, constitutes absolute reality, the question of what the "thing in itself" may be in *this* sense, [i.e. within the context of pure phenomenology] remains unanswered, except that more and more we learn to recognize it as a fallacy in formulation, an intellectual phantasm.[4]

[3] Ernst Cassirer, "Davos Disputation Between Ernst Cassirer and Martin Heidegger [1929]," in Martin Heidegger, *Kant and the Problem of Metaphysics*, trans. Richard Taft (Bloomington, IN: Indiana University Press, 1990), 171.

[4] Ernst Cassirer, *The Philosophy of Symbolic Forms*, vol. 1, *Language*, trans. Ralph Manheim (New Haven, CT: Yale University Press, 1953), 111.

Despite nuances, "Cassirer's world is a kantian phenomenal world."[5] Cassirer remains obedient to this Kantian framework, which provides consistency, but also becomes a liability. By removing the possibility of knowledge beyond the purely phenomenal image, reality is constricted in its meaning-and-value-giving capabilities. To render a symbol intelligible there must be a move from sensory particulars to both an ordered whole, as well as to that which acts upon the senses and is observed (an ontic level). This second move is not part of Cassirer's framework.

Dupré does, however, accept Cassirer's development of symbol from Kant's understanding. This should not be understood as Neokantian, but rather a basic acceptance of one of Kant's ideas. Cassirer explains his thought process:

> for me as well the productive power of imagination appears in fact to have a central meaning for Kant. From there I was led through my work on the symbolic. One cannot unravel this [the symbolic] without referring it to the faculty of the productive power of imagination. The power of imagination is the connection of all thought to the intuition. Kant calls the power of imagination *Synthesis Speciosa*. Synthesis is the basic power [*Grundkraft*] of pure thinking. For Kant, however, it [pure thinking] does not depend simply on synthesis, but depends instead primarily upon the synthesis which serves the species. But this problem of the species leads into the core of the concept of image, the concept of symbol.[6]

Cassirer starts with Kant's concept of the productive power of imagination, the power which links thought to the intuition. Cassirer must have in mind § 24 of Kant's *Critique of Pure Reason*. This section is not only the logical place to turn, but within Kant's

---

[5] William Van Roo, *Man the Symbolizer*, Analecta Gregoriana 222 (Rome: Gregorian University Press, 1981), 4. Van Roo offers a critique of the strengths and limitations of Cassirer's thought. Also see id., "Symbol According to Cassirer and Langer — II-III," *Gregorianum* 53 (1972): 654-668.

[6] Cassirer, "Davos Disputation," 172.

collected works, it is also the only location where he explicitly designates the figurative synthesis of imagination as *synthesis speciosa*. Kant distinguishes this power of imagination from the synthesis through the understanding (*synthesis intellectualis*): "As figurative, it is distinguished from the intellectual synthesis, which is carried out by the understanding alone, without the aid of the imagination."[7] The figurative synthesis (*synthesis speciosa*) combines the various forms of sensible intuition. This question of the figurative synthesis is linked then with imagination. "The figurative synthesis ... must ... be called the *transcendental synthesis of imagination. Imagination* is the faculty of representing in intuition an object that is *not itself present*."[8] This provides Cassirer with a basis for thought on symbol.

Additionally, with regard to Kant, Cassirer understands him to adhere to a static appreciation of the various forms of *a priori* sensible intuition; these synthetic *a priori* principles of the understanding are unchangeable for Kant. This is due to Kant's assumption that science and mathematics do not allow any other philosophically relevant alternatives. Cassirer moves beyond Kant and accepts a developing notion of mathematical and scientific principles as well as recognizing scientific studies on aspects of culture which had not yet been treated in Kant's day. In so doing, Cassirer extends Kant's critique of the principles of natural science and morality to encompass all human consciousness. "Whereas Kant was concerned only with the formative role of reason in scientific knowledge, Cassirer recognized a far wider range of formative activity and of concept formation."[9] Cassirer does not limit himself to a critique of reason but embarked upon a critique of culture,

---

[7] Immanuel Kant, *Immanuel Kant's Critique of Pure Reason*, trans. Norman Kemp Smith (London: Macmillan, 1953), § 24, B 152.

[8] Kant, *Critique of Pure Reason*, § 24, B 151.

[9] Van Roo, "Symbol According to Cassirer and Langer — II-III," 654.

encompassing not only science but also the symbolizing activity in language, myth, religion and art.

## b. Philosophy of Symbolic Form

Now we shall briefly present Cassirer's reflections on form and also his understanding of the three functions of consciousness which provides the basis for distinguishing the functions of symbol.

Starting with *the* beginning of philosophical speculation, which he identifies with the emergence of the concept of being, Cassirer discusses the relationship between thought and being. These were viewed as interchangeable; in a 'copy theory' of knowledge there is a similarity of content between the particular being and the thought image we have of it. With Plato, being is no longer identified with a particular existing object (as it was for the Presocratics) but it is raised to the status of a problem: what is the concept of being? Thought "no longer runs parallel to being, a mere reflection 'about' being, but by its own inner form, it now determines the inner form of being."[10] Through the inner form of thought, meaning is established and not simply mirrored. A similar realization was attained through the development of scientific thought: "The fundamental concepts of each science, the instruments with which it propounds its questions and formulates its solutions, are regarded no longer as passive images of something given but as *symbols* created by the intellect itself."[11] The 'thought' of science symbolically understands it object. Its knowledge is mediated through specific logical and conceptual structures. This view requires science to relinquish any aspirations of achieving "an 'immediate' grasp and communication of reality."[12] Another consequence of this

[10] Cassirer, *Symbolic Forms*, 1:74.

[11] Cassirer, *Symbolic Forms*, 1:75.

[12] Cassirer, *Symbolic Forms*, 1:76.

view is that different sciences will explain a physical object in varying ways depending upon the manner in which each science frames its question and subjects phenomena to a particular interpretation.

Cassirer extends this approach to the interpretation of being beyond science to every authentic function of human consciousness (the human spirit). He specifically refers to art, myth and religion.

> All live in particular image-worlds, which do not merely reflect the empirically given, but which rather produce it in accordance with an independent principle. Each of these functions creates its own symbolic forms which, if not similar to the [scientific] intellectual symbols, enjoy equal rank as products of the human spirit.[13]

Symbolic representation, then, is an essential operation of human consciousness. It operates throughout science, language, myth, religion, art and history; that is to say, it operates throughout culture. Thus, since the forms of human cultural life are symbolic, Cassirer offers a definition of human being "as an *animal symbolicum*."[14] For Cassirer, defining human beings as rational cannot properly express the forms of human cultural life. To accomplish this, he instead views human beings as 'symbolizers'.

Cassirer's theory of symbolic forms is based upon his conception of the functions of human consciousness. He does not approach consciousness from metaphysics, or epistemology, or empirical psychology, but from the view of "pure phenomenology." The three symbolic systems of myth (including religion), language (ordinary language and common sense), and science are understandable in their correspondence to the threefold structure of consciousness.

---

[13] Cassirer, *Symbolic Forms*, 1:78.

[14] "symbolizing animal," Ernst Cassirer, *An Essay on Man* (New Haven, CT: Yale University Press, 1944), 26.

These divisions in consciousness develop progressively, one from another.[15]

First, there is the expressive function (*Ausdrucksfunktion*). This is the most primitive mode of representation. Here, symbol and significance blend together. They can still be differentiated, but this is not consciously realized. Symbols directly express an object. This is present in myth and ritual where, for example, a dancer is perceived as the god whose mask is worn, or thunder is apprehended not simply as an external sign of a god's anger, but actually is the god's anger.

Second, there is the representational function (*Darstellungsfunktion*) which encounters the power of language and thus encompasses higher forms of experience. Here the symbol points beyond the immediate perception. This is operative when any language uses a word to refer to a specific object or class of objects that have particular perceptual qualities, such as the word "bed."

With the third, which is the pure significative function (*reine Bedeutungsfunktion*), we move to the realm of science. Here the focus is a system of relations as distinguished from a system of substances with attributes. The interest is not universalization but a principle of ordering. Symbols freely and systematically establish a world of meaning. While this is somewhat present in common language (when meanings are not explainable by perceiving an object, but must be defined through the meanings of other words), its primary expressions are found in modern mathematics, symbolic logic and scientific concepts. Thus there is a progression from the first function of consciousness concerned with the simple expression of a phenomenon, to the third where new meanings are reached through the systematic ordering of symbols themselves.

[15] See Ernst Cassirer, *The Philosophy of Symbolic Forms*, vol. 3, *The Phenomenology of Knowledge*, trans. Ralph Manheim (New Haven, CT: Yale University Press, 1957), 92-117; 281-327.

## c. Philosophy of Culture

Cassirer's philosophy of culture should not be considered as simply a special field or theme in his thought. Instead, it is much more fundamental: it is where his thoughts are directed and coalesce. Cassirer extends Kant's critique of reason to cultural forms. "Thus the critique of reason becomes the critique of culture. It seeks to understand and to show how every content of culture, in so far as it is more than a mere isolated content, in so far as it is grounded in a universal principle of form, presupposes an original act of the human spirit."[16] In developing a philosophy of culture, the question arises as to whether permanent order and meaning can be found in the variety of cultural expressions through time. Dupré recognizes Cassirer as "One of the first thinkers to seek the permanent meaning of the transient historical processes."[17] Cassirer attempts to account for both the unity and the diversity of cultural forms by interpreting them as symbolic forms. He identifies both aspects as present in myth; the unifying tendency is the strongest in primitive religions (seen in the equating of natural forces with deities) while more developed religions can express greater variety (witnessed in moral codes of personal responsibility). This can also be witnessed in language with the need for consistent rules as well as phonetic and semantic changes. Similarly, in art there is both a push toward creativity as well as keeping some type of continuity. Finally, in science the conservative element is quite strong, yet there is also room for occasional refinement and limited alteration. Living within this symbolizing and other activity, human beings experience the possibilities of culture. Cassirer's understanding of symbol through

[16] Cassirer, *Symbolic Forms*, 1:80.

[17] Louis Dupré, *Passage to Modernity: An Essay in the Hermeneutics of Nature and Culture* (New Haven, CT: Yale University Press, 1993), 8. [Hereafter *PM*].

the influence of Kant, the concept of form, and a philosophy of culture all will have an influence upon Dupré's thought.

## 2. *G. W. F. Hegel*

Clearly, more can be said regarding Hegel's view of symbol than that presented in the previous chapter. However, it is only necessary to keep in mind his general framework of representation which Dupré utilizes. It is specifically due to Cassirer's Neokantian propensity that Dupré turns to Hegel. Hegel reaches the conclusion that everything that exists is knowable; (every reality is rational and the rational is real). There is no unknown thing-in-itself or remaining in the image. For Hegel, reality is the self-unfolding of the Absolute Idea from God to his creation and return into itself. All objects of knowledge (all that is) are the products of the Absolute Spirit.

For Dupré, Hegel suggests the metaphysical grounding lacking in Cassirer. In developing a view of culture that would present a unified concept and at the same time respect the multiplicity of cultures, Cassirer "like all Neokantians, abandoned a 'substantialist' philosophy in favor of a search for a fundamental 'rule' of mental creativity."[18] This is not acceptable to Dupré. Dupré maintains the necessity of a metaphysical foundation. "Cassirer's [hermeneutic] was never to result in a metaphysical principle of being: its unity remains that of *rule*, albeit a more comprehensive rule than that of objective science."[19] While not appealing to the Absolute Spirit of Hegel, Dupré agrees with Hegel that there must be metaphysical ultimacy. This is an important guiding principle for Dupré's

---

[18] Louis Dupré, *Metaphysics and Culture*, The Aquinas Lecture 1994 (Milwaukee: Marquette University Press, 1994), 30. [Hereafter *MC*].

[19] *MC*, 33.

approach to the question of culture and symbolism which will be taken up below beginning on page 76.

## 3. *Susanne Langer*

We turn next to a few points in the thought of Susanne Langer (1895-1985). The logical theory of her work is dependent upon Wittgenstein and she also employs the ideas of Cassirer. Langer is utilized by Dupré because of her adherence to Cassirer and the clarity of her distinctions. One of the weaknesses that has been identified in Cassirer's thought is his lack of differentiation between sign and symbol. One of the basic distinctions which Langer provides is precisely that between sign, signal and symbol.[20]

### a. Sign: Signal, Symbol

A sign is a general term used "to denote any vehicle of meaning, signal or symbol."[21] A signal is a specific type of sign that "indicates the existence — past, present, or future — of a thing, event, or condition."[22] A signal may be either natural — such as smoke signifying fire, wet ground signaling it has rained — or artificial, that is, strictly by convention, such as road signs and

[20] In the main text of *Philosophy in a New Key*, 22-52, Langer only distinguishes between sign and symbol. In the preface to the second edition in 1951 of *Philosophy in a New Key*, she further differentiates between sign and signal. This change is brought about from her reading of Charles Morris, *Signs, Language and Behavior*. Langer replaces the term "sign" with "signal," which then allows sign to function as a more general term and signal to be a type of sign. See Susanne Langer, *Philosophy in a New Key*: *A Study in the Symbolism of Reason, Rite, and Art* (Cambridge: Harvard University Press, 1942, 1957³), x. Also see id., *Feeling and Form*: *A Theory of Art Developed From Philosophy in a New Key* (London: Routledge & Kegan Paul, 1953), 26 and 26 note 1. Dupré acknowledges Langer's modification, [see *OD*, 148] as will this study.

[21] Langer, *Philosophy in a New Key*, x.

[22] Langer, *Philosophy in a New Key*, 57.

bells. For both natural and artificial signals there is a one-to-one correspondence of the signal and its object (the item, event, or condition signified). Thus, by perceiving the signal, the signification is apprehended. Yet, particularly with artificial signals, they may indicate any one of a variety of meanings. Langer provides the example of a bell which can mean the beginning of school, a person at the door, time for dinner, etc. Unbeknown to the author at the time of her writing, with this example she also underscores the fact that signals can culturally and historically fall in and out of use. For example, she mentions that a bell can mean that a type-writer line is ended, a cash register drawer is opening, or that the knife grinder passes. Today, most typewriters automatically advance to the next line without ringing a bell, not to mention computers, and the same holds for cash registers. (I must admit to never having seen a knife grinder go down the street, none the less heard one's bell.) The variety of meanings also suggests that the significance of a signal can be misinterpreted. (For example, I quickly learned that the church bell I can hear from my room rang ten minutes before the start of liturgy and did not always signify the hour as I expected.) Misinterpretation is also possible with natural signs. (A wet sidewalk may be due to someone having washed it and not a signal of recent rain.)

In all of these cases a signal is used to *indicate* things; it simply announces or points to things, whereas a symbol actually *represents* them. The wet pavement replaces the actual rain it signals. But, in functioning as a symbol, the name of a person need not point to the physical individual as it can be a reminder or used to talk about the person. "Symbols are not proxy for their objects, but are *vehicles for the conception of objects*."[23] The symbol expresses the meaning held in the conception; it is an instrument of thought.

---

[23] Langer, *Philosophy in a New Key*, 60-61.

"Furthermore, a symbol is used to articulate ideas of something we wish to think about, and until we have a fairly adequate symbolism we cannot think about it."[24] Symbolism is necessary to formulate a certain thought process. In doing so, there must be some interest in the idea or object in order to understand the symbol and allow it to effectively express its meaning. Otherwise the symbol carries no meaning. All other animals at most can use articles or sounds as signs to simply indicate something else, whereas humans can also employ objects or language as actually representing what is signified.

## b. Art

Additionally, in Langer's work we should single out her interest in the symbolic nature of art. While it cannot be developed here, it is engaging to follow her progression of thought in three of her main works. Beginning with *Philosophy in a New Key* she investigates "symbolism as the characteristically human element in cognition ... [which leads to] the concept of art as the symbolic expression of an artist's knowledge of feeling."[25] The latter is found in her second main work *Feeling and Form*. The final culmination of her thought is presented in *Mind: An Essay on Human Feeling*. In *Mind* she combines "the efforts of a lifetime in one lasting, original synthesis"[26] as she argues for the biological foundation of feeling as expressed in aesthetic images.

Langer discusses the arts as symbolic, providing continuity with the symbolic nature of language, science and mathematics. "Art is

[24] Langer, *Feeling and Form*, 28.

[25] Susanne Langer, *Mind: An Essay on Human Feeling*, vol. 1 (Baltimore: Johns Hopkins Press, 1967), xv.

[26] Louis Dupré, review of *Mind*, vol. 1, by Susanne Langer, in *The New Scholasticism* 46 (Autumn 1972): 527.

the creation of forms symbolic of human feeling."[27] Artistic symbols possesses characteristics unique from linguistic ones. Accordingly, Langer distinguishes between presentative symbols and discursive symbols. The language of ordinary speech, science, mathematics, and other language systems are discursive. "The essence of language is statement."[28] Words articulate a successive, linear order of projection. The strength of language includes its ability to assist in the formation of abstract concepts, propositions, and facts, and apply these to the practical and theoretical realms through reasoning. Yet, its strengths can also become a liability. "It is clumsy and all but useless for rendering the forms of awareness that are not essentially recognition of facts, though facts may have some connection with them."[29] Langer finds it difficult to express in discursive language those "perceptions of our own sensitive reactions to things inside and outside of ourselves, and of the fabric of tensions which constitutes the so-called 'inner life' of a conscious being. The constellations of such events are largely non-linear."[30] The symbols of art, which are nondiscursive — color, gesture, dance, sounds, dress, poetry — are more suited to express these realities.

Langer refers to these nondiscursive symbols as presentative. Unlike discursive symbols that have an intrinsic generality, these symbols directly present an individual object; there is a simultaneous, integral presentation. "Just as the content of discourse is the discursive concept, so the content of a work of art is the non-discursive concept of feeling; and it is directly expressed by the form, the appearance before us."[31] There are a number of characteristic

---

[27] Langer, *Feeling and Form*, 40.
[28] Langer, *Mind*, 102.
[29] Langer, *Mind*, 103.
[30] Langer, *Mind*, 103.
[31] Langer, *Feeling and Form*, 82.

differences attributed to presentative symbols in contrast to discursive ones. For example, artistic creation is governed by the laws of imagination and not those of discursive logic. In this light:

> Non-discursive form in art has a different office, namely to articulate knowledge that cannot be rendered discursively because it concerns experiences that are not *formally* amenable to the discursive project. Such experiences are the rhythms of life, organic, emotional and mental ... which are not simply periodic, but endlessly complex, and sensitive to every sort of influence. All together they compose the dynamic pattern of feeling. It is this pattern that only non-discursive symbolic forms can present, and that is the point and purpose of artistic construction.[32]

An additional characteristic of a nondiscursive symbol is its 'overdeterminative' or ambivalent quality; the same form may have more that one significance. Even when a word has a variety of meanings — and particularly when the meanings are quite disparate from each other — it is limited to one specific meaning in the context of discourse. In contrast, artistic form can present opposites together and is limited only by its formal structure:

> The power of artistic forms to be emotionally ambivalent springs from the fact that emotional opposites — joy and grief, desire and fear, and so forth — are often very similar in their dynamic structure, and reminiscent of each other. Small shifts of expression can bring them together, and show their intimate relations to each other, whereas literal description can only emphasize their separateness.[33]

Related to ambivalence is the attribute of condensation. An artistic symbol is quite intricate and is able to fuse forms together by intersection, contraction, elision, suppression, and many other devices. This normally produces an intensified image expressing a complexity of feelings. Also typical of this symbolism is that

---

[32] Langer, *Feeling and Form*, 240-241.
[33] Langer, *Feeling and Form*, 242. Also see *Mind*, 103.

while words and phrases can be translated from one language system to another, all art is formally and essentially untranslatable. The meaning of artistic symbols is delineated by its particular form and cannot be adequately translated into words. For example, "because the forms of human feeling are much more congruent with musical forms than with the forms of language, music can *reveal* the nature of feelings with a detail and truth that language cannot approach."[34] This is even true of poetry, "for though the *material* of poetry is verbal, its import is not the literal assertion made in the words, but *the way the assertion is made*, and this involves the sound, the tempo, the aura of associations of the words, [etc.]."[35] Finally, with artistic symbols it is not a matter of succession but of simultaneity. That is, fundamental in artistic form is a simultaneous perception of meaning. There are aspects that intellectually could be conceived only successively if taken as a discursive symbol, but apprehension of a presentative symbol occurs in one look: by seeing in the visual arts, hearing in music, understanding in poetry. Thus, presentative symbols possess unique possibilities in distinction to the powers of discursive symbols.

On music in particular, Langer provides an extensive treatment which includes an investigation of the claim that music makes a person feel a certain way. She argues to the conclusion that the significance of music is neither that of a stimulus to elicit emotions nor of a signal to point to them. Rather, "if it has an emotional content, it 'has' it in the same sense that language 'has' its conceptual content — *symbolically*."[36] Music is an "unconsummated symbol,"[37] because while it is a symbolic form, there is no

[34] Langer, *Philosophy in a New Key*, 235.

[35] Langer, *Philosophy in a New Key*, 260-261.

[36] Langer, *Philosophy in a New Key*, 218. Also see her summary of the discussion of music in *Philosophy in a New Key*, in id., *Feeling and Form*, 27-32.

[37] Langer, *Philosophy in a New Key*, 240-241; id., *Feeling and Form*, 31.

permanent contents or conventional reference, as there is, for example, in language. This is to say that "the *assignment* of one rather than another possible meaning to each form is never explicitly made."[38] Thus, instead of calling the significance of music its "meaning," she designates it as "vital importance" in order to express the dynamic subjective experience and lack of conventional reference. Langer than takes her theory of music and generalizes it into a theory of art, including pictorial art, architecture, literature, poetry, drama, etc. This has provided a true contribution to philosophy of symbol and furnishes additional background for Dupré's thought.

## B. FRAMING SYMBOLISM WITHIN METAPHYSICS AND CULTURE

Turning directly to Dupré's own understanding of symbol, we now initially approach the issue by investigating the role it plays in other areas of his thought. There are many constants in Dupré's works, and if one uniting concept is to be singled out, it is his interest in culture. This bears a similarity to the fundamental role of culture in Cassirer's thought; (the affinity is in the placement and raising of the question, but not always in the answers). In his Introduction to Dupré's *De symboliek van het heilige*,[39] Jacques De Visscher insightfully portrays Dupré as a philosopher of culture and traces this interest through the history of Dupré's works under

---

[38] Langer, *Philosophy in a New Key*, 240. Also see id., *Mind*, 1:105: "The art symbol, however, does not rest on convention. There are conventions in art, and they do change, but they govern only the ways of creating the symbol, and not its semantic function."

[39] Jacques De Visscher, "Inleiding: De cultuurkritiek van Louis Dupré," in *De symboliek van het heilige*, trans. Guido Vanheeswijck (Kampen: Kok Agora; Kapellen: DNB/Pelckmans, 1991), 7-21. [Hereafter *SH*].

the two interrelated constants of the social and religious phenomena. Even before its publication, De Visscher was able to include comments on Dupré's 1993 *Passage to Modernity* which is a clear example of Dupré's cultural concern, here as embodied in modernity. More importantly for us, in his 1994 Aquinas Lecture, *Metaphysics and Culture*, (which was not yet available for De Visscher to include in his 1991 introduction), Dupré explicitly articulates the philosophical underpinnings of the overall cultural question. He explains that "Culture consists of the symbols that preserve and direct the life of a society. Its philosophical significance, then, corresponds to that of symbol[']s."[40]

## 1. *Metaphysics and Culture*

In *Metaphysics and Culture*, the fundamental question that Dupré raises is how can unity be articulated through the multiplicity of cultural expressions, both over time and between existing cultures. He proposes a metaphysical justification of culture because culture "receives its definitive unity and coherence only from the kind of comprehensive synthesis which metaphysics alone can convey."[41] Dupré does not propose the 'rules' of Cassirer, but ultimately knowable 'metaphysical ultimacy' in the lines of Hegel. Yet for metaphysics to provide the basis for historical cultural change without relinquishing its necessary character, metaphysics itself must be reinterpreted from its traditional understanding. A first condition for the possibility of a metaphysics of culture is to move from a static metaphysics of Aristotle and Aquinas to one which allows itself to be affected by historical change. Metaphysics must not just reflect unchangeably about changeable time; but Being (as investigated by metaphysics) itself becomes historical.

[40] *MC*, 12.
[41] *MC*, 60.

Dupré points to Hegel as "the first to abandon the static idea of philosophy."[42] Through work initiated by Husserl on the ontological significance of time, "Heidegger dealt the definitive blow to the subjective interpretation of time by showing how beyond being a subjective awareness of self-duration, the intrinsic temporality of existence (*Dasein*) discloses an essential quality of *being*."[43] However, Dupré acknowledges that more must be done to acquire a metaphysics of culture than ascertain the historicity of being. One must still account for how the variety of cultures which are often incompatible can articulate a unified revelation of being. To attempt to accomplish this, Dupré turns to cultural hermeneutics. It is through its cultural works that humanity is able to understand itself. Through language and literature, insight is made into the self, in its many faceted moral feelings and complexities. With the modern turn to the subject as the source of meaning, the study of being is pursued through the study of existence and the issue of existence in turn requires an examination of its cultural expressions. Thus, Dupré moves beyond Cassirer's philosophy of culture, by recognizing the more recent developments which justify an understanding of philosophy as within time and culture and not simply as a reflection from outside.

However, granting this inner hermeneutical reflection, the problem still remains how metaphysics can be able to discover unity in the midst of cultural multiplicity. Granted there is much intercultural exchange which occurs today, but this does not reconcile oppositions which exist between cultures. "The inner coherence of

[42] *MC*, 26. Dupré continues: "[For Hegel], Spirit, the ultimate philosophical category, is intrinsically historical. History is Spirit as it objectively proceeds to its fulfillment. ... Temporality hereby enters into the absolute without simply coinciding with the absolute itself." *MC*, 26-27.

[43] *MC*, 27. See Martin Heidegger, *Being and Time*, trans. John Macquarrie and Edward Robinson (Oxford: Basil Blackwell; New York: Harper and Row, 1962), 274-488.

one culture remains largely impenetrable to another."[44] To speak of "Greek culture" or "Roman culture" excessively universalizes specific features. Certain intrinsically related traits do exist, but there are no unified totalities of which to speak. Yet, when we refer to "modern culture" there is even a lower degree of coherence. "The term 'modern culture', has hardly any definable content beyond an almost universal aversion of traditional attitudes and values."[45] Diverse cultures and subcultures, sometimes barely able to find a common point of communication, all can be called modern. We shall not dwell upon this point, but this important terminological caution must be kept in mind throughout the remaining chapters when reference is made to "modern culture."

Thus, the primary hindrance remaining to the attainment of a complete philosophical hermeneutic of culture is the contingency of cultural symbols. From one time to another there are a variety of symbols, and within a given period great diversity exists from one society to another. This conglomeration of symbols is not experienced as universal and necessary. "The philosopher engaging on a hermeneutic quest gambles on the faith that the always hazardous interpretation of cultural symbols will pay off in *some* understanding of existence, and that, through it, he or she will gain *some* insight into being itself."[46] In addition, there remains the problem of how to regain a metaphysical principle of ultimacy in light of the modern turn to the human subject as the source of meaning. We will return to this second question in the fourth chapter.[47] Here we keep our focus on the immediate difficulty of how cultural symbols may transcend the contingency of their expression.

---

[44] *MC*, 35.

[45] *MC*, 36.

[46] *MC*, 37.

[47] On the modern interpretation of the human subject as the sole source of meaning and value, see below, pp. 203-212.

## 2. *Symbols and Metaphysical Ultimacy*

This question of cultural symbols and the possibility of a meta-physical grounding is formed within the issue of symbols and metaphysical ultimacy. "Symbols enable the mind to perceive the permanent in the transient, the universal in the particular."[48] Dupré reaches back to the beginnings of metaphysics to locate the development of the role of symbol in understanding and in the meaningful totality of perception (through architecture, sculpture, poetry, etc.) which is culture. The science of metaphysics emerged as the mere appearance of things was no longer accepted as justification for their existence. The Presocratics "conceived of the absolute as expressiveness."[49] The absolute was expressed through the primacy of water, or fire, or mathematics, etc. (Later, Plato and Neoplatonists preserve this expressive character as the Good which communicates existence and meaning to all beings.) For Parmenides the foundational principle was Being: Being is, not-Being is not. Thus, metaphysics becomes ontology. Of course there have been considerable shifts in the meaning of "Being" throughout history. "For Plato and Aristotle, *being* consisted essentially in meaningful *form*. Not that things were there but that they made sense had to be justified."[50] That things had meaning needed a justification. Yet there are two fundamental changes that occurred in the metaphysical quest which were occasioned by Christianity. The first is due to the doctrine of creation. With this doctrine, there was no longer any need to search for a justification of meaning. The meaningfulness of everything was guaranteed because God had created it. So, "the primary question was no longer why things

[48] *MC*, 9.
[49] *MC*, 1.
[50] *MC*, 1.

were meaningful, but why they were there at all."[51] The ensuing
approaches took another look at such concepts as ground, cause,
participation, being and knowledge.

The second shift prompted by Christianity is related to the first
and has primary significance for our project. The Gospel of John
set the stage for a new religious and metaphysical understanding
of reality. "In the beginning was the Word, and the Word was
with God, and the Word was God."[52] All that is has being through
the eternal Word. Language is proclaimed "the primeval symbol
of the expressiveness of the absolute."[53] The conception of the
absolute as expressiveness which had been so pronounced in the
ancient pagan tradition becomes expressiveness *through language*.
Eventually, as the language of faith is conceived as revelatory, this
quality is extended to all language. "Western thought came to
view language *itself* as revelatory and as transforming the entire
visible but mute world of appearance into a verbal metaphor."[54]
Yet the move from the symbolic nature of religious language to all
language was a slow process. While reflection on the revealed
word urged Christian thinkers in this direction, the categories for
understanding language required certain modifications. So in ancient and medieval thought the symbolic nature of language remained mostly restricted to some previously established metaphorical function. That is, words were used merely as expressing
an already established internal state of mind. Knowing was a
process of first interiorizing the known in an internal word (*verbum internum*) which was then externalized in spoken or written
language (*verbum externum*). Dupré maintains, "Not before the

---

[51] *MC*, 1.
[52] John 1:1 NRSV. See *MC*, 4 and *PM*, 102.
[53] *MC*, 4.
[54] *MC*, 4.

twelfth century did philosophers become aware of the symbolism inherent in all language."[55] Dupré indicates Abelard as pointing to this understanding. For a word to be symbolic it must be more than the outward expression of the internal word of an external reality. Not before the twelfth century was there any awareness of the fact that words had substance of their own, so to speak, other than being read. The tight link between the word and thing (*res*) was loosened. Words have a meaning beyond expressing an internal copy of reality. A word "*articulates* the reality to which it refers."[56]

Dupré suggests that it was not until the end of the Middle Ages that words were fully appreciated as articulating reality. The philosophical approaches of nominalism and early humanism made this achievement possible. As to nominalism, through a negative impulse to detach words from things, words receive an independence of their own, independent even of the concepts (inner words) that they express. "As meaning became detached from the given structure of the real, words and forms became independent symbols of expression."[57] Language could no longer be considered as merely a mirror of a reality internalized by the mind. While not an intentional plan of nominalism, "it created a wider space for metaphorical creativity."[58] As to early humanism, it embraced a positive view of language stemming from a medieval rhetorical tradition employing Roman models. Armed with this inspiration, early humanism went beyond the negative nominalistic split between word and thing and promoted language as such as creative of meaning; language positively created something new. The traditional order of reference from reality to language was reversed so

---

[55] *MC*, 6. Also see *PM*, 103.
[56] *MC*, 6. Also see *OD*, 148.
[57] *PM*, 41.
[58] *PM*, 105.

that reality itself was viewed through the prism of language. This transformation was aided by the medieval interpretation of Scripture in which the sacred word alone revealed meaning. Humanists applied this meaning giving function of biblical words to all language, including profane vernacular literature.[59] Thus, the early humanists recognized that word's have the power to make present in a new way that to which they refer. Language is capable of disclosing new levels of meaning. "Emphasizing the essential expressiveness of human nature, humanism laid the basis for a genuine philosophy of the symbol."[60] This is not to deny that poets (and religious and philosophical writers) were aware of the need for metaphor to express invisible realities. But "before Dante and the early humanists[,] poets had not been as aware of their creative potential."[61] In this brief outline of Dupré's reading of history, the primacy of the role of symbol in expressing the meaning of reality is manifested as well as the development toward a genuine philosophy of the symbol through which metaphysical ultimacy is attained.

The foregoing has been a treatment of symbol as primary metaphysical expression. But Dupré's theory of Western metaphysics will coincide with religion, for as we have indicated metaphysics has been religiously inspired. Having framed Dupré's conception of symbol within his thought on culture and metaphysical ultimacy, we turn to further develop three general patterns operative in symbol.

---

[59] Of course there was a split between those early humanists who sought the fullness of expression through the living vernacular language and those who advocated the consistency of ancient Latin, but all agreed on the primacy of the word. See *PM*, 106.

[60] *MC*, 7.

[61] *PM*, 107. For related reflections by Dupré on nominalism and humanism see *MC*, 6-7; *PM*, 102-112; "The Broken Mirror: The Fragmentation of the Symbolic World," *Stanford Literature Review* 5 (Spring 1988): 9-11.

## C. THREE GENERAL PATTERNS

Brand Blanshard has summarized Dupré's theory of religious symbolism by the following six characteristics.[62] First, a symbol is distinguished from a sign. A sign points to something beyond it, whereas a symbol does this and also represents what it presents. Second, what differentiates religious symbols from other symbols is their referring to what is transcendent. Third, verbal symbols are distinct from nonverbal ones and verbal symbols are necessary to express the attributes of God and God's relationship to humanity. Fourth, faith is required to understand the meaning of a religious symbol. Fifth, "symbolic signs and expressions actually *produce* the signified and expressed reality."[63] Sixth, even religiously symbolic truth must be coherent with itself. While these six characteristics by and large correctly describe Dupré's thought[64] they do not adequately capture the fullness of its meaning.

Instead of simply trying to refine and augment this list of characteristics, I have chosen to designate the following three points as 'patterns' to provide a more extensive and authentic presentation of Dupré's understanding of symbol. A certain amount of overlap with Blanshard's characteristics should be expected, but my patterns afford a focus on certain fundamental distinctions and insights into Dupré's thought.

---

[62] See Brand Blanshard, "Reply to Mr. Dupré['s 'Faith and Reason']," in *The Philosophy of Brand Blanshard*, The Library of Living Philosophers 15, ed. Paul Schilpp (La Salle, IL: Open Court, 1980), 1002- 1014.

[63] *OD*, 183. Quoted by Blanshard, "Reply," 1007.

[64] In characteristic three, Blanshard states that Dupré distinguishes between verbal and "imaginal" symbols. I have corrected this to read "nonverbal" since in Dupré's understanding words can also be images. See Blanshard, "Reply," 1007.

## 1. *Form*

While the importance of form in an investigation of symbol has been implied in our discussion of Cassirer and Langer as well as within Dupré's framework of metaphysics and culture, we must explicitly recognize its relevance in Dupré's appreciation of symbol. Symbols are "*forms* which refer to something that is not directly given."[65] Signs are also objective forms referring to something else. However, a sign does not change its referent, whereas with a symbol "the original reality undergoes a fundamental transmutation."[66] The symbol lifts the content to a new level of reality in and through the appearance, but also beyond the appearance. The content requires the mediation of a symbol because "the mind is intrinsically dependent upon sensuous forms"[67] due to its embodied existence. A brief outline of Dupré's understanding of form will help to place it as a component in the function and existence of symbols.

Returning to the ancient Greek philosophers, Dupré asserts, "If there is one belief Greek thinkers shared, it must be the conviction that both the essence of the real and our knowledge of it consists ultimately of *form*."[68] He goes on to explain, "Basically this means that it belongs to the essence of the real to *appear*, rather than to hide, and to appear in an orderly way."[69] It is in this light that Dupré interprets the Presocratics. Theirs is a search for an orderly state of balance because only when there is a state of harmony can a thing be truly real. For Thales, for example, water should be regarded not as a substantial principle but as presenting a state of balance. While for the early Ionians form appeared

[65] *OD*, 148 emphasis added. Also see *OD*, 150.
[66] *OD*, 150.
[67] *OD*, 150.
[68] *PM*, 18.
[69] *PM*, 18.

through immediate sense perception, for the Pythagoreans form was the appearance of the absolute through an intellectual intuition beyond appearances. This prepares the way for Plato's placement of form in an intellectual realm beyond the sensible world; the physical world is then considered real only to the degree that it participates in the pure forms. His thought on the physical world is dominated by the concept of harmonious form. Aristotle, of course, returns to the individual substance, itself composed of matter and form. Still, it is through the form that the true reality and nature of a thing is attained. Even when Plotinus places the One above all determinate knowable forms, this does not negate the identification of form with reality, but actually "extends it [form] by applying it to the very foundation of reality."[70] Thus, for the ancient Greeks form was the principle by which everything that is has meaning. Form provides the unity and balance that is necessary for things to exist.

With the Christian doctrine of creation, the question shifted from the meaningfulness of form (its orderliness) to the reason for its existence, as indicated in the previous section. But the advent of Christianity raised additional questions. One of particular significance is posed: "How could a cosmic symbolism prefigured in and centered around one individual — the Christ — conform to the universal Greek idea of form?"[71] The principle of balance and meaning, which in its perfection is one with the divine, is now proposed to be located in one individual. For Eastern Christians this question was embodied in the issue of how to artistically express spiritualized form. The iconoclast controversies grappled with the problem of representing the form of God's manifestation. Ultimately, the incarnate divine form was artistically expressed

---

[70] *PM*, 22.
[71] *PM*, 31.

because "the sacramental universality of the incarnated Word whose presence in the world had consecrated all forms proved to be a stronger argument than the uniqueness of its particular appearance."[72] For Western Christians, Dupré suggests that the problem of form provoked the practical moral issue of fallen human nature's ability to embody the divine form. Proposing a number of examples and an outline of historical development, Dupré traces the issue from a negative view of human nature to a renewed interpretation of the incarnation as a positive cosmically transforming event.[73] An openness toward nature and viewing the human person as a microcosm are presented as further pieces to the development. However, the key is the individual. Particularly through Franciscan influence, with the mysticism of Francis of Assisi and the philosophy of John Duns Scotus, "the primary significance of individual form no longer consists in disclosing a universal reality beyond itself."[74] The individual form is itself considered as primary; it is no longer subservient to the universal. Individual form is granted a definitiveness which it had not previously possessed. With this shift, individual beings throughout the natural world are not merely signs of contingency but are expressive of reality. "Thus began a daring cosmic symbolism that endowed each facet of nature with inexhaustible expressiveness. Far from being added to nature, this symbolic potential constituted its very essence."[75]

There is a further shift in the understanding of form in the modern mind as the link between form and the divine is severed. Form no longer receives meaning from the creator God as Christian thinkers had successfully argued. Instead, the human subject assumes this role as form becomes a construction of the human mind.

---

[72] *PM*, 32.
[73] See *MC*, 32-34.
[74] *PM*, 38.
[75] *PM*, 36.

With humanism, form acquires the position of being the symbol of the mind's expressive independence. There is a new freedom in approaching form; it is not simply accepted as a given, rather meaning is also imposed by the mind upon reality. "The singular significance of the humanist movement ... consists in having introduced a different notion of form. Contrary to the ancient view that conceived form as given with the real, form for the humanists was an ideal to be achieved."[76] This ideal combines form and nature to produce a receptivity to aesthetic experience.

Such an appreciation of form must be kept in mind when approaching Dupré's concept of symbol. The role of form in its relation to the meaning of reality, the human ability to touch the divine, the significance of the individual object, and the human subject, acquires a symbolic connection. "Thus form, the central concept of Greco-Christian thought, stood ready [with Modern thought] to assume yet another function in defining the nature of the real."[77] In this new function, form was more adaptable than ever because now it was unincumbered by apriori restrictions. As words acquired an independence apart from the objects and conceptions that they express, so too "forms became independent symbols of expression."[78] The form of a thing (its reality and meaning) is to be symbolically understood.

Dupré fully acknowledges form's aesthetic import. With Plato the form of beauty is linked with goodness as the highest place in the order of the real; and with his adherence to the Greek allegiance to the primacy of form, Plotinus produces what may be regarded to be the first philosophy of aesthetics. Dupré summarizes, "With the emphasis on form begins an aesthetic vision of nature

---

[76] *PM*, 44.
[77] *PM*, 41.
[78] *PM*, 41.

that dominated most of Greek antiquity, much of the Renaissance, and some of the romantic philosophies of Germany and England."[79]

It is no coincidence that Dupré's approach to form, particularly in his interpretation of the incarnation and concern for theological aesthetics, bears a marked similarity to von Balthasar's thought. In commenting upon von Balthasar's seven volume *The Glory of the Lord*, Dupré observes, "At the center of von Balthasar's enterprise stands a simple idea. By assuming human nature God transformed the very meaning of culture. Henceforth all forms have to be measured by the supreme form of the Incarnation."[80] By embracing this interpretation Dupré acknowledges the transforming effect of the incarnate divine form. "When in the Incarnation God adopted human nature, the divine presence transformed the entire cosmos into a living symbol."[81] Following Bonaventure, von Balthasar does not locate the essence of form in subjective perception but in its power to express. The expression may be concealed behind the visible appearance, yet the visible form manifests the expressiveness. This is the case with the incarnation which "allows us to speak of a *divine form*, even though the expressing God remains hidden within the expressive form."[82] This should be understood within von Balthasar's overall project of theological aesthetics. "Theological aesthetics ... consists in the science of the divine form as it stands revealed in Christ and, through that prism, reflected in cosmos and history."[83] Von Balthasar develops this theological aesthetics in his seven volume work. This background on form is particularly

[79] *PM*, 20.

[80] Louis Dupré, "The Glory of the Lord: Hans Urs von Balthasar's Theological Aesthetic," *Communio* 16 (Fall 1989): 385.

[81] Louis Dupré, review of *The Glory of the Lord: A Theological Aesthetics*, in *Religion and Literature* 19 (Autumn 1987): 68.

[82] Dupré, "The Glory of the Lord," 388.

[83] Louis Dupré, "Hans Urs von Balthasar's Theology of Aesthetic Form," *Theological Studies* 49 (June 1988): 300.

important as a frame for the discussion of aesthetics and religious art, below on pages 153-168.

## 2. *Representation*

Following Langer, Dupré distinguishes between sign and symbol and upholds the ability of symbols to actually articulate what is signified and not merely announce it. Symbols *"represent* it [the signified object] in the double sense of *making present* and *taking the place of.*"[84] Symbols express a variety of meanings and are not restricted as are signs to one specific meaning. This is in contrast to Hegel's placement of sign above symbol due to the symbol's ambiguity. Still, despite its complexity a symbol's connection to the signified is greater than that between a sign and signified. It is also precisely because of its complexity that a symbol is able to express the various facets of the signified. The symbol "truly presents what it represents and is therefore, unlike the sign, entitled to receive the respect due to the signified itself."[85] Additionally, a symbol is not limited by the sensible object; "All symbols reveal a reality *beyond* their sensuous appearance."[86] However, Dupré cautions that this does not imply that meaning precedes the symbol; this is far from being the case as meaning is actually discovered in and through the symbol itself. "A symbol never refers back to a pre-existing reality: it opens up a new one."[87] This mediation of the content by the symbol to reveal a new reality is not an optional endeavor of human existence, but is a necessary component of the mind's embodied relation to the sensible world. Thus, Dupré asserts

[84] *OD*, 149.

[85] *OD*, 149. Dupré follows Gadamer in making this assertion. See Hans-Georg Gadamer, *Truth and Method*, trans. Joel Weinsheimer and Donald Marshall (New York: Continuum, 1989²), 154.

[86] *OD*, 149.

[87] *OD*, 150.

that "The fundamental function of the symbol ... is to enable this mind to express itself."[88] This requires a plurality of symbolic structures that cannot be reduced to a single expression since the mind commands multiform articulation.

The first condition for the mind to achieve symbolic expression, whether it be in science, philosophy, art, or rituals and myths, is for it to be removed from the constant stream of sensations and to give certain data a representational function. "Impressions must be made to last beyond their fleeting appearance and to represent a whole complex of impressions."[89] There is a limitless aggregate of impressions which the mind then synthesizes into segments. This process of representation creates a complex of relations in which each impression can depict a number of others. This is not a passive process of association but "an active grasp by which the mind stabilizes and interrelates its sensations in order to be able to perceive representations rather than impressions."[90]

Similar to Cassirer, Dupré returns to Kant as the basis for this process which Kant designates the synthesis of the imagination. Dupré singles out two of Kant's texts as particularly relevant, first, the division entitled "The Synthesis of Reproduction in Imagination,"[91] from the first edition of the *Critique of Pure Reason*, and second, the part of the *Critique of Judgment* where he opposes symbols to schemata.[92] In the first passage Kant argues for a transcendental capacity of the imagination that synthesizes sense appearances into representations. If, for example, human beings one moment changed into one animal shape and the next moment

---

[88] *OD*, 151.

[89] *OD*, 152.

[90] *OD*, 152.

[91] Kant, *Critique of Pure Reason*, § A 100-102.

[92] See Immanuel Kant, *Critique of Judgment*, trans. Werner Pluhar (Indianapolis: Hackett, 1987), § 59, B 255-257.

into a different one, or a feather is one time light and another time heavy, then no empirical synthesis could take place. Thus Kant declares that there is an *a priori* basis for a synthetic unity of appearances which makes the reproduction of appearances possible. Dupré explains that "Only by means of a new temporal synthesis can percepts be detached from the continuous stream of sensation and made into independent representations."[93] The synthesis of the imagination reproduces the initial succession of the appearances into a new temporality. In the second passage Kant expresses that

> all intuitions supplied for a priori concepts are either *schemata* or *symbols*. Schemata contain direct, symbols indirect, exhibitions of the concept. Schematic exhibition is demonstrative. Symbolic exhibition uses an analogy (for which we use empirical intuitions as well), in which judgment performs a double function: it applies the concept to the object of a sensible intuition; and then it applies the mere rule by which it reflects on that intuition to an entirely different object, of which the former object is only the symbol.[94]

In contrasting schemata to symbols Kant distinguishes the principal function of symbolic activity. Symbols are indirect expressions of concepts and maintain an analogous relation to concepts, where schemata are directly transformed into concepts.

Dupré recognizes Hegel as the first thinker to further develop Kant's theory of imagination, which he accomplishes within his philosophy of representation. As discussed above, Hegel's philosophy of representation is foundational for Dupré. The mind re-presents the content of the sensuous intuition by detaching it from the restrictions of space and time. With the productive phantasy human beings are able to assemble a variety of diverse perceptions into a completely new synthesis. Additionally, Dupré appropriates Hegel's idea — advanced through his theory of representation — that

---

[93] *OD*, 153.
[94] Kant, Critique of Judgment, § 59 B 256.

symbols necessitate reflection. Hegel, however, concludes that rational thought must at some point replace the symbol while Dupré does not. Dupré maintains that "to some extent all symbols must be interpreted since the empirical appearance is never the entire symbolic reality."[95] Yet religious symbols are unique in that even for their basic understanding they always require interpretation. A person completely unfamiliar with the artistic traditions and designs of a culture may require a particular art work to be explained regarding these categories, but not beyond them. However, the uninitiated who encounters religious symbols inquires from the most basic level; for religious symbols "interpretation is *intrinsically* necessary."[96] Dupré further asserts that this "interpretation must always be linguistic, for words alone can indicate a *reality* beyond all appearances."[97] To reach their proper function of referring to a transcendent reality, religious symbols must receive the interpretative assistance of language.

This need for interpretation acknowledges the negative character of religious symbols. "Religious symbols are foremost *negative* symbols."[98] They are self-denying and are not to be considered too literally. This negative characteristic is found in all symbols, but it is a predominant quality of religious symbols as they reveal the transcendent primarily by showing what it is not. True, it is the function of all symbols to reveal, to express something that does not directly appear. Yet different types of symbols may reveal in different ways. Aesthetic symbols fully present their referent and emphasize the unity between what is signified and what appears.

---

[95] Louis Dupré, "The Life and Death of Religious Symbols," *The St. Luke's Journal of Theology* 14 (May 1971): 7.

[96] Dupré, "The Life and Death of Religious Symbols," 7.

[97] Dupré, "The Life and Death of Religious Symbols," 7.

[98] Dupré, "The Life and Death of Religious Symbols," 5. Also see *OD*, 164.

However, the contrary is true for religious symbols. The referent remains beyond reach and the discrepancy between what is actually perceived and what is intended is accentuated. Religious symbols are more negative than positive, presenting their referent by expressing what it is not and by concealing more than is revealed. It is through the interpretation of language that the basic meaning of religious symbols is presented.

It should be apparent, then, that religious symbols cannot exclusively be employed to bring about an immediate experience, otherwise their transcendent meaning is impoverished. Further, there is no teleological relationship between religious symbols and immediate experience, but it is simply a structure between the symbol and symbolized. Some assume that religious worship is meaningful only when it can be fully and immediately experienced.[99] But beyond the direct experience of a feeling of God which may result in serving the needs of others, there is a transcendent dimension that cannot be reduced to an immanent experience. The "purpose of worship and in general of all religious symbols is to *meet* the transcendent, not to *use* the transcendent for some ulterior, immanent end."[100] Dupré does not deny that direct experience and social action are necessary components of Christianity. However, the ultimate question is: "Did we confront the transcendent in faith?" Not: "Did we get anything out of it?"[101] What distinguishes religious symbols from all other symbols is not the experience which they articulate, but the articulation itself. "There is no religious experience prior to the religious symbolization."[102] Dupré agrees that there can be an immediate numinous feeling as Otto

---

[99] See e.g., Harvey Cox, *The Feast of Fools*: *A Theological Essay on Festivity and Fantasy* (Cambridge: Harvard University Press, 1969).

[100] Dupré, "The Life and Death of Religious Symbols," 6.

[101] Dupré, "The Life and Death of Religious Symbols," 6.

[102] *OD*, 164.

describes, but in itself it is not a religious experience, nor is it indispensable to the religious experience. Rather, it is through the actual articulation of the religious symbol that there is an awareness of a deeper *reality* underlying all appearances. But as explained above, such an articulation requires interpretation. Thus, once again we return to the need of religious symbols to be interpreted by language, and this is the third pattern to which we now turn for a general appreciation of Dupré's conception of symbol.

## 3. *Language*

### a. Language in General

Following upon the above discussion that framed symbolism within Dupré's thought on metaphysics and culture, it is not surprising that he proclaims, "Language is *the* symbol *par excellence*."[103] Dupré approaches language in the tradition of the writings of Cassirer and Langer. Among his direct and indirect citations of Langer and Cassirer, we first cite a substantial passage of Cassirer that Dupré notes. In it Cassirer explains language's unique ability to clarify relations:

> All the intellectual labor whereby the mind forms general concepts out of specific impressions is directed toward breaking the isolation of the datum, wresting it from the "here and now" of its actual occurrence, relating it to other things and gathering it and them into some inclusive order, into the unity of "a system." The logical form of conception, from the standpoint of theoretical knowledge, is nothing but a preparation for the logical form of judgment; all judgment, however, aims at overcoming the illusion of singularity which adheres to every particular content of consciousness.[104]

---

[103] *OD*, 157.
[104] Ernst Cassirer, *Language and Myth* (New York: Dover, 1953), 25-26.

The goal of symbolization in general is to establish relations between a variety of impressions. In particular, verbal symbolization achieves this goal through conceptualization; "conceptualization is an important function of the symbolization process and an essential one in all linguistic symbols."[105] In conceptualization, relations are symbolized within a clearly defined "system of meaning where each unit is able to convey an independent content."[106] Because these units can be combined into complex meanings that at the same time remain clear, language is able to construct a greater variety of compositions than nonverbal symbols.

A second passage of Cassirer that Dupré notes recognizes that discursive language alone does not exhaust our expressions of reality.

> The forms of things as they are described in scientific concepts tend more and more to become mere formulae. These formulae are of a surprising simplicity. A singular formula, like the Newtonian Law of gravitation, seems to comprise and explain the whole structure of our material universe. It would seem as though reality were not only accessible to our scientific abstractions but exhaustible by them. But as soon as we approach the field of art this proves to be an illusion. For the aspects of things are innumerable, and they vary from one moment to another.[107]

Conceptualization of relations is first attempted by ordinary language. Scientific language "both completes and surpasses this attempt."[108] With the highly discursive language of science there is a particularly prominent level of independence in meaning that allows its words to be detached from direct experience and create its own symbolic system. Yet, while scientific abstractions provide

---

[105] *OD*, 160.
[106] *OD*, 157.
[107] Cassirer, *An Essay on Man*, 144.
[108] *OD*, 159.

an independent and systematic view of reality, it "loses the living contact with experience which is so richly present in non-discursive symbols."[109] However, "not all language is discursive."[110] For example, languages of poetry and prayer are nondiscursive; they present their symbolic content. Dupré applies to all nondiscursive symbols, particularly the aesthetic ones, Gadamer's description of the role of the aesthetic image as opening up new ontological dimensions and making what is symbolized more present and authentic.[111] Dupré reacts against those early linguistic analysts who considered discursive language the only meaningful verbal symbols. He invokes the words of Langer in opposition to this idea that nonconceptual linguistic symbols are merely emotional cries or 'symptomatic' expressions. Langer responds: "Why should we cry our feelings at such high levels that anyone would think we were talking? Clearly poetry means more than a cry: it has reason for being articulate."[112] The different types of symbolization cannot be reduced to one another. Rather, a philosophy of symbolic forms should "distinguish symbols according to the various functions which they fulfill."[113] The process of interpretation must give proper consideration to the type of symbol that is being considered. Thus, Dupré also admits that much nondiscursive symbolism is not verbal at all. Within the field of art there are visual and auditory experiences that are neither discursive nor linguistic. These symbols do not express their meanings by conceptualizing relations in the manner of verbal symbols, but they maintain a stronger living contact with experience.

---

[109] *OD*, 159.

[110] *OD*, 159.

[111] See Gadamer, *Truth and Method*, 154. Also see *OD*, 159 note 28.

[112] Langer, *Philosophy in a New Key*, 81. Also see id., *Problems of Art* (New York: Charles Scribner's Sons, 1957), 24. See *OD*, 160.

[113] *OD*, 160.

## b. Religious Language

Dupré argues that at least within the modern Judeo-Christian tradition the term "religious language" can be applied in a standard manner to such diverse expressions as worship, dogma, Scripture, etc. based upon a common model of interpretation.

> All religious speech requires *faith* for its understanding, that is, it invites the listener to surpass the phenomenal world in a way which essentially differs from the demands of poetry, scientific language, philosophical discourse or the ordinary, functional speech we use going about our business in everyday living.[114]

Dupré explains that "Faith is never an immediate feeling or emotion. It is the awareness of a transcendent dimension to all the experiences of life, the affirmation of a deeper *reality* underlying the obvious appearances."[115] Religious language is essentially different from other language structures as it requires faith. Religious utterances lift the believer to reach toward the transcendent. Language is uniquely fitted to express reality beyond the empirical. "Symbols can be religious in many ways but only words can name the sacred directly."[116] As with Rahner, it is the efficacious word that expresses the divine.[117] "Language alone is sufficiently flexible to mean explicitly reality other than the one to which its symbols refer in a nonreligious context."[118] This statement is more fully

[114] *OD*, 202.

[115] *OD*, 164.

[116] *OD*, 202.

[117] See Karl Rahner, "The Word and the Eucharist," in *Theological Investigations*, vol. 4, 266-267. Also see id., "What is a Sacrament," in *Theological Investigations*, vol. 14, *Ecclesiology, Questions in the Church, The Church in the World*, trans. David Bourke (London: Darton, Longman & Todd, 1976), 135-148, esp. 137-138. Also see Lambert Leijssen, "La contribution de Karl Rahner (1904-1984) au renouvellement de la sacramentaire," *Questions Liturgiques/Studies in Liturgy* 75 (1994): 91-94.

[118] *OD*, 203.

understood by dividing it into two theses. The first declares that "language alone can make us fully aware of the real as such."[119] To make this point Dupré relies upon the earlier assertion that language alone conceptualizes and only through concepts is the mind able to be cognizant of its own structuring activity and thus of the real as such. This does not imply that words always name the real because they can indeed perform other roles such as articulating feelings, emotions, and aesthetic appearances. However, even in these situations language implicitly refers to the real. This affirmation of reality is a primary component of the religious act. Thus, because of their reference to a transcendent reality, religious symbols rely upon language.

The second thesis which helps to clarify Dupré's general understanding of religious language proposes that "language can directly refer to a metempirical reality."[120] Dupré acknowledges that this assertion is not readily accepted by all. Many would hold that language cannot profess a reality beyond the empirical world. In particular, the basic claim of neopositivists asserts "that all language of reality must be structured upon the pattern of the physical sciences, that it must mean a *thing* if it is to mean the real."[121] For Dupré, any attempt at compromise with such a position would be futile. Yet, there are those who accept the restrictions of neopositive philosophy and still attempt to justify religious language. However, even these reinterpret religious language in ways that deny its essential character of asserting the transcendent as real. In this context, Dupré reflects upon the writings of J. J. C. Smart, Thomas McPherson, R. M. Hare and R. B. Braithwaite. Each attempts to hold a basic positivistic outlook balanced with the acceptance of religious language.

[119] *OD*, 203.
[120] *OD*, 203.
[121] *OD*, 204.

For example, to avoid relegating religious language to the absurd, Smart proposes that the believer must avoid the question, "Does God exist?"[122] Dupré counters that in fact in moving from unbelief to belief one would appropriately inquire into the question of God's existence and this is also properly asked occasionally by believers. Further, the principle out of which Smart operates regards "language as a purely formalistic game, deprived of any relation to the real and allowing no other questions than whether or not a particular concept fits into a particular language."[123] Obviously this position does not defend the ability of religious language to declare the transcendent as real.

Within the framework of espousing statements that are not verifiable by sense experience as nonsense, McPherson also attempts to provide a sympathetic hearing for religious language by interpreting 'nonsense' as a favorable label.[124] However, in providing this answer McPherson relegates religious language to a sphere of

[122] J. J. C. Smart, "The Existence of God," in *New Essays in Philosophical Theology*, ed. Anthony Flew and Alasdair MacIntyre (London: SCM Press, 1955), 41: "The question 'Does God exist?' has no clear meaning for the unconverted. But for the converted the question no longer arises. The word 'God' gets its meaning from the part it plays in religious speech and literature, and in religious speech and literature the question of existence does not arise."

[123] *OD*, 205.

[124] Thomas McPherson, "Religion as the Inexpressible," in *New Essays in Philosophical Theology*, 140- 141: "Nonsense is a pejorative word, and people do not like being told that they are talking nonsense. Theologians like it as little as anyone else. People who insult one are one's enemies. So the positivists are enemies of religion. I want to say that this opinion may be a mistaken one ... Perhaps positivistic philosophy has done a service to religion. By showing in their own way, the absurdity of what theologians try to utter, positivists have helped to suggest that religion belongs to the sphere of the unutterable."

the unutterable that is not only beyond the rational — which is a suitable assessment of faith — but is also superfluous speculation — which denies faith's dependence upon language. As Dupré responds, "If religious man insists upon using language, his reason for doing so is not the pleasure of indulging in rationalist, super-fluous speculation, but the inability to be religious without it."[125] It is one thing to call God the unutterable mystery to demonstrate God's transcendence and another to deny the legitimacy of any religious discourse.

For Hare religious language provides no information on the objective world, but expresses the general attitude of the speaker toward life. He calls this outlook a 'blik'. Appealing to observable occurrences within the world does not unite discrepancies between 'bliks'.[126] Religious statements are neither true or false since all truth must ultimately be verifiable by empirical observations. However, for Dupré this does not agree with the lived experience of the believer who accepts an outlook because it actually can be considered true and not false, and not only contain meaning but also truth.

These attempts to marry the philosophical assertion that 'language must mean a thing if it is to mean the real' with a justification of religious language do not succeed in safeguarding the essential character of religious language which is to assert the transcendent as real.[127] To preserve this character, language must be accepted as possessing the ability to directly refer to a metempirical reality — a position which Dupré upholds.

---

[125] *OD*, 205.

[126] See R. M. Hare, "Theology and Falsification," in *New Essays in Philo-sophical Theology*, 101.

[127] Also see the attempt of R. B. Braithwaite, *An Empiricist's View of the Nature of Religion* (Cambridge: Cambridge University Press, 1955), 10. Dupré's response is found in *OD*, 206-207.

## i. Thetic

There are also others from various perspectives who question the meaningfulness of religious language.[128] This brief look at Dupré's objections to these neopositivists has provided a sufficient foil to elucidate Dupré's assertion: "The purpose of religious language is to assert the transcendent *as real*."[129] Religious assertions not only must be meaningful but meaningful by reference to a transcendent reality. "The ultimate problem is not whether a consistent religious language is possible, but whether such a language is able to deal with reality and, most importantly, with reality as it transcends the empirical world."[130] Thus for Dupré religious language is basically *thetic*. By this he understands religious language as "positing a reality beyond the subjective experience of the speaker and the objective reality of the world."[131] Religious language sets forth as true transcendent reality. Dupré does not deny that often religious language is expressed in poetry, or as a value judgment, or an imperative. While these utterances are nonthetic of themselves, they are religious precisely because of their connection to the believer's language which posits the transcendent as real. Due to its basic thetic nature, Dupré identifies prayer as the religious language *par excellence*. Prayer is preeminently a confession of God's reality, an proclamation in wonder that God is there. Finally, in its thetic constitution the categories of truth and falsity are decisively operative. This does not repudiate

---

[128] See e.g., John Randall, *The Role of Knowledge in Western Religion* (Boston: Starr King Press, 1958). In his naturalistic approach Randall presents religious symbols as only "instruments of 'insight' and 'vision' " of action and human possibility; see 117-118.

[129] *OD*, 205.

[130] *OD*, 208.

[131] *OD*, 210.

religious language as a language of commitment, but "this commitment itself presupposes an intellectual and intentional act which accepts as *true*, that is, as really existing, that to which one commits oneself."[132]

## ii. Two essential conditions

Consistent with its basic thetic nature, Dupré identifies two essential conditions of religious language. The first is the subjective involvement of the religious speaker and the second is the transcendent nature of the referent. As to the first, while it is "subjective" involvement one should not conclude that religious language is purely subjective. This was found in the neopositivistic positions argued against above. Instead, Dupré holds that "The religious act always asserts a reality *which cannot be identified with the self* even though the self must be included in it."[133] Further, this "involvement" exhibits an intimate connection between the speaker and the spoken. By subjective "involvement" Dupré is not asserting that a total commitment is required. It is a commitment only insofar as "the subject is vitally involved with what he speaks about."[134] It appears possible to make religious statements without personal commitment; in certain ways this is illustrated by the words of a sinner denying commitment or a theologian writing about religious matters. So, Dupré maintains that while the subjective involvement of religious statements ideally leads to commitment, it may not always attain such.

As to the second condition of religious language, the fact that the referent is transcendent should not be interpreted to refer to some sort of hyper-objectivity.

---

[132] *OD*, 210.
[133] *OD*, 212.
[134] *OD*, 211.

> Unlike scientific and ordinary language, religious language does not refer to an object but to a more fundamental reality in which the subjective is united with the objective. Moreover it refers to this reality as transcendent and thereby differs from aesthetic language which asserts a similar unity *within* the subject.[135]

Religious language cannot accept the reduction of all meaningful speech to object languages; "there can be no object called God."[136] Yet, while religious believers proclaim this principle, they depict God in object language, as either away in the distance or deep within. How then can religious language refer to the transcendent? How can religious statements be thetic, if the only language that sets forth transcendent reality as true is object language? What is the quality of religious language that allows it to declare the transcendent and avoid being objective?

Historically, the oldest answer is that of predication by analogy. Applied to language about God, analogy attempts to mediate the dilemma between anthropomorphism and agnosticism. That is, on the one hand, univocal predication of qualities to God and human creatures remains object language about humans, and on the other, equivocal talk which prohibits humans from saying anything meaningful about the transcendent. Dupré briefly analyzes the scholastic interpretation of Aristotle's thought. Dupré centers on Cajetan's commentary on Aquinas' *Summa Theologiae*, 1a, q. 13, arts. 5 and 6 and *Summa contra Gentiles*, I, q. 34. Cajetan proposes the classical distinction between analogy of attribution and analogy of proportionality. With analogy of attribution, a quality is predicated properly and formally of one subject and analogously of other subjects according to their relation to the first. The common example from Aristotle is the quality of health which can be assigned to food (which preserves health), medicine (which may

---

[135] *OD*, 210.
[136] *OD*, 211.

restore health), and good complexion (which may be a symptom of health).[137] With this model, Cajetan applies goodness to God in the formal sense and to creatures by an "extrinsic nomination." Dupré suggests that this type of analogy is insufficient. For to learn something about God through analogy, one must first known something about God literally. Dupré agrees with Ferré's assessment:

> The analogy of attribution allows us to remain in ignorance of the formal nature of one of the analogates; our aim, on the contrary, was to speak of these very formal characteristics of God and somehow to justify our language about them. The analogy of attribution tells us nothing we did not know before: it merely tells us that whatever is capable of producing an effect may have applied to it ("virtually") the term properly signifying that effect thanks solely to the fact that — it is able to produce that effect.[138]

All that we learn, for example, is that since God is capable of producing the effect of goodness, we may apply goodness formally to God. Additionally, with analogy of attribution there is no answer to the problem of which qualities of all his finite creations may be applied to him.

Another primary division of analogy is analogy of proportionality. Here the analogy is not between two terms but between two relations. As God is related to divine goodness so too there is a relation between human goodness and humanity. This is analogy of proper proportionality where that which is predicated is present intrinsically and formally (in its essence) in each subject. However,

---

[137] See Aristotle, *Metaphysics*, 4.2, 1003$^a$ 33-1003$^b$ 5; id., *Nicomachean Ethics*, 1096$^b$ 27, in *Aristotle*, vol. 19, The Loeb Classical Library 73, ed. E. Warmington, trans. H. Rackham (London: William Heinemann; Cambridge: Harvard University Press, 1934$^2$). Also see *OD*, 212.

[138] Frederick Ferré, *Language, Logic and God* (New York: Harper & Row, 1969), 73-74.

here too there are weaknesses in application to God language. First of all, neither the attribute or the essence or the relation between the two is known. Proportionality can unintentionally collapse into equivocation and the importance of one term over another cannot be determined. Because the two terms are not known, a second complication arises in that the relationship itself becomes problematic. Proportionality asserts that goodness is present in God in a manner which resembles its presence in humans, but not only is goodness analogous, so too is the resemblance of the relation.

These critiques of both types of analogy do not point so much to errors in formulation of the approach but to the parameters of its function.

> The obvious nature of the objections should alert us to the possibility that the function of analogy is neither to provide new information about God nor to be a complete grammar and vocabulary for the production of meaningful religious language. Rather, analogy is a rule of logic which helps us define the limits of speech about God, *should such speech ever become possible from other sources.*[139]

Dupré agrees with McInerny's assessment that the analogy of names in Aquinas is not a metaphysical principle, but exclusively expresses a logical relationship. By 'logical relations' McInerny understands "relations which are attributed to known things precisely insofar as they are known."[140] Consequently, as a logical doctrine analogy cannot add to our knowledge of the transcendent. "The analogy of names is not, then, a tool for invention; it is an instrument of discipline, a method of keeping order in one's thinking. In analogy we merely compare two sets of language: we do not compare God as he is in himself with the creatures."[141]

---

[139] *OD*, 214.

[140] Ralph McInerny, *The Logic of Analogy* (Notre Dame: University of Notre Dame Press, 1961), 41.

[141] *OD*, 214.

Through analogy no new knowledge of God is given. Instead of offering a technique for speaking directly of God, it illustrates that all speech about God remains speech about humans.

iii. Paradoxical

With such a view of analogy the problem of religious language's transcendent referent and avoidance of objective utterances still remains. The answer lies in the uniqueness of religious language characterized as odd or paradoxical language. Dupré recognizes Johann Georg Hamann (1730-1788) as the first philosopher to regard the odd nature of God talk. He identifies divine truth as appearing only through the "inner lies or contradictions of reason."[142] This idea is clearly confirmed in Christianity where the power of God is manifested in the suffering servant. Hamann also recognizes the operation of the contradiction of reason in Greek myths which anticipate the Judeo-Christian incongruity of the suffering redeemer.[143]

Søren Kierkegaard (1813-1855) is Hamann's most famous disciple and he develops the theory of paradox into the foundation of all religious expression. Kierkegaard includes even language that initially may not appear paradoxical. "For Kierkegaard all existential truth is paradoxical: an eternal truth can never be directly assimilated by an 'existing' individual, that is, a subject who lives *in time*."[144]

[142] *OD*, 216. See Johann Georg Hamann, *Konxompax*, in *Sämtliche Werke*, vol. 3, *Sprache, Mysterien, Vernunft 1772-1788*, ed. Josef Nadler (Vienna: Herder, 1950), 227.

[143] See Johann Georg Hamann, *Socratic Memorabilia: A Translation and Commentary*, trans. James O'Flaerty (Baltimore; Johns Hopkins Press, 1967), 157.

[144] *OD*, 217. For Dupré's assessment of Kierkegaard on paradox, also see Louis Dupré, "Kierkegaard, Søren Aabye," in *The New Catholic Encyclopedia*, vol. 8 (New York: McGraw-Hill, 1967), 175; id., *Kierkegaard as Theologian: The Dialectic of Christian Experience* (New York: Sheed & Ward, 1963), 131-138. [Hereafter *KT*].

Objective language cannot adequately express a matter that has crucial importance to a subject, though Kierkegaard holds to the objective nature of all language. Consequently, the subject must turn inward to assimilate existential truth. For Kierkegaard this is the Socratic paradox:

> The eternal, essential truth [for Socrates] is itself not at all a paradox, but it is a para dox by being related to an existing person. Socratic ignorance is an expression of the objective uncertainty; the inwardness of the existing person is truth.[145]

For Socrates truth is not paradoxical by nature, but it becomes such due to the existing subject, that is, a free individual placed in a certain time. Truth "originates within the existential interiority of the knower. Given this starting point, all truth, as the objective correlate of this interiorization is, to a certain extent, paradoxical, for the objective always presents itself as a challenge to a subject which is pure interiority."[146] The more the matter is of crucial importance to the subject, the more resolutely objective truth resists interiorization. Consequently, for Socrates, God — as absolute truth — becomes a complete paradox.

When Christianity is added to the equation, a new level of paradox is required. From a Socratic position, the obstacles confronted by the subject in assimilating an eternal truth already made the relationship paradoxical. With Christianity the claim is elevated; here there is a totally disproportionate relationship between the finite existing subject and the Infinite. The paradox is now absolute. This absolute divergence between humanity and God is a result of sin — the deliberate human separation from God in an act of supreme

---

[145] Søren Kierkegaard, (pseudonym Johannes Climacus), *Concluding Unscientific Postscript to* Philosophical Fragments, vol. 1, *Text*, Kierkegaard's Writings 12.1, ed. and trans. Howard Hong and Edna Hong (Princeton, NJ: Princeton University Press, 1992), 205.

[146] *KT*, 133.

independencc. Thus, the absolute paradox is that despite humanity's complete break from God, the infinite still enters into a relationship with humanity. The absolute paradox is also called "absurd." There is also a second aspect to this absurdity of faith, namely the paradox of the person of Christ; the eternal becomes incarnate in time.

> Christ's appearance is and still remains a paradox. To his contemporaries the paradox lay in the fact that this particular individual human being, who looked like other human beings, talked like them and followed the customs, was the son of God. For all subsequent ages the paradox is different, for since he is not seen with the physical eye it is easier to represent him as the son of God, but the shocking thing now is that he spoke within the thought world of a particular age.[147]

The paradox of the incarnation is not a vague unity of God and man, but rests in the ambiguity of the personal identity of the infinite God in and through the person of Christ. For Kierkegaard this paradox of Christ emphasizes "the strictly personal character of the act of faith."[148] Faith "is a complete self-surrender, it scandalizes not only the intellect but the entire moral person. Before achieving the fullness of faith man must first have faced despair."[149] Faith is a surrender to the absolute paradox.

Thus, since a transcendent referent cannot be directly communicated by object language, the "whole purpose of language in this case is to turn the subject entirely away from the objective world in which language usually applies and to drive him inside

---

[147] Søren Kierkegaard, *Søren Kierkegaard's Journals and Papers*, vol. 3, ed. and trans. Howard Hong and Edna Hong (Bloomington, IN: Indiana University Press, 1975), 400, § 3075.

[148] *KT*, 137.

[149] *KT*, 142. Also see Louis Dupré, "*The Sickness Unto Death*: Critique of the Modern Age," in *International Kierkegaard Commentary*: *The Sickness Unto Death*, International Kierkegaard Commentary 19, ed. Robert Perkins (Macon, GA: Mercer University Press, 1987), 85-106.

himself."[150] The language of religion is the language of paradox, even when it may appear to correspond to ordinary usage.

Dupré also turns to Ramsey's more recent theory of modes and qualifiers within his principle of odd language. This theory is related to analogy but different in function since in the style of Hamann and Kierkegaard it answers how religious language is created, and not how it is logically controlled. For Ramsey, while religious language is verbally similar to other ways of speaking, it is truly odd language. There is a verbal similarity in saying 'Christ sits at the right hand of the Father', and 'Tommy sits at the right hand of the Father'. However, only focusing upon the verbal similarity fails to communicate the oddity of the situation. There must be an odd language appropriate to these odd situations. More precisely, the oddity of the situation consists in an insight brought about in a disclosure. Religious language cannot be reduced to flatly descriptive statements since it is based upon disclosure situations. A summary is provided by De Pater:

> each disclosure-situation may be analyzed as follows: it begins with an appeal to empirical and verifiable facts, sometimes many, sometimes few; these facts are such that they evoke an insight (the situation comes alive, takes on depth, the light dawns, the ice breaks, the bell rings, the penny drops, etc. ...); what is disclosed is not entirely independent of the verifiable facts, yet it transcends them; ultimately, the language used to speak about what is disclosed is odd compared to the language which led to the disclosure.[151]

As an example of a disclosure situation Ramsey recounts the story of King David and Nathan the prophet in 2 Samuel 12:1-7.

---

[150] *OD*, 218.

[151] Wim De Pater, "Sense and Nonsense in talking about God," trans. the editors of the *Saint Louis Quarterly, Saint Louis Quarterly* 16 (1968): 19. See Ian Ramsey, *Religious Language: An Empirical Placing of Theological Phrases* (New York: Macmillan, 1957), 20, 62.

Nathan confronts David with his sin of having had Uriah killed after he had slept with Uriah's wife. Yet Nathan does not bluntly accuse David. Instead, he tells David an objective story about a rich man who possessed great flocks who took the only lamb of his poor neighbor to feed a guest. Outraged at the action of the rich man David pronounces sentence against him. David does not realize that Nathan is speaking of David himself. However, when Nathan explicitly states to David, "You are the man," it is a disclosure moment for David as he recognizes himself in the story and accepts his responsibility. The disclosure reveals a deeper level of meaning and also demands a response or commitment.

Also operative in Ramsey's exposition of religious language are the fundamental notions of model and qualifier. A model uses language proper to a familiar situation as a lens through which another context can be comprehended.[152] Once a disclosure takes place, models are invoked in order to express the disclosure in an articulate way. Models also function prior to a disclosure in order to facilitate understanding of the language through which the disclosure is attained. Models that lead to a finite disclosure can also assist another model to develop toward an infinite — also called cosmic — disclosure. A finite disclosure is one within a limited situation with a limited effect, such as recognizing an acquaintance in a crowd of people. By contrast, an infinite disclosure is unlimited and total, such as a happy marriage or deep friendship where an absolute value may be realized or God may be seen in the other. So, for example, the model of the reliability of nature's seasonal regularity can lead to a finite disclosure of spousal fidelity and can also act as a catalyst for the overall model of nature and fidelity to produce the cosmic disclosure of Subjectivity as an

---

[152] See Ian Ramsey, *Models and Mystery*, The Whidden Lectures 1963 (London: Oxford University Press, 1964), 54.

absolute reliability. Ramsey also distinguishes between scale models and disclosure models. The former are replicas of the original, like a model train. The latter is a more abstract way striving to uncover the deeper meaning. The work of theology is engaged in disclosure models. Theologians should employ as many of these models as possible as each one is an "inspired simplicity"[153] providing certain characteristics. The purpose of a model is "to offer a wider contextual account of the situation which links it with many other kinds of disclosure"[154] such as the wider articulation in terms of being, aim, and cause.

Language of God takes a familiar situation as a model but then qualifies it in a way that the discourse about the disclosure becomes odd in comparison with the speech that precedes the disclosure. For example, the qualifier "infinite" alerts one that the religious referent is highly unfamiliar. A qualifier is "a directive which prescribes a special way of developing those 'model' situations."[155] The qualifier makes us aware that we are talking about something which cannot satisfactorily be articulated in flatly descriptive terms — a mystery.

## iv. Relation to ordinary language

Based upon the work of Hamann, Kierkegaard, and Ramsey, Dupré concludes to the necessity of viewing religious utterances as paradoxical. In order to further express the meaningfulness of paradoxical religious language, Dupré takes a closer look into the relationship between ordinary and religious languages which we now summarize. First, from the above he readily recognizes the

[153] Ramsey, *Models and Mystery*, 45.
[154] Ian Ramsey, "Some Further Reflections on Freedom and Immortality," *The Hibbert Journal* 59 (1960-61): 354.
[155] Ramsey, *Religious Language*, 70.

essential role of ordinary language in religious speech. "It is obvious that the paradoxical can be understood only through the nonparadoxical, for its entire purpose is to draw attention to its difference."[156] Second, it is not as readily clear whether the two languages can exist without one degenerating into the other. Dupré disagrees with those authors who answer this issue by attempting to reduce the paradoxical to the nonparadoxical. Dupré maintains that while religious propositions which fulfill an auxiliary function may be reducible to nonreligious ones, this reduction is not possible for all religious assertions — otherwise "faith would consists of a few empty factual statements."[157]

Third, a dilemma presents itself since on the one hand the paradox remains a paradox only within a religious framework, and on the other "the religious paradox, by its very nature, includes all reality: faith discovers a new dimension in all aspects of life."[158] Purely religious expressions must be reconciled with all other facets of life. If the first horn of the dilemma was taken as a possible solution, then all language becomes paradoxical and we are only left with confusion. If the second was selected as an answer, then objective language assumes command and religious assertions no longer possess their distinctive meaning. Dupré's median solution relies on his assertion that religious language is not obscure language about a separate reality concealed from the nonbeliever. While religious utterances are paradoxical, this does not imply that they are cryptic or obscure. Their meaning may be disconcerting to the nonreligious, but always remains obvious and apparent. In addition, the believer is not in contact with a separate reality, but with "a transcendent *dimension* in the one and only reality

[156] *OD*, 219.
[157] *OD*, 220.
[158] *OD*, 220.

accessible to him."[159] With this understanding, the relationship of religious language to ordinary speech is primarily negative: "it shakes man's accepted view of reality, challenges the self-sufficiency of the finite and questions the definitiveness of its limits."[160] Religious speech requires the ordinary to provide a context for its expression; without ordinary language religious assertions would remain unspoken. Religious language depends upon ordinary speech but the reverse is not true. Ordinary language does not require the paradoxical, but the paradoxical needs the nonparadoxical. As support, Dupré points out that thinkers as divergent as Tillich and Flew both agree that the symbolic must be grounded in the nonsymbolic to be intelligible. "However comprehensive religious propositions may be, they never interfere with the ordinary or scientific expression of the objectively real."[161] Since there is always this division of roles between the two languages, the paradoxical language of religion can exist together with nonparadoxical language without tarnishing it. Consequently, religious and ordinary expressions are dialectically related insofar as religious language is the negation and transcendence of ordinary language. Religious utterances question the ability of ordinary speech to express reality by suggesting another dimension to existence.

Finally, these three points regarding the relationship between paradoxical and ordinary language are summarized by Dupré's acknowledgment of religious speech as "a subspecies of ordinary language in which modifiers constantly negate and sublate the direct meaning."[162] The two should not be separated insofar as religious assertions are always intrinsically dependent upon ordinary language, though the two remain distinct — religious speech is

[159] *OD*, 220.
[160] *OD*, 220.
[161] *OD*, 221.
[162] *OD*, 221.

paradoxical, odd, and penetrates into another dimension. Thus, the relationship between the two languages is dialectical with a constant interplay between the sensible and objectivity on the one side and the paradoxical and a transcendent dimension on the other.

## v. Symbolic

To complete this discussion of religious language we explicitly emphasize its symbolic nature. Here we again propose three areas of interest. First, there are brief historical comments which Dupré offers on various approaches to symbolic interpretation of scripture. Some kind of symbolic representation is found in the Greek, Hebrew and early Christian traditions. Dupré locates in early scriptural reflection an interpretation in which events mean more than the actual circumstances directly implied — what we now call a typological interpretation. Of course, all interpretation in these periods was not typological, and especially when placed in a wider historical framework, typology is understood as "a particular form of religious symbolism, the one of which Christians have been most conscious, but which is neither universal nor essential. Even in Scripture most symbolism is not of the typological variety."[163] Still, the allegorical or mystical sense of scripture indicated by the Fathers and Aquinas' spiritual sense can be recognized as typology. Some recent authors have distinguished typology as based on historical correlation, contrasted to allegory which is purely imaginative. Yet, for the Fathers allegory was never considered invalid typology.

Specifically, the Hebrew Scriptures portray Israel's own understanding of its history. There is a fresh appreciation of past occurrences in light of new events with religious interpretation. For example, Psalms 104 and 105 reinterpret the meaning of

---

[163] *OD*, 224.

creation and the exodus to express God's providence and faithfulness for the author's own time. Other examples include Wisdom, chapters 10-19 (the work of wisdom from Adam and the deliverance from Egypt is applied to the situation of the writer) and Sirach, chapters 44-50 (honoring the ancestors of Israel also provides a parallel between past and present). In addition, the continuing Hebrew tradition interpreted scripture in view of current questions. The midrashim and the targums steadily brought the 'hidden' meaning of Scripture to light.

The early Christians continued this typological interpretation. In their writings Jesus proclaims himself as the fulfillment of the law and the prophets, (Matthew 5:17-19 and Luke 24:25-27). The New Testament authors often read the presence of Jesus into Old Testament circumstances, (1 Corinthians 10:4). In the letters of Paul, Adam prefigures Christ, and Hagar and Sarah represent the Old and New Testaments respectively, (Romans 5:14; 1 Corinthians 15:22, 45 and Galatians 4:22-26). The Gospel of John suggests a deeper meaning for much of its subject matter including simple elements such as bread, fish, wine and water in anticipating Eucharist and baptism. Each event in Christ's life is interpreted to apply new meaning to both past events and future hopes.

While we cannot assert that the New Testament authors perceived every line of the Hebrew scriptures as applicable to Jesus or a Christian meaning, this idea became popular in patristic times. The Hellenistic center of Alexandria encountered both the Hebrew trend of representation and the Greek allegorical approach. This meeting "gave birth to a Christian hermeneutical consciousness."[164] Through Clement's exegesis based on the existence of a Christian gnosis and Origen's general expectation that the Old Testament was Christological in many sections, allegorical interpretation found

---

[164] *OD*, 222.

great proponents. Clement's key to revealing the secret knowledge of the truths of Christian faith lie in his wide-ranging allegorization of the literal words of scripture in explanation to the initiated. Origen wielded great influence on patristic exegesis as he moved beyond the literal meaning and employed allegory. Even the rival school of Antioch with its emphasis upon a literal approach to scripture also employed an exegesis that included θεωρία. This θεωρία was an insight or vision by which the biblical author was able to see the future through present circumstances. The writer was then able to capture both the contemporary meaning of events and also intertwine their future fulfillment. Thus the exegetes of Antioch perceived their role as uncovering both meanings. In the West, Hilary, Ambrose, and especially Augustine appropriated to themselves the allegorical exegesis of Alexandria. Hilary even declares that all of Scripture — both Old and New Testaments — prefigures the incarnation of Christ. Christ is prefigured in the sleep of Adam, the flood of Noah, the blessing of Melchizedek, the justification of Abraham, the birth of Isaac and the servitude of Jacob.[165] Augustine selects a similar view and asserts that "The New [Testament] lies hidden in the Old; the Old [Testament] is enlightened through the New."[166]

Through the middle ages the search for the spiritual meaning of scripture dominated. The philological interests of Renaissance humanism and the theological debates of the Reformation over the literal meaning of scriptural passages marked an intermittent turn away from spiritual exegesis. However, through the ensuing

[165] See Hilary of Poitiers, *Tractatus Mysteriorum*, in *Corpus Scriptorum Ecclesiasticorum Latinorum*, vol. 65, ed. Alfred Feder (Vienna: F. Tempsky, 1916), 1-38.

[166] Augustine, *Quaestionum in Heptateuchum libri septem*, 2.73 in *Corpus Christianorum, Series Latina*, vol. 33, ed. I. Fraipoint (Turnhout: Brepols, 1958), 106. Translation mine.

centuries there is a fundamental interplay between the literal
and more than literal senses of scripture.[167] A predominance of
the varieties of hermeneutical styles employed to interpret the
religious language of the Bible recognize some type of symbolic
expression.

Next, following these brief biblical comments, we return to the
two essential conditions necessary for religious language. It is only
through symbolic representation that these conditions can be met.
"Only symbols (in the strict sense) can provide religious language
with the two essential conditions ... [of] the subjective involvement
of the religious speaker and the transcendent nature of his referent."[168]
As to the first, discursive language is identified more completely
with the objective, but symbolic language — given its paradoxical
and disclosive nature — can more readily express the involvement
of the subject. This subjectivity does not limit religious symbols
to the reality of a specific subjective state. In fact, its subjective
involvement is based upon religious language's thetic quality of
positing a reality beyond the subject and indeed beyond worldly
objective reality. "It is because of its reference to a trans-objective
reality, not because of the absence of any referent, that religious
language is symbolic."[169] This leads to the second condition
which depends upon symbolization. "The ability of symbols to
express a transcendent reality is the ultimate reason why religious
man cannot dispense with them."[170] Once again the inadequacy
of discursive language to express the transcendent comes for-
ward.

---

[167] See Raymond Brown, "Hermeneutics," in *The New Jerome Biblical
Commentary*, ed. Raymond Brown, Joseph Fitzmyer, and Roland Murphy (Englewood Cliffs, NJ: Prentice Hall, 1990), 1162.

[168] *OD*, 225.

[169] *OD*, 226.

[170] *OD*, 226.

Discursive language can convincingly show the insufficiency of the objectively real. It may even conceptualize to some extent symbolic expressions of the transcendent — if they are available. But discursive language alone is incapable of giving man's relation to the transcendent its ultimate articulation. Its concepts are too closely bound to the objective reality which they are primarily created to express. Their very adequacy in this respect is their greatest drawback for religious symbolization, since the transcendent cannot be adequately expressed.[171]

Symbolic language is able to meet the requirements that discursive language is unable to attain. Despite their physical concreteness, symbolic representations are less misleading precisely because they are less determinate in their meanings. The meaning of a representation is potential, not actual; a representation is open to receiving a number of meanings placed upon it. Since meaning is superimposed upon the representation, there is no expectation of precision and consequently symbols are more flexible than concepts for religious expression. Concepts can also have meaning superimposed upon them. However, when this occurs, "the concept itself becomes symbolic and turns into a representation."[172] This consistently transpires when religious language attains the status of theological reflection. For example, even when speculation regarding the Trinity is abstract and theoretical this concept assumes a symbolic meaning. What about other religious concepts, can they be considered to be other than symbolic?

Lastly, Dupré turns to this question. He asks whether any religious concepts can be nonsymbolic. The answer impacts the degree to which symbolic language is necessary. If many religious concepts can be nonsymbolic then the importance of symbolic speech in religion is minimized; it may not be sufficient for religious

---

[171] *OD*, 226.
[172] *OD*, 226.

affirmation. This is a particularly important contemporary question in that as ancient cultures structured reality by means of symbols in the narrow sense, modern society has primarily turned to rational concepts to provide an explication of reality. Dupré investigates the response of Tillich since the question is essential to his thought. Dupré interprets Tillich as proposing the primary reference to the transcendent as nonsymbolic, which satisfies the demands of the rational mind. Dupré identifies two religious statements as nonsymbolic for Tillich. The first is the assertion that God is the Supreme being. "The statement that God is being-itself is a nonsymbolic statement."[173] This nonsymbolic statement declares that God is foundational of the real. God is not a being, but being itself; beyond every being and transcending the totality of beings. God is "the ground of the ontological structure without being subject to this structure himself."[174] In the second volume of his *Systematic Theology*, Tillich refers to the deeper interest in the question of the symbolic knowledge of God since the appearance of his first volume. He explains that "everything religion has to say about God, including his qualities, actions, and manifestations, has a symbolic character and that the meaning of 'God' is completely missed if one takes the symbolic language literally."[175] But Tillich further explains that there is a nonsymbolic assertion that can be made about God. The statement that everything we say about God is symbolic, is itself a nonsymbolic assertion. Dupré identifies this as a second nonsymbolic assertion in Tillich's thought.

[173] Paul Tillich, *Systematic Theology*, vol. 1, *Reason and Revelation, Being and God* (Chicago: The University of Chicago Press, 1951), 238. Also see id., "The Religious Symbol," trans. James Adams with Ernst Fraenkel, in *Religious Experience and Truth: A Symposium*, ed. Sidney Hook (New York: New York University Press, 1961), 314-315.

[174] Tillich, *Systematic Theology*, 1:239.

[175] Paul Tillich, *Systematic Theology*, vol. 2, *Existence and The Christ* (Chicago: The University of Chicago Press, 1957), 9.

Based upon this assessment, Dupré formulates his own opinion as a refinement to Tillich's thought. Dupré sets up his argument against the position that the basic religious affirmation of 'God as the Supreme Being' must be nonsymbolic. Dupré maintains that because of the dialectical nature of all religious affirmation no true statement can be made about God in a single proposition. The statement that 'God is the Supreme Being' does not assert the reality of the divine for the complete statement must include the negation that God is not Being in the same way that creatures are, and a re-integration of created being into the divine Being. These additional statements must also be considered as nonsymbolic but "only to the extent that they affirm divine existence, not insofar as they define it beyond what is strictly necessary for a meaningful existential affirmation."[176] Therefore, Dupré concludes to his own position that "no statement about God is *entirely* nonsymbolic, not even the primary ones, but that all discourse about God *contains* a primary, nonsymbolic dialectical affirmation."[177] This nonsymbolic quality is needed to provide humanity some connection between divine transcendence and one's world-affirmation. Without such a nonsymbolic aspect it would not be possible to affirm God at all, but this is always present in conjunction with symbolic language.

Of course, there are other assessments of Tillich's thought. It is even possible to suggest an agreement between Dupré and Tillich when one highlights Tillich's avowal that the statement 'God is being itself' is both nonsymbolic and symbolic. Tillich states, "If we say that God is the infinite, or the unconditional, or being-itself, we speak rationally and ecstatically at the same time. These terms precisely designate the boundary line at which both the symbolic and the non-symbolic coincide ... The point itself is both

[176] *OD*, 228.
[177] *OD*, 228.

non-symbolic and symbolic."[178] Some commentators criticize Tillich precisely because they understand him as attempting to interpret symbolic language of God into nonsymbolic language, which can be seen as a reversal of Dupré's critique.[179] Yet, what is important here is not primarily the various interpretations of Tillich, including the one proffered by Dupré, but how Dupré presents his own understanding of the possibility of nonsymbolic language about God, as we have seen.

## D. SUMMARY

Thus, we have presented Dupré's symbol theory in general. The works of Kant, Hegel, Cassirer and Langer as foundational to Dupré's thought have been viewed, including the role of form, culture, and distinctions such as those between signal and symbol, and presentative versus discursive symbols. Dupré's appreciation of symbols must be framed within his overarching interest in culture and search for a metaphysical grounding which is attainable only through symbolic expression. It is through the malleableness of symbols that cultural meanings are given expression and reach toward metaphysical ultimacy.

Finally, we have proposed three general patterns by which Dupré's perception of symbol can be approached. First, form must

---

[178] Tillich, *Systematic Theology*, 2:10.

[179] See e.g., William Alston, "Tillich's Conception of a Religious Symbol," in *Religious Experience and Truth*, 25: "I do not know how to read this [Tillich, *Systematic Theology*, 268, 274 303] other than an attempt to translate symbolic language into nonsymbolic language." Paul Edwards, "Professor Tillich's Confusions," *Mind* 74 (April 1965): 203-204. For an argument against the interpretations of Alston and Edwards and suggesting a different criticism, see William Rowe, *Religious Symbols and God: A Philosophical Study of Tillich's Theology* (Chicago: The University of Chicago Press, 1968), 182-193.

be recognized as symbolic in its role of presenting the essence and knowledge of reality, expressing the significance of the individual object and the human subject, and bridging the human desire to touch the divine. Second, we have acknowledged the specificity of religious symbols as representational while maintaining their primarily negative characterization. Third, we have identified within Dupré's thought the fundamental symbolic nature of all religious language. The religious usages of language is quite broad, encompassing worship, doctrine and Bible. But all religious language is united in requiring faith which inspires the believer to reach toward the transcendent. Religious speech is both thetic insofar as its purpose is to assert the reality of the transcendent, and paradoxical as its transcendent referent cannot be directly communicated by objective language. Religious language, then, characteristically unites the speaker and the spoken more closely than with ordinary language, while referring to a fundamental transcendent dimension beyond objective reality. The relation of religious language to ordinary language is dialectical because religious language negates and transcends ordinary expression. Thus, for Dupré the symbolic nature of religious language is basic to its understanding. Interpretation of the religious language of the Bible has historically exhibited this symbolic quality. Without symbols the subjective involvement of the religious speaker and the transcendent nature of the referent cannot be attained; this is true for all religious language — even the primary statements about God must contain a symbolic element, given the dialectical nature of all religious affirmation.

CHAPTER THREE

# SYMBOL THEORY APPLIED

Having investigated Dupré's symbol theory in general we now apply this research to his study of specific religious symbols; we will consider ritual, sacraments, and religious art. In this analysis the three general patterns of form, representation, and language will come into play as well as the foundational and framing elements discussed in the previous chapter. Based upon this general understanding and specific application of Dupré's symbol theory, we will be in a position to inquire into what makes a religious symbol unique from other symbols. The merits and limitations of certain referents to make a symbol religious will be viewed.

## A. SPECIFIC RELIGIOUS SYMBOLS

Now we turn to an investigation of certain religious symbols, specifically, ritual, sacraments and religious art in their symbolic significance. At first glance these issues may not appear to be appropriately investigated by philosophy, but only by religion and theology, since these areas of concern attain meaning from within these realms. Questions of sacraments and the like indeed belong to the sphere of faith. So-called philosophical proofs for the existence of God clearly have not lived up to their name otherwise it would be standard practice for people to logically hold for the necessity of God's existence. Yet, assuming faith, assuming a life view that believes in some type of transcendent as well as personally immanent

God, philosophy is then able to reflect upon faith's assertions. Accepting the theological source of his subject, Dupré embarks upon a philosophical reflection of ritual, sacraments and religious art.

## 1. *Ritual*

### a. Preliminary Comments

One specific form of symbolization is that of ritual. While the word is primary in religious symbolism, the deed is encountered first. "First among religious symbols ... are the ceremonial deeds of worship to which we refer by the general term of *rite*."[1] Dupré would certainly agree with Vergote that:

> "Ritual symbolism is always accompanied by the liturgical word that makes it explicit. Action and word give the natural elements such as water, bread, oil, etc., their proper symbolic quality. This language is of its nature sacral, in the sense that it is the language of the divine, and of God: the language of the Other-than-the-world."[2]

Because the word is primary and the deed is encountered first, there is a dialectical relation between myth and symbol. The symbolic ritual deed precedes the myth, while the myth itself develops symbolically into specific expressions. Thus, in religion the spoken myth accompanies the acted ritual. The relation of word and deed will be pertinent again under the topic of sacraments below.

By way of a further preliminary comment, we submit that ritual symbol as expressed in gesture and action is the place of union between human and transcendent dimensions. Again we turn to a distinction of Vergote apropos to Dupré's thought, namely, the difference between gestures which simply perform and those

[1] *OD*, 170.
[2] Antoine Vergote, "Secularized Man and Christian Rite," *Louvain Studies* 2 (Fall 1968): 152.

which express. A person may walk so as to go somewhere or tender money for food; these are gestures which perform an action. Actions such as these can be distinguished from actions like a child skipping with a friend or giving a present; these actions are symbolic for they both express and achieve an intention. We call them symbolic by analogy with symbolic words and objects, because they unite a bodily attitude with an intended meaning. They become symbolic signs, and rational language will never attain the richness of their communication. Ritual gesture is the second type of action; "it unifies sentiment and action. It expresses and achieves."[3] For example, standing in prayer, breaking bread, laying on hands, and anointing with oil, are actions which convey something which cannot be communicated other than symbolically. "As with every true symbol they [liturgical gestures] do not depend on anything else, but by themselves they achieve a pact with the Other recognized as himself."[4] Ritual gestures symbolize humanity's relationship with the transcendent; they point to and make present humanity's union with God. It is possible to speak in these terms, for, as Vergote suggests, "gestures are symbolic because the body carries the power to condense into superdetermined signs the whole man in his lived relationship with God."[5] Humans live an embodied existence and ritual gestures are a manner by which union with the divine is symbolized. As Panikkar has argued, "Rituals are precisely needed to sustain our living link with transcendence."[6] Thus, ritual precisely as symbolic gesture and action attempts to join the

---

[3] Antoine Vergote, "Symbolic Gestures and Actions in the Liturgy," trans. Barbara Wall, in *Concilium*, vol. 2/7, *Worship of Christian Man Today*, ed. Herman Schmidt (London: Burns & Oates, 1971), 42.

[4] Vergote, "Symbolic Gestures and Actions," 44.

[5] Vergote, "Symbolic Gestures and Actions," 44.

[6] Raimundo Panikkar, "Man As a Ritual Being," *Chicago Studies* 16 (Spring 1977): 11.

world with God who is totally Other. The "rite is also symbolic; that is to say, it is the presence of the absent. It unites the world that is present with the absent God."[7]

Further, from a phenomenological point of view it is correctly recognized that rituals are associated with human structures. Yet, because rituals aim at drawing their participants closer to the divine, these basic human actions in rituals are not complete in themselves.

> Ritual['s] ... function is not primarily to express man's feelings nor to verbalize the mentality characteristic to our age ... the rite's basic meaning is not to express what it means to be human, but rather to bring the subject into an order that transcends technical man. The rite as symbolic occurrence is not primarily an expression of human sentiments and experience, but a rendering present and manifesting of the Other, of the divine.[8]

Dupré's thought is in agreement with these assertions of Vergote. Dupré explains that "the purpose of a ritual act is not to repeat the ordinary action which it symbolizes, but to bestow meaning upon it by placing it in a higher perspective. A reduction of ritual gestures to common activity would defeat the entire purpose of ritualization, which is to transform life, not to imitate it."[9] A distinction must be made between everyday life and ritual gestures and actions in which they are symbolized.

> Rites *symbolize* joyful and sad occasions but never turn joyful or sad themselves. They express love without passion, austerity without hardship, sorrow without grief. Rites articulate real life, they mold it into their restrictive forms but they never fully merge with it.[10]

---

[7] Vergote, "Secularized Man," 150.

[8] Vergote, "Secularized Man," 150.

[9] *OD*, 171.

[10] *OD*, 171.

Dupré suggests that "a common error in the interpretation of rites [is] to consider them identical with the functions which they symbolize."[11] Adherence to this inaccuracy causes ritual to be trivialized to the ordinary. In such cases the metaphorical quality which is essential to ritualization is overlooked.

> Ritual behavior never merely repeats the ordinary gestures of life. It formalizes and schematizes them until they become "different." Ritual eating, drinking, walking and dancing removes itself from the common performance of those activities. It *determines* the ordinary and bestows new meaning upon it.[12]

Ordinary actions are raised to a new level of meaning since in ritual they operate within a formal structure arranged to express foundational meanings.

Lastly, by way of introduction we note Dupré's acknowledgement of the normative quality of ritual behavior. Ritual provides a pattern to express and enhance life experiences. "Rites dramatize the important moments of existence and thereby bring structure into life as a whole."[13] Dupré notes the Chinese philosopher Hsün Tzu (*c.* 298- 212 B.C.E.) who reflects upon the meaning and purpose of rites including their standardizing role. For Hsün Tzu rites "should not be regarded as acts possessing any supernatural efficacy, but as purely human inventions designed to ornament the social life of man and guide him in the proper expression of his emotions."[14] Hsün Tzu writes:

---

[11] *OD*, 171.

[12] Louis Dupré, "Ritual: The Sacralization of Time," *Revue de l'Université d'Ottawa* 55 (October- December 1985): 264. [Hereafter RITUAL].

[13] *OD*, 176.

[14] Burton Watson, "Introduction," in *Hsün Tzu: Basic Writings*, trans. Burton Watson (New York: Columbia University Press, 1963), 8.

Rites trim what is too long and stretch out what is too short, eliminate surplus and repair deficiency, extend the forms of love and reverence, and step by step bring to fulfillment the beauties of proper conduct. Beauty and ugliness, music and weeping, joy and sorrow are opposites, and yet rites make use of them all, bringing forth and employing each in its turn.[15]

Thus, in general for Dupré ritual behavior imparts new meaning upon ordinary actions and words, which, through standardization, reaches toward a transcendent dimension.

## b. Time in Ritual and Myth

Dupré interprets ritual as the sacralization of time, through which the transitoriness of time is overcome and an enduring meaningfulness to life is provided. The alienation caused by temporality is redeemed through time and memory. Let us explain. The core of the experience of alienation is the scattering of existence by temporality.

Of all the burdens man has to carry through life, I wonder whether any weighs heavier than the transient nature of his experience. Not only does all life inevitably move toward decline and death, but the passage of time prevents any phase of human existence from ever attaining a definitive meaning. Transitoriness and oblivion mark life as a whole as well as each one of its segments.[16]

As we march on through time we are constantly confronted with change. In almost all aspects of life — relationships, work, personal enrichment — if there is not a continual striving for success and growth, there is stagnation and regression. The words of Nietzsche's Zarathustra echoes the desire to be saved from time: "To redeem the past and to transform every 'it was' into an 'I wanted it thus!'

---

[15] *Hsün Tzu: Basic Writings*, 100.
[16] RITUAL, 261.

— that alone do I call redemption!"[17] How is one able to attain permanence and stability and overcome the annihilating impact of time? Christianity attains this goal of redemption "not by abolishing time but by interiorizing it through the function of memory."[18] Through ritual the founding events that giving meaning to life are recaptured and the past is reversed.

Time is structured and ordered by recalling the founding events of the beginning through myth and ritual. "Returning time ... overcomes the passage of time. By being reversible the so-called mythical past in fact ceases to be a past. It becomes an absolute time, not preceded by a more remote past or followed by a future."[19] Historical religions such as Judaism and Christianity find permanence in the present, not through the present itself, but by returning to the past. "The myth returns to the past in order to establish the present."[20] Dupré is not advocating that myth would always return the past and make it actually present; no one wishes to return to experiences of evil and pain. Yet all significant events, even negative occurrences, "require a foundation in the past in order to become meaningful and thereby manageable."[21] The past is able to attain a permanence and completeness which the contingency and transition of the present will never realize. Through archetypical gestures which are interpreted through sacred words there is a search for stability in the midst of flux.

Whether the myth follows the rite as a reflection upon it, or whether the two are united as one, Dupré asserts that "the rite

[17] Friedrich Nietzsche, *Thus Spoke Zarathustra*, trans. R. Hollingdale (London: Penguin Books, 1961), 161.

[18] Louis Dupré, *Transcendent Selfhood: The Loss and Rediscovery of the Inner Life* (New York: Seabury Press, A Crossroad Book, 1976), 66. [Hereafter *TS*].

[19] *TS*, 67.

[20] *TS*, 67.

[21] *TS*, 67.

possesses a meaning of its own that resists the shifts and changes of the restless narrative."[22] Ritual movement does not allegorically reenact an autonomous story, but must be respected and understood as it is in itself as structured gesture. "It is the ritual that enables the accompanying myths to return, across the lapse of time, into the actuality of the present."[23] The narrative of the sacred story transforms elusive appearances into eternal reality through the sacred gesture. "The rite alone recalls the sacred reality of the past into the present."[24] This is because, as we have acknowledged, for Dupré the myth is not the first symbolic expression of existence, since ritual precedes the myth in the dialectical articulation of reality. What the ancient myth does is interpret ritual gestures into dramatic narrative. The mythic story narrates primeval events in succession and by doing so interiorizes the steps of the ritual gesture and furnishes a dramatic quality. For these reasons Dupré asserts that "Temporality ... is an essential feature of the myth."[25] Cassirer posits this same requirement for a true exposition of myth.

> Only where man ceases to content himself with a static contemplation of the divine, where the divine explicates its existence and nature *in time*, where the human consciousness takes the step forward from the figure of the gods to the history, the narrative, of the gods — only then have we to do with "myths" in the restricted, specific meaning of the word. And if we break down the concept "history of the gods" into its component factors, the emphasis is not on the second, but on the first factor, *the intuition of the temporal.*[26]

[22] RITUAL, 262.
[23] RITUAL, 262.
[24] RITUAL, 262.
[25] *OD*, 252.
[26] Ernst Cassirer, *The Philosophy of Symbolic Forms*, vol. 2, *Mythical Thought*, trans. Ralph Manheim (New Haven, CT: Yale University Press, 1955), 104.

In fact, Dupré considers myth to be humanity's "first reflective awareness of time."[27] And based on Husserl's understanding of temporality as the essence of consciousness, the significance of myth is all the more apparent in the development of consciousness as such.

In the line of Cassirer, Eliade, and Lévi-Strauss, Dupré proposes the dialectical nature of mythic time; "the myth posits time only to abolish it immediately."[28] The present is related to a mythic past, yet the goal of this relation is not to become another stage in the succession of time, but to master entirely the indefinite continuum of temporality. Dupré is in agreement with Cassirer's specification, "for mythical time there is an absolute past, which neither requires nor is susceptible of any further explanation ... once this past is attained, myth remains in it as in something permanent and unquestionable."[29] For example, the natural characteristic of a snake crawling on the ground is presented as a result of its coercive actions, or the human condition is explained through the Fall. Once these myths are accepted there is no need to reach back further to determine a reason, since a complete "answer" has already been given. "The beginning itself needs no foundation: it is creative while all that follows is imitative."[30] Dupré cautions that from this one should not conclude that myth is "a primitive substitute for a scientific theory of causality."[31] For, while one aspect of the foundational nature includes a theoretical

[27] *OD*, 252-253.

[28] *OD*, 253. See Claude Lévi-Strauss, *The Raw and the Cooked*, Introduction to a Science of Mythology 1, trans. John and Doreen Weightman (London: Jonathan Cape, 1970), 15-16: "It is as if music and mythology needed time only in order to deny it. Both, indeed, are instruments for the obliteration of time."

[29] Cassirer, *The Philosophy of Symbolic Forms*, 2:106.

[30] *OD*, 253.

[31] *OD*, 254.

justification which evolves through historical periods and takes on the terminology of causality, there is another feature of "a more basic existential need for structures"[32] which is superior to the former.

Characteristic of myth, then, is its ability to express archetypical meanings; as Cassirer states, "The true character of mythical being is first revealed when it appears as the being of origins."[33] So, dialectically the ancient myth both abolishes the present along with other temporal stages, and provides the ultimate foundation of the present. A timeless permanence is accorded the present, thus providing its justification. Paradigmatic gestures and myths are united with the timeless acts of the beginning, recapturing their original creativity as human beings are connected with the primeval events. These ritual gestures should not be understood simply as commemorative but as foundational. Similarly, when referring to mystery cults, Cassirer explains that the ritual is "no mere imitative portrayal of an event but is the event itself ... a real and thoroughly effective action."[34] The myth that accompanies the ritual gesture must be understood in the same manner, thus Dupré appropriates Malinowski's designation of myth as "a narrative resurrection of a primeval reality."[35]

To speak in terms of the past as providing security and meaning for the present is to suggest some type of nonsequential time, some kind of eternity. As religion separates itself from purely mythic thought of temporal progression, a developed concept of eternity emerges. "It appears to be the concept of eternity which distinguishes advanced religions, even those which grant time itself a redemptive

---

[32] *OD*, 254.

[33] Cassirer, *The Philosophy of Symbolic Forms*, 2:105.

[34] Cassirer, *The Philosophy of Symbolic Forms*, 2:39.

[35] Bronislaw Malinowski, *Magic, Science and Religion*, Doubleday Anchor Books A23 (Garden City, NY: Doubleday, 1954), 101.

role, from the archaic myth with respect to temporal succession."[36]
This is not to suggest that eternity must be separate from time.
Normally, eternity is considered to be a continuation of time, but
it is a unique extension in that it "is no longer subject to succession
and development."[37] Diverse religions also take a variety of approaches to the relationship between ordinary temporality and
eternity. The roots of the Christian view of eternity include Greek
philosophy and Hebrew faith. The Greek philosophical tradition
itself contains no uniform idea of time and eternity but undergoes
development. Still, in general the Greek philosophers assigned a
positive significance to time and do not abolish or ignore time as
do certain religions of the East. Usually in Greek thought "eternity
conveys the permanence and necessity without which time would
remain wholly amorphous."[38] Even with Plato time is not entirely
integrated with eternity. Time is a characteristic intrinsic to the
cosmos and is thus mainly cosmological. With Christian authors
such as Gregory of Nyssa and Augustine time is treated as a
psychological category.[39] The Hebrew notion of time also impacted Christian thought, specifically as the Hebrew understanding
embraces time as obtaining a lasting relevance from God's deeds
in history. "History thus came to interact with an eternity which
they believed to be incarnated in time."[40] Yet this approach still requires the redemption of time. Christianity does not seek redemption

---

[36] *TS*, 67.

[37] *TS*, 67.

[38] *TS*, 68.

[39] See Augustine, *Confessions*, trans. Henry Chadwick (Oxford: Oxford
University Press, 1991), Book 11. Gregory of Nyssa, *On the Soul and the Resurrection*, in *Nicene and Post-Nicene Fathers*, Second Series, vol. 5, *Gregory
of Nyssa*, trans. Willaim Moore (London, 1892), 458; id., *Against Eunomius*,
1.42, in *Nicene and Post-Nicen Fathers*, trans. H. Ogle and Henry Wilson,
5:97.

[40] *TS*, 69.

by abolishing or escaping from temporality but through time it-self; eternity is victorious in time.

However, Dupré appropriately asks, "How can what moves in time [i.e., ritual] redeem temporality?"[41] He proposes that the answer rests "in the different time conjunction of ritual per-formances."[42] By this he is suggesting a distinction between the manner in which separate ordinary experiences are combined to-gether into one common time experience, and the fashion in which ritual defies such a union with other experiences. Ritual action is free of the uncertainty native to even the simplest of deeds. Ritual "presents the *ideal* deed, the one the gods themselves performed before the confusion of historical time."[43] As a model deed it restores order because its foundation is outside the ordinary succession of time. Everyday actions, regardless of whether the agent desires to act directly and unambiguously, always reside in a world of ambiguity and unpredictability. By contrast, the ritual deed is locked in a temporality of its own that remains detached from historical time.

But what about historical religions, such as Judaism and Christianity? Specifically, with Christianity the saving events of the life, death, and resurrection of Jesus belong to an historical and therefore irretrievable past. All major symbols in Christianity re-ceive their distinctive meaning from a particular historical event. Historical faiths advance an ardent affinity to a founding event. In Christianity the founding deed is not concealed in an unidentifiable past, but in an act executed at a precise moment of history. How-ever, "founding deeds are never *merely* historical."[44] Included in their expression is a facet that transcends history and reaches people

[41] RITUAL, 265.
[42] RITUAL, 265.
[43] RITUAL, 264.
[44] RITUAL, 265.

of all ages; the past does not exist in total separation from the present. "A rite retains religious significance only as long as through it man is able to relive the past and to re-establish the beginning."[45] Rites make the past present. Rites, then, cannot be understood simply as re-enactments or commemorations, but as *re-presenting* the salvific events. "Without re-presenting those events such a religion easily evaporates into a purely interior attitude in which salvation is remembered but not renewed."[46] While the time of history is in the past, salvation must take place in the present, and to do so the past is re-presented.

> Though history is indissolubly connected with it, salvation, if the term is to retain its meaning, must take place in the present. Christians and Jews appear to experience considerable difficulty in reconciling this present with the inherent historicity of their faiths. Often they favor the latter, regarding their faith as a new, decisive epoch of history. But in doing so they reduce the redemption of time itself to a purely temporal event and sacrifice its basic meaning.[47]

The events of salvation, such as the Incarnation, are forever historically unique; they occurred in the past and cannot be repeated. Yet through faith the believer is able to become contemporary with them.

Paul Knitter employs these thoughts of Dupré to explain what he proposes as 'mythistory'.[48] In the wider context of evaluating what is meant by 'presence' when applied to Jesus, Buddha and Krishna, while suggesting a basis for ecumenical dialogue, Knitter argues that Christianity must be perceived not simply as equating the real with the factual, but as establishing salvation through

[45] *OD*, 177.

[46] RITUAL, 265.

[47] *TS*, 77.

[48] Paul Knitter, "Jesus — Buddha — Krishna: Still Present?" *Journal of Ecumenical Studies* 16 (Fall 1979): 658-664.

myth and symbol. "While it is undeniable that Christian myth owes its origin, identity, and vitality to historical events, it would be misleading and incorrect to maintain that Christian salvation is mediated through history as such."[49] There is a constant interplay between historical facts and the meaning of the myth. "The historical Jesus and what we know about him will continue to serve crucial roles in the proclamation and living of the myth."[50] Knitter explains that of the roles that history exercises, "most importantly, [it is] a constant remembrance of what happened in the past — even when we are not absolutely certain about it — [which] is essential for preserving the identity and the continuity of Christianity."[51] Our current interest is not so much in Knitter's thesis, but in his employment of the ideas of Dupré. Knitter accepts and correctly highlights in Dupré's thought the notion that only through the mind's faculty of memory can one transcend time and have access to redemption.

> To Christians and Jews redemption remains permanently temporal and accessible only through memory. A purely existential (non-historical) interpretation of those faiths … therefore conflicts with their very nature. Even events which no historical evidence could ever firmly establish must be *recollected* rather than *constructed*. It may well be the case, as Franz Rosenzweig suggests, that no one ascended the mountain and that no one descended, yet the Sinai event, though clouded in historical darkness, remains essentially a "memorable" event. Similarly, the Christian possesses no decisive historical evidence of the resurrection and very little of the "historical Jesus" in general, yet he cannot believe without what Kierkegaard called the footnote of history."[52]

---

[49] Knitter, "Jesus — Buddha — Krishna: Still Present?" 659.
[50] Knitter, "Jesus — Buddha — Krishna: Still Present?" 663.
[51] Knitter, "Jesus — Buddha — Krishna: Still Present?" 663.
[52] *TS*, 76-77. Parentheses added by Knitter, "Jesus — Buddha — Krishna: Still Present?" 663.

The historical Jesus is necessary for Christian faith, yet the message is recollected in the mythic Christ. There is an "inherent and productive tension between the particular historical event and the universal, mythic-symbolic message."[53]

Since salvation must take place in the present, the past must be re-presented. Such a synthesis of past and present presupposes that time be acknowledged as essentially a quality of the mind. "Only the mind can transcend time without ceasing to be intrinsically temporal, because only the mind is able to hold on to the past and to anticipate the future."[54] The activity of remembering the past also encompasses more than mere retention of past events. The past is actually recreated and given a new mode of being in contrast to one that it had when it was originally present. "Ritual does more than *repeating* a transmitted gesture: it possesses an ideal, creative structure of its own."[55] Thus, to represent the past is not to pretend that the event never became past and simply continues in the storage of memory, but to make it present once again through the recreation of memory.

Dupré cautions that memory does indeed possess shortcomings. First of all, it is impossible for the temporal mind to exhaustively recall all of the past. All stories of history that one has learned and even events that one has personally experienced cannot completely be remembered. Secondly, it is sometimes not valuable or even fatalistic to remember all events of the past. Memories of pain and rejection may not be liberating; "to remember the past is not yet to redeem it."[56] Thirdly, the converse is also true: remembering

[53] Knitter, "Jesus — Buddha — Krishna: Still Present?" 664.
[54] *TS*, 69.
[55] Louis Dupré, "Ritual, Time and Modern Culture," in *Philosophy and Culture*, vol. 4, Proceedings of the 27th World Congress of Philosophy, ed. Venant Cauchy (Montreal: Éditions Montmorency, 1988), 687.
[56] *TS*, 71.

too much may also be harmful insofar as it may cause one to avoid living in the present. To withdraw into the past is to hide from the present as well as the future. Instead of one of these approaches to memory, religious recollection furnishes what is needed for memory to be redemptive and provide the permanence of eternity.

> Experiences come and go, and memory is the awareness of their constant destruction. Yet it is in the double awareness of this continuous passage of the self into nothingness and of the permanence of the remembered self that the religious mind attains the still point where the passing comes to rest and the past is forever preserved. Such a transcending of time is achieved not by the mere reminiscence of the past but by a new perspective on the present.[57]

The self is able to perceive the totality of its history as contingent in its awareness of the nothingness of its beginning. "Religious recollection consists in a conversion, via the past, toward a more interior self which is no longer subject to the passage of time, because it rests in eternity."[58] Through religious remembrance the completeness of the past allows the present to realize final significance. "Only if through this past man succeeds in touching a timeless present, does he consider that past redeemed and himself whole again."[59] Thus, ordinary 'memory' has become true 'recollection' — the religious inward journey into the past that, beyond searching for an archetypal past, attempts to return to the center of existence from which one *personally* feels removed by time. Augustine describes memory as containing the mind's latent knowledge of both itself and God.[60] Dupré observes in the spiritual tradition of William of St. Thierry, Alexander of Hales, Bonaventure and others, the appreciation that "recollection is both the image of,

---

[57] *TS*, 73.
[58] *TS*, 73.
[59] *TS*, 78.
[60] See Augustine, *On the Trinity*, 14.13, 17.

and the encounter with, the mystery that give birth to the Eternal Word in time."[61] Here, ritual's return to and representation of the past is interiorized by personal recollection. One is not mutually exclusive of the other. "The distinction between personal recollection and historical memory need not be exclusive. One inevitably leads to the other."[62] On the one hand, the ritual is never an abstract activity solely meaningful for society in general but seeks to provide meaning for one's existence, and on the other, the personal mystical experience primarily should not be interpreted as individualistic but in union with the faith community's ritual expression. The remembrance of God's action is "most effective when it is ritually revived."[63] In religions humans are able to move from the contingency of life lived in the irreversibility of time to ritual where time is reversible as it represents the founding events of the past as symbolic actions affirm a relation with a transcendent dimension.

c. Play

The symbolic gestures of ritual are executed in a formalized manner according to rules. From a psychological perspective in his ontogeny of ritualization, Erik Erikson describes play age as one of the stages of growth necessary for proper adult ritual expression. At this stage children learn to be expressive through dramatic elaboration.[64] Earlier, from a different vantage point, Dupré notes that Johan Huizinga (1872-1945) explains the form and function of play as the first, highest, and holiest expression of

[61] *TS*, 78. See e.g. Bonaventure, *The Mind's Road to God*, Library of Liberal Arts 32, trans. George Boas (Indianapolis: Bobbs-Merrill, 1953), 23.

[62] *TS*, 75.

[63] *TS*, 74.

[64] See Erik Erikson, "The Development of Ritualization," in *The Religious Situation: 1968*, ed. Donald Cutler (Boston: Beacon Press, 1968), 711- 733.

the human awareness of the sacredness of things.[65] A connection between the structures of play and religious ceremony can be made based upon various features.

Specifically, Dupré identifies some of these characteristics which we enumerate and summarize as the following five features. First, both play and ritual embody an existence apart from everyday life. In contrast to the labors of the day, be they physical toil or mental arrangement of facts and data, games and rites create a world of make believe. In this new realm "the player does not dismiss the *real* as such ... [but] affirms a different reality which cannot be reduced to the ordinary one."[66] For the player the world of the game is real to the exclusion of the ordinary universe. Likewise, the religious act reaches for another dimension. Dovetailing with the first, the second shared feature is its existence in a space and time all its own. The card table, or playground, or stage are delineated areas of activity, just as the sacred space is marked by church walls, or specified by the baptistery or sanctuary. Dupré turns again to Huizinga:

> All play moves and has its being within a play-ground marked off beforehand either materially or ideally, deliberately or as a matter of course. Just as there is no formal difference between play and ritual, so the 'consecrated spot' cannot be formally distinguished from the play-ground.[67]

Evidently, the time of ritual is not that of the ordinary present, and the game, while perhaps restricted to a specific time interval, carries out specific movements according to its own time rules.

Third, the feature of celebration is common to play and ritual. There is a festivity in liturgical celebration that is related to the exuberance of play. When applied to ritual the word "celebrate"

---

[65] See Johan Huizinga, *Homo Ludens: A Study of the Play Element in Culture*, trans. R. F. C. Hull (London: Kegan Paul, 1949), 17-46.

[66] *OD*, 173.

[67] Huizinga, *Homo Ludens*, 28.

should not be taken in its everyday usage of having a good time or fun, but it does possess a joyful dimension. The joy of ritual is not a superficial emotion, but it always contains some sorrow or pain; it is a truly human experience. Theologies of glory and of the cross exist together. In this way, it is proper to speak of anointing of the sick, and even death as a celebration.[68]

Correlated with this is the fourth feature of seriousness. In the midst of festivity and play there is an imposing seriousness that is inherent to one's involvement. A religious ritual reaching for the divine is a solemn activity not to be entered into with frivolity. While some may not value the constraints of rubrics, there is an expectation that ritual uniformity is evident in the midst of diversity. Even in play there is a most strenuous sobriety that demands strict adherence to the rules of the game. Even ignorance of the proper play is not countenanced.

Lastly, the fifth parallel between ritual and play that can be gleaned from Dupré's reflections is the attribute of dramatization. Specifically in play age Erikson identifies the acquisition of the capacity for dramatic elaboration that provides the foundation for an appreciation of drama in adult ritualization. Dramatization "lifts seasonal and historical events out of the indifferent succession of time and conveys [to] them a permanent structure."[69] Ritual lifts the present to the stability secured through representing the primeval stories. The gestures and words of the ritual performance constitute dramatic expression. In its own way, play also acts out its own story through proper order. "Into an imperfect world and into the confusion of life it brings a temporary, a limited perfection. Play demands order absolute and supreme."[70] The dramatic order of

[68] See Piet Fransen, "Sacraments As Celebrations," *Irish Theological Quarterly* 43 (1976): 151-170.

[69] *OD*, 174.

[70] Huizinga, *Homo Ludens*, 29.

both play and ritual is pursued for its own merits, though certain practical effects may result. The player may receive an award or a physical healing may result, for example. Yet the drama remains primary, otherwise the play becomes 'professional' and the ritual degenerates into magic.

Given these similarities between play and ritual it is not surprising that Van der Leeuw states that a game bound by rules is always a rite.[71] But this is not acceptable to Dupré, for despite the similarities which have been enumerated they do not necessarily imply a common origin and there are significant differences between play and ritual. As to their origin, Dupré refers to the work of Lévi-Strauss who distinguishes ceremonial rites and ritual games from ordinary games in archaic society. "In free games talent or chance separate the players and result in a disjunctive effect. In ritual, on the contrary, events are structured in a way which in the end conjoins the participants and obliterates the initial distinctions in a universal harmony."[72] The result of ritual action is always a state of equilibrium, which is not necessarily the case with regular play. Dupré ventures beyond Lévi-Strauss and suggests a further distinction between ceremonial rites and ritual games. He suggests that "all games, even the ritual ones, display a looser symbolic structure which may eventually allow the play element to go its own unpredictable way. Mere play is the play-rite deprived of its symbolic potential."[73] It is the strength of its relationship to

---

[71] See Van der Leeuw, *Religion in Essence and Manifestation*, § 48, 1: "For a game bound by rules, is, as such, always a rite, conduct, dominance."

[72] *OD*, 174. Dupré follows Lévi-Strauss in making this assertion. See Claude Lévi-Strauss, *The Savage Mind*, The Nature of Human Society Series, n. trans. (London: Weidenfeld, 1972²), 32.

[73] *OD*, 175. Dupré understands his interpretation as similar to "Émile Benveniste's claim that play results from the separation between myth and ritual: once the rite loses its mythic symbolism it becomes a 'mere' play." *OD*, 175 note 58. See Émile Benveniste, "Le jeu comme structure," *Deucalion* 2 (1947): 165- 166.

symbol that determines the difference between ceremonial rites and ritual games.

Further, the original relationship between play and ritual cannot be reduced to a consideration of rite as religious and play as non-religious. To do so would be to impose upon the archaic attitude a distinction that is foreign to its perspective. In other words, if 'religion' signifies a separation between the realms of the religious and the secular, then neither play nor rite were initially considered religious, because primitive humanity "knows only one sphere of existence which within itself admits the distinction between sacred and profane, but not the one between religious and secular."[74] The question, then, is not whether an ancient ritual action is religious or secular, but rather whether play and ritual both contribute in the same fashion to giving basic structure to existence. Dupré regards both as "instrumental in the discovery of such elementary distinctions as the one between the sacred and the profane,"[75] but he does not pretend to provide a developed answer as to *how* each may uniquely contribute to this discovery, since it is primarily a question for which anthropologists and sociologists must lead in providing an answer.

Once human consciousness does reflect upon the nature of the sacred, additional general differences between play and ritual surface. First of all, humans consider themselves the inventor of the game, human decision defines the rules and determines the stakes. By contrast, within the religious realm humans experience a feeling of helplessness and need before the powers that are completely overwhelming. Even though the rubrics are written through human determination there is a certain duty inherent in the ritual to act as the divine power desires. Additionally, play brings a sense of

[74] *OD*, 175.
[75] *OD*, 175.

relaxation and entertainment. Ritual may set before one the sacred mystery that is fascinating to contemplate, but this is not done in leisure. There are tensions such as guilt and unworthiness, fear and uncertainty which keep one in dread of the sacred. Lastly, the view that one embraces of ordinary reality from within play and ritual differ considerably. In play one can escape completely from the desires and concerns of everyday living. There are no worries, and questions of ultimate existence are given no voice. A different approach is taken by religion. The religious person either brings the cares of the day to worship or bracketing worldly concerns turns to surrender to the divine for meaning and purpose. Ordinary life is separated from ritual not to escape from daily living but to be renewed in strength and wisdom to return to the ordinary responsibilities that can then be integrated with the sacred.

## d. Other Functions of Ritual

Finally, Dupré summarily states some of the other functions of ritual.[76] One is its role in structuring activity for the group. A ritual that is developed by an individual for strictly private usage does not integrate as rituals should, but instead isolates one from the community. A common unity is fostered through participating together in formalized structured activities. Through rites of passage the individual is incorporated into one group from another and the personal events of life are given a public quality. Another function of ritual is to explain humanity's relation to nature — out of which humanity emerges and upon which humanity continually depends. Through ritual humanity is able to relive union with nature while also preserving the detachment needed to establish culture. Once again, Dupré does not develop these ideas because he understands them primarily as the domain of anthropology and sociology.

[76] See *OD*, 177-179.

Lastly, regarding ritual we must explicitly state what Dupré designates as its 'religious' function or meaning. "The religious meaning of all rites ... [is] to establish the real by means of transformation."[77] Rites of passage such as initiation, marriage, and death particularly express the sacralization of change as one moves from one group to another. Through these transformations marked by rites the meaning of existence is established at the core of reality. Dupré advocates a close affiliation between conceptualization and the constitution of the real, which he regards as an outcome of Kant's theory of the categories. However, he opposes the conclusion that this constitution is produced by a purely intellectual process. Instead, "the existential awareness of the real results from meaning-constituting acts which are by no means purely intellectual."[78] For a significant event to be experienced as completely real it must be celebrated — one must become fully involved. Dupré also refers to Eliade's description of the religious meaning of common rites as a reestablishment of existence by reliving the initial acts which give life meaning. For example, regarding Christian baptism Eliade explains:

> For the Christian, baptism is a sacrament because it was instituted by the Christ. But, none the less for that, it repeats the initiatory ritual of the ordeal (i.e., the struggle against the monster), of death and of the symbolic resurrection (the birth of the new man).... The revelation conveyed by the Faith did not dispel the "primary" meanings of the Images; it simply added a new value to them. For the believer, it is true, this new meaning eclipsed all others: it *alone* valorised the Image, transfiguring it into Revelation.[79]

[77] *OD*, 178.

[78] *OD*, 179.

[79] Mircea Eliade, *Images and Symbols*: *Studies in Religious Symbolism*, trans. Philip Mairet (New York: Sheed & Ward, 1961), 158-159.

An ultimate source of reality is avowed by ritual. There is both the presentation of a new action and at the same time a return to the foundations. Thus, myths of the origin accompany ritual since that which is definitely real has existed from the beginning.

## 2. Sacraments

As we begin this section, note that it will have a limited focus, for Dupré does not claim to be a sacramental theologian but a philosopher of religion. Even from a theological perspective philosophical reflection is essential for a sound sacramentology. Perhaps this is one reason why, in the midst of referring to a variety of works regarding sacraments, Dupré primarily relies upon the philosophically grounded sacramental work of Edward Schillebeeckx for his overall understanding of sacramental theology.[80] With this in mind we turn to the following primary points that Dupré proffers from his philosophical stance.

### a. As Ritual Action

Sacraments are a specific type of ritual; every ritual is not sacramental. "A sacrament differs from other rites in that the ritual action itself is believed to yield a numinous influence."[81] While Dupré's main interest is to understand the Christian term sacrament, he acknowledges that even among primitives the notion of a rite that imparts a supernatural power is prevalent. Regardless of how such a power is envisioned, in all cases it produces some type of

---

[80] Dupré specifically consults Edward Schillebeeckx, *De sacramentele heils-economie: Theologische bezinning op S. Thomas' sacramentenleer in het licht van de traditie en van de hedendaagse sacramentsproblematiek* (Antwerp-Bilhoven: 't Groeit, 1952). Also see id., *Christ the Sacrament of the Encounter with God*, trans. Paul Barrett, Mark Schoof, and Laurence Bright (London: Sheed & Ward, 1963).

[81] *OD*, 182.

salvation. This is indeed present in the Christian conception of sacrament. "In the sacramental rite a common function of life obtains a salvific effect which it did not possess in an ordinary, nonsymbolic situation, and which is somehow directly connected to the action."[82] There is always the danger of equating such sacramental rites with magic. At its roots a magic rite makes something appear, disappear, or transforms one object into another. A proper performance of the actions and words of the theurgist — once he has received the secret power — assure the desired effect. Only emphasizing this direct connection of performance and effect, expressed in scholastic terminology as *ex opere operato*, has never been accepted as a valid interpretation of Christian sacraments which must also include the intention of the minister and the disposition of the recipient. "The salvific influence of the sacramental action does not originate in the nature of the rite *considered in itself*, as is the case in magic. Rather does the rite partake in a transcendent reality from which it derives an efficacy surpassing its ordinary power."[83] A genuine religious attitude does not confuse the difference and refuses to reduce sacraments to magic rites.

## b. Sacramental Efficacy

Among the Christian churches there are varying opinions regarding the efficacy of sacraments, but most ascribe sufficient efficacy to grant that they are more than mere metaphorical signs of salvation. Primary to any theological interpretation of sacraments is the philosophical principle that "*all* symbolic actions do more than signify: they also to some degree *realize* what they signify."[84]

---

[82] *OD*, 182.

[83] *OD*, 182.

[84] *OD*, 183.

There is an intrinsic unity of symbol and symbolized which must be acknowledged. Actions such as a handshake or embrace do not figuratively 'express' or 'represent' friendship, but presupposing the action is not feigned, "they also 'seal' it and effect its full realization ... symbolic signs and expressions actually *produce* the signified and expressed reality."[85] The epistemic function of symbolic activity — the basic act of signification — is only one of its features. "The symbol signifies, expresses, *and realizes.*"[86] Of specific importance for understanding sacraments is to properly regard symbols as intrinsically unifying the components of which it is constituted, and not in the fashion of a simile or allegory by which two things that are essentially distinctive are extrinsically combined. Thus, meaning is attained by a synthetic insight that grasps all components at once, and not by discursively adding one to another. Applied to sacraments, this approach is important since sacraments symbolize a reality which is impossible to directly access and therefore could not be symbolized by a discursive addition of components. Instead, the influence that this other dimension exerts upon human existence is communicated through ordinary functions and acts of life.

If one were to force upon sacraments a view of symbols solely based in a concept oriented model of thinking that simply connects two components extrinsically, then sacramental efficacy would be understood "as a mere *addition* to the ordinary one, resulting from some extrinsic divine decree. Yet sacraments are symbolic *in their very essence* and, consequently, differ intrinsically from the acts which they ritualize."[87] For example, a theology may simply add a supernatural level onto the ordinary act taken over by the ritual. This is done when there is an exclusive emphasis on the institutional

85  *OD*, 183.
86  *OD*, 183.
87  *OD*, 183-184.

quality of sacraments which searches for proofs of Christ's founding act of a certain sacrament; the divine institution is considered paramount. This same extrinsic approach to sacraments has also had the opposite effect insofar as the natural meaning of the sacraments is considered paramount. In this case the sacramental character is once again viewed as being superimposed upon ordinary actions, but where older theologies promoted a supernatural addition, now secularized approaches repress it. The stress is placed upon the natural activity of washing, eating, drinking, touching, etc.

However, an appreciation of the intrinsic nature of religious symbolism, while not denying an institutional element to sacraments, expresses "the primary truth that sacramentality is a universal form of symbolism."[88] Thus, the certain forms which can logically claim historical institution cannot profess to be the totality of sacramental expression. Once the Catholic sacraments where enumerated as seven there still remained a plenty of 'sacramentals'. Regarding the more secularized approach of emphasizing the natural meaning of the sacraments, an intrinsic understanding would add the corrective that first and foremost sacraments are a symbolic expression of a transcendent reality. "Sacraments must be recognized as intrinsically connected with the sacred before the specific nature of their symbolism of washing, eating, etc., can be understood."[89] Dupré turns to Schillebeeckx for verification:

> We must hold that the bodily washing in baptism, as the symbolic realization of Christ's own act, is more than bodily washing is on the merely human plane; it is indeed the gift of grace in tangible visibility, the outward sign of something inward.[90]

[88]  *OD*, 185.
[89]  *OD*, 184.
[90]  Schillebeeckx, *Christ the Sacrament of the Encounter with God*, 75.

From a sacramental perspective, the transcendent reality precedes the ordinary, visible form which is a consequence of the incarnated nature of human existence including the human relation to the transcendent. Dupré refers to Rahner for the proper ordering of first the transcendent reality and then the visible form.

> *As* God's work of grace on man is accomplished (incarnate itself), it enters the spatio- temporal historicity of man as sacrament, and *as* it does so, it becomes active with regard to man, it constitutes itself.... For at no stage can the sign be seen apart from what is signified, since it is understood *a priori* as a symbolic reality, which the signified itself bring about in order to be really present itself.... In a word, the grace of God constitutes itself actively present in the sacraments by creating their expression, their historical tangibility in space and time, which is its own symbol.[91]

While accepting the main point, as a philosopher of religion Dupré's methodology requires him to distance himself from such comments as "God's work of grace on man is accomplished," and "the grace of God constitutes itself as actively present." Dupré interprets such expressions descriptively and concentrates upon the existential commitment that is underneath them. In addition, the sum of Dupré's reflections upon sacramental efficacy cannot not be perceived as recommending what *ought* to exist religiously. His "method of critical reflection is restricted to the discovery of logical structures in faith *as it actually exists*."[92] Yet, the application of his philosophical reflection upon religion does identify particular misconceptions regarding sacramental efficacy. "Only where the religious manifestly degenerates into the nonreligious (as when sacraments are used as magic devices) or where theological interpretations of religious realities betray the original intuition can the

---

[91] Rahner, "The Theology of the Symbol," 242.
[92] *OD*, 185 note 78. Also see the introduction to *OD*, xx.

critic reject *what is.*"[93] Thus, while exposing certain inadequacies in various theological approaches he does not decide, for example, the larger debate between the Catholic Church and the Reformation on the sacraments.

## c. Word and Deed

However, the question remains *how* can sacraments be interpreted as an intrinsic unity of symbol and symbolized. There are two quite divergent components that are united as one. First, there is the 'signified' which is transcendent and is impossible to express satisfactorily in concrete form. Second, there is the human action which still maintains a complete intentionality of its own when removed from a sacramental context. How can this duality be reconciled beyond adding one element to the other? Dupré advocates an intrinsic unity of the elements based upon the reality of the sacramental *word*. "Only words can direct the intentionality of immanent acts toward a transcendent reality without first asserting their ordinary noema. The unique flexibility of language enables it to establish a symbolic meaning which directly (and not successively) subsumes the ordinary one."[94] It is through linguistic interpretation that an act can be understood as meaningful apart from its natural expression. "Language alone is equipped with the symbolic apparatus to say the unspeakable and to structure the invisible. Once the word is spoken, all human acts are able to participate in its transcendent meaning."[95] The word transforms the meaning of the act.

This does not deny that even before the religious person is able to linguistically articulate a religious attitude he or she is already

---

[93] *OD*, 185 note 78.
[94] *OD*, 186.
[95] *OD*, 186.

'religious'. But as one's religious consciousness develops, to provide an adequate articulation, it becomes necessary to express in speech such distinctions as that between the sacred and the profane. "We may therefore formulate as a law that all religious symbols are either verbal or require verbal interpretation."[96] Within the confines of its system, scholastic theology acknowledged the essential role of language as the word is identified as the form of a sacrament as distinct from the matter. Dupré also notes that for Rahner the sacramental deed itself becomes word:

> The sacramental action too has the character of a word. It designates something, it expresses something, it reveals something that is of itself hidden ... [The sacramental signs] are all freely created signs, in the same sense that 'words' are, which are not merely signs of the thing, but likewise always signs of the free personal self-disclosure of a person, in contrast to things, which have always automatically made themselves known and cannot be closed in on themselves. In other words: since grace is always free and personal self-communication of God, its divulgation is always free and personal and hence essentially word.[97]

The deed is carried by the transcendent intentionality of the word and transforms the original worldly meaning. The complete action enters into the new intentionality once the word is spoken. Thus, Dupré concludes that "the word is primary in religious symbolism even though the deed was first."[98]

## 3. Religious Art

The final specific application of Dupré's understanding of symbols will be made to religious art. The texts that are pertinent to this discussion will be separated into four areas of interest.

[96] *OD*, 186.
[97] Rahner, "The Word and the Eucharist," 266-267.
[98] *OD*, 187.

In the first, the larger question of aesthetics particularly as understood by von Balthasar provides a frame for Dupré's thought. In
the second, Dupré investigates the relation of aesthetic perception
to ordinary perception. This interest in aesthetics in essential to an
understanding of religious art because "religious art symbols are
essentially aesthetic."[99] Their uniqueness lies "in that they express
aesthetically what was originally a religious experience."[100] Thus,
the third section will distinguish between religious and aesthetic
experience. The fourth is closely connected with the third and further
unfolds the symbolic character of religious art by searching for a
distinction between religious and nonreligious art. These four
divisions do not follow a chronological presentation of Dupré's
writings, but synthesizes his ideas by the progression of topics we
have chosen to develop. In addition, far from being mutually exclusive, these various writings are in concert together which explains why references from works classified in one division may be
cited in another. We will now briefly view each of these in turn.

a.  Aesthetics and Form

The basic framing of aesthetics within the conception of form
has been provided above on pages 85-90 and will not be repeated.
Dupré further explains that "nowhere is the connection between
form and content more intimate than in the aesthetic image."[101]
Aesthetic expression does not mean that an artist first feels emotions
that are subsequently expressed. The expressed feelings in art are
constituted within the expressive articulation and not before. "It is
mistaken to regard a work of art as if it 'expressed' the feelings of
love or hate which preceded and initiated it. The *aesthetic* feeling

[99]  *OD*, 228.
[100]  *OD*, 228.
[101]  *OD*, 151.

fully develops only in the expression itself."[102] Associative processes may account for certain aesthetic impressions, "but ultimately one must accept an irreducible originality in the combination of feeling and form. The music of Mendelssohn creates the very feelings which it reveals."[103] The form and the content are not separated, but the "sensuous form of a symbol is by its very nature self-transcending."[104] The finite appearance of the form reaches beyond itself toward the infinite content.

## b. Aesthetic and Ordinary Perception

Dupré's understanding of the relation between aesthetic and ordinary perception should be distinguished from a physicalist view of perception. For example, Vincent Tomas expresses the relationship as follows:

> [1] When we see things in the "common way," our attention is directed toward the stimulus objects that appear to us, or toward what they signify, and we do not particularly notice the ways in which these objects appear ... [2] When we see things aesthetically, our attention is directed toward appearances and we do not particularly notice the thing that presents the appearance, nor do we care what, if anything, it is that appears.[105]

Tomas does not distinguish between two orders of perception, but regarding what is real to be the physical he assumes this to be the

---

[102] *OD*, 151. Also see Louis Dupré, "Aesthetic Perception and Its Relation to Ordinary Perception," in *Aisthesis and Aesthetics*, The Fourth Lexington Conference on Pure and Applied Phenomenology 1967, ed. Erwin Strauss and Richard Griffith (Pittsburgh: Duquesne University Press, 1970), 176: "No feeling is fully aesthetic until it is expressed. We may say, then, that the aesthetic feeling is born in its expression." [Hereafter AESTHETIC].

[103] AESTHETIC, 176.

[104] *OD*, 151.

[105] Vincent Tomas, "Aesthetic Vision," in *Aesthetics and the Philosophy of Criticism*, ed. Marvin Levich (New York: Randam House, 1963), 256.

object of ordinary perception. "Tomas simply identifies the *thing* with the pigments, the physical words, the vibrations in the air, and relegates the three-dimensional picture, the fugue, the tale to the realm of appearance or illusion."[106]

Dupré is more in line with Kant's appreciation of a transitional stage between sense experience and objectified experience which he attributes to imagination. "Aesthetic perception is neither ordinary perception nor pure reflection. It combines the detachment of the latter with the intuitive immediacy of the former."[107] Mikel Dufrenne offers an interpretation and application of Kant's thought by demonstrating how through a process of temporalization the imagination detaches the object from the immediate experience.[108] In providing a critique of Dufrenne's theory Dupré explains that the aesthetic object cannot be deprived of the fancies of the empirical imagination. "Art would be very dull if it were reduced to pure form without play."[109] Also, while there is a separation between the aesthetic object and the ordinary world, the two are never completely detached. "The self-sufficiency of the aesthetic object does not eliminate the intentional reference of this object to the world of ordinary perception."[110] Artistic representation pre-supposes and refers to ordinary perception. In the temporal as well as the spatial arts the "artistic forms, however abstract, always refer to the one world of ordinary perception in which they were first discovered."[111] For example, both a musical composition and a novel both possess an inherent rhythm of succession, but this must be based on ordinary experience. Without such, the novel is

---

[106] AESTHETIC, 171.

[107] AESTHETIC, 172.

[108] See Mikel Dufrenne, *Phénoménologie de l'expérience esthétique*, vol. 2 (Paris, 1953), especially 434. Also see AESTHETIC, 172-173.

[109] AESTHETIC, 173.

[110] AESTHETIC, 173.

[111] AESTHETIC, 173.

unintelligible, and in a similar fashion, the rhythm of a musical composition must have a connection to the rhythmic succession of ordinary perception.

> No work of art ... can claim a full aesthetic immanence: the intentional reference to the world of ordinary perception is an intrinsic part of all aesthetic experience. But some arts are more representational than others and not every art form intends the world of ordinary perception as explicitly as the portrait.[112]

Aesthetic perception needs ordinary perception as a foundation and available for support to assure its connection to a wider view of reality. "What distinguishes the aesthetic experience [from an ordinary one] is that it is never a pure perception, but a perception colored by a subjective disposition."[113] The aesthetic perception always requires the involvement of the self — not a commitment of giving and receiving, but an interiorization of the aesthetic object in the subject.

## c. Aesthetic and Religious Experience

There are certain similar and dissimilar features between aesthetic and religious experiences as well as possessing relational qualities. Each area provides further insight into determining the nature of religious art.

Regarding the similarities, first of all, both aesthetic and religious experiences produce a complete awareness that gives a meaning to life beyond its ordinary purpose, beyond its ordinary boundaries. Concomitant with this depth of meaning is the shared ability to "create order out of chaos by integrating existence in an all-comprehensive synthesis."[114] In other words, in the presence of

[112] AESTHETIC, 173-174.
[113] AESTHETIC, 174.
[114] *OD*, 229.

great art and in the religious experience one encounters an awareness
of the ultimately real. By moving beyond the bifurcation of objective
knowledge and subjective desire these experiences bring new insight. F. David Martin's words are accepted by Dupré:

> Both [religious and aesthetic experiences] are intimate and ultimate;
> both are attuned to the call of Being; both are reverential in attitude
> to things; ... both give enduring value and serenity to existence; and
> thus both are profoundly regenerative. The participative experience,
> then, always has a religious quality, for the participative experience
> penetrates the religious dimension.[115]

Because both attempt to retrieve a deeper attitude of being, they
also have the tendency to be absolutist in their claims as they
search for ultimates.

Regarding the dissimilarities, there are two main qualities which
suggest a clear division between the aesthetic and religious experiences. The first is Dupré's distinction between religious and
aesthetic symbolism — the aesthetic symbol sufficiently explicates
the feeling it expresses, where the religious symbol can never
completely symbolize its transcendent content — which he makes
in response to Schleiermacher. The second dissimilarity is the
different manner in which each approaches reality. The artist is able
to present reality; even in its complexities art can command
contradictory facets in an aesthetic harmony. However, art can never
resolve the conflicting forces of life. The artist "articulates feelings
and brings a new *appearance* to reality, but he introduces no new
reality. The artist brackets existence and devotes all his efforts to
essence."[116] By contrast, religious faith does not merely resign itself
to reality, but asserts a new meaning to life through a transcendent
reality in which resolution to conflict and new purpose is attained.

---

[115] F. David Martin, *Art and the Religious Experience* (Lewisburg, PA: Bucknell University Press, 1972), 69.

[116] *OD*, 231. Also see *TS*, 52.

Yet, are there not exceptions to this dissimilarity? Dupré asks, "Does art become assertive when it aesthetically articulates an affirmation of faith?"[117] This concern can be raised at different levels. First of all, there are works of art which have a religious subject but do not intrinsically depend upon a religious view of life. For example, one does not need to be a religious believer to admire and value Rafael's "Disputation of the Blessed Sacrament" or Caracci's "Pietà." There are also works where the artist's belief in the religious subject is significant as in the van Eyck's "The Adoration of the Lamb" or the fugues of Bach, but still the aesthetic form is solid enough to make an impression on the nonbeliever as well as the believer. Lastly, Dupré singles out aesthetic works which express religious belief in words, specifically, poetic expression. For example, Eliot writes in the last lines of "Little Gidding":

> And all shall be well and
> All manner of thing shall be well
> When the tongues of flame are in-folded
> Into the crowned knot of fire
> And the fire and the rose are one.[118]

Dupré concurs with Ronald Hepburn's assessment:

> The poet is not in such command of his material as we were tempted to think. His image is not self-authenticating. Its extreme beauty and integrating power must not lead the reader to imagine that its *extra*-poetic truth has been established, that the integrative power of the poetry is pragmatic proof of the truth of what it expresses. If God does not exist or if his nature is other than Christianity paints it, then the flame and the rose will not be one, and the most potent alchemy of images cannot make them one.[119]

[117] *OD*, 231.

[118] T. S. Eliot, "Little Gidding," in *Four Quartets* (New York: Harcourt, Brace, 1944²), 44.

[119] Ronald Hepburn, "Poetry and Religious Beliefs," in *Metaphysical Beliefs*, ed. Stephen Toulmin (London: SCM Press, 1957), 146.

Religious poems may or may not contain explicit religious assertions as Eliot's, but in either case the poetic character of a religious poem does not abide "in the religious assertion as such, but rather in its rhythm, images, and symbols."[120] Dante's *Divina Commedia* can be enjoyed without partaking in the author's religious views. Based upon these reflections Dupré concludes that art does not assert new meaning in reality even when it contains an affirmation of faith because such an affirmation can be distinguished from the aesthetic articulation itself. "Art appears to be religious only if it intrinsically *depends* upon an affirmation of faith, yet the affirmation itself is never part of the aesthetic expression. Aesthetic belief differs from religious belief even though the former may be directly influenced by the latter."[121] Even when art has a religious subject, it persists in an essentially aesthetic approach of basically presenting reality; this remains distinct from a religious expression that actually asserts new meaning through a transcendent dimension.

Yet, religious art is not purely an aesthetic concern. In comparing and contrasting the aesthetic and religious experiences Dupré determines a certain relationship between the two. There is an intimate connection that has developed out of an original unity. "All through the primeval era of a culture's development, art forms an essential part of a symbolic integration to which we now, in retrospect, give the name 'religious'."[122] 'Art' and 'religion' were indistinguishably connected as a total view of life was expressed. Dupré applies to all the arts in an archaic society Van der Leeuw's comment regarding dance which he considers the most primitive religious expression.

[120] *OD*, 232.

[121] *OD*, 232.

[122] Louis Dupré, "The Enigma of Religious Art," *Review of Metaphysics* 29 (September 1975): 27. Also see *OD*, 229; and *TS*, 52.

That the dance has religious meaning does not mean that it can express only religious feelings. On the contrary, all feelings, from the most solemn to the most frivolous, find their expression in the dance. The religious is not a particular sensation alongside other sensations, but the summation of them all. Thus the dance can also serve a purpose which we, too, would call religious.[123]

As with ritual, the artistic expression is originally one in the overall understanding of life before it is broken up into a variety of segments.

After making the distinction between the sacred and the profane, following the dissipation of the original unity, a close connection between artistic expression and the religious attitude still exists. "Faith continues to express itself in liturgical action, stylized according to aesthetic standards."[124] In and through the ritual actions, words, music, images, etc., the religious community proclaims and fosters its beliefs. Even with the advent of secular art, a common ground with religion remains. In painting, literature, stage, and cinema the images of superhuman gods and demons, angels and prophets, salvation and damnation continue to endure.

At an initial level Dupré identifies a common 'border' between aesthetic and religious experience. As a model he points to the expression and feeling of the sublime, in which "the content overwhelms the expression so much that it eclipses the purely aesthetic form."[125] While the aesthetic image does not point beyond itself and indicate in its structure the transcendence of the reality to which it refers — as is the case with religious symbols — in expressing the sublime the aesthetic image "breaks through the finite

---

[123] Gerardus Van der Leeuw, *Sacred and Profane Beauty: The Holy in Art*, trans. David Green (New York: Holt, Rinehart & Winston, 1963), 17. See *OD*, 229.

[124] *OD*, 230.

[125] *OD*, 233.

form to lose itself in a transcendent beyond."[126] The aesthetic and religious symbols almost coincide as the transcendent content becomes the object of both. Still, the aesthetic value is not dissolved by the experience of the sublime.

Beyond a common border, there is a deeper relationship between the aesthetic and religious experiences. "Despite the differences in symbolization, aesthetic images are constantly used to express religious experiences."[127] The religious artist unites basic symbols acquired from faith into uniquely new compositions. Also, to successfully rejuvenate its traditional symbols, the religious activity of symbolization relies upon the creativity of the aesthetic imagination. "The entire Christian iconography as well as the liturgy consist of aesthetic variations on religious symbols."[128] Dupré suggests that this unity between the aesthetic and religious symbolizations is so close that we could refer to a "double symbolization." Faith requires artistic expression to symbolize its experiences. Thus, this union runs even deeper:

> Because faith *needs* the artistic expression, art ends up changing faith itself.... Artists change the tradition which they express, not because they prefer to ignore the original message but because they consider it inadequately expressed in the art forms of the past.[129]

The religious experience is shaped and transformed by its artistic expression. Artistic modifications "open new perspectives on the content of faith."[130] Through history such reinterpretations have often been met with resistance. The content of faith is incorrectly identified with its traditional expression. "Almost every innovation

---

[126] *OD*, 233.
[127] *OD*, 233.
[128] *OD*, 233.
[129] *OD*, 234.
[130] *OD*, 234.

in religious art has been accompanied by cries of blasphemy."[131] Dupré considers this conflict to be inevitable since both religion and art are absolutistic insofar as neither desires to relinquish its control over what it regards to be its own domain. As Van der Leeuw asserts, "Holy power no more allows itself to be ruled by art than art allows itself to be constrained by holy power."[132] Religions have often sought to suppress their own desire to express the infinite in finite form; witness the extreme success of the iconoclastic movements in Judaism and Islam as well as Christianity's grappling with the question. Even when artistic expression has been allowed, concern for its aesthetic value has not always been notable.[133] Albeit in a negative way, these approaches help to illustrate the paramount importance of the interplay between faith and its artistic expression. Since it is of such consequence and since a great variety of aesthetic tastes exists even within cultures and generations, a conservative response to permitting artistic expression and even more so to allowing change has been the general norm.

Literary art has overall been accepted as necessary to expressing faith. In particular, poetry has sometimes been singled out as being intrinsically religious. True enough, in a religious culture religious symbols contribute the inspiring force and main content of the poetic imagination, but this does not make poetry in and of itself religious.

> Religious language may be called poetic in the widest sense of the term to the extent that it is metaphorical and symbolic rather than discursive. Yet poetry is not *per se* religious. Its basic orientation is to enlighten the empirical world by making its visible and audible forms transparent of a deeper reality. Religious language may develop into

---

[131] *OD*, 234.
[132] Van der Leeuw, *Sacred and Profane Beauty*, 268.
[133] See below, pp. 237-238.

full-fledged poetry, as it does in a number of sacred writings. But its main purpose is not so much to enlighten experience as to refer to a "beyond" of experience.[134]

From different perspectives, both religion's overall restrained approach to changing its artistic expression and the tendency to advance the intrinsically religious nature of all poetry suggest an inherent union of the religious and aesthetic experiences.

### d. Religious and Nonreligious Art

Armed with this understanding of the similarities, dissimilarities and the strong relationship between the aesthetic and religious experiences, Dupré considers possible characteristics which may properly distinguish between religious and nonreligious art.

First of all, the presence of a religious subject cannot adequately account for the distinction. Just because the subject is an image of a madonna does not require that the aesthetic representation reach beyond itself to express a greater meaning.

Secondly, the effect of the artistic image upon the beholder is equally a poor candidate to determine its religiosity. What is religiously inspiring to one person may provide no such impulse to another. Even when a work of art motivates one to pious feelings it is often difficult to identify these feelings as separate from simply being morally uplifting, noble, or the like. The context often casts the deciding vote if, for example, a certain piece of music will be considered religiously inspiring or not. Music played in a church on an organ may evoke a specifically pious response, but the same melody may produce a raucous result when played in a tavern on a piano. The German drinking song which has become "A Mighty Fortress Is Our God" is a good case in point. Yet, to another culture drums or other instruments may reveal the transcendent instead.

---

[134] *OD*, 238.

Just because art may be inspiring to some does not provide an objective demarcation of its religious character.

Thirdly, the intention of the artist cannot sufficiently account for the religious feature in art where it exists. An artistic creation does not simply express a previously completed feeling but contains significance within itself. In addition, in common estimation some religious artists are held to have been authentically religious persons, such as Fra Angelico and Bach, while others have not been deemed as obviously devout, such as Perugino.

Given these three insufficient approaches to the question we now look for hints of some positive factors to distinguish religious from nonreligious art. Yet, granting the multifaceted interpretations of religious feelings and cultural variations which have been acknowledged, Dupré concludes that "no *universal* rules could determine a form of expression as exclusively religious."[135] Still, certain objective criteria exist. One such basic condition is that the artist must have a genuine understanding of the religious experience in order to determine the aesthetic expression. This does not require the artist actually to be a religious person, but he or she must be acquainted with the religious experience. Beyond an acquaintance with the religious experience the artist must also be able to express it aesthetically. "Not the quality of the artist's preceding feelings determines the religious nature of his work, but his ability to probe and articulate the religious attitude in the creative process itself."[136]

In accepting this knowledge of the religious experience as basic to the existence of religious art, there still remains the question of what is unique to religious art's aesthetic presentation. Dupré recommends that "Religious art differs from other art in stressing

---

[135] *OD*, 239.
[136] *TS*, 54.

the inadequacy of its form with respect to the expressed content."[137] Key to distinguishing religious and nonreligious art is to recognize that, regarding the content, genuinely religious artistic works are those *"explicitly manifesting the transcendent."*[138] The artistic form never succeeds in reaching the transcendent content. The religious artistic creation must balance this deficiency of the form in relation to the content on the one hand, and on the other must also preserve "an aesthetic harmony between form and content, without which the symbol would cease to be artistic altogether."[139] Dupré acknowledges certain basic ways by which religious artists strive to achieve this balance; four of these procedures emphasize the inadequacy of the form while a second set embraces a more positive approach.

One method by which the transcendent content may be conveyed is through "the *monumental* character of the form."[140] Through the grandeur of the marble or stone, for example, an attempt is made to portray the vastness of the transcendent. Another procedure used by religious art is the incompleteness of the form; it is unfinished or open-ended. The beholder recognizes that the form cannot contain the immensity of the content and searches beyond the aesthetic expression to a new dimension. "Aesthetic satisfaction yields to a desire to penetrate into a trans-aesthetic area."[141] An additional device to underscore the transcendency of the content which cannot be adequately revealed by the form, while at the same time sustaining aesthetic harmony between content and form, is what Dupré calls the *"expressiveness* of religious art."[142]

---

[137] *OD*, 240.
[138] *TS*, 53.
[139] *OD*, 240.
[140] *OD*, 240. Also see Van der Leeuw, *Sacred and Profane Beauty*, 206-207.
[141] *OD*, 241.
[142] *OD*, 241.

By employing unusual contrasts (such as unnatural shadings or highlights) or by distorting the forms (such as elongating a figure), the artist strives to express a metempirical reality. "By changing the ordinary the artist attempts to evoke the extraordinary."[143] Finally, the inadequacy of the form may be expressed through the manner in which the material itself is used. A block of marble may take on new shapes and contours or the solid stone building embody movement as each reaches toward infinity.

There are also a variety of positive means by which artists attempt to express the divine. One that is quite extensive in its employment is the symbol of light. It appears throughout history over an expanse of cultures to refer to the divine. There are additional techniques utilized to apprehend the permanence of a spiritual realm. These include the frontal position of figures with an immobility and lack of perspective and sometimes without the presentation of individual resemblance, while time is often suspended to express the eternal.

Yet, none of these methods — whether in expressing the form's inadequacy or in positive symbolization — is intrinsically religious. In and of itself the form's monumental character, or its incompleteness, or unique expressiveness, or even the symbolization of light or position, does not dictate that all people over time and cultures (and even within the constancy of these factors) will respond to a particular artistic image as religious. Thus, while we must distinguish between religious and nonreligious art, there are no universal rules that differentiate between the two. "No technique, style, or representation is *per se* religious. The concept of religious art is valid but must forever remain relative."[144] Art is deemed religious "only within a specific cultural context with

[143] *OD*, 242.
[144] *OD*, 242.

particular religious doctrines."[145] However, certain symbols do indeed appear more regularly as expressive of the transcendent, though "symbols that are by *their very nature* religious cannot exist."[146] The repeated use of a particular symbol endows a certain religious significance. Finally, there are certain objective criteria which set religious art apart, including the need for the artist to possess a genuine understanding of the religious experience which enables the production of works that explicitly manifest the transcendent.

## B.  THE UNIQUENESS OF RELIGIOUS SYMBOLS

What makes religious symbols such as ritual, sacraments, and religious art distinctive from nonreligious symbols? What is the unique referent which allows a symbol to be a religious expression? This referent must be universally applicable to all religious acts and also contribute a significant role in their expression. There are many referents frequently employed in an attempt to signal the religious significance of something, such as the holy, the numinous, faith and piety. Within Dupré's works many important religious expressions are discussed, such as revelation and redemption, but there are three main referents which are quite significant and the possibility of the uniqueness of each to transform a symbol into a religious symbol will now be considered. We will clarify why the first two are not actually regarded by Dupré as the unique referent of religious symbols since they are not universally applicable to religion. It is the third which gives rise to specifically *religious* understanding.

[145] *TS*, 56.
[146] *TS*, 56.

## 1. *God*

First, we turn to the term 'God'. Dupré refers to 'God' as "key religious concept." He writes:

> the concept of God originates exclusively in, and is developed solely by, the religious act. It never is a philosophical discovery and no philosophical argument can prove it to be true or false. Yet philosophy provides this key religious concept with a logical structure enabling it to justify the central position which faith claims for it.[147]

'God' is a symbolic term which is specifically religious. It receives a principal status in religion by the profession of faith and justification through philosophy, though philosophy does not prove the existence of God. 'God' can express many images including "God's absolute priority as value and as power."[148] Following Van der Leeuw, Dupré acknowledges power "as one of the most elementary attributes of the religious 'object'."[149] Yet, for Dupré power along with will is not ultimate, for the two "are religious only to the extent that they reveal a deeper form of *being*."[150] This is one instance of how the meaning of 'God' shifts in primary meaning from power to being, or any number of interpretations.

The variety of meanings that 'God' may express is also apparent through a cursory glance of its historical development. Early religions do not necessarily even use the expression 'God'.[151] In and of itself this fact already illustrates that 'God' is not universally found in religious symbolism. Further, once arriving at the concept of God, after a long preparation, it has undergone constant revision through the ages. Polytheism is more sophisticated than the

[147] *OD*, 11.
[148] *OD*, 327.
[149] *OD*, 324.
[150] *OD*, 14.
[151] Dupré follows Van der Leeuw, *Religion in Essence*, § 11, 4: "God ... is a late comer in the history of religion."

animistic distinction between living and dead bodies. The qualified monotheism of the Hebrews is more exclusive but allows for some polytheism; the God which matters, their own, is an exclusively conceived expression and is highly personal. Even today after centuries of Christianity, signs of dissatisfaction with applying the word 'person' to God have surfaced theologically and philosophically. Christians can explain that the term person applies in its fullest sense to the incarnation, but to speak of God as person is sometimes considered insufficient and obsolete. For example, the Trinity considered as three *persona* (persons) frequently has been marked as a poor Latin translation of ὑπόστασις. It is also deficient when applied to God as such. Jewish belief cannot but interpret the Trinity as three gods since personhood is the basis for Jewish monotheistic faith.

Thus, 'God' cannot be the unique referent which allows a symbol to be a religious expression because it is both a late comer to religious expression and one which shifts in meaning. Within Dupré's thought it would be easy to equate his references to "the other dimension" with God. Brand Blanshard does this in his critique of Dupré, when he interprets Dupré as asserting, "When the man of faith reports that he has experienced the presence of God, no one standing outside that experience is in a position to deny that he has experienced what he says he has."[152] However, Dupré never makes such an assertion that one actually has seen what one has experienced, but simply that an experience cannot be denied and that the experience is experienced as given.[153] Furthermore, such an identity of God and the other dimension forces a universality of meaning into 'God' which Dupré clearly does not maintain.

[152] Blanshard, "Reply," 1008.
[153] See e.g., *OD*, 108-109. Dupré's response to Blanshard's comments and the above reflections on the concept of God were discussed at a meeting between Prof. Dupré and the author on January 3, 1995, in Kortrijk, Belgium.

## 2. *Sacred*

The domain of the sacred must be seriously considered as a candidate for being *the* referent which allows a symbol to be a religious expression. With W. Robertson Smith's distinction between the sacred and the common, and Durkheim's refinement contrasting the sacred and the profane, ethnologists presented a universal principle for the understanding of religion.[154] Phenomenological studies of religion have also accepted it as the central principle of interpretation. By 'sacred' Dupré basically accepts what he considers to be the general meaning employed by most studies of comparative religion: "a *direct, immediate experience*, characterized by some degree of passivity.... in most religious cultures ... [the] sacred is ... that which encompasses all human experiences and gives them their ultimate integration."[155]

### a. Initial Position

Dupré himself in a work of 1968 also employs this interpretation, equating the sacred with ultimate reality:

> I shall show that its [religion's] "object," the sacred or ultimate reality, is so comprehensive that it can be defined only in contrast to ordinary, that is profane, reality. At the same time the sacred as *ultimate* reality transcends all oppositions within the real: it is the all-integrating factor of existence.[156]

Here, to express the religious experience it is necessary to place the sacred *in contrast* to the profane; yet, this contrast takes place

---

[154] See W. Robertson Smith, *Lectures on the Religion of the Semites*, Burnett Lectures 1888-1889 (London: Black, 1927³); Émile Durkheim, *The Elementary Forms of the Religious Life*, trans. Joseph Swain (London: Allen & Unwin, 1915).

[155] *TS*, 21-22. For further nuances see below, p. 176.

[156] Louis Dupré, "Secular Man and His Religion," *Proceedings of the American Catholic Philosophical Association* 42 (1968): 78.

in one domain as "no aspect of life escapes the religious determination altogether."[157] The sacred and profane exist in one sphere
of existence.

In *The Other Dimension* (1972), Dupré continues to judge the
sacred as the unique referent of religious symbols. This referent is
universally applied to the highest type of reality which bestows
reality upon all others; "the sacred is constituted when man considers one kind of reality so far superior that all others become
real only to the extent that they participate in it."[158] Once again,
while the sacred is the distinguishing factor between religious and
nonreligious symbols, at the same time it abides united with its
defining opposite.

> Originally all symbols belonged to the same sphere of existence. To
> most men even today religious symbols structure and distinguish not
> by juxtaposing two relatively unrelated spheres of the real — one
> religious, the other secular — as they seem to do for Western man,
> but by differentiating *within* the one sphere of the real that which is
> fully real, powerful, and meaningful — the *sacred*, from that which
> is not so real, immediate, and superficial — the *profane*. The
> transcendence of the sacred over the profane, its fundamental negation,
> does not relegate the two to different universes. The sacred is *in* the
> profane. It stands out but belongs to the same universe as its other
> dimension.[159]

At a 1974 colloquium he reiterates much of the thought found
in *The Other Dimension*. The sacred remains the referent which
allows a symbol to be a religious expression. In addition, the
sacred and profane remain united within one realm. This time he
makes his point with words inspired by Henri Bouillard's presentation at the same conference in which Bouillard asserts that the

---

[157] Dupré, "Secular Man and His Religion," 81.
[158] *OD*, 255. Also see *OD*, 13-20.
[159] *OD*, 165.

simple opposition of the sacred and profane split into two domains as promoted by Durkheim and others does not account for the true nature of the religious act. God is the creator of the sacred as well as the profane and must be understood as divine in regard to both; a simple opposition to the profane would limit the domain of the divine.[160] Dupré grants this and also agrees with the position that the divine cannot be conceived of without the sacred. It is through the sacred that the divine is reached; the divine cannot be separated from the sacred without losing its ultimate meaning. However, on this question there is further development in Dupré's thought which fundamentally alters his basic position.

## b. Revised Position

In *Transcendent Selfhood* (1976), he makes a clear switch and no longer regards the sacred to be the unique referent of religious symbols. He explicitly states, "My present work continues what earlier publications initiated. Yet on one fundamental point I have to change my position.... I no longer consider the sacred a primary category of transcendence today."[161] He offers two reasons why he has revised his view:

> Though much in our past justifies referring to the object of the religious attitude as sacred, the equation cannot be assumed to be universal. Not only does it fail to account for the primitive mentality, but, of more immediate concern, it appears less and less appropriate to describe modern man's awareness of transcendence.[162]

---

[160] See Henri Bouillard, "La catégorie du sacré dans la science des religions," in *Le sacré: études et recherches*, Actes du XIVᵉ Colloque Organisé par le Centre International d'Études Humanistes et l'Institut d'Études Philosophiques de Rome, ed. Enrico Castelli (Paris: Aubier, 1974), 42-50. Also see Dupré, "Idées sur la formation du sacré et sa dégéneration," in *Le sacré: études et recherches*, 371.

[161] *TS*, x.

[162] *TS*, 18.

Based on a revised interpretation of primitive cultures and — on the other side of history — on the contemporary understanding of transcendence, Dupré argues that the referent of the sacred is not universally applicable to the religious understanding.

As to the first, Dupré challenges the application of the sacred to primitive society. In centering on primitive society his argumentation is strengthened since this is the strongest alleged connection between a society and the sacred. As noted above, in his earlier works Dupré was able to harmonize the assertion of the sacred as the uniquely religious referent with the fact that the sacred and profane where united in one domain and did not exist in separate spheres of existence by arguing that *within* the one domain the sacred-profane distinction can be made, thereby allowing the sacred to stand out as the referent which allows a symbol to be a religious expression. However, now he regards such an attempt at harmonization to be forced, particularly within primitive society.

> To be sure, primitives, as all people, regard certain area of experience more important than others. It is not unwarranted to attribute a religious significance to a distinction which may in some instances lead to the one between the sacred and the profane. But the two do not coincide, for the original distinctions take place within one diffusely "sacred" sphere. I see little use for a category that covers all aspects of primitive society and for which its members possess neither name nor concept. To say this is not to make the absurd claim that nothing is sacred to the savage, but, on the contrary, to assert that, in varying degrees, all of life is [sacred] and, consequently, that nothing is entirely profane.[163]

Dupré continues to acknowledge that within the one sphere of primitive society certain acts may have a greater religious meaning than others, but to apply the sacred-profane distinction to such an attitude is anachronistic; such a precise designation of the sacred

---

[163] *TS*, 19.

is not possible within primitive society. For Dupré, there is no longer an adequate reason to award the sacred the status of the unique referent of religious symbols.

Dupré admits that general favor has been bestowed upon the ideas of the above mentioned ethnologists who have pioneered the sacred-profane distinction within primitive society, but he argues against them from within their discipline and even from their own positions. Dupré asserts that while Durkheim popularized the distinction between the sacred and the profane and considered the very essence of religion as constituted by this separation, Durkheim "nevertheless assigns to the taboos which are supposed to enact it not only the function of separating the sacred from the nonsacred but also that of introducing structure and hierarchy *within* the sacred realm."[164] Durkheim writes: "All these interdictions have one common characteristic; they come, not from the fact that some things are sacred while others are not, but from the fact that there are inequalities and incompatibilities between sacred things."[165] Among others, E. Evans-Pritchard draws out from such statements by Durkheim what Durkheim himself never admitted.

> Surely what he [Durkheim] calls 'sacred' and 'profane' are on the same level of experience, and, far from being cut off from one another, they are so closely intermingled as to be inseparable. They cannot, therefore, either for the individual or for social activities, be put in closed departments which negate each other, one of which is left on entering the other.[166]

In the primitive mind a strict dichotomy does not exist. Claude Lévi-Strauss considers the application of the sacred and profane to primitive society as an inadmissible transposition of contemporary

[164] *TS*, 19.

[165] Durkheim, *Elementary Forms of the Religious Life*, 340.

[166] E. Evans-Pritchard, *Theories of Primitive Religion* (Oxford: Clarendon Press, 1965), 65.

categories. Dupré concludes "that the very theories from which the universality of the sacred/profane distinction was derived are being questioned today."[167]

In addition, the phenomenological approaches which have presented the unique importance of the sacred do not argue from all religious expressions — including the primitive mentality — but only from a particular stage of religion. On this point Dupré states: "Mircea Eliade, whose penetrating insights and seductive style have done so much to secure the sacred a primary place in the study of religion, supports its crucial significance by arguments that are convincing only when they are drawn from advanced religions."[168] Even among advanced religions Dupré does not believe that a universal significance can be attributed to the referent of the sacred. In certain forms of Buddhism, for example, there is no use or need of such a term in ancient canonical writings.

The same difficulty is encountered when an attempt is made to universalize the Judeo-Christian conceptions of the sacred and profane. In contrast to the general understanding of the sacred, biblical and other Christian literature holds the sacred as the main attribute of God which God reveals, and is not primarily an object of experience. Also, from a biblical perspective the sacred can be revered as the wholly other, establishing an infinite gap between God and creation. This too affords a distinctive stance from the view of most religious cultures in which the sacred primarily encompasses and integrates all human experiences. Dupré concludes that given all of these shifts of meaning in 'the sacred', particularly in its forced application to the primitive mentality, it cannot "still

---

[167] *TS*, 20.

[168] *TS*, 20. Dupré points to Jonathan Smith, "The Wobbling Pivot," *The Journal of Religion* 52 (April 1972): 143, who argues against Eliade's employment of the sacred/profane opposition in a particular instance.

remain sufficiently coherent and specific to function as a primary religious category."[169]

Dupré's second reason why he no longer considers the sacred as the unique referent of religious symbols is based on his observation that in the modern situation the possibility of a worldly experience of transcendence has been significantly reduced. In this secular spirit "art, science, philosophy, and morality have virtually lost all need for religious support in their development."[170] In the modern experience humans have claimed control of the universe and have no urgent need to relate meaning to a transcendent dimension. Without a notable call for a transcendent integration the perception of the sacred declines toward imperceptibility. Return to the sacred becomes a private decision and enterprise. "If anything is 'sacred' to the modern believer, it is only because he *holds* it to be so by inner conviction and free decision, not because he passively *undergoes* its sacred impact."[171] We will return to this modern predicament in the next chapter.

Note that Dupré does not deny his previous claim that the religious experience is neither objective nor subjective. He is not looking for a more subjective principle and thus removes the objective referent of the sacred.

> Yet contrary to a common opinion today, it is not the *objective* nature of the sacred that makes it unfit to symbolize an experience which the modern mind tends to regard as purely interior. Even in its most intimate self-possession the embodied mind requires objective symbols. But the sacred is *one* symbolic complex in which man expresses his encounter with transcendence; it is not the only one.... Indeed, some religious cultures seem to do very well without it.[172]

---

[169] *TS*, 22.
[170] *TS*, 23.
[171] *TS*, 29.
[172] *TS*, 18-19.

He strengthens his plea for viewing the religious attitude as dialectical (neither wholly objective nor wholly subjective) by listing the sacred as one referent of religious symbols among others. The problem with claiming the sacred as the unique referent of religious symbols in modern times is the decline of the role of the sacred in expressing the transcendent.

> What we are claiming, then, is not the disappearance of the category of the sacred altogether: we continue to give the name to persons and objects as we include them in our relation to ultimate transcendence. But since that transcendence itself is no longer *perceived as sacred*, the whole process of naming sacred, or holding sacred, is demoted from the primary level of experience to the secondary level of interpretation.[173]

Thus, Dupré develops his thought and reaches the conclusion that religious expression need not always be described in relation to the sacred. There is no evidence that the sacred is the unique referent of religious understanding in primitive society nor in a secularized world view.

## 3. *Transcendence*

Given our previous discussion of the religious symbols of ritual, sacraments and religious art, it should be of no surprise that we will discover transcendence to be the unique referent of religious symbols in the thought of Louis Dupré. Recall that ritual is the place of union between human and transcendent dimensions; sacraments express transcendent reality; and religious art presents a transcendent content. In fact, we have already acknowledged that this manifestation of a transcendent content specifically distinguishes religious from nonreligious art. In addition, in investigating the possibility of God and the sacred as the unique

[173] *TS*, 29.

referent of religious symbols, the role of transcendence has been in the foreground. The referent of God, while not universal, when employed does consistently refer to some type of transcendence. Similarly, in those instances where it is appropriate to apply 'the sacred' to the religious act, it invokes a transcendent dimension.

## a. Transcendence as Universal

Unlike the referents of God and the sacred, Dupré considers transcendence to be present in all religions, at least in some form. Transcendence is a more universal referent when one takes into account that there are degrees of transcendence. For example, in the primitive mentality there is a very low grade of transcendence. In general, the forces which control life such as sun and rain are immanently present but are to some extent revered as 'other'. Allowing for Dupré's more nuanced use of 'the sacred' when referring to primitive society, Eliade's observation is still pertinent: "The sacred tree, the sacred stone are not adored as stone or tree; they are worshipped precisely because they are *hierophanies*, because they show something that is no longer stone or tree but the *sacred*, the *ganz andere*."[174] By contrast, in Islam there is a high intensity of transcendence that is accepted, and within Christianity there are varying degrees of transcendence. The Catholic acceptance of neo-Platonic approaches to reality, including participation in the divine, has historically placed it underneath the general Protestant perception of transcendence, though this distinction is vanishing.

---

[174] Mircea Eliade, *The Sacred and the Profane: The Nature of Religion*, trans. Willard Trask (New York: Harcourt, Brace & World, 1959), 12. Perhaps for 'sacred' we could read the 'revered' or 'religiously significant' in order to avoid applying the sacred/profane distinction to the primitive mind.

The universality of transcendence — as an analogous term — is also suggested from the vantage point of metaphysics. "Transcendence, understood in the most general sense as the distance between appearance and what justifies appearance, is basic to the metaphysical enterprise."[175] The very beginning of the recognition of transcendence arises when it is determined that the appearance of things requires a justification; this is also the very beginning of metaphysics. In varying degrees, a transcendent principle is offered in response to the question, 'What is it that accounts for what exists?' Answers such as the absolute as expressed in water, or mathematics, or the Good have been proposed. Parmenides shapes the reply in terms of Being. Plato and Aristotle "reformulated Parmenides' distinction between being and non-being as the relation between the *reality* of appearances and the *reality* of the ground. Plato had done so in terms of participation, Aristotle of causality."[176] Among the many other nuances that can be made, Dupré singles out the impact of Christianity.

> [Christians] changed the very meaning of *ground* [in metaphysics]. With the idea of immanent ground they combined that of *transcendent* cause. To be sure, ground and cause had been united from the beginning of Western philosophy and Plato as well as Aristotle had at least implied a dependence of reality on a transcendent principle. Christian thinkers, however, explicitly declared this transcendent principle *constitutive* of the very nature of the real. To the existing transference from appearance to ground they added a vertical reference.[177]

With this Christian expression, a stronger intensity of transcendence is presented as the nature of the real itself is constituted by it.

[175] *PM*, 162.

[176] *MC*, 2.

[177] *MC*, 5. This generalization should not be applied to all Christian thinkers. With Aquinas, for example, "even when he conceived the dependence in causal terms, the cause remained immanent in the effect and was functioning also as ground." *MC*, 2.

Thus, for Dupré, transcendence — at least in varying degrees — is accorded the status of universality in religion; and as a universal referent for religious understanding it is the most viable candidate for being the unique referent of religious symbols. In addition to its quality of universality, we now turn to view some of the functions of the religious referent of transcendence to determine if it contributes a significant role in religious expression. The goal at this stage is not to provide an exhaustive list of its roles but to give an overall indication of its importance for Dupré. (Even though the word transcendent is referenced only once in the index to *The Other Dimension* — regarding its essential use in religion — Dupré employs the word and its cognates almost 450 times in that work alone.)

## b. Transcendence as Key

The uniqueness of transcendence as a religious referent is evident from some of its operations. The dialectical nature of religion is suitably expressed through the referent of transcendence. Viewed from its objective pole, religion must be understood as a consideration of the transcendent. Religion's "one universal objective trait [is], namely, a relation to some sort of transcendent reality." This same relation to transcendence also identifies the subjective character of religion: "Precisely because the content of faith is transcendent, its appropriation requires a subjective commitment."[178] Further, the nature of the religious act necessitates reference to transcendence.

> A full understanding of the religious act, then, is impossible without taking into account a transcendent intervention (be it as subjective attraction or as objective revelation), since it is precisely this transcendent terminus which in the believer's mind gives its specific meaning to the religious act.[179]

[178] *OD*, 57.
[179] *OD*, 108.

A response to the transcendent is made through and demanded by the religious act. "By its very nature this act requires a commitment to the transcendent which does not allow the believer to remain silent."[180]

Religious language is also dependent upon reference to transcendence. "All religious assertions, to the extent that they are still meaningful to the believer, inform him about his own situation with regard to the transcendent, not about objective facts lying outside his existence."[181] Religious language is not ordinary language about the empirically verifiable world, but is dialectically related to it since the religious transcends ordinary language.

> The term *transcendent*, so essential for religion, develops dialectically and takes various meanings in different contexts. It is always transcendent *in relation to* what surrounds it. Any attempt to give it a definitive, positive content in ordinary language is bound to fail because ordinary language can deal only with ordinary life, while the transcendent is precisely what stands out of the ordinary.[182]

Religious language possess a dialectical nature precisely because the terminus of the religious quest is transcendent.

There is also a secure relationship between transcendence and faith. Through faith, human language is able to name the transcendent content that is revealed.

> Since all human discourse is equipped to refer *directly* only to intramundane relations, the question arises how the transcendent can survive being expressed in the language of immanence.... Faith alone provides the key to unlock the transcendent meaning of the revealed. It alone separates the transcendent content from the immanent appearances in which it resides.[183]

Faith is the means by which the transcendent dimension in revelation is made manifest. Through faith a relationship with the transcendent

[180] *OD*, 72.
[181] *OD*, 42.
[182] *OD*, 16.
[183] *OD*, 293-294.

is claimed. This is a separate step from a philosophical argument concluding to the transcendence of Being or to a transcendent ground. Pure metaphysics encounters the transcendent through the two basic models of being or of consciousness. Yet, neither one of these models reaches a positive content. "Philosophy can do no more than articulate the primal awareness of transcendence. Only the religious act can transform it into an awareness of God."[184] Metaphysical reflection becomes religious when the transcendent is perceived as self-revealing. Both the believer and nonbeliever integrate their experiences into separate sets of ultimate beliefs.

> Faith interprets the same data which confront the nonbeliever, but it interprets them differently by subordinating them to an ultimate principle which is neither the totality nor an inherent part of the empirical order. Thus it gives a new meaning to existence in relating it to the transcendent.[185]

It is not that faith presents any essentially new facts or information; instead faith presents a new *attitude* in which assertions *about* the transcendent are understood in terms of the believer's own relation *to* the transcendent.

Many additional connections between transcendence and the interpretation of religious thought can be made, such as in relation to myth, mysticism, and hope. In short,

> [transcendence] refers to that particular quality by which the source and terminus of the religious relation surpasses absolutely the mind's and all other reality. It introduces separation into the most intimate union, negation into the most affirmative assertion. It provides the dynamic tension without which the religious act would grow slack and eventually collapse in its own immanence. Transcendence marks religious practice before it becomes a principle of reflection.[186]

---

[184] *OD*, 137. Also see *OD*, 127-132.

[185] *OD*, 48.

[186] Louis Dupré, "Transcendence and Immanence as Theological Categories," *Catholic Theological Society of America Proceedings* 31 (June 9-12, 1976): 1.

Consequently, in Dupré's thought transcendence must be accorded the status of the unique referent of religious symbols because it is both universally applicable to all religious acts and also contributes a key role in their expression.

## c. Transcendence as Unique Referent

Chapter One established the necessity of employing symbols in general for religious understanding. The theological justification was argued given the primary role of some type of mysticism in religion and the symbolic nature of mysticism, thus requiring religious expression to be symbolic. Additionally, in Dupré's general symbol theory, the three patterns of form, representation, and language all point to the primary role of symbol for the understanding of religious thought as do the specific religious symbols of ritual, sacraments and religious art investigated in this chapter. Philosophical justification was also developed to demonstrate the primacy of symbol in expressing religious understanding. This was based upon Dupré's reading of Schleiermacher and Hegel. Further philosophical grounding for the primary function of symbol is suggested by Dupré's appreciation of the thought of Cassirer and Langer and its necessity for explicating a metaphysics of culture.

There is no other expression that is equal to nor more primary than symbol for religious understanding. All religious expression must be understood symbolically. "Symbolic creativity is the single gate through which the transcendent must enter consciousness, for symbols alone can convey meanings which sufficiently surpass the empirical appearance to express a transcendent content."[187]

However, symbolism in general is not sufficient for the interpretation of religious thought. Its referent must be indicated in order to specify a symbol's religious nature. Transcendence has

[187] *OD*, 297.

been demonstrated as this necessary referent. In turn, transcendence is approached through the vision of faith. "Religious man attains the transcendent only *in faith*."[188] Dupré explains: "By themselves symbols, ideas, or events, however unusual, cannot point beyond the immanent universe to which they belong.... What makes words and deeds surpass their intra-mundane appearance is the constitutive act of faith."[189] Through faith the symbol is accorded the required reference to the transcendent.

It should be clear now why Dupré states: "Transcendence is the religious category *par excellence*."[190] Transcendence is the religious category *par excellence insofar as* it is *the* factor which distinguishes religious symbols from other symbols. Transcendence is the referent through which we conceptualize all religious symbolization, while allowing for the fact that different degrees of transcendence exist. For the religious person, "only symbols ... can provide religious language with ... the transcendent nature of his referent."[191] Symbols are *the* primary expression for the interpretation of religious thought insofar as they possess a transcendent referent.

The dialectical characteristic of religion implies that religion cannot be defined from only one direction. In speaking of transcendence one must also speak of immanence. "The immanence of God in all that is, is as essential as his transcendence."[192] Without this balance the transcendent quality of religion can eclipse its authentic expression. "If not allowed to come to rest in a new

---

[188] *OD*, 106.

[189] *OD*, 294.

[190] Dupré, "Transcendence and Immanence," 1.

[191] *OD*, 225.

[192] Louis Dupré, "Hope and Transcendence," in *The God Experience: Essays in Hope*, The Cardinal Bea Lectures 2, ed. Joseph Whelan (New York: Newman Press, 1971), 223.

immanence, the obsession with transcendence turns into an all-consuming fire, destructive of the very culture which ignited it."[193] For example, a deficient portrayal of immanence may result in God being considered as present in oneself or members of one's group, but in no one else. This leads to religious warfare, intolerance and persecutions.

Finally, note that Dupré refers to transcendence as both a religious category and a "theological category."[194] David Burrell objects that "transcendence is not a religious category, but a theological one."[195] He argues that "transcendence refers not to a distinguishing feature of divinity, but to a formal feature of all discourse about divinity."[196] The first, Burrell would ascribe to the domain of religion and the second to theology. The theological category of transcendence names "the relation between God and all that is but is not God,"[197] i.e., the relation between God and creation. Dupré agrees that transcendence is a theological category as Burrell presents it. Yet, it must also be considered to be a religious category, for without this category religion cannot be spoken of in any universal way. To articulate the religious experience appeal must be made to the language of transcendence.

## C. SUMMARY

In applying Dupré's understanding of symbol to religion we have viewed the specific religious symbols of ritual, sacraments,

---

[193] Dupré, "Transcendence and Immanence," 1.

[194] Dupré, "Transcendence and Immanence," 2.

[195] David Burrell, "A Response (I) to Louis Dupré['s 'Transcendence and Immanence as Theological Categories']," *Catholic Theological Society of America Proceedings* 31 (June 9-12, 1976): 11.

[196] Burrell, "A Response (I) to Louis Dupré," 11.

[197] Burrell, "A Response (I) to Louis Dupré," 11.

and religious art. With their own particular nuances each elucidates a deep appreciation of the symbolic nature of religious expression. For example, there is a homogeneity of action and word in ritual symbolic expression. The ritual unites humanity and the transcendent as the transitoriness of time is surmounted by representing the founding events which provide meaning and purpose to existence. As formally structured activity, ritual can be compared and contrasted to the functions and aims of play. Sacraments are a specific type of ritual which maintain an intrinsic unity of symbol and symbolized. This is accomplished through language which alone can direct the deed toward a transcendent reality without first asserting the deed's ordinary meaning. In investigating religious art, Dupré builds upon the intimate connection between form and content present in the aesthetic expression. He distinguishes between aesthetic and ordinary perception and identifies that artistic expression is necessary for faith to symbolize its experiences. Yet, of course, all art is not religious. Though no universal rules spanning history and culture can distinguish religious art from nonreligious, one basic objective criterion is that the artist, while not necessarily a religious person, must be acquainted with the religious experience and be able to render an aesthetic expression of it. This aesthetic presentation of religious art is unique from other art insofar as its form is always striving to express, but never attaining, its content that explicitly manifests the transcendent.

Finally, in this chapter transcendence has been credited as the unique referent which sets a symbol apart as religious. While both God and the sacred are important referents of religious symbols, they are not universally applicable to all religious expression. The referent of transcendence does function universally and is key in all religious expressions. The question remains how the modern worldview may have affected religious symbolism in its search to express the transcendent. The final chapter develops Dupré's appreciation of this problem.

# CHAPTER FOUR

# INABILITY TO MAKE RELIGIOUS SYMBOLS:
# THE MODERN PREDICAMENT

Given Dupré's understanding of the symbolic nature of all religious expression with its transcendent referent, it is valuable to inquire into the viability of this approach for modern Western culture. While arguably there is as much symbolism today as in the past, it is now a very diminished symbolism that does not refer to the transcendent because of the splintering of transcendence into a realm separate from nature. All reality is objectified and the subject becomes the sole master-giver of meaning. Various attempts have presented themselves to provide the recovery of transcendence. For his solution, Dupré proposes a return to the inner life because such a turn succeeds in keeping a unified world view where secular culture has failed. Devout humanism, particularly as embodied by Ignatius of Loyola, is historically one such successful model. Each person today must look inward to reestablish a connection with the transcendent and recover the full meaning of religious symbols.

The foregoing are the ideas that will be developed in this chapter. We will do so by tightening the threads which weave together Dupré's world view, including the fibers of form, transcendence, mysticism, and of course, symbol. We will begin by exploring Dupré's analysis of Western culture. Under this section we will present the characteristics which distinguish modernity from premodernity, namely, the separation of transcendence from nature and also the division of the human subject from nature, leaving nature to refer only to the cosmos. While we will discuss each under a different heading, both were occasioned by many of the same historical events and outlooks. Armed with this interpretation, a closer investigation will be possible of Dupré's assessment of the qualities and challenges of the modern situation. The second main section of this chapter will explore the feasibility of the recovery of a sense of the transcendent which is a prerequisite for authentic symbolic expression. Here, after identifying the short-comings of a few popular attempts, we will discuss the alternatives envisioned by Dupré for the revitalization of modern Western culture. In this discussion the purpose is not to attempt an exhaustive treatment of Dupré's many significant reflections upon culture, but furnish those insights most essential to our plan.

## A. FROM PREMODERNITY TO MODERNITY

To understand Dupré's conception of the modern situation, it is imperative to comprehend his broader world view as understood through philosophy, theology and history. In the opening pages of *Transcendent Selfhood*, Dupré asserts that the modern age has lost a sense of transcendence. Culture has turned to objectivism, signaling not so much an absence of subjectivity but more an in-appropriate view of the self devoid of content and meaning. He continues by offering a Marxist interpretation of reality as an example of this loss of transcendence and selfward turn. In ad-dition, numerous articles by Dupré treat one or another aspect of the turn to modernity, the crisis of modern culture, and/or the possibility for a renewed cultural outlook. His recent book *Passage to Modernity* can been recognized as a clarification and expansion of these introductory pages of *Transcendent Selfhood* and as a synthesis of many of these previously published articles.

As we begin this investigation of Dupré's analysis of culture, we must acknowledge with him the general use of diverse and often contradictory definitions of 'culture'. Dupré employs the definition of anthropologist Ruth Benedict as a succinct but comprehensive summary of a variety of definitions. She writes that culture "is a more or less consistent pattern of thought and action."[1] Culture, then, "includes all the ideas, norms, values, rules of conduct, and expectations prevalent in any given society."[2] A narrow sociological interpretation may limit these norms and values to those necessary for managing the material conditions of existence. But a culture does far more than this; it "consists of the symbols that preserve and direct the life of a society."[3] Culture looks beyond individual tasks and interests toward a spiritual fulfillment; "it holds out a spiritual surplus that urges humans beyond the satisfaction of immediate needs."[4] Culture is above all a spiritual enterprise.

Of course, 'culture' carries different meanings at different times, or more precisely, between different sets of expectations, outlooks and presuppositions. "The Greek *paideia* [to teach], as well as the Latin *cultus animi* and *cultura animi* (derived from the agricultural *colere* [to grow]) stress the need to harmonize erudition and education with the demands of an established, social nature."[5] Yet the modern notion of culture is to create a new second nature. Here the shift is made from one fabric of culture to another — and, extending the

[1] Ruth Benedict, *Patterns of Culture* (New York: Houghton Mifflin, 1934), 53.

[2] Louis Dupré, "Ascent and Decline of a Self-Centered Culture," in *Individuality and Cooperative Action*, ed. Joseph Earley (Washington, D.C.: Georgetown University Press, 1991), 137.

[3] *MC*, 12.

[4] *MC*, 14.

[5] Louis Dupré, *Marx's Social Critique of Culture* (New Haven, CT: Yale University Press, 1983), 1.

metaphor, I would describe it as a shift from cotton and wool (natural plant and animal fibers) to polyester and rayon (humanly engineered synthetics). In other words, while the ancient understanding of culture endeavored to cultivate a given nature, the modern notion pursued the creation of a new second nature. To understand the modern predicament we must first understand more completely some of the factors which gave it birth.

## 1. *Nature: Cosmic, Human, Transcendent*

In distinguishing modern culture from the premodern, Dupré argues that it is not enough to view some of its effects. It is also not sufficient simply to assert that modernity began with the Renaissance. Instead, one must inquire into the basic principles operative through different periods of history. The differentiation of one era from another is not marked simply by the passage of time. For Dupré, the key to understanding the demarcation lines between epochs in history is to identify them as shifts in how "nature" is perceived: "In the relation between the old and the new I can think of no intellectual factor that has played a more decisive role than the transformation of the concept of *nature*."[6]

When the period we now call ancient was modern, something changed for it to be marked from the then premodern. The epoch

---

[6] Louis Dupré, "The Dissolution of the Union of Nature and Grace at the Dawn of the Modern Age," in *The Theology of Wolfhart Pannenberg: Twelve American Critiques*, ed. Carl Braaten and Philip Clayton (Minneapolis: Augsburg Publishing House, 1988), 96. Also see e.g., Leo Strauss, *Natural Right and History* (Chicago: The University of Chicago Press, 1950), 81-119; Thomas Prufer, *Recapitulations: Essays in Philosophy*, Studies in Philosophy and the History of Philosophy 26 (Washington, D.C.: The Catholic University of America Press, 1993), 71: "The articulation of the history of philosophy into epochs (ancient, medieval, modern, post-modern) [is] on the basis of shifts in the senses of 'nature'."

we now call ancient begins with the acceptance of φύσις as an all comprehensive, creative principle; Thales being the first Greek thinker known to make this proclamation. This original approach understands φύσις to be one unified whole simultaneously forming (answering how things came about) and informing (answering why things are the way they are) all that is. At this stage we will now translate φύσις by 'nature'. However, already with Plato and Aristotle limits begin to be placed upon the meaning of nature which requires it to be coupled with an additional term for it to equal nature as all encompassing.

Among other constraints, Plato denies that nature can function as the ultimate norm of conduct.[7] There is an ulterior principle to nature that moves itself as well as other beings. Dupré summarizes the argument: "Since self-movement belongs exclusively to living beings, soul, the principle of life, must be regarded to be more primitive than nature."[8] If soul is elementary to nature then nature is dependent upon this higher spiritual order. At the same time, Plato maintains that it is the existence of soul which is most eminently *natural*. Thus within the original concept of nature there are now "two distinct principles: a transcendent one that functions as the cause of motion, and one that depends on it as its effect."[9] Similar to Plato's division of the meaning of nature within itself, with Aristotle there is a clear introduction of a second term to add to nature to produce an all comprehensive principle. His definition of nature limits it to a principle of motion in those beings capable of self-induced motion and rest, and he

---

[7] See Plato, *The Laws*, Book 10, in *Plato: In Twelve Volumes*, vol. 11, *Laws II, Books VII-XII*, The Loeb Classical Library 192, ed. E. Warmington, trans. R. Bury (London: William Heinemann; Cambridge: Harvard University Press, 1926). Also see *PM*, 16-17.

[8] *PM*, 17.

[9] *PM*, 17.

includes in this the four elements.[10] While nature is directing these organic processes to their projected end, the term κόσμος is introduced to account for "the ordered totality of being that coordinates those processes as well as the laws that rule them."[11] In the classical era the Greek perception of κόσμος ordered more than the physical universe which we now designate by cosmos. For the Greeks κόσμος was a comprehensive term that "included theological, anthropic as well as physical meanings."[12] This multifarious conception of κόσμος is coupled with φύσις to express nature in its entirety.

Thus, nature, understood as φύσις begins as an all comprehensive principle. However, even with the ancients the original unity of φύσις begins to disintegrate when it requires the addition of κόσμος to remain the all encompassing principle of nature. Nature remains a unified whole but now is seen as possessing cosmic, human and transcendent elements in an inseparable totality. It is this composite appreciation of nature and not the original concept of φύσις which is the direct ancestor of the modern understanding of nature.

## 2. *Transcendence Torn From Nature*

The next step in the dissolution of nature is to remove one of its component elements — cosmic, human and transcendent — and this action marks one of the turns toward the birth of modernity. This step is qualitatively different from the move begun with Aristotle to add concepts in order to safeguard nature's comprehensive

---

[10] See Aristotle, *Physics*, in *Aristotle: The Physics*, vol. 1, The Loeb Classical Library, trans. Philip Wicksteed and Francis Cornford (London: William Heinemann; Cambridge: Harvard University Press, 1957[2]), 2.1, 192[b]: "Nature is the principle and cause of motion and rest to those things, and those things only in which she inheres primarily, as distinct from incidentally."

[11] *PM*, 17. See Aristotle, *Physics*, 2.1.

[12] *PM*, 18.

character. Now, instead of protecting the inclusivity of nature, this new shift severs the integrity of nature by ripping the element of transcendence out of nature and relegating it to a separate realm. Dupré identifies a number of conditions which allowed transcendence to be removed in this way. We will confine our presentation to the tensions between two main relationships: the causal link between God and creation, and that between nature and grace. These factors are not so much explanations of the change as they are conditions which made the shift possible.

### a. Synthesis with Aristotle: Causality

One instrumental factor in the separation of the divine from nature was the particular causal relation attributed between God and creation. "For the Greeks as well as for Jews and Christians, some form of causality had always been the principal category for expressing the link between God and the world."[13] However, in reflecting upon the Christian doctrine of creation, whereby God freely created all that is, medieval theologians could not maintain the complete immanence of the cause in the effect as did their Greek predecessors. For the Christian, the existence of God alone without the world is meaningful — it is God's free decision to create. In creating the world God is no greater than God would be without the world. For the Greeks, nature 'emerged' and possessed divine sufficiency; a freely creating God would have destroyed this. Christianity does not deny this logic but reinterprets nature as being 'brought to emerge' by the free act of God. Still, Christians could not completely deny a divine presence in creation since God's creative act conveys God's being. Christian thinkers of the Middle Ages were challenged to reconcile this tension of nature's divine sufficiency and the acts of a transcendent God.

[13] *PM*, 172.

Aquinas succeeded in explaining the Christian perception of the relation between God and creation through a synthesis with Aristotelian efficient causality, but not without balancing this concept with Platonic participation. "Aquinas hesitated considerably between Plato's participation and Aristotle's efficient causality for conceptualizing the creature's dependence on God."[14] In Aquinas' later thought in the *Summa Theologiae* he mainly embraces efficient causality:

> God exists in everything; not indeed as part of their substance or as an accident, but as an agent is present to that which its action is taking place. For unless it act through intermediaries every agent must be connected with that upon which it acts, and be in causal contact with it: compare Aristotle's proof that for one thing to move another the two must be in contact [*Physics*, 7.2, 243ᵃ]. Now since it is God's nature to exist, he it must be who properly causes existence in creatures, just as it is fire itself [that] sets other things on fire.[15]

Yet, even here participation is perceptible, as the passage continues: "But being is innermost in each thing and most fundamentally inherent in all things since it is formal in respect of everything found in a thing. ... Hence it must be that God is in all things, and innermostly."[16] Thus, "even within an Aristotelian conceptualization, participation continues to balance efficient causality in Thomas' description of God's presence in his creation."[17]

---

[14] *PM*, 173.

[15] Thomas Aquinas, *Summa Theologiae: Latin Text and English Translation*, trans. Blackfriars (New York: McGraw-Hill, 1964), I, q. 8, a. 1.

[16] Aquinas, *Summa Theologiae*, I, q. 8, a. 1, [for this English translation I have followed the 3 vol. edition of the Fathers of the English Dominican Province (New York: Benziger Brothers, 1947)].

[17] *PM*, 173.

## b. Synthesis with Aristotle: Nature and Grace

The question of the causal relation between God and creation and the general attempt to synthesize Christian and Aristotelian concepts impacted the debate over the relationship between nature and grace. This covers an intricate and complex history. Dupré comments in *The Other Dimension*: "The entire history of Christian theology could be written in terms of the emphasis which one or another of the aspects of grace received."[18] In many ways, this is what Dupré begins to write twenty-one years later in *Passage to Modernity*. Here we cannot even present the highlights but only touch on a few pertinent facts which provoked transcendence to be placed outside of nature.

Dupré asserts that "some time during the thirteenth century the first signs of the theological dispute concerning the relation between nature and grace appear."[19] The problem arose in attempting to incorporate the philosophy of Aristotle into Christian theology. Among other obstacles was the fundamental barrier imposed by conflicting concepts of nature. "In Latin theology the term nature had originally referred to human nature in the concrete context of a creation that itself was gratuitous."[20] By contrast for Aristotle "each nature is endowed with its own immanent teleology, the end of which had to be proportionate to the natural means for attaining it."[21] Aristotle's understanding was not broad enough to

---

[18] *OD*, 460. Dupré continues in summary: "In Catholic theology since the late Middle Ages the notion of gratuitousness has predominated. In Lutheran theology the accent was on justification and forgiveness of sin. The ideas of liberation and restored freedom permeate all the predestination theologies from Augustine to Calvin. The primary idea of divinization seems to be best preserved among Orthodox theologians thanks to their uninterrupted contact with the Greek Fathers."

[19] *PM*, 170.

[20] *PM*, 170.

[21] *PM*, 170.

allow human nature to attain a life of heavenly bliss since this could not be achieved by the powers of human nature alone without God's help. Aquinas reconciled these positions by allowing nature some immanent human end — namely, the ends of virtue and contemplation in the good city advanced by Aristotle — but this ideal is inferior to the more fundamental end which is not realized by human effort alone.[22] Thus, "in Aquinas the term *supernatural* does not refer to a new order of being added to nature but to the means for attaining the one final end for which the power of nature alone does not suffice."[23] The terms 'nature' and 'supernatural' are two formally distinct aspects of one reality.

Despite this successful synthesis with Aristotelian philosophy, a separate aspect of Aquinas' structure threatened the balance of its complex unity:

> Rather than considering the Incarnation a decisive but by no means discontinuous moment in a process of divine self-communication that had started with creation, as Scotus (and later also Erasmus) was to do, Aquinas saw it essentially as a divine response to the effects of the fall. Without the fall the Incarnation would not have occurred. Viewed from this perspective, redemption might be interpreted as a supernatural cure for a natural disease and, as such, as initiating a wholly different order of grace.[24]

However, beyond this problem within Aquinas' formulation, radical followers of Aristotle's philosophy (the Averoists) began to question Aquinas' synthesis of Aristotle with the content of Christian revelation. Particularly Aquinas' colleagues at the University of Paris, Siger of Brabant and Boethius of Dacia,

---

[22] See Aquinas, *Summa Theologiae*, I-II, ques. 62-63. Also see *PM*, 171.

[23] *PM*, 171. See Aquinas, *Summa contra Gentiles*, 3, ch. 150, § 5: "Some supernatural form and perfection must be super added to man whereby he may be ordered suitably to the aforesaid end."

[24] *PM*, 172.

perceived nature as the object of philosophy, which existed in a
distinct order of being from the content of Christian revelation;
they did not conceive of any reason why these two orders should
be made compatible. Though Aquinas argued successfully against
such a severe division between philosophy and theology, the thought
of his adversaries disturbed the belief in the viability of the al-
liance between Aristotelian philosophy and theology. (Neither was
confidence raised in 1277 when Étienne Tempier, the archbishop
of Paris, condemned some of Aquinas' Aristotelian theses.) However, the real separation of the divine from nature was not due to
differences in the interpretation and application of Aristotle but
"in the end was mainly the work of those who had led the resistance
against Aristotelianism, namely, the nominalists."[25]

## c. Disintegration of Medieval Syntheses

When the Aristotelian framework was abandoned the synthesis
between God as cause of creation and human action deteriorated,
and so did the one between grace and nature. The nominalist
theologies of the fourteenth and fifteenth centuries advanced the
idea of an unrestricted divine power to an extreme never before
witnessed. This slowly matures until the relation between Creator
and creature is barely intelligible; the actions of creatures appeared to be on a completely separate sphere which has no relation
to God's power.[26] This view basically suggests that "a supreme
power allows the natural processes of this world to follow their
'own' course, until it threatens to collide with God's 'own' projects
of salvation or damnation — at which point God himself in turn

---

[25] *PM*, 174.

[26] See *PM*, 173: "Never before the modern age did Christians consider a
notion of extrinsic causality adequate to express the intimate, permanent presence
of God to his creation."

takes hold of the events."[27] Secondary causes are placed in an independent order distinct from God as primary cause. This idea of an absolute divine power also incites the separation of grace from nature. Unconditioned divine power operates independent of any known laws or routine, leaving nature without an intrinsic intelligible ground for the understanding of why things are as they are or for predicting what will occur. Only the observation of actual facts provides some clue into nature's actions. Grace becomes equally unpredictable as it is "granted by an inscrutable divine decree ... randomly dispensed or withheld regardless of the recipient's moral conduct."[28] Divine cause, human action, nature, and grace begin to be seen differently in light of God's unrestricted power — a difference which undermines the synthesis between transcendence and nature.

Dupré develops the historical story of how the supernatural order was torn from the natural one. He begins with Scotus in the thirteenth century who prepares the way by producing his view of the Incarnation in opposition to Aquinas' theory. Scotus argued that the definition of 'human nature' must apply to Christ exactly the same as it does to all others who are endowed with this nature. While requiring a divine intervention, the potential to be assumed by a divine person — or to be elevated in grace — is by definition possessed by all humans in all instances.[29] "Scotus's solution came with a price, for it detached nature as such from what Christians regarded as its linkage to a divine destiny."[30] There are many intricacies and nuances as this concept progresses through

---

[27] Dupré, "Transcendence and Immanence," 9.

[28] *PM*, 174.

[29] See John Duns Scotus, *God and Creatures: The Quodlibetal Questions*, trans. Felix Alluntis and Allan Wolter (Princeton: Princeton University Press, 1975), 434-435. Also see *PM*, 175-176.

[30] *PM*, 175.

different thinkers, not the least of which is William of Ockham.[31] Yet, what is essential for our project is *that* the syntheses explained above were fractured. Dupré summarizes and connects these rifts.

> The idea of an independent order of secondary causes gradually led to a conception of nature as fully equipped to act without special divine assistance. But if the actual order of nature functioned as an independent entity directed only by its own teleology, the elevation to grace had to be regarded as a divine addition to the realm of nature. Logic required that theology treat this additional order separately from that of nature.[32]

Steadily, a distinction is forming between a natural human end and humankind's revealed destiny. The term 'supernatural' begins to refer to a separate order as nature's intrinsically transcendent dimension is pulled from it. Eventually, in the sixteenth century theologians explicitly distinguish between two distinct ends resulting in the concepts of 'pure nature' and 'supernatural' becoming concrete independent realities.[33]

Thus, by the end of the Middle Ages, nominalism had effectively banished God from creation. Even Aquinas' main sixteenth century commentators were affected; contrary to their teacher's synthesis with Aristotelian philosophy, they considered nature as a concrete

---

[31] Dupré agrees with "recent studies of Ockham . . . [that] have shown how unjustified it is to call him the 'father of theological nominalism', but there is no doubt that his position prepared the concept of nature as a self-sufficient reality." *PM*, 176.

[32] *PM*, 177.

[33] See *PM*, 171, 178. Dupré further suggests in *PM*, 178: "[Pure nature] might have remained a theological abstraction if Renaissance naturalism had not given it an acceptable content, and seventeenth-century philosophy a rational justification. Once the idea of an independent, quasi-autonomous order of nature gained a foothold in Catholic theology, it spread to all schools except the Augustinian."

reality in its own right and grace as an addition that superimposed a different reality upon nature.[34] The transcendent had been successfully removed from nature and transferred to a "supernatural" domain.

### d. Attempts to Regain the Syntheses

Dupré investigates a number of attempts to reclaim the comprehensive view of nature which would include a transcendent dimension. "We may well regard the early period of modern thought — from the 15th through the 17th centuries — as a prolonged attempt to recover the lost unity."[35] He discusses three major attempts which he groups as humanist religion, the early Reformation, and Jansenist theology. Each is effective to some extent but in the end all are fraught with problems prohibiting a reunification.[36] Even before these attempts at a new synthesis, Nicholas of Cusa (1401-1464) proposed an intellectual framework in which such a reunion would be successful. Still, while Cusa appears to be the champion of the story in overcoming many of the obstacles of nominalist theology of the late Middle Ages, a number of difficulties plague its acceptance by others of his age, not the least of which being a general dismissal of spiritual

---

[34] See Sylvester of Ferrara, *Summa contra Gentiles cum Commentariis Ferrariensis*, in Thomas Aquinas, *Opera Omnia*, ed. Pope Leo XIII, vols. 13-15 (Rome: Riccardi Garroni, 1918-1930). Thomas Cajetan, *Summa Theologiae cum Supplemento et Commentariis Caietani*, in Thomas Aquinas, *Opera Omnia*, ed. Pope Leo XIII, vols. 4-12 (Rome: S. C. de Propaganda fide, 1888-1906).

[35] Dupré, "The Dissolution of Nature and Grace," 102.

[36] See *PM*, 190-220. On Jansenism also see Louis Dupré, "Jansenism and Quietism," in *Christian Spirituality*, ed. Louis Dupré and Don Saliers, 121-130; id., "Jansenius, an Intellectual Biography," *The Journal of Religion* 13 (1993): 75-82.

theologies such as his own.[37] Dupré does acknowledge that a provisional synthesis is attained particularly by devout humanists,[38] but the fracturing of nature is too prominent to be ubiquitously rejoined.

## e. Implications for Religious Symbols

This very split between nature and the supernatural affects the possibility of religious symbolization because the relationship between the transcendent and creation is denied. All that remains is a transcendent creator who sets the world in motion and retreats to a separate sphere of existence. The transcendent component can no longer be an integrative power for human and cosmic reality. With transcendence relegated to a realm outside of nature, it no longer encompasses the finite realm and is excluded from the meaning-giving process. In addition, due to the split, the medium for speaking of transcendence ceases to endure. The transcendent referent essential for the existence of religious symbols can no longer be articulated. The dialectical interplay between God's transcendence and God's immanence is necessary for religious expression. Severing any potentiality for God's immanence eliminates the possibility of religious symbolism. Symbolism in general still is viable, but without transcendence it is reduced in its significance and the very possibility of religious symbolism is impeded.

[37] See Louis Dupré, "Introduction, and Major Works of Nicholas of Cusa," in *The American Catholic Philosophical Quarterly* 64 (Winter 1990): 1-6; id., "Nature and Grace in Nicholas of Cusa's Mystical Philosophy," in *The American Catholic Philosophical Quarterly* 64 (Winter 1990): 153-170; id., "The Mystical Theology of Cusanus's *De visione Dei*," in *Eros and Eris: Contributions to a Hermeneutical Phenomenology: Liber amicorum for Adriaan Peperzak*, Phaenomenologica 127, ed. P. van Tongeren, et al. (Dordrecht, Holland: Kluwer Academic Publishers, 1992), 105-117; and *PM*, 186-189.

[38] See below, pp. 249-256.

Thus, the tearing of transcendence out of a comprehensive understanding of nature is the first split signaling the dawn of modernity. With transcendence completely removed to another sphere, nature's significance is limited to the cosmic and human.

## 3. *Human Subject Torn from Cosmos*

Concomitant with the first split, there is a second tearing of meaning from nature which signals the dawn of modernity. With God removed into another realm separate from nature, the human subject becomes the sole meaning-giving agent. Humankind is exalted to a position as the sole master of nature. Devoid of its transcendent and human elements, nature is reduced to signifying only the cosmos. Reason is no longer immanent in the cosmos which is now respected only as an object; instead, the human subject is the exclusive source of reason imposed upon reality. Far from becoming deified, the human subject itself loses all meaning as it is reduced to a mere function of the process of objectification. Since the real contains no meaning of its own, the only place for stability and encounter with transcendent meaning is the lived experience of one's own subjectivity. In summarizing Dupré's development of these points we will inquire into the passage through objectivism to the subject's mastery over nature and the subsequent loss of selfhood.

### a. Transition to Objectivism

The transition to objectivism began with the Greek philosophers. Inquiring into the intrinsic nature of things they embarked upon the beginnings of methodic thought. This approach "consisted in the marvelous capacity to be interested in the world *as it is in itself* rather than as it fleetingly impresses itself upon the perceiver's momentary condition."[39] In a word, it was the discovery of objectivity. The main focus of inquiry was the world around. Though there are convincing examples of investigation of the inner life (one need only think of the Orphic mysteries and many of the questions of Socrates), "they remained exclusive, reserved to a spiritual elite."[40] Once the character of the subject was perceived it "seems to have meant little more than the window through which they saw the world."[41] The main question to ponder was the meaning of the world around; this assuredly lead to the formulation of generalized concepts of Being and universals beyond the sensible world, but rarely inward to the selfhood of humanity.

This changed with the advent of Christianity when for the first time Western culture attempted to appraise inwardness as its nucleus. Despite incorporating certain perspectives incongruous with this concern for selfhood, "an intense spiritual life continued to protect the concept of an irreducible subject against the encroachments of an ever imminent objectivism."[42] By the end of the Middle Ages an inward mystical expression had received affirmation but there was an even more ardent objectification of religious structures and indeed of all of nature. Dupré develops a nuanced presentation of the objectivist trend of the fifteenth and sixteenth centuries and its passage into a scientific objectivism. He explains that "the objectivism of the modern age (especially scientism) is not 'continuous' with late medieval religious thinking. In fact, it reacted strongly against it, especially against Scholasticism. But it was definitely prepared by it."[43] Leonardo da Vinci (1452-1519), Giordano Bruno (1548-1600), and Marsilio

[39] *TS*, 3.
[40] *TS*, 3.
[41] *TS*, 3.
[42] *TS*, 3; also see *TS*, 22-26.
[43] *TS*, 106 note 4.

Ficino (1433-1499) are influential transitional figures in Dupré's exposition of the move toward a new knowledge of nature. For the early humanists and also Renaissance artists there is a constructive dialectical tension between nature and mind. Nature remains a source of wonderment and receptivity but increasingly becomes reducible to a scientific problem to be solved by the human mind. Dupré identifies this as a new phase in a continuous tradition, but not a break. For example, "the artist complemented and corrected nature, yet he never ceased to consider himself an integral part of it."[44] The same could be said of the mathematician, astronomer and alchemist who confronts and orders nature but "supported the aesthetic ideal of a harmoniously coherent universe."[45] Form is no longer given with the real as it was for the ancients; "form for the humanists was an ideal to be achieved."[46] Nature itself is deemed created in accordance with aesthetic rules, yet nature was still regarded as the model of formal perfection. However, with the philosophy of the seventeenth century an explicit break occurs as mind alone becomes the source of perfection and meaning.

b. Mastery Over Nature

Galilei Galileo (1564-1642), Francis Bacon (1561-1626) and René Descartes (1596-1650) are among the thinkers whom Dupré discusses as pivotal in the metamorphosis of the exultation of science over art, and mathematically calculable mechanical ends over an independent natural teleology. With the seventeenth century a break ensues as the human subject assumes the role of sole form-giving principle and reduces the given meaning of nature "to a subordinate, increasingly instrumental, position."[47] At the root

[44] PM, 50.
[45] PM, 57.
[46] PM, 44.
[47] PM, 50.

of the physical universe Galileo postulates a mathematical core. Reality is reduced to only those characteristics which can be placed within a mathematical grid. In contrast to Galileo, Bacon adopts a methodology of experiment and induction. Bacon calls for an unlimited control over nature because he presupposes that nature possesses no purpose of its own. "His opposition to teleological interpretations and concomitant belief in unrestricted human power over nature originated in the voluntarist view of creation";[48] the reason why existing things are as they are is simply because God has willed it so. "This placed the entire responsibility for conveying meaning and purpose to the world entirely on the human person, the only creature endowed with purposiveness."[49] With Descartes' particular manner of classifying between the *res extensa* (properties intrinsic to nature itself) and the *res cogitans* (ascribed to nature only as the cause of subjective sensations that do not coincide to the original substance), the object is sharply distinguished from the subject. In so doing, "we detach the observer from nature in such a way that he ceases to remain an integral part of it."[50] The scientific knowledge of nature (*res extensa*) is restricted to extension and motion which is irreducibly separated from thought (*res cogitans*). The physical world is deprived of an internal teleology which is reserved to the *res cogitans* and at the same time it is endowed with an unprecedented bodily concreteness insofar as extension is the essence of physical substance.

Dupré further develops and interweaves the thought of these figures. These general comments are sufficient for our project to appreciate that the universe is no longer experienced as a harmoniously coherent system; it is now mathematical uniformity that rules the stars and all reality.

[48] *PM*, 72.
[49] *PM*, 74.
[50] *PM*, 77.

The modern idea of science was not the outcome of a single factor. It rested on a practical, voluntarist view of nature as well as on a theoretical, mechanistic one that related all parts of nature to each other. The two combined resulted in an instrumentalism that was fundamentally at variance with the ancient conceptions of *cosmos* and *technē*.[51]

The *idea* of science, that is science as conceived in its ideal state before any actual achievement, assumes that its methodology will produce an order and structure for all reality. If God's will is the reason why nature exists in the way it does (volutarism) and each and every part of nature serves the function of the whole (mechanism), then natural processes are exclusively determined by efficient causality (instrumentalism). "Within the closed circuit of instrumental thought the very idea of final end becomes meaningless. Each moment serves as a signal referring to another signal."[52] Ends and means, contemplation and action, technique and theory, each serves its counterpart. Form is reduced simply to the function it fulfills. Just as God set up nature to act in a determined way, the human mind can order and direct nature as it wills. In fact, with God withdrawn from nature only related as an active principle of existence, "the intrinsic intelligibility of such a creation could no longer be taken for granted and the task of conveying meaning to it fell *entirely* upon human reason."[53] Humanity is unrestrained in its quest to conquer nature by rational methods as the mind exclusively "defines the limits of the intelligible and even of the real."[54]

c. Loss of Selfhood

This primacy of the human over nature removes the human into a realm outside of nature, thus reducing nature's significance to

[51] *PM*, 75.
[52] *PM*, 75.
[53] *MC*, 43, emphasis added.
[54] *PM*, 43.

only its cosmic element. However, once removed from nature the human subject loses its own meaning. The more nature is considered as an object, opposed to the human subject, the more the subject also looses its own content and meaning. The subject itself is reduced "to the mere function of *constituting objectivity* in the theoretical and the practical order."[55] Dupré accepts Max Horkheimer's summary:

> The more all nature is looked upon ... as mere objects in relation to human subjects, the more is the once supposedly autonomous subject emptied of any content, until it finally becomes a mere name with nothing to denominate. The total transformation of each and every realm of being into a field of means leads to the liquidation of the subject who is supposed to use them. This gives modern industrialist society its nihilistic aspect. Subjectivization, which exalts the subject, also dooms him.[56]

The subject forfeits its own meaning as reason becomes only an instrument to organize the objective world.

Beginning with Plato, Dupré traces a variety of historical dynamics which lead to the loss of self. The self is gradually transformed to be regarded as subject. Severed from the world and the transcendent, as described in the previous sections, the rational subject assumes the power of establishing and defining that which previously had provided the content of the subject itself. Descartes turns to the thinking self in beginning to formulate clear and distinct ideas. Selfhood is narrowed to designate individual solitude and the other is reduced to the status of object. Baruch Spinoza (1632-1677) is heralded by Dupré as one of the "few modern thinkers [who] avoided the pitfall of severing the person as

[55] Louis Dupré, "The Modern Idea of Culture: Its Opposition to its Classical and Christian Origins," in *Ebraismo, Ellenismo, Cristianesimo II*, ed. Marco Olivetti, *Archivio di Filosofia* 53 (1985): 477.

[56] Max Horkheimer, *The Eclipse of Reason* (New York: Continuum, 1947), 93. Also see Dupré, "The Modern Idea of Culture," 477.

creative principle from the rest of nature."[57] But, it was not enough to stem theological egocentrism from inevitably leading to a moral one. With the eighteenth century, Immanuel Kant (1724-1804) restricted the moral act to the intention and thereby withdrew morality to an inner realm of consciousness detached from the physical and social order, thus solidifying the privatization of freedom. At another level, his postulation of the transcendental self is produced by pure reason alone in an attempt to achieve a coherent synthesis of the various experiences of psychological activities; yet while it is universal it is devoid of a content of its own.

Romanticism reacted against the cultural trend toward a rational and objective approach to life. "Romantic poets and philosophers attempted to liberate the self from its oppressive life-draining task of constituting an objective universe."[58] With Jean-Jacques Rousseau (1712-1778) the individual self is deemed worthy of attention, free of any constrictive rules of reason or moral justification. "Yet here modern consciousness experienced what may well have been its most bitter disenchantment: the autonomous subject that had been so totally engaged in the task of bestowing meaning upon all things had no content left in itself."[59] The self is now only able to view itself in the same way it relates to everything else to which it gives meaning and value — as an object. The psychological sciences have attempted to comprehend the subject, but they have only succeeded in discounting it to an object of analysis and examination, essentially the same as other objects. Dupré concurs with Kolakowski's assessment:

[57] *PM*, 143. However, Spinoza lacked a subjective dimension in his understanding of nature which "prevented his *Ethics* from providing the moral synthesis demanded by modern culture." (*PM*, 143). Spinoza's category of the substance through which he chose to express divine reality was the objective category *par excellence*. See Dupré, "The Modern Idea of Culture," 481.

[58] Dupré, "The Modern Idea of Culture," 478.

[59] Dupré, "The Modern Idea of Culture," 478.

It seems that once our world picture has been cleared of so-called anthropo morphisms, the anthropos himself disappears as well. The critique was carried out in order to achieve a scientific attitude; it results in self-defeat, though, for this attitude becomes then as baseless as any other. It was defined with reference to the goals of knowledge, yet no goals can be defined in scientific terms.[60]

The act of separating the human from the cosmic aspired to categorize reality scientifically without the encumbrance of metaphorical language which usually was anthropomorphically oriented. However, not only did the modern project deanthropomorphize the subject's view of reality, it also dehumanized it. The human subject itself was exposed to the same scientific objectification process foisted upon cosmic reality resulting in the subject's inability to propose any meaning and value.

When Karl Marx (1818-1883) absolutizes the primacy of *praxis* over *theoria* the subject itself is included in the productive act. The subject ceases to precede creative activity in becoming the outcome of it. "Marx radicalized the modern rule that meaning and value are not *given* with the nature of reality, but *constituted* by the living deed."[61] The human being creates both the self and the world through productive activity.

Thus, through this long history there are profound transformations in the way the self is understood.

The humanists mediated the self's expressive power through its integration with nature and through its intrinsic dependence on a transcendent reality. The self of rationalist philosophy, however, serves a foundational purpose: the existence of the world and of God have to be established and defined by the thinking subject.[62]

---

[60] Leszek Kolakowski, "The Search for Meaning," *Religione e cultura* 27 (1979): 29, quoted in Dupré, "The Modern Idea of Culture," 478.

[61] Dupré, "The Modern Idea of Culture," 479. Also see id., *Marx's Social Critique of Culture*, 5-14, 67-71, 276-288.

[62] *PM*, 119.

But as the thinking self dispensed meaning to reality it searched for its own value. "The image of the person that emerged in the sixteenth century became increasingly more enclosed within itself. Eventually it narrowed its teleology to one of self-preservation or self-fulfillment, either social or individual."[63] Inevitably, as the self objectifies all reality, it becomes prey to its own design and develops into an entity lacking of content.

## d. Implications for Religious Symbols

By removing the human subject from nature in the manner described, the possibility for religious symbols is inhibited. All symbols become either purely objective as in the approach of scientific symbols, or they become purely subjective which is the assessment of artistic symbols today. Yet, religious symbols are dialectical in essence; they are neither definable through a purely objective sacred reality nor a purely subjective state of consciousness. When the human subject proclaims to be the sole source and dispenser of meaning and value all connection to a transcendentally presented or naturally endowed meaning is severed. Each group, indeed each individual, assumes permission to create symbolic relationships. "Symbolic universes became sovereign realms, beholden only to self-made rules."[64] Restricted only by self-given principles, "innovation and diversity have resulted in an unprecedented explosion of symbolic creativity."[65] However, instead of attaining the permanence of meaning offered by the transcendent referent of religious symbols, "a projected symbolic structure in the end appears to be no more than the contingent utterance of a contingent subject."[66]

---

[63] *PM*, 164.
[64] *MC*, 44.
[65] *MC*, 44.
[66] Dupré, "The Broken Mirror," 22.

By the human subject becoming the supreme referent of meaning and the transcendent removed to another realm, the stability of religious symbols and all symbols is weakened. "Once the belief in a transcendent, ultimate norm weakens, symbolic creations become autonomous but, inevitably, also fragmentary."[67] Once the human subject has itself become objectified even the meaning and value it asserts is jeopardized.

Thus, the tearing of the human subject out of nature is the second split signaling the dawn of modernity. The intrinsic rationality of the natural order is replaced by one of the subject's own making. However, as a result the human subject also becomes devoid of meaning. "In becoming pure project, the modern self has become severed from those sources that once provided its content."[68]

## 4. *Conclusion*

To speak of a passage *to* modernity, one must consider *from* what this passage arose and how the two states are distinguishable from one another. The demarcation of history into periods of ancient, medieval, and modern is best characterized by shifts in the appreciation of nature. Western philosophy begins in the search for of an underlying principle of meaning. It is φύσις understood as the all encompassing principle of nature which initially fulfills this role. However, the unity of this original outlook breaks apart into the cosmic, human, and transcendent elements of nature. The complexities of medieval culture both assist in restoring the previous synthesis and intensify its further fracturing. Long before Descartes and the Enlightenment, Dupré points to late medieval thought, inspired by Scotus, Ockham, and nominalism in general, as paving the way for later claims that the source of human meaning rests in

---

[67] Dupré, "The Broken Mirror," 23.
[68] *PM*, 119.

creative self-expression. This is the legacy that gives rise to modernity: the tearing of transcendence into a dimension separate from nature and the further bifurcation of the human over worldly actualities. The previous cohesive understanding of reality collapses, resulting in its separation into disunited component parts.

## B. THE MODERN SITUATION

From the foregoing it should be apparent why Dupré states that "Modernity is an *event* that has transformed the relation between the cosmos, its transcendent source, and its human interpreter."[69] While a twofold separation from nature has been outlined — namely, the transcendent and human subject both removed from nature — the two separations are interconnected. Combined together this new outlook marks the beginning of modernity. "Only when the early humanist notion of human creativity came to form a combustive mixture with the negative conclusions of nominalist theology did it cause the cultural explosion that we refer to as modernity."[70] Its significance must not be underestimated. "The cultural revolution of the modern age was an event of ontological significance that changed the nature of Being itself."[71] The tearing of transcendence and the severing of the human from nature do not simply indicate a phase in contingent historical conditions, but actually manifests a break from a previously held world view. Change "marks a new epoch in being."[72]

---

[69] *PM*, 249. For a summary of historical usages of the term "modern" see *PM*, 146.

[70] *PM*, 3.

[71] *PM*, 7.

[72] *PM*, 7.

## 1. *Late Modernity or Postmodernity*

Clearly the story of Western culture continues beyond the first half of the seventeenth century. (In fact, Dupré plans to resume the narrative in his next book.) However, with the seventeenth century all the primary factors which resulted in modernity were in place. It must be made perfectly clear that what has been described above regarding the turn to modernity is quite applicable and active in contemporary culture. For Dupré, the cultural conditions that gave birth to modernity are fundamentally those outlined above. He concurs with Henri Daniel-Rops who considers the 1648 Peace of Westphalia the conclusion to the formation of the modernity.

> The Treaties of Westphalia finally sealed the relinquishment by statesmen of a noble and ancient concept, a concept which had dominated the Middle Ages: that there existed among the baptized people of Europe a bond stronger than all their motives for wrangling — a spiritual bond, the concept of Christendom. Since the fourteenth century, and especially during the fifteenth, this concept had been steadily disintegrating…. The Thirty Years' War proved beyond a shadow of a doubt that the last states to defend the ideal of a united Christian Europe were invoking that principle while in fact they aimed at maintaining or imposing their own supremacy. It was at Münster and Osnabrück that Christendom was buried. The tragedy was that nothing could replace it; and twentieth-century Europe is still bleeding in consequence.[73]

Some will object that culture has lived through yet another shift. A break from the modern project to a rejection of all ultimates — the postmodern. Dupré remains unconvinced that a strict demarcation between the modern and 'postmodern' can be made.

---

[73] Henri Daniel-Rops, *The Church in the Seventeenth Century*, trans. J. Buckingham, vol. 1 (Garden City, NY: Doubleday, 1965), 200-201.

Dupré situates contemporary culture in a period of *late* modernity. The tearing of the transcendent and human elements out of nature that occurred in the break between the premodern and modernity directly effect the fundamental presuppositions of the contemporary world view. In contrast, 'postmodernity' may profess to ask or answer questions which either complete modernity and mark a new beginning, or break with modernity and take a unique turn. In a departure from his previous writings in which he advocated a radical discontinuity between modernity and postmodernity, Rorty recently articulated a more continuous understanding:

> The term [postmodern] ... has been so over-used that it is causing more trouble than it is worth.... It seems best to think of Heidegger and Derrida simply as post-Nietzschean philosophers — to assign them places in a conversational sequence which runs from Descartes through Kant and Hegel to Nietzsche and beyond rather than to view them as initiating or manifesting a radical departure.[74]

Yet, the continuity Rorty suggests is not simply from modernity to 'postmodernity' but extends all the way from the Greeks. He proposes a continuity between the premodern and modern, identifying some changes in course but no radical interruptions. Dupré neither accepts an unbroken history from premodernity to modernity nor a strict distinction between modernity and post/late modernity. Dupré argues "that there is discontinuity between modern and premodern and continuity between modern and postmodern."[75]

Leading up to the current critiques of modernity, the classic critiques focus only on one or another aspect of the modern condition and not on the totality of its situation. Hegel, often regarded

---

[74] Richard Rorty, *Essays on Heidegger and Others*, Philosophical Papers 2 (Cambridge: Cambridge University Press, 1991), 1-2.

[75] Louis Dupré, "Postmodernity or Late Modernity? Ambiguities in Richard Rorty's Thought," *Review of Metaphysics* 47 (December 1993): 277.

as the first philosopher to engage in a systematic reflection on modernity, limits his critique by retaining "the principle of subjectivity, both in its Cartesian epistemic and in its Lutheran religious formulations, as the great discovery of modern thought."[76] According to Hegel only the Enlightenment's narrowing of the principle of subjectivity is responsible for the alienation of the modern mind. Marx, with his own unique adaptation of Hegel, also criticizes and furthers the project of modernity. While attempting to restore the person to the wholeness possessed in pre-modernity, the subject itself is the outcome of social-economic *praxis*. His critique is basically limited to the person's alienation from the natural world and by extension the social world. In venturing a critique, Freud admonishes civilization for its repressive character but also remained within the modern premise of an independent physical world. Friedrich Nietzsche (1844-1900) provides a deeper critique by inquiring into the foundations of modern thought and tracing them back to Greek and Christian sources. Still, "in Nietzsche's critique the modern epoch merely intensified and completed a process that had begun in the fifth century B.C. Nietzsche attributes no particular significance to the early modern epoch: the seeds of nihilism have been present since Socrates."[77] Thus, Dupré concludes that each of these classic

---

[76] Dupré, "Postmodernity or Late Modernity?" 278. See G. W. F. Hegel, *The Phenomenology of Spirit*, trans. A. Miller (Oxford: Clarendon Press, 1977), 15: "That Substance is essentially Subject, is expressed in the representation of the Absolute as *Spirit*—the most sublime Notion and the one which belongs to the modern age and its religion."

[77] *PM*, 4. Also see *TS*, 12-14. Dupré, "Postmodernity or Late Modernity?" 279. Also see Friedrich Nietzsche, *The Birth of Tragedy*, trans. Francis Golffing (Garden City, NY: Doubleday, 1956), 94: Socrates is "the vortex and turning point of Western civilization." While Nietzsche later rejects many of his assertions from *The Birth of Tragedy*, he maintains the continuity from Socrates to modern nihilism; see *TS*, 12.

critics "described our condition as having now become problematic, yet none identified the problem with modern culture as such."[78]

The current critics of modernity include those who follow Nietzsche's understanding of Western culture as a continuous process which from the beginning was headed for the problematic rationalism of contemporary culture. Heidegger provided such a comprehensive critique.[79] Presently, Derrida and Rorty reflect from within this view. Dupré's analysis is more in accord with others who distinguish a deep fissure between premodern and modern thinking. The modern predicament is due to the breakup of the ancient conception of nature; it is not the necessary outcome of historical progression in thought (though the conditions for its possibility were created by earlier Greek and Christian thought). In this group Dupré includes both defenders of modernity such as Jürgen Habermas, Hans Blumenberg and John Randall, as well as its critics like Leo Strauss, Eric Voegelin, and Alasdair MacIntyre. Dupré differs from this second group as a whole in that he "further distinguishes the early humanist conception that transformed the nature of the interaction among the components of the traditional synthesis from the later idea of a subject conceived as sole source of meaning and value."[80]

Dupré summarizes his appraisal of classic and contemporary critiques of modernity:

> Critics of modernity implicitly accept more of its assumptions than they are able to discard. Even those who globally reject its theoretical principles continue to build on them. Post-modern critics are unambiguous enough, it seems, in repudiating the primacy of the subject, the reduction of the real to the objective, as well as the logocentric

---

[78] *PM*, 5.

[79] See e.g., Heidegger's interpretation of how "Being" is understood through history: id., *Being and Time*, 21-35.

[80] *PM*, 5.

emphasis on epistemological issues. Yet does the self-referential
nature of thought and language assumed by several post-modern
authors not return speech to the central position from which the
theory had expelled the speaking subject? Has the post-modernist
critique gone beyond desublimating modernity while still remaining
part of it? Whatever the answer to these questions may be, I trace
the problematic features of modern thought to a more recent epoch
than Nietzsche's followers usually do. Its seeds lie buried not in the
sands of ancient or early medieval rationalism but in a set of as-
sumptions newly formulated at the closing of the Middle Ages.[81]

Thus, in contrast to his assessment of classical critiques of
modernity, Dupré recognizes the entire breakup of nature and not
just one aspect of it, while remaining aware of the risk of falling
prey to modernity's premises. In contrast to certain postmodern
critiques, Dupré does not attribute from the premodern to the modern
an essential continuity of thought. He does agree with those who,
despite a diversity of ideas, can be categorized together as embracing
the opposite approach of discontinuity. For Dupré, therefore, in
the weaving of the cloth of Western culture there is a break in the
pattern between the premodern and modern. Once the modern has
been definitively established (not before the seventeenth century)
there has not been any further break (different phases, but no
break). The current historical situation is best characterized as
'late modernity'.

Dupré asserts that "the modern program appears not so much
obsolete as unfinished."[82] To complete the modern project a
correction is needed which "will require a more equitable recognition of the meaning-and-value-giving function of all three of
the component factors than the absolute dominance of the subject
has hitherto admitted."[83] The cosmos must be appreciated as

[81] *PM*, 6. Also see *PM*, 250.
[82] *PM*, 251.
[83] *PM*, 251.

possessing meaning beyond what a reduction to pure objectivity imparts. Also, as the source and support of the world's givenness, the transcendent element cannot be removed from the meaning-giving process. "The achievement of such a more comprehensive synthesis remains part of the program of the modern age."[84] From this perspective the present and future project remains a modern one. Possible methods to accomplish a correction to complete the modern project will be viewed in the third part of this chapter beginning on page 240.

Rather than abandon any hope for ultimate understanding through a metaphysical grounding, the modern predicament should be interpreted as a challenge to establish a more dynamic conception of metaphysical ultimacy.

> Post-modern critics, aware of the inconsistency of a philosophy that continues to assume what it explicitly rejects — the ultimately static, unchanging quality of the real — have abandoned the epistemological project of modern philosophy altogether. Their critique has exposed the incoherence between two fundamental presuppositions of modern epistemology, namely, [1] that the subject alone determines meaning and value yet [2] the real remains ultimately static and identical. Most of them have rejected one as well as the other. While sharing their critique of the metaphysical assumptions of modern philosophy, I think nevertheless that the metaphysical question of the modern experience ought to be reopened.[85]

In discussing the possibility of a metaphysics of culture, Dupré identifies that "the fragmentation of the classical synthesis in the late modern epoch lies at the root of our present metaphysical poverty."[86] The same can be applied to religious symbols. Given the tight connection between metaphysics and religion for Dupré,

---

[84] *PM*, 251.
[85] *PM*, 162.
[86] *MC*, 48.

'metaphysics' can be replaced by 'religious symbols' and we can read: the fragmentation of the classical synthesis lies at the root of our present poverty in religious symbols. With this understanding of the modern situation we will now take a direct look at the main consequence it produced for religion in general and religious symbols in particular.

## 2. The Loss of the Sense of Transcendence

The most penetrating result of the change which marks the modern epoch is the disappearance of a sense of transcendence: "The loss of transcendence, then, more than a particular fact among others, is the event which symbolizes the direction of our entire culture."[87] As we have demonstrated, this loss is a consequence of the removal of the transcendent element from nature and the objectification of the cosmos.

There is an additional factor which has reinforced objectivism and accelerated the loss of transcendence, namely, "the fundamental historicalness of human existence."[88] A variety of intellectual developments occurred in the eighteenth and nineteenth centuries which affected the understanding of history. "The intellectual developments that took place during that recent period brought to an extreme of relativism the sense of historical uniqueness that Christianity had fostered for centuries."[89] The increasing perception that the variety of religions are interconnected, the employment of scientific methods to the study of Scripture, and even the overall repercussions of the theory of evolution "abruptly confronted the modern mind with the historical nature of a relation which it had heretofore conceived beyond history."[90] From its beginning

[87] *TS*, 14.
[88] *TS*, 6.
[89] RITUAL, 267.
[90] *TS*, 6.

Christianity was firmly established as a religion rooted in history. Even in its pilgrimage through time, revelation was unchangeable and permanent. Yet, with the onset of historical criticism people, places and events were placed under a microscope and dissected as over and done, completed and irretrievable. There was an "inextricable integration of events with a complex and unrepeatable context."[91] The past was no longer viewed in its living vitality and applicability to current experience. The past is significant only as a relic which leads to the present which in turn is important for the ultimate concern of the attainment of future goals. "While literary critics of the seventeenth century could still argue about the greater significance of the ancient or the modern writers, the Romantics discovered the past as definitively completed and therefore unrepeatable."[92] Every past event is perceived as part of a unique cultural totality that excludes any authentic imitation in a later period. The result for religion in general was that believers in the modern age either submit to the judgment of history and lower the position of their faith to the realm of secular events, or they safeguard their faith from the contingency of history by placing it in a closed sequence of decrees divinely foreordained, once for all time.[93]

Without the sense of a transcendent dimension that unites reality, religion no longer has the power to permeate all of existence. Instead, the human subject objectifies all reality and becomes the sole source of meaning and value for all areas of life.

> Science, art, philosophy, and morality have emancipated themselves from their religious origins to the extent that apparently they can exist as well without religion as with it. The scientist is no longer

---

[91] RITUAL, 267.

[92] RITUAL, 267; also see *PM*, 145-159.

[93] See *TS*, 6. For an application of this principle of historicism to ritual see below, pp. 226-227.

puzzled by the parallelism between the laws of nature and the laws of the mind, since he knows that all laws are laws only for the mind. Economic goods are not considered any more a gift of divine largesse, but man's own response to self-created needs. What artists dimly felt in the past, they now bluntly assert, namely, that the work of art is not an imitation of nature, subject to an extrinsic code, but that it creates its own norms and reality. In his moral behavior also man has assumed full responsibility over himself: he has no more use for a divinely imposed, unchangeable code of conduct. Even religion can be accommodated in this man-centered universe as a symbolic expression of the human mind, structured according to immanent schemas.[94]

Frequently the terms "secular," "secularism," "secularization," etc., are used to refer in some manner to this occurrence, though they have been defined and redefined many times. Particularly with the sixty's the conversation expanded in vastness. Our project has two modest goals with regard to secularity. First, insofar as the term signifies the religious crisis of modern Western culture, it is important to comprehend the effects that the loss of a sense of transcendence has had on religion in general and religious symbols in particular. Thus, the first goal is to view these effects and this will be done in the next two main sections respectively. Second, insofar as secularization is sometimes viewed as the manner in which traditional religion has been transformed to act in a new manner to sustain modern structures, we will mention some of the attempts of secular theologians to recover or reinterpret transcendence. The second goal is to identify these views and this will be accomplished below.[95] Here we turn to the first goal which explains the current situation, later we will investigate possible solutions.

[94] *OD*, 21.
[95] See below, pp. 242-246.

## 3. *Effects of the Loss of Transcendence on Religion in General*

The primary effect that the loss of a sense of the transcendent has had upon religion in general is that the believer has in a very real way become a-theistic insofar as God plays no role in everyday concerns: "The most crucial issue in the modern problematic ... [is] whether the idea of God has any meaning left."[96] The problem is "not in the loss of the actual belief in God, but in the loss of the very possibility of that belief."[97] The atheism of our culture is the abolition of true transcendence.

Historically, in the eighteenth century the idea of God by and large ceased to be an integral concern for the intellectualized mind set. Rationalist deism can be characterized as 'latent atheism'. This progressed into the belligerent atheism of the nineteenth century. With the twentieth century this anti-theism has been replaced by a radical disposal of the very idea of God. In the last century, the atheist continued to determine a vision of life through a negative relationship to faith in God. In the current century, belief in God is not even a negative or polemical concern.

> The void between an immanent awareness and the affirmation of a transcendent reality also affected past experience. Yet that experience was sufficiently determined by the surrounding culture to carry the believer across the void by his or her participation in an objective communion of faith. Experience, interpretation, and decision occurred in one continuous act. That connection today is broken. An identical experience justifies the believer's faith as well as the unbeliever's unbelief.[98]

Dupré asserts that present day atheism is the necessary result of the entire development of Western culture. Modern atheism is itself a

[96] Louis Dupré, "Spiritual Life in a Secular Age," *Daedalus* 111 (Winter 1982): 30. [Hereafter SPIRITUAL].

[97] Dupré, "The Religious Crisis of Our Culture," 214.

[98] SPIRITUAL, 24.

religious phenomenon. "Believers even more than unbelievers have
failed their God — or in Nietzsche's terms 'murdered him' — by
lowering him to a scale of being where he can no longer be truly
sacred."[99] With God relegated to a sphere outside of nature and
the human subject having so fully objectified the world and having
become the only creator of meaning and value, even spiritual
phenomena are under its control. Contemporary atheism "no longer
expects an integral world view from science, and it is even beginning to abandon the previous identification of science with
human progress."[100] Dupré argues that the transition from a belligerent atheism to a totally self-sufficient humanism was prepared
by the three prophets of suspicion, Freud, Marx and Nietzsche.
While each clearly expressed his own forceful atheism, they also
envisioned a humanism beyond a polemical attitude. Dupré summarizes: "Contemporary humanism is less polemical, more comprehensive, but also more thoroughly immanent than that of the
recent past."[101]

Thus, because religion itself has lost its connection to the transcendent, the believer must somehow integrate this atheism with a
religious perspective. Similar to traditional negative theology,
modern atheism has created a silence about God in which words
have lost their meaning.[102] Anticipating Dupré's suggestions for
regaining transcendence, he identifies that for believers today "the
desert of modern atheism provides the only space in which most
of them are forced to encounter the transcendent."[103] To regain a

---

[99] Dupré, "The Religious Crisis of Our Culture," 214.

[100] SPIRITUAL, 21.

[101] SPIRITUAL, 21.

[102] See below, p. 268.

[103] SPIRITUAL, 27. Also see Louis Dupré, "The Closed World of the Modern
Mind," *Religion and Intellectual Life* 1 (Summer 1984): 21: "If they [people
today] still want to seek a transcendent dimension, they have no other entrance to
it but that of their own atheism."

sense of transcendence the modern believer must pass through silence and experience God's absence in order to search out a new presence, just as spiritual seekers of the past once found in the desert. Before continuing with Dupré's recommendations for the possibility of a renewed contemporary faith, we return now to the three specific religious symbols which have been previously discussed in order to reflect on how they are affected by the modern situation.

## 4. *Effects of the Loss of Transcendence on Religious Symbols*

With religious faith in general having undergone such a radical shift in meaning, it comes as no surprise that modern culture's inability to support a transcendent dimension of reality has severely affected the power of religious symbols. The following three sections must be read in light of what has been previous developed, particularly in this chapter and Chapter Three.

## a. Ritual

"The secularization of the modern age has radically changed our attitude toward ritual."[104] The observations of Mary Douglas are applicable:

> One of the gravest problems of our day is the lack of commitment to common symbols. If this were all, there would be little to say. If it were merely a matter of our fragmentation into small groups, each committed to its proper symbolic forms, the case would be simple to understand. But more mysterious is a wide-spread, explicit rejection of rituals as such. Ritual has become a bad word signifying empty conformity. We are witnessing a revolt against formalism, even against form.[105]

---

[104] RITUAL, 266.

[105] Mary Douglas, *Natural Symbols: Explorations in Cosmology* (New York: Random House, 1971²), 19.

With the transcendent removed to a realm totally separate from nature and with the objectification of the human subject along with the entire physical world, ritual words and gestures no longer possess their original referents. The awareness of the fundamental historicalness of human existence that has reinforced this objectivism and subsequent loss of transcendence has profoundly obstructed a symbolic understanding of ritual particularly in relation to time and play.

With regard to time, objectivism and a heightened historical relativism has impeded the possibility for ritually transcending time and space. If the sole source of meaning-and-value-giving is the human subject, there is no need to look for ritual reenactment to provide the founding events that give meaning to life. Even more disastrous, if history is only composed of contingently irreversible events, there is no possibility for ritually reversible time. No activities, including rituals, can any longer transcend "the closed circuit of ordinary, homogeneous time."[106] Archetypical meaning that unites all epochs ceases to exist as all reality is objectified. The uniqueness of the events of historical faiths such as Christianity are radicalized and become merely nonretrievable historical occurrences. Past events possess a particularity that can never be represented. "Not only could the same event never occur twice in its existential singularity; it was not even seriously comparable to any more recent event, since its very essence restricted it to an irreversible past."[107] By the historicism of secular culture restricting all events to their one-time appearance in history, the possibility of overcoming time through ritual loses its meaning. With the past definitively closed, the search for meaning shifts from the present ritual experience of representation and remembrance to the only other possibility — the future.

[106] RITUAL, 266.
[107] RITUAL, 267.

Progress and effective action characterize this exclusive commitment toward the future. Temporality is subject to human control and life is reduced to a planned career. The result is the demise of ritual and the ceaseless increase of instability and transition. Dupré accepts Berger's appraisal of the modern estimation of time:

> There is no reason to doubt what battalions of psychologists have been telling us for decades, namely that the pace of modern living is detrimental to mental well-being and may also be harmful to physical health. Futurity means endless striving, restlessness, and a mounting incapacity for repose. It is precisely this aspect of modernization that is perceived as dehumanizing in many non-Western cultures.[108]

The result is that "no place, no occupation, no relation provides the security of lastingness. Everything is in transition."[109] Generally, along with all other activities, ritual is divorced from its intrinsic meaning and reduced to a goal directed activity. For religious ritual this often entails petitioning God to solve problems or grant needs in this life or as a means to acquire heavenly happiness — all goal oriented, disregarding, or at least impairing, ritual's power to offer thanksgiving and praise, meaning and value.

With regard to the play aspect of ritual, "objectivism has weakened our ability to conceive of any human activity as totally nonfunctional and gratuitous."[110] This aspect of the modern mentality has undermined the inclination to play. It is no coincidence that the characteristics of play which have disappeared from the modern scene are those shared with ritual, since the common threads portray nonpragmatic and nonproductive qualities. The shared feature of embodying an existence apart from ordinary life becomes superfluous in a modern world view; it provides no new meaning or

---

[108] Peter Berger, *Facing up to Modernity: Excursions in Society, Politics and Religion* (New York: Basic Books, 1977), 74. See RITUAL, 268 note 11.

[109] RITUAL, 268.

[110] RITUAL, 266.

purpose as all reality is placed under the objectivist umbrella and from there receives its full expression. The space and time of play is not qualitatively different from nonplay time, because both are constructed and determined by the human subject. There is neither a useful advantage to accepting the feature of celebration or the opposite quality of seriousness for the human mind naturally takes control of every situation. Additionally, while dramatization is necessary to the ordering of play and the ritual contact with primeval events, when these endowments are taken over by the human subject dramatization no longer produces a tangible result. The drama of religious ritual is reduced to superfluous action unless it can demonstrate its worth. This might explain the rise in religion's need to authenticate itself through its quantifiable results — be they physical healings produced in the ritual drama or the success of social action programs instituted in response to or in place of the drama.

Play, of course, has not completely disappeared from culture. It still is regarded as a necessary component of life. Yet it is necessary because it provides a function, and it does not possess meaning apart from this purpose. Play continues to provide relaxation and entertainment precisely because these are necessary for proper maintenance of the human subject. We need play in order to be more productive. Play allows an escape from the constant worries and questions that accompanies the responsibility of being the sole meaning-giving agent. And throughout play the human actor remains completely in charge. It is true that the human player follows the rules, but they are rules invented by the human subject! Cheating is not necessarily judged negatively by the individual participant because it is just another way of reinventing the rules for oneself. One plays to win which instills self-confidence, demonstrates superiority, and may even provide monetary reward — all goals to be pursued. Even when winning is not held as the primary aspiration other aims are promoted, sometimes as being higher. This is particularly true for children's games where the object may be to build physical strength, learn a mental skill, instill the usefulness of working as a team, etc. Still, the game itself — the drama of the play — is not esteemed as an end in itself but only as a means to an end. Despite the admirable nature of many of these goals, they remain objectifiable and quantifiable goals. Concretely, these characteristics which remain fundamental in modern play are precisely those qualities which distinguish play from ritual. Relaxation, entertainment, escape from life, and the human invention of rules are features of play but not of religious ritual.

Still, in some small ways modern culture searches for the primordial time and gratuitous play of ritual beyond its functionality. "Unwittingly our contemporaries still look for the ritual catharsis that men of a former age consciously sought in rites or in ritual drama."[111] The exclusive turn toward the future and overarching concern for function inhibits the acceptability of ritual. So, instead of turning to religious ritual many in the secular age turn to the drama of movies, television, or theater. Both modern dramas and ancient theater act out the inner conflicts and concerns of life. Yet in the ancient theater answers were somehow related to a transcendent or cosmic design. This is no longer possible in the modern world view. The stage and screen are often approached as psychological projections enabling the individual to explore their own complexities in the privacy of a dark theater, or to depict in public images a private feeling of deficiency in meaning (which is a reversal of drama's original role). "Yet even on that reduced scale something remains of the magic power inherent in pure 'acting', as opposed to 'doing' or 'making'."[112] These are modest attempts by modern culture to ritually enact concerns about life's meaningfulness.

[111] RITUAL, 269.
[112] RITUAL, 269.

There are other experiences which the modern world attempts to turn into religious ones and restore some of the lost features of ritual. For example, there are the social and family rituals that mark a significant occurrence such as a birth or death, anniversary or birthday. Such secular rituals structure a group's activity and allow an event to be experienced as fully real through its celebration. Besides possessing the aspects of play which differentiate it from ritual, modern sporting events are ritual activity insofar as ritual is a function of society establishing a group identity for an individual.

Anthropologists and sociologists often consider ritual as a function of society. "One function of ritual in the present world is to give a sense of identity and community to those who would otherwise have none."[113] Ritual is essential both for individual and social well-being. Through ritual personal and communal identity is formed. It attempts to forge a bond in an otherwise fragmented society. This interpretation of ritual is logically derived from modernity's turn to objectivity and functionality. Ritual supports the health of the individual and society. Dupré agrees that "ritual, individual and society interpenetrate one another."[114] There is an essential interconnectedness.

However, ritual is more than the handmaid of societal well-being. Thus, Dupré further asserts that "at the same time ritual transcends the merely social, or rather, in ritual the social *transcends itself*."[115] Dupré understands this statement as constituting Turner's distinction between *societas* and *communitas*.[116] *Societas* is the structured externally defined entity. By contrast *communitas* is the inner realm

[113] Leonel Mitchell, *The Meaning of Ritual* (Wilton, CT: Morehouse-Barlow, 1977), 114.

[114] RITUAL, 264.

[115] RITUAL, 264.

[116] Victor Turner, *Dramas, Fields and Metaphors: Symbolic Action in Human Society* (Ithaca: Cornell University Press, 1974), 52-53.

of anti-structure. In describing ritual as a process or movement from one state to another, three stages arc distinguished, namely, separation, liminality and reaggregation. In simple terms, in the separation stage one breaks away from normal everyday life, away from structures and systems of status. In the liminal or threshold or in-between-ness stage, separated from the normal organized structures one engages in a relation with others without status roles or tensions (at least symbolically). People relate in "an un-differentiated, ecstatic oneness that is called *communitas*."[117] One important goal is for this *communitas* to continue even after the ritual is completed. "The bonds of communitas ... are anti-structural in the sense that they are undifferentiated, equalitarian, direct, nonrational (though not irrational), I-Thou relationships."[118] In the last stage of reaggregation (incorporation) one moves back to everyday living and ideally carries along a new bond and in-novative approaches to status and tensions. Still, as the social transcends itself, it can merely be reduced to a function of society when reincorporation is held as the goal. This functionality is even more apparent when *communitas* is divided into spontaneous and normative. Spontaneous *communitas* may simply arise within a given, unforeseen situation which might occur, such as when a previously unrelated group of people is faced with attempting to survive after a natural disaster. The bond that is formed serves the purpose of enabling each individual member of the group to work together for the common good. By contrast, normative *communitas* occurs within an activity specifically chosen to create a liminal experience in which *communitas* will develop. This is the case for religious ritual. At this liminal point the human subject cannot

[117] Gerald Arbuckle, "Communicating Through Ritual," *Human Development* 9 (Summer 1988): 22.

[118] Turner, *Dramas, Fields and Metaphors*, 53.

remain the meaning-giving agent but must surrender to a transcendent dimension. Of course, provided the fragmentation of a coherent world view and the secular acceptance of reality constituted independent of a transcendent source, modern culture in and of itself can neither promote nor support such a conception of ritual. Another ground must be provided for the religious person today.

## b. Sacraments

As religious ritual in general has been severely discounted by the modern situation so too sacraments as a specific type of ritual have been reduced in significance. In fact, the effect upon sacraments has perhaps been even more devastating, since with sacraments the ritual action is effective and actually realizes the transcendent presence it signifies.

A sacrament as efficacious ritual action in which the word directs the immanent act toward a transcendent reality is no longer supported by the current cultural view. The tearing of the transcendent into a realm separate from nature has resulted in the inability of modern people to be receptive to any sacramentology. Secularism proposes the extreme position whereby sacraments are limited to the meaning of their earthly words and gestures. Without a transcendent referent, the natural symbols of bread, wine, water and oil will have only a limited effect today. Sacramental words and gestures are not accorded symbolic meaning in their very essence; the intrinsic connection with the divine is denied. Instead, the sacramental character is viewed as being added onto ordinary actions and objects. Secularism has taken the further step of removing any transcendent addition, thus leaving only the worldly meaning. This can be understood as a radical anthropological approach to the sacraments at the expense of their transcendent meaning. Sacraments become only a secular expression of existence.

The overall view of nature reduced to signifying only a cosmic dimension has desacralized the secular understanding of the world and sacraments along with it.

> We seldom encounter the sacred in an objectively given, universally attainable reality, as the miraculous statue or the rustling of leaves in an oak forest were to our ancestors.... Almost nothing appears directly sacred to us. In this respect we find ourselves at the opposite extreme of archaic man for whom at least in some sense everything is sacred. We no longer share a coherent, sacred universe with all other members of our society or our culture, as religions in the past did. Nor are particular times, places, or persons *experienced* as sacred, as they were until recently even in Christianity and Judaism.[119]

The larger loss of the sense of transcendence in nature is to blame for the loss of a sense of transcendence in sacraments. Of course, there are people in contemporary culture who are able to reestablish sacramental depth. Yet, as the solution below will discuss, such individuals do so rarely by *perceiving* the source of sacralization in the symbolic reality itself, but in *deciding* to hold objects and events as symbolic of transcendence.[120] However, in choosing to accept a transcendent dimension in sacraments or in any other area of religion all foundations have been removed except those established through a personal spiritual life.

> The joining of a religious community, the reception of sacraments, even the acceptance of an established doctrine, mean something essentially different from what they meant for our ancestors, for symbolic gestures and doctrinal representations, accepted by deliberate decision rather than conveyed by direct experience, turn into empty shells, unless they are constantly replenished by a rather intensive and deliberate spiritual awareness.[121]

---

[119] *TS*, 29.
[120] See below beginning on p. 260.
[121] SPIRITUAL, 30.

People today often turn to less formalized structures that are more in keeping with their own inward spirituality than to preestablished forms from a previous cultural era.

The opposite extreme is also a possible outcome of the fracturing of nature: sacraments can turn into magic. If God exists in another dimension completely separated from the world, then any divine presence produced in and through human actions and words must be purely of a supernatural origin. The priest becomes the shaman who has special access to the divine sphere. However, accepting such a magical interpretation of sacraments would undermine the human subject's role as sole source of meaning and value. The need to look for answers from the theurgist neither reunites the fractured elements of nature nor considers the secularized notion of human autonomy.

## c. Religious Art

Within a secularized world view, art struggles to manifest the transcendent — the quality that makes it specifically religious art. Since there is no single method that art employs to express this transcendent dimension, the religious quality of art is particularly dependent upon cultural interpretations to determine what makes a symbol religious. In art, more than in any other object or event, the ambiguity of the contemporary situation is revealed.[122] On the one hand, art comes under the spell of the objectified, grasping attitude which characterizes existence. On the other hand, art is a primary weapon in humanity's fight against this dehumanization.

As to the first, art is subjected to the same forces that affect modern culture. Art itself is unable to create the transcendence that our culture lacks. In its struggle to manifest the transcendent

---

[122] In this section I will follow *SH*, 107-108. [*SH*, 107-108 contains a new conclusion to the material previously appearing in *TS*, 50-65].

dimension, the very possibility of religious art is brought into question. "The profound secularization of our age makes it questionable whether art can still be called religious even in that minimum sense in which all authentic art of the past could be considered 'potentially religious'."[123] A remark by Peter Berger is fitting:

> Like so-called religious persons, artists *can* adapt their work so that it merely celebrates current forms of power, so that it merely sanctifies our technical advances, our affluence, our dominance ... By this means, however, art will only enlarge the vacuum rather than fill it.[124]

Art easily results in pure formalism which is itself only a step away from the objectivism against which it reacts. The extreme forms of structuralism in literature and the post-expressionalist tendencies in painting are themselves part of the process of dehumanization.

In the new era artistic representation is preoccupied with formalism; it is detached from the listener and viewer and enclosed in its own independent meaning and space. The modern artist disregards the listener's or viewer's predisposition. Separated from the beholder, art eventually stands by itself and "ceases to refer beyond itself in space and time."[125] Instead of presenting reality in its historical context and articulating human feelings within the world, "things simply *are*, indifferent to the human observer, self-contained in an inhuman solitude."[126] The work of art no longer refers to the mind of its creator nor to the outside world. This self-sufficiency is illustrated not only in pictorial representation, but also in literature's flirtation with the antinovel or antinarrative that

---

[123] *TS*, 60.

[124] Langdon Gilkey, "Can Art Fill the Vacuum?" in *Art, Creativity, and the Sacred: An Anthology in Religion and Art*, ed. Diane Apostolos-Cappadona (New York: Crossroad, 1984), 192.

[125] *TS*, 61.

[126] *TS*, 61-62.

reduces existence to a succession of incoherent circumstances, and architecture's unprecedented emphasis on the material of construction. Having objectified reality, art removes itself one step further from any religious effort to provide a new meaning to reality through a transcendent dimension. Art as such is not sufficient to break through the circle of closed existence. It needs a transcendence which it cannot create out of itself.

Yet, it would be abrupt to suggest that no religious art exists today. "Art remains the great protest against the dehumanization of modern life."[127] Dupré suggests that certain works of painting, sculpture and music produced in modern times demand a religious interpretation, if one is at all open to their meaning. Still, these works are not representative of the majority of current art; today there is little significant art that is traditionally religious. The *possibility* of a religious viewing also exists of some abstract and expressionist art.[128] But, while these "may provide the openness in which transcendence may be rediscovered; ... [they do] not show the transcendent itself."[129] There is of course a third group of religious art which confronts people today, namely the images presented from past ages. These masters from past centuries do not use the same voice and keep the same power as before, but their message remains. Sometimes these artistic expressions only remain as museum pieces, aesthetically pleasing, but without religious significance. Despite their drawbacks each of these three types of art attempt in some way to express the depth of the religious dimension. Regardless of their personal philosophy of life, contemporary

[127] *SH*, 107: "De kunst blijft het grote protest tegen de ontmenselijking van het modern leven." Translation mine.

[128] See *TS*, 63-64 where Dupré refers to the abstractionists Rothko, Kline, and Kandinski and the expressionists Arshile Gorky, Francis Bacon, Willem de Kooning and Germaine Richier.

[129] *TS*, 64.

artists and poets in some way point to the possibility of transcendence insofar as they take a stand against an objectivistic manner of seeing and thinking. Additionally, even in museums, artistic expression of past ages remains a word from another world — a world in which the other dimension of life is still possible.

Today, perhaps more than ever a heightened awareness exists of the aesthetic quality of religious art. Unfortunately, the opposite is true of the modern ability to recognize in the aesthetic expression an explicit manifestation of the transcendent. A cursory glance at Church documents through history suggests an overall lack of concern for the aesthetic dimension of religious art. For example, while the documents of the Council of Constantinople IV (869-870) reconfirmed the cult of images following the iconoclastic bids of the Byzantine emperors, they are not an occasion for promoting aesthetic excellence:

> For, just as through the written words which are contained in the book [of the gospels], we all shall obtain salvation, so through the influence that colours in painting exercise on the imagination, all, both wise and simple, obtain benefit from what is before them; for as speech teaches and portrays through syllables, so too does painting by means of colours.[130]

Even with the Council of Trent sacred images are primarily considered as objects of instruction, edification, or veneration.[131] Dupré follows Gilson's conclusion from these documents that the Church values religious art exclusively based upon its ability to

---

[130] Decrees of the Council of Constantinople IV, in *Decrees of the Ecumenical Councils*, vol. 1, *Nicaea I to Lateran V*, ed. Norman Tanner (London: Sheed & Ward; Washington, D.C.: Georgetown University Press, 1990), 168, can. 3.

[131] See Decrees of the Council of Trent, Session 25, December 3, 1563 in *Decrees of the Ecumenical Councils*, vol. 2, *Trent-Vatican II*, Norman Tanner, ed. (London: Sheed & Ward; Washington, D.C.: Georgetown University Press, 1990), 775: "Bishop should teach with care that the faithful are instructed and strengthened by commemorating and frequently recalling the articles of our faith

instruct and edify. Concern to regulate the expressions of faith has incited religious leaders to be wary of art. More recently, the Second Vatican Council has reaffirmed faith's reliance upon artistic expression and, of greater significance, has demonstrated a stronger concern for the aesthetic dimension of religious art.[132] The intimate relation between faith and art suggests a greater openness to different models of expression between cultures and through each generation. In the end, there are no universal rules that distinguish between religious and nonreligious art, but it is precisely in its quest to express the transcendent that religious art is struggling today, since modern culture itself has lost contact with this transcendent dimension of life.

## 5. *Conclusion*

Firmly entrenched in late modernity, the contemporary situation is characterized by a loss of the sense of transcendence as the human subject assumes control and objectifies the world. Even the believer can be viewed as atheistic as God ceases to be a part of the cultural understanding of life. Without a transcendent referent the possibility of religious symbols to carry meaning has been crushed. Culturally speaking, religion has been reduced to one experience among others. It is occasionally powerful but unable to be *the* integrating factor of cultural life as it had been in the past.

through the expression in pictures or other likenesses of the stories of the mysteries of our redemption; and that great benefits flow from all sacred images, not only because people are reminded of the gifts and blessings conferred on us by Christ, but because the miracles of God through the saints and their salutary example is put before the eyes of the faithful, who can thank God for them, adore and love God and to practise devotion."

[132] *Constitution on the Liturgy*, in *Decrees of the Ecumenical Councils*, 2:842, nos. 112-129; 124: "Ordinaries should see to it, in their encouragement and support of authentic worshipping art, that their aim is noble beauty rather than mere sumptuousness."

In the modern world, religion no longer exercises its integrating function — so essential to its survival — primarily by means of ecclesiastical power or discipline, or even by means of doctrinal authority. Rather, it does this by means of a personal decision to *adopt* a traditional doctrine and to *use* it for guidance and integration of the various aspects of social and private conduct.[133]

It must be reiterated that the loss of a sense of transcendence that characterizes modernity and issues in a new type of atheism along with an inability to make religious symbols is a *cultural* phenomenon. It is a fact that religion has ceased to be the integrating factor of *public* life; the only question that remains is whether value may be integrated in any other way.

To profess a belief in God and to observe certain rules of ritual and moral conduct is not sufficient to regain it. Faith itself is permeated by objectivism. What is needed is a conversion to an attitude in which existing is more than taking, acting more than making, meaning more than function — an attitude in which there is enough leisure for wonder and enough detachment for transcendence.[134]

Religious symbols themselves have lost their transcendent referent and therefore are not capable of providing an integration to life. Modern Western culture does not furnish the space for transcendence to be recognized.

Culture requires freedom, but freedom requires spiritual space to act, play, and dream in. Such a space is not provided by leisure alone: leisure itself becomes suffocating without spiritual content. The space for freedom is created by transcendence. What is needed most of all is an attitude in which transcendence *can be recognized again*. The question of actual faith is entirely secondary to the recovery of freedom by detachment from the purely objective.[135]

---

[133] SPIRITUAL, 24-25.
[134] *TS*, 17.
[135] *TS*, 17.

How then can religion survive in a secular society? The endurance of society is no longer predicated upon a religious integration. The basic values of society and its institutions have ceased to require a religious brace. Neither does faith provide unique solutions to contemporary problems such as environmental pollution, ethnic tensions, and urban plight. The virtues of religion may be highly praised today, but precisely because the secular culture has assumed that which was previously held to be religiously virtuous. However, religion may still be the ultimate integrating force for the religious *individual*. "Our predicament is due not to a lack of faith but to a lack of inwardness."[136] It is to this idea and other attempts at providing hope for the future that we conclude this chapter.

## C. HOPE FOR THE FUTURE

In *Passage to Modernity*, Dupré does not profess to have a perfect working plan for the problems of our culture. He views his presentation of the turn from premodernity to modernity and reflections upon the modern situation as more of a hermeneutic than a critique. In remaining faithful to this plan, the book necessarily does not represent the fullness of his response to modernity, though he does point to certain historical movements as providing a provisional synthesis. However, throughout a preponderance of his works Dupré has more than demonstrated that far from avoiding an answer to the modern situation he gathers his insights and scholarship to meet the challenge.

Looking for a 'solution' to the modern 'problem' is itself a manifestation of the modern outlook, insofar as this continues to

---

[136] *TS*, 17.

express belief in human ability to conquer the world by action and assault. Nevertheless, neither a paralysis caused by trepidation of taking a misstep or complacency with the current situation will restore a sense of transcendence. Thus, in this section we will provide a cursory survey of attempts to regain or reinterpret transcendence from within the secular experience. Dupré provides an alternative response through the historical example of devout humanism, though it failed to be widely embraced since such "mystical theology" was ostracized from theology proper. His main answer is to regain transcendence through the inner life of the self which reaches out to provide an integration with culture.

## 1. Failed Attempts to Regain Transcendence

Each of the following attempts fails in one way or other to translate transcendence into a meaningful notion necessary for religious symbols. This is not to deny that there are positive aspects contained in each. The goal of this section is neither to develop completely the thoughts of others nor to offer a full critique, but to glance at an assortment of ideas that are significant for Dupré's reflections.

One general solution which is proposed from various quarters — probably due to its clarity and simplicity — is to return to the visible rock of past ages. This is illustrated from exhortations to renounce technology,[137] to popular argumentations to restore the Tridentine liturgy. However, a return to earlier, safer or less complicated structures will not address the needs of the contemporary situation.

---

[137] See e.g., Jerry Mander, *In the Absence of the Sacred: The Failure of Technology and the Survival of the Indian Nations* (San Francisco: Sierra Club Books, 1991) and the bibliography he provides, pp. 411-426.

> Those who, by updating past thoughts, hoped to neutralize such baneful features of modern thought as the opposition between subject and object or the loss of a transcendent component underestimated the radical nature of the modern revolution. Its problems cannot be treated as errors to be corrected by a simple return to an earlier truth. That truth is no longer available; it has vanished forever.[138]

A tide of fundamentalism is rising from an ocean filled with various streams of thought. Antimodernist views appear in Islam and political power lobbies. The goal is to reestablish objective certainty by denying historical change. They close themselves to the values and beliefs of their modern world. Others, without any desire to turn the clock back, attempt to isolate the secular from their deeper existence. Instead of providing a successful solution, this "schizoid attitude is bound to become untenable before long"[139] because there is no incorporation or reconciliation of personal beliefs with those of one's culture. Even before personally turning to one's deeper beliefs one must first acknowledge the loss of transcendence. "This is particularly painful to the believer who tends to hide his head in the sand of a past spiritual tradition in order to avoid the sight of his own atheism."[140] Certain theologians, philosophers and other specialists do approach the problem by first acknowledging the question of transcendence. They provide solutions beyond this general attempt of a return to the past.

Sometimes the response of secular theologians is to eliminate the notion of transcendence altogether as meaningless (as with van Buren below), but usually they endeavor to reinterpret it in order to make it worthwhile. Bonhoeffer is commonly considered the initiator of this-worldly theology in allowing secularity to be

---

[138] *PM*, 6-7. Also see *TS*, 16-17. Dupré, "The Modern Idea of Culture," 483.
[139] SPIRITUAL, 23.
[140] *TS*, 17.

considered a Christian category. His goal was not to eliminate God but to take God away from a supernatural realm that has lost its meaning. Genuine types of transcendence accept the life God gives and is not a foundation for escape. From a Catholic theological perspective, Teilhard de Chardin also furnished a forceful inspiration for world directed theology. Often misinterpreted as advocating the embrace of the world at the complete neglect of any quest for the transcendent, he actually was a defendant of transcendence while constantly seeking to reconcile it with an immanence that required a new place in religion and philosophy. He did not deny transcendence but reformulated an understanding of it. The vital question was whether the higher, long dreamed of life of union and consummation sought Above should be pursued Ahead in the prolongation of the forces of evolution — or perhaps both.

Guidance from mentors such as these was accepted in varying degrees and sparked a number of different and often contradictory responses. Still, the common thread remains that "all radical theologians consider secularization the essence of the Christian message for our time."[141] This has been expressed in both critical and creative ways. Paul van Buren is the "critical" theologian of the group and argues from empiricist linguistic philosophy that the gospel can possess only a secular meaning today. He reasons that since no verifiable object or human experience corresponds to the theological concept of God, all theological talk about God has become meaningless. However, he does interpret statements of religious commitment as meaningful because, unlike God talk, they serve a

---

[141] Dupré, "The Problem of Divine Transcendence in Secular Theology," in *The Spirit and Power of Christian Secularity*, ed. Albert Schlitzer (Notre Dame, IN: University of Notre Dame Press, 1969), 102. Compare Dupré, "Meditations on Secular Theology," 1469.

definite communicative function.[142] This interpretation enables him
to provide the statements of the Gospel with a purely empirical sense
— a call to action — understandable to the modern person.

However, it is doubtful that a true religiosity can survive such a
radical secular interpretation — nonetheless Christianity — since
transcendence cannot be jettisoned and still maintain the authentic
religious symbolization necessary to its expression. Some try to
solve this problem by suggesting that transcendence was never
abandoned in the midst of their talk of the here-and-now. For
example, Edward Farley, Kenneth Hamilton, and David Cairns
draw on the resources of their day to demonstrate that the motif of
transcendence had not disappeared.[143] Reminiscent of Pascal's
statement about the God of Abraham, Isaac, and Jacob and not of
the philosophers, Farley and Hamilton wish to defend the healthy
existence of transcendence into our day by distinguishing between
biblical-kerygmatic transcendence and philosophical-experiential
transcendence. More prominent secular approaches such as John
A. T. Robinson and Harvey Cox suggested transcendence could be
relocated, rephrased, or remythologized.[144] Robinson accepts the

[142] See van Buren, *The Secular Meaning of the Gospel.* Also see above, pp. 99-
101, including Hare and Braithwaite whom van Buren follows in their empirical
views which allow for meaningful statements of religious commitment. But van
Buren also goes beyond them, insofar as he qualifies the element of faith as
meaningful only to the extent that it is secularized. See Dupré, "Meditations on
Secular Theology," 1469.

[143] See Edward Farley, *The Transcendence of God: A Study in Contemporary
Philosophical Theology* (Philadelphia: Westminster Press, 1960; London: Epworth
Press, 1962); Kenneth Hamilton, *Revolt Against Heaven: An Enquiry Into Anti-
Supernaturalism* (Grand Rapids: Eerdmans, 1965); and David Cairns, *God Up
There? A Study in Divine Transcendence* (Philadelphia: Westminster Press;
Edinburgh: St. Andrew Press, 1967).

[144] See John A. T. Robinson, *Honest to God* (Philadelphia: Westminster
Press, 1963); Harvey Cox, *The Secular City* (New York: Macmillan, 1965); id.,
*Feast of Fools*; id., *Religion in the Secular City: Toward a Postmodern Theology*
(New York: Simon & Schuster, A Touchstone Book, 1984).

transcendent nature of God and revelation. What he rejects is "otherworldly" transcendence that replaces the creative responsibility of the human subject. Cox is clear that secularization is the mature evolution of the Christian faith and not a regression of it. Both Robinson and Cox fail to elucidate in what such a transcendence consists which can be reconciled with a radical this-worldly Christianity.

Thomas Altizer is another who denies any need for a transcendent dimension. He adopts a more radical attitude and explicates a mythology without transcendence. He interprets the Incarnation as meaning that the divine has become completely identical with the human.[145] By contrast, Gordon Kaufman argues for the existence of a transcendent dimension even when mythology is abandoned.[146] His argument begins by asserting that the mythological cosmological dualism dividing earth and heaven belonged to a previous unscientific age and is incompatible with the secular world view. It was through this dualism that thinkers located transcendence. However, Kaufman declares that we can locate transcendence without mythology. He argues that it is our understanding of finite limit that we apply to the ultimate limit. This gives meaning to "God" and here lies our notion of transcendence today. Further, it is only through communication that we know the transcendent reality of another. It is therefore only through revelation that genuine knowledge of God is possible (that God exists). When myth is abandoned, the secular still provides an understanding of transcendence. In attempting to salvage religion for modern persons, Kaufman sifts out all mythological elements from religion.

[145] See Thomas J. J. Altizer, *The Gospel of Christian Atheism* (Philadelphia: Westminster Press, 1966).

[146] See Gordon Kaufman, "On the Meaning of 'God': Transcendence Without Mythology," in *New Theology No. 4*, ed. Martin Marty and Dean Peerman (New York: Macmillan, 1967), 69-98.

Yet, Kaufman himself even questions after this reduction whether Christian faith can have a real role to play in our secular culture. The image of transcendence that he advocates is not associated with any social concern and is not needed since a secular humanism is quite effective without it. However, it is misleading to suggest that immanence is linked to radicality and transcendence to a conservatism.

Religious sociologists and anthropologists have also provided their share of direct input. In March of 1969 the Vatican Secretariat for Non-Believers sponsored a colloquium on the culture of nonbelief. Among the participants were Robert Bellah and Peter Berger. For his part, Bellah made an urgent appeal that theology consider the human response to the transcendent.[147] His concern was not in reiterating the traditional picture of transcendence held by theology, but in investigating the modern experience of transcendence. Previous to the conference Berger confronted the casual dismissal of the transcendent by theology.[148] He suggested that such human endeavors as humor, play, order, outrage and hope are signals of transcendence that have been overlooked. He argued that the secular model of society far from being exhaustive must also admit of a turn to the supernatural and the transcendent. Others also have taken up the dissatisfaction of modern people with their present life and suggest that this malaise forces people to pose the question of

[147] See the paper delivered at the conference: Robert Bellah, "Transcendence in Contemporary Piety," in *The Religious Situation: 1969*, ed. Donald Cutler (Boston: Beacon Press, 1969), 896-909; revised version printed in *Transcendence*, ed. Herbert Richardson and Donald Cutler (Boston: Beacon Press, 1969), 85-97. Also see id., *Beyond Belief: Essays on Religion in a Post-Traditional World* (New York: Harper & Row, 1970).

[148] Peter Berger, *A Rumor of Angels: Modern Society and the Rediscovery of the Supernatural* (Garden City: Doubleday, 1969). Also see id., *The Sacred Canopy: Elements of a Sociological Theory of Religion* (Garden City, NY: Doubleday, 1967).

transcendence which leads many back to some type of religious world view.[149] However, just by questioning the adequacy of a purely immanent world view, discontent itself does not constitute a rediscovery of the sacred.

## 2. Dupré's General Assessment

Trying to regain transcendence through a return to past structures by repudiating the current situation results in an extreme isolationism of the individual from society and avoids the complexity of the problematic. If *I* discover a sense of transcendence for *me*, this is well and good for *me*, but this is cultural suicide. Perhaps I may even convince others to join me in reviving structures from a bygone era. But this only produces a fundamentalism characterized by its unwillingness to dialogue with culture precisely because it is incapable of integrating with culture. Likewise, Dupré remains skeptical of theological and sociological attempts to regain a sense of transcendence in and through the secular world view itself. This is the overall position of those mentioned in this brief survey, aside from van Buren and Altizer who basically exclude the possibility of transcendence at all. If such a restoration is possible in this manner, then

> the so-called secularity of the present age means nothing more than that the established faiths which integrated an entire society and externally controlled the whole conduct of its members are disappearing, while new movements, perhaps less doctrinal and certainly less universal, but no less religious, are gradually taking their place.[150]

However, Dupré regards the outcome of secularity to be more profound than a simple shift in the functional and structural

---

[149] See e.g., Robert Nisbet, *The Social Bond* (New York: Knopf, 1970) and Andrew Greely, *Unsecular Man* (New York: Schocken Books, 1972). Also see *TS*, 108 note 12.

[150] *TS*, 25.

expression of religious faith. He explains, "I believe the secularist revolution to have effected a more radical change, one that has not been reversed by recent trends."[151] It has not been successful because the attempted return to the sacred itself is born from a completely secular attitude. The secular view proclaims that it has expanded the immanent to include even the religious experience. After renouncing the traditional expression of the transcendent, people in the secular world continue to feel the need for that other dimension which is not attainable through humanistic or social interests. Yet, in searching to regain this lost dimension there is no intention of conceding any aspect of the secular lifestyle; there is no "commitment to the transcendent as to *another* reality."[152] Instead, feelings of self-expansion are cultivated which may indeed be shared with others who possess a similar state of mind, but the experience remains private and religious symbols only borrowed from the past with little or no commitment to their content. "Much of what passes for a revival of the sacred in our age is only marginally religious, and the so-called sacred presence usually turns out to be no more than a romantic remembrance or an aesthetic imitation of past experiences."[153] Religion in the secular age is primarily reduced to an individual experience useful for the formation of moral codes and social concern, or abandoned for a secular humanism that can accomplish the same results.

Thus, neither an inward denial of the present situation nor the secular incorporation of the transcendent are workable solutions for Dupré. Still, much of the responsibility falls to the individual acceptance of transcendence, since modern culture no longer integrates transcendence as it had in the past. Without this cultural support, the burden of regaining transcendence does fall to the

[151] *TS*, 25.
[152] *TS*, 26.
[153] *TS*, 26.

individual. Likewise, it would be wrong to deduce that secularization necessarily excludes a relation to the transcendent, since despite exaggerations some of the roots of secularization are within religion itself and these roots cannot omit religion's necessary relation to the transcendent. While not providing an answer, each provides a contribution to the recovery of transcendence for the contemporary believer. Thus, Dupré weaves some threads of these attempts into his response.

## 3. *Dupré's Alternative*

Dupré proposes a healthy balance between an individual withdrawal and a totally secular attitude in which to locate transcendence. He promotes an inward turn without denying that we do in fact live in a secular culture. It is precisely the inner life or the lived experience of one's own subjectivity that is the condition of openness to transcendency. Neither can the role of secular culture be ignored in the attempt to restore transcendence. The religious person must blend his or her inward resolution with existence in culture. This integration is assisted by culture insofar as certain features of traditional negative theology emerge as secular theology grapples with the question of the role of transcendence in culture. In developing these aspects of Dupré's alternative we will first turn to a brief recognition of how an earlier integration was accomplished by devout humanism and how this presents a certain pattern of technique that can be incorporated into today's response. Then we will conclude with a summary of what Dupré proposes as the key for recovering transcendence in the contemporary world.

### a. Historical Precedent: Devout Humanism

Without attempting a thorough historical investigation we turn to devout humanism as establishing a certain precedence for addressing the contemporary situation. The root term "Christian humanism" has developed with more than its fair share of ambiguity. Some authors understand Christian humanism as an exclusively spiritual phenomenon which combined traditional religious piety with a modern commitment to secular responsibility, with or without an association with humanism proper.[154] Other authors view the term as referring beyond a spiritual movement to "all writers who, in whatever capacity, shed light on the religious quality of Renaissance culture, including such dubious candidates as Rabelais."[155] The more precise spiritual trend has been distinguished from the general movement by receiving the name "devout humanism." Originally devout humanism designated Francis de Sales and his direct and indirect followers such as J.-P. Camus and Yves de Paris. Dupré interprets devout humanism more broadly and applies the term "to a spiritual movement that included a variety of religious schools united only by a new concept of nature and, in the practical order, by new ideals and methods of Christian piety."[156] Thus, this discussion of devout humanism explicates all spiritual movements (compared to a comprehensive interpretation of Christian humanism) of the early modern age that share a similar vision of the powers of redeemed nature (without restriction to Francis de Sales and his school). Dupré investigates Ignatius of Loyola and Francis de Sales as paradigmatic of the spiritual life of the Counter-Reformation. While certain differences between the two approaches will be apparent, our goal is to acknowledge their

---

[154] See Henri Bremond, *A Literary History of Religious Thought in France*, vol. 1, *Devout Humanism*, trans. K. Montgomery (New York: Macmillan, 1928). Bremond is commonly credited with having coined the term "devout humanism."

[155] *PM*, 223. This position is taken by Francis Herman, *Histoire doctrinale de l'humanisme chrétien*, 4 vols. (Tournai: Casterman, 1947).

[156] Louis Dupré, "Ignatian Humanism and its Mystical Origins," *Communio* 18 (Summer 1991): 165. Also see *PM*, 224.

mutual contribution to a spiritual synthesis of the modern break up
of the transcendent and human realms from nature.

## i. Ignatius of Loyola

For Dupré, "the most original Catholic response to the religious
challenge of the modern age was unquestionably the one given by
Ignatius of Loyola [1491-1556]."[157] With transcendence severed
from nature, Ignatius was surrounded by theological attempts to
regain a sense of transcendence by formulating grace as a separate
order of being that was dispensable in the order of nature. As the
threads of this tentative synthesis unraveled, Protestant Reformers
uncompromisingly espoused the primacy of grace. Ignatius appropriated this same position, but unlike the Protestant spiritual
solution he would not sacrifice the basic integrity of nature. "Only
a mystical vision of God's all-inclusiveness allowed him to harness
the tensions under an all-comprehensive unity."[158]

While his spiritual vision was expressed in the anthropocentric
language of modern culture, instead of yielding to the emerging
secular world view he actually inverted the modern ideal of self-
realization. "Ignatius transforms the anthropocentric ideal of
creative self-development by placing it within a radically theocentric
perspective."[159] This is worked out in his spiritual writings. Though
his contemplative spirituality was based upon medieval sources,
he adopts a definitively modern view in placing the person at the
center of the universe. No fixed place or established life is imposed upon Ignatian followers but they must shape themselves
under the guidance of God's spirit. The *Spiritual Exercises* assume

[157] *PM*, 224. For this section see both Dupré, "Ignatian Humanism," 164-182
and *PM*, 224-226.

[158] Dupré, "Ignatian Humanism," 181.

[159] *PM*, 226.

that by a methodic, systematic training of will power, people are capable of controlling their own lives.[160] This idea of employing a system of rules and maxims intended to lead a person to a defined goal is intrinsically modern: effective strategies are to be discerned from ineffective ones and an awareness of the limited time available for productive action is always present. The *Exercises'* "insistence on making the most effective use of one's spiritual potential resembles so closely contemporary secular attitudes as to cast suspicion on its religious nature."[161]

However, far from capitulating to naturalism or human self-sufficiency, "The *Exercises* present a uniquely modern synthesis of freedom and grace, far superior to the one achieved by the theology of the time."[162] It is not the case that nature's potential is only methodically directed toward a transcendent goal. Instead, the goal for Ignatius is the glory of God and this end "intrinsically transforms the very method for attaining it."[163] He inverts the modern understanding of the human subject as sole meaning giving agent insofar as grace is now required to first liberate nature from a state of unfreedom so that nature may attain its potential. Freedom is redefined as a divinely inspired surrender and no longer a capacity for self-realization. In this surrender, action itself becomes grounded in passivity. True freedom, then, "consists in acting under the motion of grace."[164] Each person must choose between a narrow freedom restrict to self-centered objectives or a renewed freedom elevated to transcend the self.

---

[160] See Ignatius of Loyola, *The Spiritual Exercises*, in *Ignatius of Loyola*: *Spiritual Exercises and Selected Works*, The Classics of Western Spirituality, trans. George Ganss (New York: Paulist Press, 1991), 114-214.

[161] *PM*, 224.

[162] *PM*, 224.

[163] *PM*, 225.

[164] *PM*, 225.

God, not the human subject, is both the foundation of human nature and the goal of its accomplishments. Human beings are created by God to give praise and service to God. First there is a movement descending from God and only secondarily one ascending from humans. The love that moves and causes one to choose must descend from above, from the love of God. These images of descent and return permeate the two fundamental visions that shaped the spirituality of Ignatius. At Manresa he witnessed the entire creation as proceeding from God the Father and, through the Son, returning to its divine origin. Fifteen years later the vision of La Storta transformed his contemplative vision into a life of action. "Or, more correctly, it converted the apostolic action upon which Ignatius was ready to engage into contemplation."[165] Action itself is perceived as participating in the "outgoing" movement of the trinitarian life of God. Humans are called to fulfillment not by resting in divine quiet but by descending with the Son into creation in order to sanctify it. Here Ignatius finds sanction for the worldly mission he embraces and advocates.

In this manner, the devout humanism of Ignatius of Loyola completely avoided the problematic separation of nature and the supernatural. "Ignatius's mystical vision articulated in the language of the modern age turns the modern primacy of the subject on its head and results in a more radically God-centered view of reality than the natural theology of the Scholastics or even the spiritual theology of Gerson and his followers."[166] Ignatius succeeded in filling the new form of humanism with a more radically mystical religious content.

[165] *PM*, 225.
[166] Dupré, "Ignatian Humanism," 173.

## ii. Francis de Sales

With Francis de Sales (1567-1622) the new trust in human nature continues to advance as he also attempts to bridge the separation between nature and the order of grace. In his *Introduction to the Devout Life* he writes a plan of piety for those who live in the world and are surrounded by its affairs.[167] Francis seeks in outward manners and wholesome living to express the divine inner grace. For the theological foundation of his thought one must turn to his more theoretical *Treatise of the Love of God*.[168] Here he explains that human nature is dynamically oriented toward the love of God:

> We have been created to the image and likeness of God. What does that mean but that we stand in a relation of extreme correspondence with his divine majesty? ... Even as the person cannot become perfect except through God's goodness, that goodness itself can nowhere better activate its external perfection than in our humanity.[169]

Grace transforms nature from within and the result is a single reality that is both human and divine. Charity is the agent of sanctification and is "infused" into a person. Yet, charity is also a "virtue" and as such requires the active cooperation of the natural inclinations that are "the wild branches" on which we must graft the roots of God's eternal love. Grace rules spiritual life, not by forcing the will, but by attracting it. "When the will follows the attraction and consents to the divine motion, it follows freely, just as it freely resists when it resists — even though our consent to grace depends much more on grace than on the will."[170]

[167] See Francis de Sales, *Introduction to the Devout Life*, trans. Michael Day (Westminster, MD: Newman Press, 1956). For this section see both Dupré, "Introduction," in *Christian Spirituality*, xiv-xvii and *PM*, 227-229.

[168] See Francis de Sales, *Treatise of the Love of God*, trans. H. Mackey (London: Greenwood Press, 1942).

[169] Francis de Sales, *Treatise of the Love of God*, 1.15.

[170] Francis de Sales, *Treatise of the Love of God*, 2.12.

However, Francis never succeeds in providing a clear theological basis for understanding the relation between free will and grace. He lacks the speculative grounding to mediate between human effort or divine predestination as the principal agent of salvation or reprobation. Without committing to any particular theological approach Francis simply wants to assert that supernatural grace appeals to natural inclination.[171] The fundamental basis for his synthesis is practical piety, and because of this there is a second problem inherent in Salesian humanism. "While Francis succeeded in restyling the modern synthesis of nature and grace in accordance with the new type of personhood, [through a practical piety] he utterly fails to do the same for either cosmos or society."[172] His synthesis remains strictly on the level of interiority; it takes place between God and the soul. True enough he is apt to employ analogies with the life of nature.[173] Yet, while he accepts the physical world, he does not integrate it theologically. The cosmic world remains outside the purview of the spiritual realm which is restricted to the relationship between the individual soul and God.

Francis is successful when he keeps his focus set on practical piety wherein grace and nature are in fact united. The issue of sin does not upset the Salesian synthesis in the way that it thwarted so

[171] Though Francis does not appeal to any specific theological school, "his formulation that God grants his grace to those who will respond, appears to depend on Molina's questionable assumption of a divine foreknowledge in accordance with which God, in a second moment, grants grace." *PM*, 227-228. In other words, there is a time sequence whereby God first desires to save all people, then, in foreseeing those who will respond, God grants efficacious grace only to them. See Francis de Sales, *Treatise of the Love of God*, 8.3.

[172] *PM*, 228-229.

[173] See e.g., Francis de Sales, *Introduction to the Devout Life*, 3.39 where the elephant is held as an example for modesty in marriage; id., *Treatise of the Love of God*, 2.19 where the lioness is a model for frequent confession and in id., 3.22 the salamander reminds us that sin ruins friendship.

many others. In this practical spirituality sin does not impede
nature's divine impulse, though the dynamism of nature does require assistance to accomplish what it could do normally in its
original state. Neither is nature considered as self-sufficient in
Francis' writings; there is no idea of pure nature. Thus, it is possible
to call God's assistance "supernatural" in Salesian humanism, but
the love practiced through this divine support remains natural.

iii. Implications for today

Ignatius of Loyola and Francis de Sales exemplify the force of
devout humanism that integrates the action of God with modern
living. "Spiritual theologies alone succeeded in recapturing in the
lived experience of devotional practice the synthesis that systematic theology had lost in speculation."[174] However, these spiritual
solutions were not merged into the dominant theological reflection
of their day, nor did they pass unscathed by cultural forces into the
twentieth century. In general, "[devotional] thought itself becomes
marginalized, if not expelled altogether, from the main currents of
Christian thought."[175] Devotional and mystical movements are
relegated to the sidelines of theology and failed to wield any substantial influence in producing a mainline theological synthesis.

There are also specific nuances which have impacted the
prosperity or deterioration of devout humanism through the years.
The approach of Francis united the modern image of the human
subject within a spiritual vision but it failed to accommodate the
new cosmological and societal dimensions. Much of Francis'
theological unworldliness was assimilated by later spiritual masters,
including Jansenists and Quietists, but the link with cosmos or
society was rarely fully reestablished and they never possessed his

[174] *PM*, 189.
[175] Dupré, "The Dissolution of the Union of Nature and Grace," 121.

human warmth. Ignatius' version of this incarnated mysticism was more successful. He brought not only God and the soul together, but succeeded in uniting an entire world view. With this accomplishment the Ignatian vision played an active role in a new scientific world picture. More importantly for our concern, his insight directed the aesthetic culture of the Baroque. Fully acknowledging the tensions and inconsistencies of Baroque culture, Dupré interprets it as the last comprehensive synthesis through a spiritual vision whereby a dual center exists — both human and divine. The human person stands at the center of meaning but "that center remains vertically linked to a transcendent source from which, via a descending scale of mediating bodies, the human creator draws his power."[176] However, the Baroque integration unraveled because it lacked the stability as well as flexibility of a theological base.

What about the feasibility of the Ignatian and Salesian syntheses for today's culture? Have they continued to shape and inform the modern situation? The answer must be "yes and no." They have survived into late modernity as providing stable guiding principles but the rising secularist trend has been a formidable opponent. Particularly the spiritual humanism of the Jesuits — born of the combined heritage of nominalist theology and Renaissance paganism — continues to leave a distinctive mark upon the understanding of the modern world. Still, today this global insight of Ignatius is often reduced to an internal relation between God and the soul or degenerated into an extreme worldliness. This encompassing vision has basically succumbed to secularism. Yet, individuals can indeed continue to embrace this view and herein lies the primary lesson of devout humanism for contemporary persons: the recovery of a contemplative spirit.

---

[176] *PM*, 237; also see 238-248.

> If the union of nature and grace, vital to the survival of the Christian message, was maintained only as long as theology retained a contemplative, practico-spiritual dimension, then the future success of that theology in influencing a now largely dechristianized culture may well depend on its ability to reincorporate the contemplative aspect that once belonged to its very essence.[177]

Devout humanism sets a precedence for contemplation as a successful means through which transcendence is united with the world and human subject. This contemplative life of devout humanism is not self-centered but moves out from itself to a life of devotion to work and service. The asceticism of monastic piety was replaced by one of self-denial through devotion to work, sanctification of life in the world, and a living not only for salvation but also for a higher life in the spirit of the pure love of God's pleasure.[178]

## b. Contemporary Key: Transcendent Selfhood

Finally, from the provisional synthesis inherited from devout humanism the key for the contemporary solution is manifested: the recovery of the inner life. Three points will help to explain this further. First, the inward turn must not be perceived as a total withdrawal from society; it always returns to reinterpret and reground culture. Second, revelation appreciated as both experience

---

[177] Dupré, "The Dissolution of the Union of Nature and Grace," 121.

[178] Of course, Ignatius and Francis are not the only influential spiritual writers of this century. However, they are the primary example of those who rethought spiritual life in modern terms. Dupré explains in *PM*, 230: "For others, no less influential in the century, the medieval, fully integrated cosmos had never broken down. Teresa of Avila . . . and John of the Cross . . . thought within the earlier synthesis. Certainly, their affective, subjective language substantially differs from the objective, Neoplatonic one of Eckhart, Ruusbroec, and their fifteenth century disciples. Yet their worldview remains unaltered, and they illustrate spiritual life's independence of the new cultural environment. Neither Teresa nor John had to confront the full challenge of modernity."

and message suggests the divine givenness of the inward turn beyond its human expression. Third, this inner life prompted by the complete absence of transcendence in secular culture places it in the tradition of negative theology. Particularly in the first and third area an intimate affinity is established between the modern believer and the mystics of former generations.

## i. Personal not individual

All religious people today are forced to turn inward because there is no place else to turn, as the culture has ceased to support the possibility of a transcendent dimension to life. Many people today do have intense religious experiences, but "what uniquely distinguishes our present situation is the nature of the experience."[179] No longer is the experience direct and self-interpretative as it was in the past. The sole grounding for the religious person today is an individual active commitment to transcendent reality. "Generally speaking, this new relation is marked more by personal reflection and deliberate choice than by direct experience."[180] Of course, religious persons of every time have been confronted with making a personal free decision of faith. Neither immediacy of perception nor intensity of feeling were considered to match personal assent to the revelation. Nevertheless, faith was supported by an abundance of direct experiences present in the religiously imbued cultural environment. Today such cultural encouragement has disappeared.

The interpretation of an experience as being one of a transcendent dimension is separated from the experience itself. Without a cultural foundation, ambiguity and an openness to a multiplicity of interpretations are the new hallmarks of experience. "An identical experience justifies the believer's faith as well as the unbeliever's

[179] SPIRITUAL, 23.
[180] SPIRITUAL, 23.

unbelief."[181] Doubt regarding the correct interpretation of an experience is removed only by a subsequent decision of full commitment. "Religious men and women will continue to attribute a 'sacred' quality to persons, objects, and events closely connected with their relation to the transcendent. But they will do so because they *hold* them sacred, not because they *perceive* them as sacred."[182] The sacred possess a totally private character when it is still experienced today. Thus, the religious person now *chooses* those doctrines and symbolic expressions that he or she finds meaningful for himself or herself, while in the past ecclesiastical institutions, verbal revelation, and nature determined the inner experience. "The religious person embraces only those doctrines which cast light upon his inner awareness, joins only those groups to which he feels moved from within, and performs only those acts which express his self-transcendence."[183] Consequently, religion is now often considered as possessing a certain eclectic nature, or even an arbitrary appearance by those who judge by past objective standards. "The external and institutional elements of religion seem to have been reduced to an instrumental role."[184] Dupré is not suggesting that there will come a time when religion will ever be without communally established symbols. Rather, his point is that "those who opted for a religious dimension in their lives will use institutions and symbols to the extent of their *personal* needs."[185]

---

[181] SPIRITUAL, 24.

[182] SPIRITUAL, 24.

[183] *TS*, 29-30.

[184] SPIRITUAL, 24.

[185] SPIRITUAL, 24. Here Dupré also notes that a significant result of the tailoring of religion to personal needs has been an unprecedented rise in the acceptance of religious pluralism—a pluralism which even helped the modern secular crisis along, but only after the subjective individual took precedence over objective institutions.

However, the recovery of the inner life of the self is not simply an individual enterprise. In fact, insofar as it is a personal quest it is not at all individualistic. Dupré explains that the notion of person includes both individuality and selfhood. "As individual man belongs to the world; as self he surpasses it."[186] Individuality is the objective pole of personhood and self is the subjective one. A biological, physiological, and even at times philosophical description of the person may describe "person" as an individual substance of a rational nature. But this incorporates only an objective understanding of person. By contrast, the inner life of the self embraces the person as subject. Selfhood is self-awareness which is achieved not by analysis, control and critical doubt, but by recollection. "Religious recollection consists in a conversion, via the past, toward a more interior self which is no longer subject to the passage of time, because it rests in eternity."[187] Recollection makes the discovery of the self possible. Its primary aim is not to evoke memories as much as it is to review the totality of temporal succession — that is, to open the inner self to transcendence. "Thus to know oneself is to remember oneself, and to remember oneself entirely is to remember one's origin."[188] Here self-immanence turns to self-transcendence, and the discovery of this self-transcendence makes the recovery of God possible. Thus, "the ground of the self far surpasses the boundaries of individual personhood."[189]

Despite the contemporary preoccupation with the self, the interest in it predominately focuses on everyday consciousness and fails to grasp the more profound spiritual dimension of the self. Yet, there has been a recent upsurge in investigating the passive side of

[186] *TS*, 31.
[187] *TS*, 73.
[188] *TS*, 73.
[189] *TS*, 103.

selfhood which Dupré characterizes as recognition of the ultimate insufficiency of the human being and necessary dependence upon a transcendent source.[190] To further explicate the distinctiveness of selfhood which transcends itself, Dupré distinguishes between the ordinary self and the mystical self.[191] In the mystical self the mind is emptied of all objects and is open to some type of passively infused experience. A difference between the two levels of ordinary and mystical experience is universally suggested by metaphors of qualitative distinctness: height, depth, isolation, and secrecy. For example, Pseudo-Dionysius interprets Plotinus with his dominate metaphor of the soul ascending beyond images and understanding; Teresa of Avila (1515-1582) speaks of the inner castle, Catherine of Siena (*c*. 1347-1380) of the interior home, Johannes Tauler (*c*. 1300-1361) of the ground of the soul, John of the Cross (1542-1591) of darkness and concealment. This mystical understanding of the self is precisely what the contemporary believer must regain in order to attain a sense of transcendence. "The ultimate message of the mystic about the nature of selfhood is that the self is *essentially* more than a mere self, that transcendence belongs to its nature as much as the act through which it is immanent to itself, and that a total failure on the mind's part to realize this transcendence reduces the self to *less* than itself."[192]

This transcendent selfhood is also akin to mysticism in demanding that any inward experience must have a further outward expression. "The total religious attitude requires outward expression in worship

---

[190] See e.g., Thomas Moore, *Care of the Soul: A Guide for Cultivating Depth and Sacredness in Everyday Life* (New York: Harper Collins, 1992); Mihaly Csikszentmihalyi, *The Evolving Self: A Psychology for the Third Millennium* (New York: Harper Collins, 1993), 207-251.

[191] See *TS*, 95-100.

[192] *TS*, 104.

and social behavior, as much as inward commitment."[193] The source of a sense of transcendence is inward, but it must be actualized in outward expression.

> The sources of modern man's faith lie in the individual and his conviction, not in the Church as social institution, and even less in a society determined by the Church. One might call such a faith private, but not if that term excludes very tangible public effects.[194]

Even if religion does not possess technical solutions to issues of justice and peace, for the believer, religion provides an inward motivation and inspiration to action. With the mystics of past generations, the modern believer must struggle against an all too exclusive emphasis on inwardness; (the Eastern Church found it easier to harmonize contemplation and action). "Being all too inclined, like our secular contemporaries, to reduce life, including spiritual life, to a soulless objectivity, we cannot but profit from the spiritual message of those who, exposed to similar temptations, vigorously asserted the primacy of the divine life in us."[195] Dupré argues that the idea of the common good must incorporate in-dividual rights *without* separating them from their social context.[196] The religious person today must turn inward to a personal inter-pretation of experience to recover a sense of transcendence, but, like the mystics of past generations, this is not an individualistic turn, for there is an essential outward move to action and an in-tegration of this renewed vision with one's culture.

---

[193] *OD*, 60. Also see Louis Dupré, "Openness and Closedness of the Religious Community," in *Miscellanea Albert Dondeyne*: *Godsdienstfilosofie*: *Philosophie de la religion*, Bibliotheca Ephemeridum Theologicarum Lovaniensium 35, ed. Jan Walgrave, Antoine Vergote, and Ben Willaert (Louvain: Leuven University Press, 1987²), 67-74.

[194] *OD*, 26.

[195] *DL*, 88-89.

[196] See Louis Dupré, "The Common Good and the Open Society," *Review of Politics* 55 (Fall 1993): 687-712.

## ii. Unity of experience and message

The danger always exists that the religious person will not reinterpret culture in light of his or her inward turn but live an individual existence devoid of cultural integration. This amounts to cultural suicide as epitomized by some fundamentalist movements which repudiate any need to incorporate their understanding of truth within the larger cultural context. Yet, even when one makes his or her own peace with culture from within and provides it with a new religious meaning that it has lost, there is still the possibility that this personal integration will be viewed only as an assemblage of independent, private worlds, each one as valid as another. Because modern culture has itself lost its basic unity, can the personal interpretation by the believer of his or her experience of transcendence do anything more than add to culture's multiform expression? In other words, if culture does not provide the ground for interpreting one's experience, is there any givenness on which to base one's personal interpretation of experience and conclude that it is of a transcendent dimension? Posed more specifically, to what extent are religious symbols mere human constructions and to what extent are they given?

The answer lies in the nature of revelation, particularly in the unity that exists between the original experience and the message. There is no priority given to one over the other in revelation. Though completely human in their experience, religious symbols are interpreted as totally given. To fully appreciate this, we must first acknowledge that simply "any state of mind that lifts a person beyond the unquestioning acceptance of existence"[197] is not necessarily a valid experience of transcendence. The inward turn of the believer cannot force the transcendent to disclose itself. Instead, there is a necessary revelation that is given.

[197] *TS*, 24.

"As self-manifestation of the divine, all religion must be revealed."[198] At the same time, the mind itself must be self-transcending in nature to receive the transcendent; that is, there is a transcending movement of the mind which urges it to listen for a transcendent message. The result is "a complex dialectic of active and passive religious attitudes."[199] In the dialectic of revelation there is a constant interplay between that which is revealed and the receiver of the revelation.

Of particular importance is the understanding that revelation is both a message and an experience. If the message is dismissed to a secondary level, then the primary position is extended to a multi-faceted experience that has the possibility of becoming anything; this is unacceptable to Dupré. His position is clearly articulated in his disagreement with Schillebeeckx.[200] It is not the intent of this project to investigate the complexities of the nuances between the two, but only to appreciate Dupré's position.[201] Dupré asserts the unity of revelation as a message and an experience in contrast to Schillebeeckx' proposal that "Christianity is not a message which has to be believed, but an experience of faith which becomes a message, and as an explicit message seeks to offer a new possibility of life-experience to others who hear it from within their own

---

[198] *OD*, 282.

[199] *OD*, 282.

[200] See Louis Dupré, "Experience and Interpretation. A Philosophical Reflection on Schillebeeckx' *Jesus and Christ*," *Theological Studies* 43 (March 1982): 30-51.

[201] It is interesting to note that the most recent response in the debate is offered by Schillebeeckx in the final volume of his trilogy. Unfortunately, here Schillebeeckx does not address the main argument. Though Dupré generally agrees with Schillebeeckx' brief resolution, it is not a solution to Dupré's main disagreement. Schillebeeckx avoids the actual issue of the unity of the revealed experience and message. See Edward Schillebeeckx, *Church: The Human Story of God*, trans. John Bowden (London: SCM Press; New York: Crossroad, 1990), 38. Dupré's reflections on *Church* were given in an interview by the author in Kortrijk on January 3, 1995.

experience."[202] Dupré does not accept this emphasis on experience for it unnecessarily and irreconcilably complicates the question: "How can a historical person [Jesus], living in a culturally different age, initiate a truly universal experience, especially at a time when most people have become fully estranged from the religious culture in which his message was delivered?"[203] (Schillebeeckx is aware of the complexities of the question.) One extreme answer would be to deny any definite authority to the historical text for our present experience. But this is not feasible when the focus of the experience is a historical person as it is in Christianity. On the other side, the believer's present experience cannot be the ultimate norm of what is accepted of the original expression, since this expression itself is the very basis of the believer's experience. The definitive aspects of the original expression must still be distinguished from its historical interpretation through obsolete models and concepts.

Dupré proposes that the answer lies in distinguishing different types of interpretation and associating revelation equally with experience and the third type of interpretation. First, there is a reflective type of interpretation which follows subsequent to an experience. Second, there is that type of interpretation which gives structure, emphasis, and meaning to the primary experience; experience still enjoys a priority, though now it is an ontological priority and not a temporal one. There is a third form of interpretation which is more fundamental and renders the experience possible. Because of its transcendent nature, revelation must provide together both the experience and its given possibility, i.e., its primary interpretative orientation. "Revelation is intrinsically, not secondarily, a universe

---

[202] Edward Schillebeeckx, *Interim Report on the Books* Jesus *and* Christ, trans. John Bowden (New York: Crossroad, 1981), 50.

[203] Dupré, "Experience and Interpretation," 31. For the answer to the question we will follow this text.

of discourse, divine expression, and hence message."[204] This message cannot be detached from the experience itself, and, rather than being a part of the process of expression as such, it directs that process by determining which cultural models will be accepted or rejected.

The nature of revelation, precisely in the unity between experience and message, provides the key to understanding to what extent religious symbols are merely human constructions and to what extent they are given. In a Christian context the religious symbolization of the revelation, though totally human in its form is nevertheless interpreted as totally given. The revelation is more than an experience. It is intimately united with the message. In turning inward the religious person must be open to the revelation of the transcendent, revealing both the experience and its divine expression. This does not deny that creativity is an essential component of revealed truth. On the one hand, all symbolic expression is human and as such subject to change. On the other hand, revelation encompasses both the experience and the message and the expression must remain authoritative. The two are compatible by recognizing "a development *within* the revealed (or authoritative) expression, supported by a creation of new symbols."[205] Religious symbols can expand beyond their original meanings as long as they develop within limits placed by revelation, "lest the original symbols become an empty facade behind which any meaning may develop."[206]

---

[204] Dupré, "Experience and Interpretation," 44.

[205] Louis Dupré, "The God of History," *Commonweal* 85 (February 10, 1967): 522.

[206] Louis Dupré, "The Religious Meaning of Secularity," in *Religion in Contemporary Thought*, ed. George McLean (Staten Island, NY: Alba House, 1973), 321. Dupré has many further insights into the nature of revelation, see especially *OD*, 278-332.

### iii. Negative theology and mysticism

Finally, present day atheism and the response of a selfward turn should be understood in light of the mystical tradition and negative theology. In the complete silence of secular culture regarding the transcendent, one encounters the same darkness and negative knowledge of God that is present in the religious tradition. As the mystics started their spiritual journey from within, so do modern believers, but not because believers today are disposed in the same manner as mystics of past ages. Instead, in the absence of cultural support there is no choice but to turn within. "The mystics start their spiritual journey from within, and that is the only place where the believer *must* begin, whether he wants to or not."[207] As the modern believer begins this selfward passage the same absence that exists outward is encountered within. It is only by recognizing one's own loss of the very idea of God that there is hope for recovering transcendence. "It is precisely in this deliberate confrontation with this inner silence of absence that I detect the true significance of the believer's current urge toward a spiritual life. For only after having confronted his atheism can the believer hope to restore the vitality of his religion."[208] In this negative encounter another dimension is discovered.

Just as the mystics of the past, the modern believer who embarks upon this quest cannot remain in pure negation. Without some positive affirmation, secular atheism will never be fully surpassed. The dichotomy between the finite and infinite is itself negated and the finite's complete dependence upon the infinite is affirmed. For the modern believer this is concretely manifested in a new perspective upon the world. Underneath ordinary reality the existence of another dimension is recognized. The contemplative finds at the

[207] SPIRITUAL, 25.
[208] SPIRITUAL, 25.

core of every creature an otherness that invites a response of acceptance instead of the more typical human interaction of control and dominance, success and dominance. This is neither an open minded secular humanism nor a new idea of God. It is merely a selfless approach to others and nature which provides a new perceptiveness for detecting transcendence.

Far from abandoning traditional religious models, this attitude is in harmony with them. Even though Christianity has been most widely exposed to the erosion of modern secularism, its outlook exemplifies viewing the world from the perspective of obedience to a higher calling, submission to a law that surpasses the person, and the search for the transcendent center of all selfhood. Before accepting the model as transcendent the believer must first discover it as viable in his or her own world. Even though much of the traditional language is preserved in the new attitude, Dupré does not consider this simply "a theological adjustment to different circumstances." Through the centuries theology's articulation of its vision of transcendence has been challenged, but the vision has not. However, in modern times "the very reality of the transcendent is at stake, not a specific conceptualization of it."[209] The possibility itself of a relation to the transcendent is attacked today.

Any attempt to recover transcendence has become an existential choice in modern times. Without outward support or a clearly defined experience of the sacred, one must turn inward to the darkness of a personal spiritual journey. Many mystics of the past have made this quest based on some desire, but now the modern seeker is required to do so because there is no other alternative. While the path is the same and the modern contemplative is a kindred spirit with the mystics of the past, it is a mistake to assume that the ancient masters and monasteries possess all the solutions

[209] SPIRITUAL, 30.

to the modern plight. "The doctrines, life-styles, and methods of a previous age were conceived within the reach of a direct experience of the sacred. This has for the most part ceased to exist."[210] Yet, the modern journey to recover transcendence must follow the one group of people who have achieved such an inward union with the transcendent — the mystics.

## 4. *Conclusion*

The future of religion rests upon the modern believer's ability to regain a sense of transcendence. With the very possibility of transcendence removed from the cultural outlook of modernity one logical solution is to attempt a return to past structures and a pretechnological way of life. But to turn back the clock and erase change is to deny one's culture. This does not provide hope for the future but an isolationism from the present by attempting a retreat to an irretrievable past. Another solution to regain a sense of transcendence is offered by secular approaches to theology and other disciplines. Through a variety of methods these advocate that transcendence is present in the secular view itself. However, the modern crisis runs deeper. The problem is not simply to accept the restructuring of traditional religious expressions and institutions, but to recover the transcendent dimension of life that secularity cannot provide.

By advocating an inward turn and a subsequent personal addition of a religious meaning to secular culture, Dupré's own solution accepts and moves beyond both the answers of a return to the past and secular theology. Both an inner decision and integration with society are needed, but without degenerating into individualism or assuming that culture still possesses its previous force.

[210] SPIRITUAL, 31.

Our project has come full circle insofar as the first chapter based the theological argument for symbol as a primary category of religious understanding upon the role of mysticism in religion. Now, in this last chapter we find that Dupré's resolution of the modern predicament of the loss of transcendence and resulting inability of the modern person to make religious symbols is founded upon the same avowal of mysticism. As with the great mystics, the modern believer must discover that "the creature in its inner reality points beyond itself."[211] This inner turn does not proclaim the modern view of the human subject as sole agent of meaning-giving, for otherwise there would be no openness to a transcendent dimension beyond the human.

Therefore, the cosmic, human, and transcendent elements of nature are once again united through the selfward turn. Instead of denying the principle of subjectivity that is a fact of the modern condition, Dupré reinterprets subjectivity as harmonious with a transcendent givenness that includes the creative subject. "The centrality of the subject in modern thought seems indeed essential and irreversible. But the principle of subjectivity excludes a comprehensive unity *only* if it reduces reality to objectivity."[212] The human subject retains its meaning-giving role, but not as the sole agent. A central position is secured for the self within a reality conceived as fundamentally, though not immediately, given. "Transcendence is not merely what lies beyond the world, but first and foremost what supports its givenness."[213] The human subject, the immanent world and transcendent being are united in an inseparable bond.

---

[211] Louis Dupré, "Christian Spirituality Confronts the Modern World," *Communio: International Catholic Review* 12 (Fall 1985): 342.

[212] *MC*, 56. Emphasis added.

[213] *PM*, 251.

Through this inward turn transcendence is safeguarded for the personal religious experience. However, this should not be interpreted as an answer to the broader cultural question of a sense of transcendence. While we have acknowledged a relationship between metaphysics and religion specifically regarding the question of transcendence, a primary difference between the possibility of metaphysics and the effectiveness of religious symbols must be recognized. A personal notion of transcendence can be recovered through the inward turn, however the wider cultural understanding cannot. True, the believer must reintegrate restored transcendence with his or her own culture. But on the broader philosophical level, there is still the need for a principle of transcendence that is accepted as standing above culture and as uniting culture. "The possibility of metaphysics ... rests on the presence of a genuine transcendence as an essential factor operative within culture itself."[214] Precisely in this problematic the question of a metaphysics of culture parts company with our project. But we must respect the dilemma, for if culture still possessed its integrating force there would be no need to search for transcendence through the inward self, because culture would still provide this transcendence. Today, culture remains disunited without a metaphysical synthesis but the individual can retain a personal notion of transcendence.

The continuation of the cultural search for transcendence does not deny that the religious community on a smaller level provides a group identity. Starting first from selfhood the idealized experience is given concrete expression and form. "It would be incorrect to assume that the community loses its role in the highly personal spiritual religion of the present, for as soon as the believer adopts a model such as Christ ... he joins a community, becomes a member of a group of like-minded individuals in the present."[215]

[214] *MC*, 57.
[215] SPIRITUAL, 30.

The inward model which the believer holds ceases to be a mere ideal as the link with a religious community — through sacraments and an extensive system of symbols — transforms it into a present reality.

Dupré's final assessment of the religious situation of the modern world offers comfort as well as a stern warning:

> The search for a deeper spiritual life is, in fact, more than a passing phenomenon on today's religious scene; it is a movement for religious survival. For without the support of a sustained personal decision, a religion that remains unassisted by the surrounding culture and is constantly under attack in the believer's own heart is doomed to die.[216]

The modern inability to make religious symbols is a consequence of the cultural phenomenon of the loss of a sense of transcendence. However, there is hope. To the believer, faith remains the all-integrating force of life and religious symbols retain the power of their expression, although not exactly as they had in the past. Now, symbols possess meaning from a deeper personal interiorization and a more intimate unity of immanence and transcendence — the knowledge and experience of which have perhaps only been equalled by the masters of mysticism.

[216] SPIRITUAL, 31.

# THE TAPESTRY
# OF DUPRÉ'S THOUGHT

The tapestry of Dupré's depiction of religious symbols is woven together with the resplendent threads of transcendence, culture, self and mysticism. To view symbols of transcendence as the primary expression of religious understanding is to appreciate the role of symbol in metaphysics, in every aspect of religion, and as part of the very fabric of culture. If the task of this book was to explicate and scrutinize the tools of the weaver's craft, we now have the pleasure of admiring the tapestry as a whole — in its beauty as a work of art.

The tapestry depicts symbols of transcendence as the primary expression of all religious understanding. Its design is inspired by religion appreciated as a dialectical and symbolical perception of absolute reality. As dialectical, religion is neither purely objective nor purely subjective. There is no object in and of itself that is religious nor is it simply a state of consciousness. It is a dynamic association of the mind to reality that changes its emphasis and function according to a variety of cultural and personal factors. Religion is also dialectical insofar as it expresses the relationship between immanent and transcendent dimensions. Given the distance between the two, an opposition is always present in the most intimate union between creator and created. Transformed into an awareness of God, the religious affirmation of transcendence demands a commitment. For the religious believer, this commitment in faith raises religion beyond simply being *a* particular aspect of

life to providing *the* meaning-giving factor of human existence —
even possibly in the modern world. However, it is an understatement
to say that it was easier for the Christians of the Middle Ages to
accept the power of religion in their lives. Religion was in fact *the*
integrating force of life. Operative as the seam which held the very
fabric of culture together it shaped and directed every aspect of existence. Its failure to maintain its position of cultural prominence was
caused by the two main factors which mark the passage to modernity: the loss of a sense of transcendence and the elevation of the
human subject to the role of sole agent of meaning and value giving.

The story which the tapestry portrays is interpreted differently
through the ages. In the shift from the premodern to the modern,
religion becomes one field of study among others, complete with
its own subject and method of investigation. The ancient conception
of the all encompassing principle of nature, complete with transcendent, cosmic, and human elements is ripped apart. Transcendence
is relegated to a sphere of existence outside of the realm of nature.
With nature reduced to its cosmic and human components, the
human subject becomes the sole master of the world, objectifying
everything in its grasp — which is the world in its entirety. Yet, in
the process of objectifying reality, the human subject falls victim
to its own plan of success. Trapped in a world of its own making,
the subject itself becomes objectified. Refusing to acknowledge
the very dimension that once was its source and meaning of life,
the subject is diminished to a mere function of the process it hailed
as its freedom and salvation. The loud proclamations of its sover-
eignty only serve to strengthen the chains that bind it to its own
parsimonious plans and self-destructive designs. Thus, nature is reduced to its cosmic element and, in placing itself over and
against nature, the human subject crumbles into meaninglessness.
This is the plight of the contemporary world, best described as
'late modernity'.

However, all is not lost. The tapestry is woven with the warp thread of transcendence. As the lengthwise warp threads of a tapestry are the necessary substructure for weaving and are completely concealed by the more numerous weft threads, so too, while unseen, transcendence is the very foundation for religious symbols and the unifying force of culture. Where the culture once provided a sense of the transcendent dimension, now the individual person must seek to regain the transcendence that culture now denies — or rather completely disregards, for the modern problematic is not the loss of belief in God but the loss of the very *possibility* of such a belief. What is at stake is not how we envision God, but if God can be envisioned at all. As the mystics of past generations chose to turn inward to unite with God, now modern believers have no choice but to embrace a similar spiritual turn inward as they find themselves in a desert imposed by culture: the desert of modern atheism which denies the very possibility of transcendence. Still, the process of restoring transcendence to its original luster cannot deny one's current culture. Just as the restoration of an ancient tapestry requires the assistance of modern technology, so too the personal attempt to recover a sense of transcendence cannot expect to deny history and return to a more amenable time. Isolationism is not a solution. Having regained a personal sense of transcendence, one must turn outward to make some type of an integration with one's culture, otherwise all that is gained is a staunch fundamentalism closed in upon itself.

Neither can this selfward turn be individualistic. Individualism is only one branch of the wider notion of personhood. An inner turn is not accomplished by the objective pole of personhood which is individuality, but by the subjective inner life of self. Here in the silence of one's self-immanence, recollection reveals self-transcendence which makes the rediscovery of the transcendent dimension possible. This personal reinterpretation of transcendence is not an independent venture, for the nature of revelation provides a corrective and unifying force. Beyond self-achievement, the religious person today must strive to serve all peoples. This is in agreement with the classical understanding of the common good which incorporates individual rights without separating them from their social context. Of even greater religious significance, this also follows in the course laid out by spiritual masters of past generations who endeavored, with varying degrees of success, to harmonize contemplation and action.

The weft threads of mysticism, self and culture which are united and stabilized by the warps of transcendence, far from obscuring the symbolic quality of the religious attitude, promote and provide clarity to it. Mysticism can speak only symbolically, and since a mystical impulse is a part of the core of religion, religion itself remains symbolic it is expression, regardless of how literally it may state its dogmas. The human self as an embodied spirit comprehends its form and all meaningful form symbolically. A central symbolic expression of the self is language, and all advanced religious symbols are linguistic or based upon language. Culture is comprised of the symbols that direct and preserve the life of a society. Through symbols the permanent and universal is perceived in the transient and particular, allowing for the possibility of culture. Most importantly, its reference to a transcendent terminus makes a symbol religious. Neither reference to the sacred nor to God, for example, possess the universality of meaning and significance for religious understanding enjoyed by the referent of transcendence. Symbols are *the* primary religious expression insofar as they indicate transcendence — the unique referent which allows a symbol to be a *religious* symbol. Since they reach beyond empirical verification, symbols of the transcendent require language that can express what is paradoxical. The basic paradox is that God's immanence in everything is as essential as God's transcendence.

This interplay between creature and creator is possible as well as necessary given the dialectical nature of religion.

Therefore, as all thought begins from the fullness of language as symbolic, all religious expression must be understood symbolically, and the unique feature which distinguishes religious symbols from all other symbols is their transcendent referent. With the loss of transcendence in modernity, the possibility of truly meaningful religious symbols is impeded. The prospect for recovering a sense of transcendence in modernity rests upon a personal decision for an inward life. This answer to the reunification of the transcendent, human, and cosmic elements of nature does not deny the modern appreciation of the centrality of the human subject. Instead of attempting the near impossibility of reversing this understanding, we need only to safeguard against the subject's complete reduction of reality to an object and its concurrent claim as *ultimate* principle of meaning and value. When a transcendent givenness is accepted as embracing the creative subject — and this is not in principle excluded by the notion of a meaning-giving subject — then an effective synthesis can be achieved. Religious people today have personally attained this goal, but Western culture still searches for a principle of transcendence that stands above it as a unifying force.

The art of tapestry making in the West has traditionally combined the artistic talents of painters or designers with those of the weaver. Aside from those instances in the Renaissance when the weaver was considered merely the imitator who reproduced the painter's creation in cloth, the skills of painter and weaver unite in a cooperative and complimentary enterprise, as witnessed by the fine art of tapestry making in Belgium and France. In a similar fashion Dupré combines the disciplines of theology and philosophy. He considers himself a philosopher who critically reflects upon religion. As a philosopher, his is the skill of the weaver who reflects upon the preparatory drawing of the cartoon not as something to be copied but as a tool open to a variety of interpretations. Dupré reflects upon the works of anthropologists, psychologists, and theologians, as well as philosophers from a number of traditions. While maintaining a proper philosophical distance, he also admits a personal exposure to the religious experience upon which he reflects. Through the centuries some weavers have expressed their talents completely from within the painter's design, others have taken a greater distance and produced extremely wide interpretations, and still others have mediated between the two approaches. Dupré is a weaver of the third type. He is not precisely a theologian who reflects upon matters of faith from within his own tradition nor is he a philosopher of religion who attempts to completely disassociate himself personally from religious experience. He is more of a philosophical theologian deliberating philosophically upon fundamental religious questions while directing his argument informed from a particular tradition.

Dupré's basic approach is grounded in a phenomenological methodology which identifies the meaning of the religious act in the act itself. Experience is therefore promoted as primary, though in and of itself experience cannot manifest its own foundation. Faith is also necessary to interpret the experience in order for the transcendent referent, which is beyond empirical experience, to be understood. Dupré's technique of investigation is also broad enough to move outside a phenomenological approach, a step which he finds necessary in order to reach the ontological foundation of religious experience. In specifically examining Schleiermacher's conception of religion, Dupré assesses it as incomplete and finds a more suitable expression in Hegel's perception of religion as representation. His general appreciation of symbol receives its philosophical bases from the works of Cassirer, Hegel and Langer. This provides him with a firm foundation on which to develop his own evaluation of symbol. In addition to other authors, he has further recourse to the works of von Balthasar on aesthetics and Kierkegaard on the paradoxical nature of religious language.

This is the tapestry of the thought of Louis Dupré: the tapestry of symbols of transcendence as the primary expression of religious understanding. Far from being a functional blanket hung on the wall to keep a balanced temperature through the fluctuation of seasons, it is a dynamic artistic design that blows with the winds of change, because it recognizes this change not simply as the passage of time, but as the creation of a new sense of being.

# BIBLIOGRAPHY OF LOUIS DUPRÉ

A. BOOKS AND ARTICLES BY LOUIS DUPRÉ
Complete List to June 1997    IN CHRONOLOGICAL ORDER

(In a given year, books appear first, then essays in collections, followed by articles. Reprinted works are cross referenced to the original citation. Review articles are cross referenced to section B.)

## 1952-1960

A1.  "Godsdienst en historische vooruitgang." *Studia Catholica* 27 (March 1952): 95-99.

A2.  "Naar de oorsprong van Hegel's staatsbegrip." *Tijdschrift voor Philosophie* 14 (December 1952): 627-673.

A3.  *Het vertrekpunt der marxistische wijsbegeerte: De kritiek op Hegels staatsrecht.* Philosophische Bibliotheek. Antwerp: Standaard-Boekhandel, 1954.
     (This doctoral dissertation accepted at the Katholieke Universiteit te Leuven, Higher Institute for Philosophy in 1952 was published with the aid of the Belgian national *Foundation Universitaire* in 1954 and was awarded the biennial J. M. Huyghe Prize in 1956.)

A4.  "S. Kierkegaard: Schets van zijn innerlijke ontwikkeling." *Streven* 9 (December 1955): 217-225.

A5.  "La dialectique de l'acte de foi chez Soeren Kierkegaard." *Revue Philosophique de Louvain* 54 (August 1956): 418-455.

A6.  "Nieuwe Duitse Kierkegaardliteratuur." *Bijdragen* 18 (1957): 290-298. [Review Article].   → see B6.

282

A7.   *Kierkegaards theologie of de dialectiek van het christen-worden.*
      Theologische Bibliotheek. Utrecht: Het Spectrum; Antwerp:
      N. V. Standaard-Boekhandel, 1958.
  a.   ▶Also appears in English as *Kierkegaard As Theologian: The Dialectic
       of Christian Existence.* New York: Sheed & Ward, 1963; reprint,
       London: Sheed & Ward, 1964.   → see A10.


## 1961-1963

A8.   "Philosophy's Uses and Abuses." *Commonweal* 75 (October 6,
      1961): 36-38.
  a.   ▶Also appears in *Georgetown* 2 (1966): 2.   → see A34.

A9.   "The Challenge of Marxism." *Cross Currents* 12 (Summer 1962):
      327-335.

A10.  *Kierkegaard As Theologian: The Dialectic of Christian Existence.*
      New York: Sheed & Ward, 1963; reprint, London: Sheed &
      Ward, 1964.   → see A7.a.

A11.  "Husserl's Notion of Truth—Via Media Between Idealism and
      Realism?" In *Teaching Thomism Today.* The Proceedings of
      the Workshop on Teaching Thomism Today conducted at The
      Catholic University of America, 1962. Edited by George
      McLean. Washington, D.C.: The Catholic University of America
      Press, 1963, pp. 150-182.
  a.   ▶Pp. 150-161 also appear with slight modifications as "The Concept
       of Truth in Husserl's Logical Investigations." *Philosophy and
       Phenomenological Research* 24 (March 1964): 345-354.   → see
       A17.
  b.   ▶A brief summary is found on p. 371.   → see A12.

A12.  "Phenomenology." In *Teaching Thomism Today.* The Proceed-
      ings of the Workshop on Teaching Thomism Today con-
      ducted at The Catholic University of America, 1962. Edited
      by George McLean. Washington, D.C.: The Catholic Univer-
      sity of America Press, 1963, p. 371.   → see A11.b.

A13. "The Philosophical Stages of Man's Self-Discovery." *Proceedings of the American Catholic Philosophical Association* 37 (April 1963): 211-224.
  a. ▶Also appears as "The Philosophical Stages of Self-Discovery." *Thought* 39 (September 1964): 411- 428.  → see A20.
  b. ▶Also appears in *New Dynamics in Ethical Thinking*. Vol. 1. Edited by George McLean. Lancaster, PA: Concorde, 1974, pp. 17-30. → see A97.

A14. "The Constitution of the Self in Kierkegaard's Philosophy." *International Philosophical Quarterly* 3 (December 1963): 506-526.
  a. ▶Also appears with modifications as "Kierkegaard on Man's Encounter with the Transcendent." In *Religion in Contemporary Thought*. Edited by George McLean. Staten Island, NY: Alba House, 1973, pp. 101-115.  → see A87.

## 1964

A15. *Contraception and Catholics: A New Appraisal*. Baltimore: Helicon Press, 1964.
  a. ▶Also appears in Spanish as *Los Catholicos y la Anticoncepcion*. Buenos Aires: Editorial Paidos, 1966.  → see A31.
  → see A16.a.  → see A19.a.

A16. "Toward a Re-examination of the Catholic Position on Birth Control." *Cross Currents* 14 (Winter 1964): 63-85.
  a. ▶Also appears with slight modifications in *Contraception and Catholics*. Baltimore: Helicon Press, 1964, pp. 29-32, 35-37, 39-63, 73-87. → see A15.

A17. "The Concept of Truth in Husserl's Logical Investigations." *Philosophy and Phenomenological Research* 24 (March 1964): 345-354.  → see A11.a.

A18. "Toward a Revaluation of Schleiermacher's Philosophy of Religion." *The Journal of Religion* 44 (April 1964): 97-112.
  a. ▶Also appears as Chapter 1 of *A Dubious Heritage*. New York: Paulist Press, 1977, pp. 9-29 and as part of the Introduction, pp. 1-2.  → see A127.

A19.   "From Augustine to Janssens." *Commonweal* 80 (June 5, 1964): 336-342.
  a.   ▶Also appears with modifications in *Contraception and Catholics*. Baltimore: Helicon Press, 1964, pp. 13, 63-70.  → see A15.

A20.   "The Philosophical Stages of Self-Discovery." *Thought* 39 (September 1964): 411- 428.  → see A13.a.

A21.   "Philosophy of Religion and Revelation: Autonomous Reflection vs. Theophany." *International Philosophical Quarterly* 4 (December 1964): 499-513.
  a.   ▶Also appears in *Insight* 3 (Winter 1965): 1-8.  → see A29.
  b.   ▶Pp. 503-506 also appear with slight modifications as *The Other Dimension*. New York: Doubleday, 1972, pp. 106-110.  → see A77.
  c.   ▶Pp. 501-503 also appear with modifications in *A Dubious Heritage*. New York: Paulist Press, 1977, pp. 76-78.  → see A127.
  d.   ▶Compare this with "Phenomenology of Religion: Limits and Possibilities." *American Catholic Philosophical Quarterly* 66 (Spring 1992): 175-188.  → see A273.a.

## 1965

A22.   "Some Comments on Doctrinal Renewal." In *The Problem of Population*. Vol. 3, *Educational Considerations*. Notre Dame, IN: University of Notre Dame Press, 1965, pp. 136-144.
  a.   ▶Also appears as "Philosophical Analysis of the Catholic Moral Problem of Contraception." *Insight* 6 (Fall 1967): 57-59.  → see A46.

A23.   "Blondel, Maurice." In *The Catholic Encyclopedia for School and Home*. Vol. 1. New York: McGraw-Hill, 1965, pp. 734-735.

A24.   "Camus, Albert." In *The Catholic Encyclopedia for School and Home*. Vol. 2. New York: McGraw-Hill, 1965, pp. 211-212.

A25.   "Kierkegaard, Soren." In *The Catholic Encyclopedia for School and Home*. Vol. 6. New York: McGraw-Hill, 1965, pp. 146-148.

A26.  "Positivism." In *The Catholic Encyclopedia for School and Home*. Vol. 8. New York: McGraw-Hill, 1965, pp. 601-604.

A27.  "Natural Law and Birth Control." *Philosophy Today* 9 (Summer 1965): 94-100.
  a.  ►Compare this with "Natural Law and Contraception." *Proceedings of the American Catholic Philosophical Association* 39 (1965): 166-170.  → see A28.a.

A28.  "Natural Law and Contraception." *Proceedings of the American Catholic Philosophical Association* 39 (1965): 166-170.
  a.  ►Compare this with "Natural Law and Birth Control." *Philosophy Today* 9 (Summer 1965): 94-100.  → see A27.a.

A29.  "Philosophy of Religion and Revelation: Autonomous Reflection vs. Theophany." *Insight* 3 (Winter 1965): 1-8.  → see A21.a.

## 1966

A30.  *The Philosophical Foundations of Marxism*. New York: Harcourt, Brace & World, 1966.
  a.  ►Also appears in Dutch as *De filosofische grondslagen van het marxisme*. Filosofie en Kultuur 11. Translated by Jan De Piere. Antwerp: De Nederlandsche Boekhandel; Bilthoven: H. Nelissen, 1970.  → see A64.
  b.  ►Also appears in Korean as *Mark-jui-eui- chol-hak-jok ki-cho*. N. p., 1986.  → see A200.

A31.  *Los Catholicos y la Anticoncepcion*. Buenos Aires: Editorial Paidos, 1966.  → see A15.a.

A32.  Mann, Jesse and Gerald Kreyche, general eds. Francis Eterovich, Louis Dupré, et al., contributing eds. *Approaches to Morality: Readings in Ethics from Classical Philosophy to Existentialism*. New York: Harcourt, Brace & World, 1966.

A33.  "Reflections on Blondel's Religious Philosophy." *The New Scholasticism* 40 (January 1966): 3-22.

A34.   "Philosophy's Uses and Abuses." *Georgetown* 2 (1966): 2.
       → see A8.a.

A35.   "New Publications in Phenomenology." *The New Scholasticism*
       40 (April 1966): 199- 216. [Review Article].   → see B9.

A36.   "The Church and Birth Control." *Nazareth Magazine* 1 (1966):
       9-14.

## 1967

A37.   "Comment." On George Kline's "Some Critical Comments on
       Marx's Philosophy." In *Marx and the Western World*. Edited
       by Nicholas Lobkowicz. Notre Dame, IN: University of Notre
       Dame Press, 1967, pp. 432-435.

A38.   and Winfield Best. "Birth Control." In *The Encyclopœdia Britan-
       nica*. Vol. 3. Chicago: William Benton, 1968[14], pp. 704-711.

A39.   "Feuerbach, Ludwig Andreas." In *The New Catholic Encyclope-
       dia*. Vol. 5. New York: McGraw-Hill, 1967, pp. 904-905.

A40.   "Hegelianism and Neo-Hegelianism." In *The New Catholic En-
       cyclopedia*. Vol. 6. New York: McGraw-Hill, 1967, pp. 990-
       993.

A41.   "Kierkegaard, Søren Aabye." In *The New Catholic Encyclopedia*.
       Vol. 8. New York: McGraw-Hill, 1967, pp. 174-176.

A42.   "The Problem of a Philosophy of Christianity: A New Study on
       Henry Duméry." *The Modern Schoolman* 44 (January 1967):
       161-168. [Review Article].   → see B10.

A43.   "The God of History." *Commonweal* 85 (February 10, 1967):
       516-522.
   a.  ►Also appears in *God, Jesus, and Spirit*. Edited by Daniel Callahan.
       London: Geoffrey Chapman, 1969, pp. 24-37.   → see A56.

A44. "How Indissoluble is a Catholic Marriage?" *National Catholic Reporter* 3 (March 8, 1967): 5.
  a. ►Also appears in Dutch as "Hoe onontbindbaar is het katholiek huwelijk?" *De Maand* (April 1969): 174-181. → see A61.

A45. "Situation Ethics and Objective Morality." *Theological Studies* 28 (June 1967): 245- 257; notes on p. 336.
  a. ►Also appears in *Christian Witness in the Secular City*. Edited by Everett Morgan. Chicago: Loyola University Press, 1970, pp. 220-232. → see A68.
  b. ►Also appears in *Situationism and the New Morality*. Contemporary Problems in Philosophy. Edited by Robert Cunningham. New York: Appleton-Century-Crofts, 1970, pp. 90-102. → see A69.

A46. "Philosophical Analysis of the Catholic Moral Problem of Contraception." *Insight* 6 (Fall 1967): 57-59. → see A22.a.

**1968**

A47. ed. and intro. *Faith and Reflection*, by Henry Duméry. Translated by Stephen McNiernery and M. Benedict Murphy. New York: Herder & Herder, 1968.
→ see A71.a.

A48. "The Existentialist Connections of Situation Ethics." In *The Future of Ethics and Moral Theology*. Chicago: Argus Communications Co., 1968, pp. 106-113.

A49. "The Indissolubility of Christian Marriage and the Common Good." In *The Bond of Marriage: An Ecumenical and Interdisciplinary Study*. Edited by William Bassett. Notre Dame, IN: University of Notre Dame Press, 1968, pp. 181-199. ["Comment and Discussion," pp. 200-204]. → see A55.a.

A50. "Husserl's Thought on God and Faith." *Philosophy and Phenomenological Research* 29 (1968): 201-215.
  a. ►Pp. 203-214 also appear with slight modifications in *A Dubious Heritage*. New York: Paulist Press, 1977, pp. 80-91. → see A127.

A51. "Religion in a Secular World." *Christianity and Crisis* 28 (April 15, 1968): 73-77.

  a. ►Also appears in Dutch as "Religieus geloof in een seculiere wereld." *Streven* 22 (January 1969): 356- 362. → see A60.

  b. ►Pp. 73-74 also appear as "Religion in a Secular World." In *Human Values in a Secular World.* Edited by Robert Apostol. New York: Humanities Press, 1970, pp. 11-12. → see A67.a.

A52. "Meditations on Secular Theology." *The Christian Century* 85 (November 20, 1968): 1469-1472.

  a. ►Also appears with modifications as "The Problem of Divine Transcendence in Secular Theology." In *The Spirit and Power of Christian Secularity.* Edited by Albert Schlitzer. Notre Dame, IN: University of Notre Dame Press, 1969, pp. 100-108. → see A59.

A53. "Marx and Religion: An Impossible Marriage." *Commonweal* 88 (April 26, 1968): 171-176.

  a. ►Also appears as "Can a Marxist Be a Christian?" In *New Theology, No. 6.* Edited by Martin Marty and Dean Peerman. New York: Macmillan, 1969, pp. 151-164. → see A58.

  b. ►Also appears with slight modifications as "Marxism and Religion." In *Religion in Contemporary Thought.* Edited by George McLean. Staten Island, NY: Alba House, 1973, pp. 87-100. → see A86.

A54. "Secular Man and His Religion." *Proceedings of the American Catholic Philosophical Association* 42 (1968): 78-92. → see C4.

  a. ►Pp. 85-88, 90-91 also appear as "Religion in a Secular World." In *Human Values in a Secular World.* Edited by Robert Apostol. New York: Humanities Press, 1970, pp. 13-17. → see A67.b.

  b. ►Pp. 78-83 also appear with modifications as *The Other Dimension.* New York: Doubleday, 1972, pp. 1-2, 13-20. → see A77.

  c. ►Compare this with "Idées sur la formation du sacré et sa dégéneration." In *Le sacré: Études et recherches.* Actes du XIVᵉ Colloque Organisé par le Centre International d'Études Humanistes et l'Institut d'Études Philosophiques de Rome. Edited by Enrico Castelli. Paris: Aubier, 1974, pp. 369-376. → see A95.a.

A55.   "Till Death Do Us Part?" *America* 118 (February 17, 1968): 224-228.
  a.   ▶Also appears as "The Indissolubility of Christian Marriage and the Common Good." In *The Bond of Marriage: An Ecumenical and Interdisciplinary Study*. Edited by William Bassett. Notre Dame, IN: University of Notre Dame Press, 1968, pp. 181-199. ["Comment and Discussion," pp. 200-204].   → see A49.

## 1969

A56.   "The God of History." In *God, Jesus, and Spirit*. Edited by Daniel Callahan. London: Geoffrey Chapman, 1969, pp. 25-37.   → see A43.a.

A57.   "Catholics and Birth Control After *Humanae Vitae*." In *Exploding Humanity*. Edited by Henry Regier and Bruce Falls. Toronto: Anansi, 1969, pp. 57-64.

A58.   "Can a Marxist Be a Christian?" In *New Theology, No. 6*. Edited by Martin Marty and Dean Peerman. New York: Macmillan, 1969, pp. 151-164.   → see A53.a.

A59.   "The Problem of Divine Transcendence in Secular Theology." In *The Spirit and Power of Christian Secularity*. Edited by Albert Schlitzer. Notre Dame, IN: University of Notre Dame Press, 1969, pp. 100-112. ["Discussion," by van der Marck, Dupré, Sullivan, Caponigri, et al., pp. 113-122].   → see A52.a.
  a.   ▶Compare this with "The Religious Meaning of Secularity." In *Religion in Contemporary Thought*. Edited by George McLean. Staten Island, NY: Alba House, 1973, pp. 311-322.   → see A88.a.

A60.   "Religieus geloof in een seculiere wereld." *Streven* 22 (January 1969): 356-362.   → see A51.a.

A61.   "Hoe onontbindbaar is het katholiek huwelijk?" *De Maand* (April 1969): 174-181.   → see A44.a.

A62.   "Themes in Contemporary Philosophy of Religion." *The New Scholasticism* 43 (Fall 1969): 577-601. [Review Article]. → see B19.

A63.   "Hegel's Concept of Alienation and Marx's Critique." Abstract of Papers to be Read. *The Journal of Philosophy* 66 (November 6, 1969): 778-779.   → see A79.a.


## 1970

A64.   *De filosofische grondslagen van het marxisme*. Filosofie en Kultuur 11. Translated by Jan De Piere. Antwerp: De Nederlandsche Boekhandel; Bilthoven: H. Nelissen, 1970.   → see A30.a.

A65.   "Aesthetic Perception and Its Relation to Ordinary Perception." In *Aisthesis and Aesthetics*. The Fourth Lexington Conference on Pure and Applied Phenomenology 1967. Edited by Erwin Straus and Richard Griffith. Pittsburgh: Duquesne University Press; Louvain: Nauwelaerts, 1970, pp. 171-177.

A66.   "Where are We Going Together?" In *The Emerging Woman*. Edited by Martha Stuart and William Liu. Boston: Atlantic Little Brown, 1970, pp. 305-315.

A67.   "Religion in a Secular World." In *Human Values in a Secular World*. Edited by Robert Apostol. New York: Humanities Press, 1970, pp. 11-19.
   a.   ►Pp. 11-12 also appear as "Religion in a Secular World." *Christianity and Crisis* 28 (April 15, 1968): 73-74.   → see A51.b.
   b.   ►Pp. 13-17 are from "Secular Man and His Religion." *Proceedings of the American Catholic Philosophical Association* 42 (1968): 85-88, 90-91.   → see A54.a.
   (Pp. 18-19 are notes.)

A68.   "Situation Ethics and Objective Morality." In *Christian Witness in the Secular City*. Edited by Everett Morgan. Chicago: Loyola University Press, 1970, pp. 220-232.   → see A45.a.

A69. "Situation Ethics and Objective Morality." In *Situationism and the New Morality*. Contemporary Problems in Philosophy. Edited by Robert Cunningham. New York: Appleton-Century-Crofts, 1970, pp. 90-102. → see A45.b.

A70. "Metaphysics and Religious Faith." In *The Future of Metaphysics*. Edited by Robert Wood. Chicago: Quadrangle Books, 1970, pp. 263-273.
a. ►Also appears in *The Other Dimension*. New York: Doubleday, 1972, pp. 112-113; 130-131; 138-147. → see A77.

A71. "Autonomy of Man and Religious Dependence in the Philosophy of Henry Duméry." In *Evolution in Perspective: Commentaries in Honor of Pierre Lecomte de Noüy*. Edited by George Shuster and Ralph Thorson. (Includes papers and comments read during a conference held at Notre Dame University on October 1967.) Notre Dame, IN: University of Notre Dame Press, 1970, pp. 161-169. [Commentary by T. Langan, pp. 170-171].
a. ►Pp. 163-169 also appear in *Faith and Reflection*. New York: Herder & Herder, 1969, pp. xxvi- xxxiii. → see A47.

## 1971

A72. "Hope and Transcendence." In *The God Experience: Essays in Hope*. The Cardinal Bea Lectures 2. Edited by Joseph Whelan. New York: Newman Press, 1971, pp. 217-225.

A73. "De krisis in de universiteit, krisis van onze beschaving." *Onze Alma Mater* [Louvain] 25 (May 1971): 75-82.

A74. "The Life and Death of Religious Symbols." *The St. Luke's Journal of Theology* 14 (May 1971): 3-9.

A75. and John Brough. "Recent Books in Phenomenology." *The New Scholasticism* 45 (Winter 1971): 147-156. [Review Article]. → see B23.

A76.   "Philosophy and the Religious Perspective of Life." Presidential
       Address. *Proceedings of the American Catholic Philosophical
       Association* 45 (1971): 1-8.


## 1972

A77.   *The Other Dimension: A Search for the Meaning of Religious
       Attitudes.* New York: Doubleday, 1972.
   a.   ▶Also appears abridged in French as *L'autre dimension: Essai de philo-
        sophie de la religion.* Cogitatio fidei 90. Translated by Marcelle
        Jossua. Paris: Cerf, 1977.   → see A128.
   b.   ▶Also appears abridged as *The Other Dimension: A Search for the
        Meaning of Religious Attitudes.* New York: Seabury Press, 1979.
        → see A139.
   c.   ▶Also appears in Chinese as *Jen ti tsung chiao hsiang tu.* Translated by
        Fu Pêi-jung. N. p., 1986.   → see A201.
   d.   ▶Also appears in Polish as *Inny Wymiar.* Translated by Sabina Lewan-
        dowska. Cracow: Znak, 1991.   → see A259.
   e.   ▶Also appears in partial, revised Dutch edition as *De symboliek van het
        heilige.* Translated by Guido Vanheeswijck. Introduction by Jacques
        De Visscher. Kampen: Kok Agora; Kapellen: DNB/Pelckmans, 1991.
        → see A260.
   f.   ▶Also appears in Korean as *Chong-kye-ae-suh-ui Sang-jing-kwa Shin-hwa.*
        N. p., 1995.   → see A290.
       → see   A21.b.   → see  A54.b.   → see  A70.a.   → see  A95.b.   → see
       A110.d.   → see  A163.a.   → see  A164.a.   → see  A178.b.   →
       see A197.d.   → see A204.a.   → see A227.a.


A78.   Preface to *Religion and Human Autonomy: Henry Duméry's
       Philosophy of Christianity,* by René De Brabander. The Hague:
       Martinus Nijhoff, 1972, pp. vii-ix.


A79.   "Hegel's Concept of Alienation and Marx's Reinterpretation of
       it." *Hegel-Studien* 7 (1972): 217-236.
   a.   ▶Also appears as "Hegel's Concept of Alienation and Marx's Critique."
        Abstract of Papers to be Read. *The Journal of Philosophy* 66
        (November 6, 1969): 778-779.   → see A63.

A80. "Reflections on a Catholic/Humanist Dialogue." *America* 126 (June 24, 1972): 653- 654.
a. ►Also appears in *The Humanist* 32 (July 1972): 36-40. → see A81.

A81. "Reflections on a Catholic/Humanist Dialogue." *The Humanist* 32 (July 1972): 36-40. → see A80.a.

A82. "Dialectical Philosophy Before and After Marx." *The New Scholasticism* 46 (Autumn 1972): 488-511. [Review Article]. → see B29.

A83. "The Cosmological Argument After Kant." *International Journal for Philosophy of Religion* 3 (Fall 1972): 131-145.

**1973**

A84. "Religion as Representation." In *The Legacy of Hegel*. Proceedings of the Marquette Hegel Symposium 1970. Edited by J. O'Malley, K. Algozin, H. Kainz, and L. Rice. The Hague: Martinus Nijhoff, 1973, pp. 137-143.
a. ►Also appears in *A Dubious Heritage*. New York: Paulist Press, 1977, pp. 56-63. → see A127.

A85. "A Critique of All Teleological Arguments for the Existence of God." In *Zetesis: album amicorum door vrienden en collega's aangeboden aan Prof. Dr. É. de Strycker*. Edited by T. Lefevre, G. Sanders, G. J. de Vries, et al. Antwerp: De Nederlandsche Boekhandel, 1973, pp. 322-331.
a. ►Also appears with modifications as "The Teleological Argument." In *The Challenge of Religion: Contemporary Readings in Philosophy of Religion*. Edited by Frederick Ferré, Joseph Kockelmans, and John Smith. New York: Seabury Press, 1982, pp. 128-138. → see A162.

A86. "Marxism and Religion." In *Religion in Contemporary Thought*. Edited by George McLean. Staten Island, NY: Alba House, 1973, pp. 87-100. → see A53.b.

A87.  "Kierkegaard on Man's Encounter with the Transcendent."
      In *Religion in Contemporary Thought*. Edited by George
      McLean. Staten Island, NY: Alba House, 1973, pp. 101-115.
      → see A14.a.

A88.  "The Religious Meaning of Secularity." In *Religion in Contem-
      porary Thought*. Edited by George McLean. Staten Island,
      NY: Alba House, 1973, pp. 311-322.
   a.  ►Compare this with "The Problem of Divine Transcendence in Secular
       Theology." In *The Spirit and Power of Christian Secularity*. Edited
       by Albert Schlitzer. Notre Dame, IN: University of Notre Dame
       Press, 1969, pp. 100-112.  → see A59.a.

A89.  "Philosophical Considerations." In *Beginnings of Personhood*.
      Edited by Donald McCarthy. Houston: The Institute of Religion
      and Human Development, Texas Medical Center, 1973, pp. 18-
      44.

A90.  "A New Approach to the Abortion Problem." *Theological
      Studies* 34 (September 1973): 481-488.
   a.  ►Also appears in Dutch with modifications as "Een bijdrage tot het debat
       over abortus." *Kultuurleven* 43 (August-September 1976): 640-649.
       → see A124.

A91.  "The Moral Argument, the Religious Experience, and the Basic
      Meaning of the Ontological Argument." *Idealistic Studies* 3
      (September 1973): 266-276.

A92.  "The New Humanist Manifesto." *Commonweal* 99 (October 19,
      1973): 55-58.  → see A93.  → see C26.  → see C25.
      → see C15.
   a.  ►Also appears in *Current* (December 1973): 22-27.  → see A94.
   b.  ►Also appears as "A Basic Misunderstanding." *Humanist* 34 (January-
       February 1974): 10-11.  → see A100.

A93.  "Reply [to Howard Radest, Harold Quigley, and Paul Kurtz]."
      *Commonweal* 99 (December 21, 1973): 321-322.  → see
      A92.  → see C26.

A94.  "The New Humanist Manifesto." *Current* (December 1973): 22-27.  → see A92.a.

## 1974

A95.  "Idées sur la formation du sacré et sa dégéneration." In *Le sacré*: *Études et recherches*. Actes du XIVᵉ Colloque Organisé par le Centre International d'Études Humanistes et l'Institut d'Études Philosophiques de Rome. Edited by Enrico Castelli. Paris: Aubier, 1974, pp. 369-376.
  a.  ►Compare this with "Secular Man and His Religion." *Proceedings of the American Catholic Philosophical Association* 42 (1968): 78-92. → see A54.c.
  b.  ►Compare this with *The Other Dimension*. New York: Doubleday, 1972, pp. 13-20.  → see A77.

A96.  "Openness and Closedness of the Religious Community." In *Miscellanea Albert Dondeyne: Godsdienstfilosofie: Philosophie de la religion*. Bibliotheca Ephemeridum Theologicarum Lovaniensium 35. Edited by Jan Walgrave, Antoine Vergote, and Ben Willaert. Louvain: Leuven University Press, 1974, 1987², pp. 67-74.
  a.  ►Also appears with slight modifications as "Transcendent Selfhood and Religious Community." *Listening* 13 (Winter 1978): 38-47.  → see A138.

A97.  "The Philosophical Stages of Man's Self-Discovery." In *New Dynamics in Ethical Thinking*. Vol. 1. Edited by George McLean. Lancaster, PA: Concorde, 1974, pp. 17-30.  → see A13.b.

A98.  "The Argument of Design Today." *The Journal of Religion* 54 (1974): 1-12.

A99.  "The Mystical Experience of the Self and Its Philosophical Significance." *Proceedings of the American Catholic Philosophical Association* 48 (1974): 149-165.

a. ►Also appears as "The Mystical Knowledge of the Self and Its Philosophical Significance." *International Philosophical Quarterly* 14 (December 1974): 495-511. → see A105.

b. ►Also appears in *Psychiatry and the Humanities.* Vol. 1. Edited by Joseph Smith. New Haven, CT: Yale University Press, 1976, pp. 101-125. → see A117.

c. ►Also appears as Chapter 8 of *Transcendent Selfhood.* New York: Seabury Press, 1976, pp. 92-104. → see A112.

d. ►Also appears as "The Mystical Knowledge of the Self and Its Philosophical Significance." In *Understanding Mysticism.* Edited by Richard Woods. Garden City, New York: Image Books, 1980; London: The Athlone Press, 1981, pp. 449-466. → see A149.

A100.    "A Basic Misunderstanding." *Humanist* 34 (January-February 1974): 10-11. → see A92.b. → see C26.a.

A101.    "[Editorial:] Humanism and Religion—On Barricades." *Humanist* 34 (March-April 1974): 37-38.

A102.    "Has the Secularist Crisis Come to an End?" *Listening* 9 (Autumn 1974): 7-19.

a. ►Also appears in *Catholic Council of Intellectual and Cultural Affairs Bulletin* 16 (Fall 1974): 60-68. → see A103.

b. ►Also appears in *Heterodoxy: Mystical Experience, Religious Dissent and the Occult.* Listening Press Studies in Religion and Culture 2. Edited by Richard Woods. Listening Press, 1975, pp. 7-19. → see A108.

A103.    "Has the Secularist Crisis Come to an End?" *Catholic Council of Intellectual and Cultural Affairs Bulletin* 16 (Fall 1974): 60-68. → see A102.a.

A104.    "Recent Literature on Marx and Marxism." *Journal of the History of Ideas* 35 (October-December 1974): 703-714. [Review Article]. → see B33.

A105.    "The Mystical Knowledge of the Self and Its Philosophical Significance." *International Philosophical Quarterly* 14 (December 1974): 495-511. → see A99.a.

**1975**

A106.   "L'intériorisation du temps dans la représentation religieuse."
In *Temporalità e Alienazione*. Edited by Enrico Castelli. *Archivio di Filosofia* [43] (1975): 121- 128.

a.   ▶Also appears in *Temporalité et aliénation*. Actes du XV<sup>e</sup> Colloque Organisé par le Centre International d'Études Humanistes et par l'Institut d'Études Philosophiqes de Rome. Edited by Enrico Castelli. Paris: Aubier, 1975, pp. 121-128.   → see A107.

A107.   "L'intériorisation du temps dans la représentation religieuse."
In *Temporalité et aliénation*. Actes du XV<sup>e</sup> Colloque Organisé par le Centre International d'Études Humanistes et par l'Institut d'Études Philosophiqes de Rome. Edited by Enrico Castelli. Paris: Aubier, 1975, pp. 121-128.   → see A106.a.

A108.   "Has the Secularist Crisis Come to an End?" In *Heterodoxy: Mystical Experience, Religious Dissent and the Occult*. Listening Press Studies in Religion and Culture 2. Edited by Richard Woods. Listening Press, 1975, pp. 7-19.   → see A102.b.

A109.   Foreword to *The Case Against Possessions and Exorcisms: A Historical, Biblical, and Psychological Analysis of Demons, Devils, and Demoniacs,* by Juan Cortés and Florence Gatti. New York: Vantage Press, 1975, pp. v-vi.

A110.   "The Enigma of Religious Art." *Review of Metaphysics* 29 (September 1975): 27-44.

a.   ▶Also appears in Dutch as "Religieuze kunst vroeger en nu." *Kultuurleven* 43 (June 1976): 388-402.   → see A121.

b.   ▶Also appears in Spanish as "El enigma del arte religioso." Translated by Magdalena Holguín. *Ideas y Valores* [Bogota, Columbia] 64-65 (1984): 99-115.   → see A183.

c.   ▶Also appears as Chapter 5 of *Transcendent Selfhood*. New York: Seabury Press, 1976, pp. 51-65.   → see A112.

d.   ▶Compare this with *The Other Dimension*. New York: Doubleday, 1972, pp. 228-237 and especially pp. 238-242.   → see A77.

A111.   "Alienation and Redemption Through Time and Memory: An Essay on Religious Time Consciousness." *Journal of the American Academy of Religion* 43 (December 1975): 671-679.

  a.   ►Also appears as "Of Time and Memory." In *Zeitlichkeit und Entfremdung in Hermeneutik und Theologie*. Kerygma und Mythos VI-8. Theologische Forschung 59. Edited by Franz Theunis. Hamburg: Herbert Reich, 1976, pp. 59-67.  → see A116.

  b.   ►Also appears as Chapter 6 of *Transcendent Selfhood*. New York: Seabury Press, 1976, pp. 66-78.  → see A112.

## 1976

A112.   *Transcendent Selfhood: The Loss and Rediscovery of the Inner Life*. New York: Seabury Press, A Crossroad Book, 1976.

  a.   ►Also appears revised in Dutch as *Terugkeer naar innerlijkheid*. With Edith Cardoen. Antwerp: De Nederlandsche Boekhandel, 1981, 1983². → see A155.

→ see A99.c.   → see A111.b.   → see A110.c.   → see A113.c.   → see A119.a.   → see A125.c.   → see A161.a.

A113.   "The Religious Crisis of Our Culture." In *The Crisis of Culture*. Analecta Husserliana 5. Papers and Debate of the Third International Conference Held by the International Husserl and Phenomenological Research Society 1974. Edited by Anna-Teresa Tymieniecka. Dordrecht, Holland: D. Reidel Publisher, 1976, pp. 205-218. ["Discussion" by Dupré, Dove, Bakan, Yosh, et al., pp. 227-238].

  a.   ►Also appears in *Yale Review* 65 (Winter 1976): 203-217.  → see A126.

  b.   ►Also appears with modifications in Dutch as "De krisis van onze kultuur." *Onze Alma Mater* [Louvain] 30 (October 1976): 188-198.  → see A122.

  c.   ►Also appears with modifications in *Transcendent Selfhood*. New York: Seabury Press, 1976, pp. 1- 15.  → see A112.

  d.   ►Compare this with "Secularism and the Crisis of Our Culture: A Hermeneutic Perspective." *Thought* 51 (September 1976): 271-281.  → see A125.d.

A114. "La sécularisation et la crise de notre culture." In *Herméneutique de la sécularisation*. Actes du Colloque Organisé par le Centre International d'Études Humanistes et par l'Institut d'Études Philosophiques de Rome. Paris: Aubier, 1976, pp. 141-152. → see A118.a.

A115. "De krisis van onze kultuur en transcendente zelfwaarneming." Lessenreeks gehouden. Louvain: Nieuwe Filosofische Kring, 1976. [Lecture notes for class, includes previously published articles]. → see A122.

A116. "Of Time and Memory." In *Zeitlichkeit und Entfremdung in Hermeneutik und Theologie*. Kerygma und Mythos VI-8. Theologische Forschung 59. Edited by Franz Theunis. Hamburg: Herbert Reich, 1976, pp. 59-67. → see A111.a.

A117. "The Mystical Experience of the Self and Its Philosophical Significance." In *Psychiatry and the Humanities*. Vol. 1. Edited by Joseph Smith. New Haven, CT: Yale University Press, 1976, pp. 101-125. → see A99.b.

A118. "La sécularisation et la crise de notre culture." In *Ermeneutica della secolarizzazione*. Edited by Enrico Castelli. *Archivio di Filosofia* [44] (1976): 141-152. → see A125.a.
  a. ▶Also appears in *Herméneutique de la sécularisation*. Actes du Colloque Organisé par le Centre International d'Études Humanistes et par l'Institut d'Études Philosophiques de Rome. Paris: Aubier, 1976, pp. 141-152. → see A114.

A119. "The Wounded Self: The Religious Meaning of Mental Suffering." *The Christian Century* 93 (April 7, 1976): 328-331.
  a. ▶Also appears as Chapter 4 of *Transcendent Selfhood*. New York: Seabury Press, 1976, pp. 42-49. → see A112.

A120. "Transcendence and Immanence as Theological Categories." *Catholic Theological Society of America Proceedings* 31 (June 9-12, 1976): 1-10. [Replies by David Burrell and Anne Carr, pp. 11-19]. → see C6. → see C7.

a.  ►Also with modifications in French as "Transcendance et Objectivisme." In *L'ermeneutica della filosofia della religione*. Edited by Enrico Castelli. *Archivio de Filosofia* [45] (1977): 265-272.  → see A129.

b.  ►Also with modifications in German as "Transzendenz und Objektivismus." In *Religion und Gottesfrage in der Philosophie: Neue Deutungen und Probleme der Religionsphilosophie*. Kerygma und Mythos VI-10. Theologische Forschung 62. Edited and translated by Franz Theunis. Hamburg: Herbert Reich, 1978, pp. 105-110.  → see A135.

A121.  "Religieuze kunst vroeger en nu." *Kultuurleven* 43 (June 1976): 388-402.  → see A110.a.

a.  ►Also appears as Chapter 3 of *De symboliek van het heilige*. Kampen: Kok Agora, 1991, pp. 90-107.  → see A260.

A122.  "De krisis van onze kultuur." *Onze Alma Mater* [Louvain] 30 (October 1976): 188- 198.  → see A113.b.  → see A115.

A123.  "Religion, Ideology, and Utopia In Marx." *New Scholasticism* 50 (Autumn 1976): 415-434.

a.  ►Also appears as "Marxist Theory and Religious Faith: A Plea for Ideology and Utopia." In *Faith and the Contemporary Epistemologies/Foi et épistémologies contemporaines*. Conférences McMartin, 1975. Collection φ Philosophica. Edited by Benoît Garceau. Ottawa: Éditions de l'Université d'Ottawa, 1977, pp. 55-69.  → see A131.

b.  ►Also appears shortened and modified in French as "Théorie marxiste et idéologie religieuse: Opposition dialectique ou conflit antagoniste?" In *Religione e politica*. Edited by Marco Olivetti. *Archivio di Filosofia* [46] (1978): 219-226.  → see A136.

c.  ►Also appears shortened and modified in German as "Marxistische Theorie und Religiöse Ideologie: dialektischer Gegensatz oder Antagonistischer Konflikt?" In *Glaube und Politik - Religion und Staat*. Kerygma und Mythos VII-1. Theologische Forschung 63. Edited by Franz Theunis. Translated by G. Memmert. Hamburg: Herbert Reich, 1979, pp. 138-143.  → see A141.

A124.  "Een bijdrage tot het debat over abortus." *Kultuurleven* 43 (August-September 1976): 640-649.  → see A90.

A125.  "Secularism and the Crisis of Our Culture: A Hermeneutic Perspective." *Thought* 51 (September 1976): 271-281.

a.   ►Also appears with modifications in French as "La sécularisation et la crise de notre culture." In *Ermeneutica della secolarizzazione*. Edited by Enrico Castelli. *Archivio di Filosofia* [44] (1976): 141-152.   → see A118.

b.   ►Also appears with modifications in German as "Die Säkularisierung und die Krisis unserer Kultur." In *Zum Problem der Säkularisierung*. Kerygma und Mythos VI. Edited and Translated by Franz Theunis. Hamburg: Herbert Reich, 1977, pp. 92-100.   → see A130.

c.   ►Also appears with modifications as Chapter 1 of *Transcendent Selfhood*. New York: Seabury Press, 1976, pp. 2-17.   → see A112.

d.   ►Compare this with "The Religious Crisis of Our Culture." In *The Crisis of Culture*. Analecta Husserliana 5. Papers and Debate of the Third International Conference held by the International Husserl and Phenomenological Research Society 1974. Edited by Anna-Teresa Tymieniecka. Dordrecht, Holland: D. Reidel Publisher, 1976, pp. 205-218.   → see A113.d.

A126.   "The Religious Crisis of Our Culture." *Yale Review* 65 (Winter 1976): 203-217.   → see A113.a.


**1977**

A127.   *A Dubious Heritage: Studies in the Philosophy of Religion after Kant*. New York: Paulist Press, A Newman Book, 1977.
→ see A18.a.   → see A21.c.   → see A50.a.   → see A84.a.   → see A162.a.

A128.   *L'autre dimension: Essai de philosophie de la religion*. Cogitatio fidei 90. Translated by Marcelle Jossua. Paris: Cerf, 1977.
→ see A77.a.

A129.   "Transcendance et Objectivisme." In *L'ermeneutica della filosofia della religione*. Edited by Enrico Castelli. *Archivio de Filosofia* [45] (1977): 265-272.   → see A120.a.

A130.   "Die Säkularisierung und die Krisis unserer Kultur." In *Zum Problem der Säkularisierung*. Kerygma und Mythos VI. Edited and Translated by Franz Theunis. Hamburg: Herbert Reich, 1977, pp. 92-100.   → see A125.b.

A131.  "Marxist Theory and Religious Faith: A Plea for Ideology and
       Utopia." In *Faith and the Contemporary Epistemologies/Foi
       et épistémologies contemporaines.* Conférences McMartin, 1975.
       Collection φ Philosophica. Edited by Benoît Garceau. Ottawa:
       Éditions de l'Université d'Ottawa, 1977, pp. 55-69.  → see
       A123.a.

A132.  "Jezus nog steeds in doodsstrijd?" *De Nieuwe Boodschap* 104
       (February 1977): 39- 41.
   a.  ►Also appears in English as "Jesus Still in Agony? Meditation on a Negro
       Spiritual." In *In Honor of Saint Basil the Great.* Word and Spirit 1. Still
       River, MA: St. Bede's Publications, 1979, pp. 191-195.  → see A143.

A133.  "Idealism and Materialism In Marx's Dialectic." *Review of
       Metaphysics* 30 (June 1977): 649-685.
   a.  ►Also appears in *Marx's Social Critique of Culture.* New Haven, CT:
       Yale University Press, 1983, pp. 125-162.  → see A173.

A134.  "A New Interpretation of Meister Eckhart." Review of *Meister
       Eckhart on Divine Knowledge,* by C. Kelley. In *Yale Review*
       67 (December 1977): 280-282.

## 1978

A135.  "Transzendenz und Objektivismus." In *Religion und Gottesfrage
       in der Philosophie: Neue Deutungen und Probleme der
       Religionsphilosophie.* Kerygma und Mythos VI-10. Theologische
       Forschung 62. Edited and translated by Franz Theunis. Hamburg:
       Herbert Reich, 1978, pp. 105-110.  → see A120.b.

A136.  "Théorie marxiste et idéologie religieuse: Opposition dialectique
       ou conflit antagoniste?" In *Religione e politica.* Edited by Marco
       Olivetti. *Archivio di Filosofia* [46] (1978): 219-226.  → see
       A123.b.

A137.  "Rationality in Marx's Concept of History." *Tijdschrift voor
       Filosofie* 40 (September 1978): 418-451.  → see A140.a.

A138.  "Transcendent Selfhood and Religious Community." *Listening* 13 (Winter 1978): 38- 47. → see A96.a.

## 1979

A139.  *The Other Dimension: A Search for the Meaning of Religious Attitudes.* New York: Seabury Press, abridged paperback edition, 1979. → see A77.b.

A140.  "Rationality in Marx's Concept of History." In *La rationalité aujourd'hui/Rationality To-day.* Proceedings of the International Symposium on "Rationality To-day" held at the University of Ottawa 1977. Collection φ Philosophica 13. Edited by Théodore Geraets. Ottawa: University of Ottawa Press, 1979, pp. 136-158. ["Discussion" by Nielsen, Dupré, Habermas, Apel, pp. 158-162].

   a.  ►Also appears in *Tijdschrift voor Filosofie* 40 (September 1978): 418-451. → see A137.

   b.  ►Also appears in *Marx's Social Critique of Culture.* New Haven, CT: Yale University Press, 1983, pp. 60; 66-96. → see A173.

A141.  "Marxistische Theorie und Religiöse Ideologie: dialektischer Gegensatz oder Antagonistischer Konflikt?" In *Glaube und Politik - Religion und Staat.* Kerygma und Mythos VII-1. Theologische Forschung 63. Edited by Franz Theunis. Translated by G. Memmert. Hamburg: Herbert Reich, 1979, pp. 138-143. → see A123.c.

A142.  "A Critique of Marx's Economic Theory of Society." In *Il Pubblico e il Privato.* Edited by Marco Olivetti. *Archivio di Filosofia* [47] (1979): 127-140. ["Discussion," pp. 141-142].

   a.  ►Also appears in Dutch as "Een kritiek op Marx' economische maatschappijtheorie." *Tijdschrift voor Diplomatie* 9 (May 1981): 556-566. → see A159.

A143.  "Jesus Still in Agony? Meditation on a Negro Spiritual." In *In Honor of Saint Basil the Great.* Word and Spirit 1. Still River, MA: St. Bede's Publications, 1979, pp. 191-195. → see A132.a.

A144.  "Het atheïsme als religieus fenomeen." *Tijdschrift voor Theologie* 19 (April/May/June 1979): 113-123.

   a.  ►Also appears in *Atheistische religiositeit?* Studies in Culture. Edited by L. Apostel, R. Pinxten, R. Thibau, F. Vandamme. Ghent: Communication & Cognition, 1981, pp. 83-94.  → see A156.

   b.  ►Also appears in *Terugkeer naar innerlijkheid.* Antwerp: De Nederlandsche Boekhandel, 1981, pp. 37-51.  → see A155.

   c.  ►Also appears in *Opium of zuurstof? Geloven vandaag.* Edited by Jean-Pierre Goetghebuer. Louvain: Davidsfonds, 1987, pp. 27-44.  → see A210.

A145.  "The Idea of Historical Progress in Marx and Marxism." *Yale Review* 69 (Autumn 1979): 33-43.

## 1980

A146.  "Negative Theology and Affirmation of the Finite." In *Experience, Reason and God.* Studies in Philosophy and the History of Philosophy 8. Edited by Eugene Long. Washington, D.C.: The Catholic University of America Press, 1980, pp. 149-157.

   a.  ►Also appears in *Esistenza, mito, ermeneutica: Scritti per Enrico Castelli 2.* Edited by Marco Olivetti. *Archivio di Filosofia* [48] (1980): 373-381.  → see A150.

A147.  "Faith and Reason." In *The Philosophy of Brand Blanshard.* The Library of Living Philosophers 15. Edited by Paul Schilpp. La Salle, IL: Open Court, 1980, pp. 996-1001.  → see C3.

A148.  "Philosophy and Religious Faith." In *The Human Person and Philosophy in the Contemporary World.* Proceedings of the Meeting of the World Union of Catholic Philosophical Societies, 1978. Edited by J. Życiński. Cracow: The Pontifical Faculty of Theology, 1980, pp. 352-384.

A149.  "The Mystical Knowledge of the Self and Its Philosophical Significance." In *Understanding Mysticism.* Edited by Richard Woods. Garden City, New York: Image Books, 1980; London: The Athlone Press, 1981, pp. 449-466.  → see A99.d.

A150. "Negative Theology and Affirmation of the Finite." In *Esistenza, mito, ermeneutica: Scritti per Enrico Castelli 2*. Edited by Marco Olivetti. *Archivio di Filosofia* [48] (1980): 373-381. → see A146.a.

A151. "From Marx to Freud." *Philosophical Psychology* 1 (Summer 1980): 1-11.

A152. "Marx's Critique of Culture and Its Interpretations." *Review of Metaphysics* 34 (September 1980): 91-121.
  a. ►Also appears in *Marx's Social Critique of Culture*. New Haven, CT: Yale University Press, 1983, pp. 216-230; 238-247; 285-287. → see A173.

A153. National Conference of Catholic Bishops, [Louis Dupré principal author]. "Pastoral Letter on Marxist Communism." Washington, D.C.: United States Catholic Conference, November 18, 1980.

## 1981

A154. *The Deeper Life: An Introduction to Christian Mysticism*. Preface by Henri Nouwen. New York: Crossroad, 1981.
  a. ►Also appears in Dutch as *Licht uit licht: Een inleiding in de christelijke mystiek*. Translated by Edith Cardoen. Antwerp: Patmos, 1983. → see A172.
  b. ►Also appears in Polish in a combined edition with *The Common Life* as *Głębsze życie*. Translated by Maria Tarnowska. Cracow: Znak, 1994. → see A281. → see A179.a.
  → see A198.a.

A155. *Terugkeer naar innerlijkheid*. With Edith Cardoen. Antwerp: De Nederlandsche Boekhandel, 1981, 1983². → see A112.a. → see A144.b.
  (Winner of the "Prijs De Standard 1982.")

A156. "Het atheïsme als religieus fenomeen." In *Atheïstische religiositeit? Studies in Culture*. Edited by L. Apostel, R. Pinxten, R. Thibau, F. Vandamme. Ghent: Communication & Cognition, 1981, pp. 83-94. → see A144.a.

A157.   "Intimations of Immortality." In *Filosofia e religione di fronte alla morte. Archivio di Filosofia* [49] (1981): 259-277.

A158.   De Visscher, Jacques. "Vandaag moet de christen het atheïsme in zichzelf onderkennen: Vraaggesprek met de godsdienst-filosoof Louis Dupré." *Kultuurleven* 48 (February 1981): 127-135. [Interview].   → see C10.

A159.   "Een kritiek op Marx' economische maatschappijtheorie." *Tijdschrift voor Diplomatie* 9 (May 1981): 556-566.   → see A142.a.

A160.   "Marx's Idea of Alienation Revisited." *Man and World* 14 (1981): 387-410.
   a.   ►Also appears in *Marx's Social Critique of Culture*. New Haven, CT: Yale University Press, 1983, pp. 15-57.   → see A173.


**1982**

A161.   "The Transcendent and the Sacred." In *The Challenge of Religion: Contemporary Readings in Philosophy of Religion*. Edited by Frederick Ferré, Joseph Kockelmans, and John Smith. New York: Seabury Press, 1982, pp. 38-49.
   a.   ►Also appears as Chapter 2 of *Transcendent Selfhood*. New York: Seabury Press, 1976, pp. 18-30.   → see A112.

A162.   "The Teleological Argument." In *The Challenge of Religion: Contemporary Readings in Philosophy of Religion*. Edited by Frederick Ferré, Joseph Kockelmans, and John Smith. New York: Seabury Press, 1982, pp. 128-138.   → see A85.a.
   a.   ►Also appears in *A Dubious Heritage*. New York: Paulist Press, 1977, pp. 152-165.   → see A127.

A163.   "The Dialectic of the Mystical Experience." In *The Challenge of Religion: Contemporary Readings in Philosophy of Religion*. Edited by Frederick Ferré, Joseph Kockelmans, and John Smith. New York: Seabury Press, 1982, pp. 247-255.
   a.   ►Also appears in a longer version as Chapter 12 of *The Other Dimension*. New York: Doubleday, 1972, pp. 484-545.   → see A77.

A164.    "History as Revelation." In *The Challenge of Religion: Contemporary Readings in Philosophy of Religion*. Edited by Frederick Ferré, Joseph Kockelmans, and John Smith. New York: Seabury Press, 1982, pp. 269-277.
    a.    ▶Also appears in *The Other Dimension*. New York: Doubleday, 1972, pp. 209-313.   → see A77.

A165.    "Geestelijk leven in een geseculariseerde tijd." Translated by Bernard de Cock. *Jeugd en Cultuur* 27 (1982-1983): 31-46. → see A171.c.

A166.    "Experience and Interpretation. A Philosophical Reflection on Schillebeeckx' *Jesus and Christ*." *Theological Studies* 43 (March 1982): 30-51.
    a.    ▶Also appears in partial Dutch translation as "Ervaring en interpretatie: Een filosofische bezinning op de christologische studies van Edward Schillebeeckx." *Tijdschrift voor Theologie* 22 (October- November-December 1982): 361-375.   → see A169.

A167.    "Spiritual Life in a Secular Age." *National Institute for Campus Ministries Journal* 7 (Summer 1982): 5-20.   → see A171.a. → see C11.   → see C20.   → see C22.   → see C24. → see C28.

A168.    "Some Recent Philosophical Discussions of Religion." *Journal of the History of Ideas* 43 (July-September 1982): 505-518. [Review Article].   → see B49.

A169.    "Ervaring en interpretatie: Een filosofische bezinning op de christologische studies van Edward Schillebeeckx." *Tijdschrift voor Theologie* 22 (October-November-December 1982): 361-375.   → see A166.a.

A170.    "Hegel's Absolute Spirit: A Religious Justification of Secular Culture." *Revue de l'Université d'Ottawa* 52 (October-December 1982): 554-565. ["Discussion" by Lauer, Dupré, Harris, Bodei, et al., pp. 565-574].
    a.    ▶Also appears in *Neoplatonismo e religione*. Edited by Marco Olivetti. *Archivio di Filosofia* 51 (1983): 351-363.   → see A176.

b.   ►Also appears in *Hegel: The Absolute Spirit/L'esprit absolu*. Proceedings of the International Symposium on the Meaning of Absolute Spirit in Hegel held at the University of Ottawa 1981. Collection φ Philosophica 26. Edited by Théodore Geraets. Ottawa: University of Ottawa Press, 1984, pp. 127-138. ["Discussion," pp. 138-147]. → see A181.

A171.   "Spiritual Life in a Secular Age." *Daedalus* 111 (Winter 1982): 21-31.

a.   ►Also appears in *National Institute for Campus Ministries Journal* 7 (Summer 1982): 5-20.   → see A167.

b.   ►Also appears in *Religion and America: Spiritual Life in a Secular Age*. Edited by Mary Douglas and Steven Tipton. Boston: Beacon Press, 1983, pp. 3-13.   → see A175.

c.   ►Also appears in Dutch as "Geestelijk leven in een geseculariseerde tijd." Translated by Bernard de Cock. *Jeugd en Cultuur* 27 (1982-1983): 31-46.   → see A165.

d.   ►Also appears in *Ignatian Spirituality in a Secular Age*. SR Supplements 15. Edited by George Schner. Waterloo, Ontario: Wilfrid Laurier University Press, 1984, pp. 14-25.   → see A182.

## 1983

A172.   *Licht uit licht: Een inleiding in de christelijke mystiek*. Translated by Edith Cardoen. Antwerp: Patmos, 1983.   → see A154.a.

A173.   *Marx's Social Critique of Culture*. New Haven, CT: Yale University Press, 1983; reprinted 1985.
→ see A133.a.   → see A140.b.   → see A152.a.   → see A160.a.   → see A178.b.   → see A227.a.

A174.   "The Spiritual Crisis of our Culture." The Fourth Annual Moran Lecture. Pennsylvania: King's College, 1983.

A175.   "Spiritual Life in a Secular Age." In *Religion and America: Spiritual Life in a Secular Age*. Edited by Mary Douglas and Steven Tipton. Boston: Beacon Press, 1983, pp. 3-13. → see A171.b.

A176. "Hegel's Absolute Spirit: A Religious Justification of Secular Culture." In *Neoplatonismo e religione*. Edited by Marco Olivetti. *Archivio di Filosofia* 51 (1983): 351-363. → see A170.a.

A177. "Krisis van het kristendom, krisis van de westerse mens." *Kultuurleven* 50 (May 1983): 319-330.

A178. "Marx's Theory of Economics as Socio-Cultural Activity." *South African Journal of Philosophy* 2 (August 1983): 123-129.
   a. ►Also appears in Dutch and modified as "Marx en de economie als socio-culturele activiteit." In *Terugkeer van de ethiek: Denken over economie en samenleving*. Edited by Luk Bouckaert. Louvain: Acco, 1989, pp. 149-161. → see A238.
   b. ►Also appears in *Marx's Social Critique of Culture*. New Haven, CT: Yale University Press, 1983, pp. 1656-166; 198-214. → see A173.

## 1984

A179. *The Common Life: The Origins of Trinitarian Mysticism and its Development by Jan Ruusbroec*. New York: Crossroad, 1984.
   a. ►Also appears in Polish in a combined edition with *The Deeper Life* as *Głębsze Życie*. Translated by Maria Tarnowska. Cracow: Znak, 1994. → see A281. → See A154.b.
   → see A187.a.

A180. "The Absolute Spirit and the Religious Legitimation of Modernity." In *Hegels logik der philosophie: religion und philosophie in der theorie des absoluten geistes*. Veröffentlichungen der Internationalen Hegel-Vereinigung 13. Edited by Dieter Henrich and Rolf-Peter Horstmann. Stuttgart: Klett-Cotta, 1984, pp. 224-233.

A181. "Hegel's Absolute Spirit: A Religious Justification of Secular Culture." In *Hegel: The Absolute Spirit/L'esprit absolu*. Proceedings of the International Symposium on the Meaning of Absolute Spirit in Hegel held at the University of Ottawa

1981. Collection φ Philosophica 26. Edited by Théodore Geraets. Ottawa: University of Ottawa Press, 1984, pp. 127-138. ["Discussion," pp. 138-147].   → see A170.b.

A182.   "Spiritual Life in a Secular Age." In *Ignatian Spirituality in a Secular Age*. SR Supplements 15. Edited by George Schner. Waterloo: Wilfrid Laurier University Press, 1984, pp. 14-25. → see A171.d.

A183.   "El enigma del arte religioso." *Ideas y Valores* [Bogota, Columbia] 64-65 (1984): 99- 115.   → see A110.b.

A184.   "Wegen naar geloof in een ontheiligde cultuur." *K.T.R.C. Pastoraal* (January 15, 1984): 5-12. [This is a pro manuscripto of radio programs for the Catholic radio in Flanders].

A185.   "De Gebroken spiegel: Een essay over het ontstaan en de deconstructie van de moderne symboliek." *De Uil van Minerva* 1 (Summer 1985): 191-203.

   a.   ▶Also appears as "Het ontstaan en vergaan van de moderne symboliek." In *Academiae Analecta*. Mededelingen van de Koninklijke Academie voor Wetenschappen, Letteren en Schone Kunsten van België. Klasse der Letteren 49 (1987): 37-49.   → see A211.

   b.   ▶Also appears in English as "The Broken Mirror. The Fragmentation of the Symbolic World." *Stanford Literature Review* (Spring-Fall 1988): 7-24.   → see A233.

   c.   ▶Also appears in *De symboliek van het heilige*. Kampen: Kok Agora, 1991, pp. 25-35.   → see A260.

A186.   "Of Time and Eternity in Kierkegaard's *Concept of Anxiety*." *Faith and Philosophy* 1 (April 1984): 160-176.

   a.   ▶Also appears as "Of Time and Eternity." In *The Concept of Anxiety*. International Kierkegaard Commentary 8. Edited by Robert Perkins. Macon, GA: Mercer University Press, 1985, pp. 111-131.   → see A192.

A187.   "From Silence To Speech: Negative Theology and Trinitarian Spirituality." *Communio: International Catholic Review* 11 (Spring 1984): 28-34.

a. ▶Also appears in *The Common Life*. New York: Crossroad, 1984, pp. 9; 20-28. → see A179.

A188. "The Closed World of the Modern Mind." *Religion and Intellectual Life* 1 (Summer 1984): 19-29.

A189. "Religion as Alienation, Ideology, and Utopia in Marx." *Logos (USA)* 5 (1984): 29- 40.

A190. "The Despair of Religion." *The Owl of Minerva* 16 (Fall 1984): 21-30.

A191. Letter to the Editor, regarding Thomas Sheehan, "The Revolution in the Church." Review of *Eternal Life?*, by Hans Küng. In *New York Review of Books* 31 (November 22, 1984): 56. → see B52.

## 1985

A192. "Of Time and Eternity." In *The Concept of Anxiety*. International Kierkegaard Commentary 8. Edited by Robert Perkins. Macon, GA: Mercer University Press, 1985, pp. 111-131. → see A186.a.

A193. Preface to *Jan van Ruusbroec: The Spiritual Espousals and other Works*. The Classics of Western Spirituality. Translated by James Wiseman. New York: Paulist Press, 1985, pp. xi-xv.

A194. "The Modern Idea of Culture: Its Opposition to its Classical and Christian Origins." In *Ebraismo, Ellenismo, Cristianesimo II*. Edited by Marco Olivetti. *Archivio di Filosofia* 53 (1985): 469-483.

a. ▶Also appears condensed as "Western Civilization: The Spiritual Crisis of our Culture." In *Minds Without Borders: Educational and Cultural Exchange in the Twenty-First Century*. The Fulbright 40th Anniversary Washington Conference Proceedings. Edited by Anne Rogers Devereux and George Seay. Washington, D.C.: USIA–Smithsonian Institution–Woodrow Wilson International Center, 1988, pp. 32-39. → see A229.

b.   ▶Also appears as "The Modern Idea of Culture: Its Opposition to Its Classical and Christian Roots." In *Modernity and Religion*. Edited by Ralph McInerny. Notre Dame, IN: University of Notre Dame Press, 1994, pp. 1-18.   → see A286.

A195.   "Over wonen en wachten: Feestrede uitgesproken bij de 850ste verjaring van de abdij van Averbode." *Averbode* 12-13 (1984-1985): 44-49.

A196.   "A Conservative Anarchist, Eric Voegelin 1901-1985." *CLIO* 14 (Summer 1985): 423-431.

a.   ▶Also appears in Dutch as "Eric Voegelin (1901-1985): een konservatieve anarchist." *Kultuurleven* 52 (December 1985): 946-954.   → see A199.

A197.   "Ritual: The Sacralization of Time." *Revue de l'Université d'Ottawa* 55 (October- December 1985): 261-269.

a.   ▶Also appears in *Man and World* 19 (1986): 143-153.   → see A203.

b.   ▶Also appears in *Taal, mythe en religie*. Huldeboek Roger Thibau. Studies in Culture. Edited by F. Decreus and F. Vandamme. Gent: Communication & Cognition, 1986, pp. 177-188.   → see A202.

c.   ▶Also appears with modifications as "Ritual: The Divine Play of Time." In *Play, Literature, Religion: Essays in Cultural Intertextuality*. SUNY Series The Margins of Literature. Edited by Virgil Nemoianu and Robert Royal. Albany: State University of New York Press, 1992, pp. 199-212.   → see A269.

d.   ▶Compare this with *The Other Dimension*. New York: Doubleday, 1972, pp. 170-187.   → see A77.

e.   ▶Also appears in summary as "Ritual, Time and Modern Culture." In *Philosophy and Culture*. Vol. 4. Proceedings of the 27th World Congress of Philosophy. Edited by Venant Cauchy. Montreal: Éditions Montmorency, 1988, p. 687.   → see A228.a.

A198.   "Christian Spirituality Confronts the Modern World." *Communio: International Catholic Review* 12 (Fall 1985): 334-342.

a.   ▶Sections of this article also appear in *The Deeper Life*. New York: Crossroad, 1981, esp., pp. 51-73.   → see A154.

A199.   "Eric Voegelin (1901-1985): een konservatieve anarchist." *Kultuurleven* 52 (December 1985): 946-954.   → see A196.a.

**1986**

A200.  *Mark-jui-eui- chol-hak-jok ki-cho.* N. p., 1986.  → see
A30.b.

A201.  *Jen ti tsung chiao hsiang tu.* Translated by Fu Pêi-jung. N. p.,
1986.  → see A77.c.

A202.  "Ritual, The Sacralization of Time." In *Taal, mythe en religie.*
Huldeboek Roger Thibau. Studies in Culture. Edited by F.
Decreus and F. Vandamme. Gent: Communication & Cog-
nition, 1986, pp. 177-188.  → see A197.b.

A203.  "Ritual, The Sacralization of Time." *Man and World* 19 (1986):
143-153.  → see A197.a.

A204.  "Wiara." Translated by Sabina Lewandowska. *Znak* [Cracow]
38 (1986): 3-22.
   a.  ►Also appears in *The Other Dimension.* New York: Doubleday, 1972,
       pp. 38-61. "Wiara" is a Polish translation.  → see A77.

A205.  "Marx's Critique of Objectivism and the Rise of Cultural
Alienation." In *Intersoggettività socialità religione.* Edited
by Marco Olivetti. *Archivio di Filosofia* 54 (1986): 653-
667.
   a.  ►Also appears as "Objectivism and the Rise of Cultural Alienation." In
       *George Lukás and his World: A Reassessment.* American University
       Studies 19. General Literature 9. Edited by Ernest Joós. New York:
       Peter Lang, 1987, pp. 77-98.  → see A224.
   b.  ►Also appears as "Objectivism and the Rise of Cultural Alienation." In
       *Lukács Today: Essays in Marxist Philosophy.* Sovietica 51. Edited
       by Tom Rockmore. Dordrecht, Holland: Kluwer, 1988, pp. 70-85.
       → see A225.

A206.  "Reflections on President Giamatti's Statement [on the Loss of
and Need for a Humanist Education at Yale]." *Prism* [New
Haven, CT] 1 (March 1986): 9-11.

## 1987

A207. "Commentary on [De Nys'] 'Speculation and Theonomy at the Close of Hegel's System'." In *Hegel's Philosophy of Spirit*. SUNY Series in Hegelian Studies. Edited by Peter Stillman. Albany: State University of New York Press, 1987, pp. 215-219.

A208. "Christian Education Toward Interiority." In *Educating the Inner Self: A Source of Personal Dynamism and Social Commitment*. Proceedings of the International Study Days held in Mexico 1986. Tracts of the O.I.E.C. 2. Brussels: Office international de l'enseignement catholique, 1987, pp. 13-26. → see A218.b.

a. ▶Also in French as "Education a l'interiorite dans une perspective chretienne." In *Eduquer l'homme intérieur: Source de dynamisme personnel et d'engagement social*. Texte Intégral des Journées Mondiales d'etudes organisées à Mexico 1986. Cahiers pédagogiques de l'O.I.E.C. 2. Brussels: Office international de l'enseignement catholique, 1987, pp. 13-27. → see A209.

A209. "Education a l'interiorite dans une perspective chretienne." In *Eduquer l'homme intérieur: Source de dynamisme personnel et d'engagement social*. Texte Intégral des Journées Mondiales d'etudes organisées à Mexico 1986. Cahiers pédagogiques de l'O.I.E.C. 2. Brussels: Office international de l'enseignement catholique, 1987, pp. 13-27. → see A208.a.

A210. "Het atheïsme als religieus fenomeen." In *Opium of Zuurstof? Geloven vandaag*. Edited by Jean-Pierre Goetghebuer. Louvain: Davidsfonds, 1987, pp. 27-44. → see A144.c.

A211. "Het ontstaan en vergaan van de moderne symboliek." In *Academiae Analecta*. Mededelingen van de Koninklijke Academie voor Wetenschappen, Letteren en Schone Kunsten van België. Klasse der Letteren 49 (1987): 37-49. → see A185.a.

A212. "Marx, Karl." In *The Encyclopedia of Religion*. Vol. 9. Edited by Mircea Eliade. New York: Macmillan, 1987, pp. 238-240.

A213. "Mysticism." In *The Encyclopedia of Religion*. Vol. 10. Edited by Mircea Eliade. New York: Macmillan, 1987, pp. 245-261.
a. ►Also appears in French with modifications as "Mystique et pensée Chrétienne." In *Encyclopédie philosophique universelle*. Vol. 1, *L'univers philosophique*. Edited by André Jacob. Paris: Presses Universitaires de France, 1989, pp. 1656-1661. → see A236.

A214. "Philosophy and its History." In *At the Nexus of Philosophy and History*. Edited by Bernard Dauenhauer. Athens: University of Georgia Press, 1987, pp. 20-41.
a. ►Compare this with "Is the History of Philosophy Philosophy?" *Review of Metaphysics* 42 (March 1989): 463-482. → see A241.b.

A215. "The 'Truth' of Religion." In *Morality Within the Life- and Social World: Interdisciplinary Phenomenology of the Authentic Life in the "Moral Sense."* Analecta Huserliana 22. Papers of the 15th International Phenomenology Congress, 1985. Edited by Anna-Teresa Tymieniecka. Dordrecht, Holland: D. Reidel, 1987, pp. 457-463.

A216. *"The Sickness Unto Death*: Critique of the Modern Age." In *International Kierkegaard Commentary: The Sickness Unto Death*. International Kierkegaard Commentary 19. Edited by Robert Perkins. Macon, GA: Mercer University Press, 1987, pp. 85-106.

A217. "Alternatives to the *Cogito*." *Review of Metaphysics* 40 (June 1987): 687-716.

A218. "Catholic Education. What is it? What Should it be?" *CCICA Annual [Catholic Commission on Intellectual and Cultural Affairs]* (June 1987): 61-72.
a. ►Also appears with slight modifications as "Catholic Education and the Predicament of Modern Culture." *The Living Light* 23 (June 1987): 295-306. → see A219.
b. ►Also appears with slight modifications as "Christian Education Toward Interiority." In *Educating the Inner Self: A Source of Personal Dynamism and Social Commitment*. Proceedings of the International

Study Days held in Mexico 1986. Tracts of the O.I.E.C. 2. Brussels: Office international de l'enseignement catholique, 1987, pp. 13-26. → see A208.

A219. "Catholic Education and the Predicament of Modern Culture." *The Living Light* 23 (June 1987): 295-306. → see A218.a.

A220. Review of *Lectures on the Philosophy of Religion,* 3 vols., by Georg Wilhelm Friedrich Hegel. New translation by R. Brown, P. Hodgson, J. Stewart. In *Religious Studies Review* 13 (July 1987): 193-197. [Review Essay]. → see B57.

## 1988

A221. and James Wiseman, eds. *Light from Light: An Anthology of Christian Mysticism.* New York: Paulist Press, 1988.
→ see A230.

A222. "Truth In Religion and Truth of Religion." In *Teodicea oggi?* Atti del Colloquio 1988 dell'Instituto di Studi Filosofici di Roma. *Archivio di Filosofia* 56 (1988): 493-518.
  a. ▶Also appears in *Phenomenology of the Truth Proper to Religion.* SUNY Series in Philosophy. Edited by Daniel Guerrière. Albany: State University of New York Press, 1990, pp. 19-42. → see A249.
  b. ▶Pp. 495-502, 516-518, (21-28, 41-42 in Guerrière edition) also appear in a shorter version as "Note on the Idea of Religious Truth in the Christian Tradition." *Thomist* 52 (July 1988): 499-512. → see A232.
  c. ▶Pp. 493-494, 502-516, (19-20, 28-41 in Guerrière edition) also appear in a shorter version as "Reflections on the Truth of Religion." *Faith and Philosophy* 6 (July 1989): 260-274. → see A243.

A223. "The Dissolution of the Union of Nature and Grace at the Dawn of the Modern Age." In *The Theology of Wolfhart Pannenberg: Twelve American Critiques, with an Autobiographical Essay and Response.* Edited by Carl Braaten and Philip Clayton. Minneapolis: Augsburg Publishing House, 1988, pp. 95-121.
→ see C23.

a. ►Pp. 97-113 also appear as "Nature and Grace: Fateful Separation and Attempted Reunion." In *Catholicism and Secularization in America: Essays on Nature, Grace, and Culture.* Edited by David Schindler. Huntington, IN: Our Sunday Visitor; Notre Dame, IN: Communio Books, 1990, pp. 54-58; 61-67. → see A252.

b. ►Also appears in part in *Passage to Modernity.* New Haven, CT: Yale University Press, 170-174, 192-193, 201-202, and 216-218. → see A274.

A224. "Objectivism and the Rise of Cultural Alienation." In *George Lukás and his World: A Reassessment.* American University Studies 19. General Literature 9. Edited by Ernest Joós. New York: Peter Lang, 1987, pp. 77-98. → see A205.a.

A225. "Objectivism and the Rise of Cultural Alienation." In *Lukács Today: Essays in Marxist Philosophy.* Sovietica 51. Edited by Tom Rockmore. Dordrecht, Holland: Kluwer, 1988, pp. 70-85. → see A205.b.

A226. "Karl Marx." In *Meesters van de westerse filosofie.* Brussels: Instructieve Omroep B.R.T., 1988, pp. 21-41.

A227. "Marx and the Reintegration of Culture." In *Philosophy and Culture.* Vol. 2. Proceedings of the 27th World Congress of Philosophy. Edited by Venant Cauchy. Montreal: Éditions Montmorency, 1988, pp. 311-315.

a. ►Also appears in *Marx's Social Critique of Culture.* New Haven, CT: Yale University Press, 1983, pp. 1-4, 7-8. → see A173.

A228. "Ritual, Time and Modern Culture." In *Philosophy and Culture.* Vol. 4. Proceedings of the 27th World Congress of Philosophy. Edited by Venant Cauchy. Montreal: Éditions Montmorency, 1988, p. 687.

a. ►This is a summary of "Ritual: The Sacralization of Time." *Revue de l'Université d'Ottawa* 55 (October-December 1985): 261-269. → see A197.e.

A229. "Western Civilization: The Spiritual Crisis of our Culture." In *Minds Without Borders: Educational and Cultural Exchange in the Twenty-First Century.* The Fulbright 40th Anniversary Washington Conference Proceedings. Edited by Anne Rogers Devereux and George Seay. Washington, D.C.: USIA–Smithsonian Institution–Woodrow Wilson International Center, 1988, pp. 32-39.   → see A194.a.

A230.   "General Introduction and Commentary" In *Light from Light: An Anthology of Christian Mysticism.* Edited by Louis Dupré and James Wiseman. New York: Paulist Press, 1988, pp. 3-26. → see A221.

A231.   "Hans Urs von Balthasar's Theology of Aesthetic Form." *Theological Studies* 49 (June 1988): 299-318.   → see A247.c.

a.   ▶Pp. 305, 309 also appear as "Nature and Grace: Fateful Separation and Attempted Reunion." In *Catholicism and Secularization in America: Essays on Nature, Grace, and Culture.* Edited by David Schindler. Huntington, IN: Our Sunday Visitor; Notre Dame, IN: Communio Books, 1990, pp. 68-73.   → see A252.

b.   ▶Also appears condensed in Spanish as "La teología de la forma estética, de Hans Urs von Balthasar." Translated and condensed by Antonio Bentué. *Selecciones de Teología* [Barcelona] 29 (March 1990): 67-80.   → see A253.

A232.   "Note on the Idea of Religious Truth in the Christian Tradition." *Thomist* 52 (July 1988): 499-512.   → see A222.b.

A233.   "The Broken Mirror. The Fragmentation of the Symbolic World." *Stanford Literature Review* 5 (Spring-Fall 1988): 7-24. → see A185.b.

## 1989

A234.   and Don Saliers, eds. and intro. *Christian Spirituality III: Post-Reformation and Modern.* World Spirituality: An Encyclopedic History of the Religious Quest Vol. 18. New York: Crossroad, 1989, 1991. London: SCM, 1990.   → see A239.

A235.   "*Unio mystica:* The State and the Experience." In *Mystical Union and Monotheistic Faith: An Ecumenical Dialogue.* Edited by

Moshe Idel and Bernard McGinn. New York: Macmillan; London: Macmillan, 1989, pp. 3-23.
a. ▶Also appears with modifications as "The Christian Experience of Mystical Union." *The Journal of Religion* 69 (January 1989): 1-13. → see A240.

A236. "Mystique et pensée Chrétienne." In *Encyclopédie philosophique universelle.* Vol. 1, *L'univers philosophique.* Edited by André Jacob. Paris: Presses Universitaires de France, 1989, pp. 1656-1661. → see A213.a.

A237. Preface to the Morningside Edition of *Philosophy and Revolution: From Hegel to Sartre, and from Marx to Mao,* by Raya Dunayevskaya. Irvington, NY: Columbia University Press, 1989³, pp. xv-xx.

A238. "Marx en de economie als socio-culturele activiteit." In *Terugkeer van de ethiek. Denken over economie en samenleving.* Edited by Luk Bouckaert. Louvain: Acco, 1989, pp. 149-161. → see A178.a.

A239. "Jansenism and Quietism." In *Christian Spirituality III: Post-Reformation and Modern.* World Spirituality: An Encyclopedic History of the Religious Quest Vol. 18. Edited by Louis Dupré and Don Saliers in collaboration with John Meyendorff. New York: Crossroad, 1989, pp. 121-142. → see A234.

A240. "The Christian Experience of Mystical Union." *The Journal of Religion* 69 (January 1989): 1-13. → see A235.a.

A241. "Is the History of Philosophy Philosophy?" *Review of Metaphysics* 42 (March 1989): 463-482.
a. ▶Also appears in Dutch with slight changes as "De filosofie en haar geschiedenis." *Tijdschrift voor Filosofie* 51 (March 1989): 41-63. → see A242.
b. ▶ Compare this with "Philosophy and its History." In *At the Nexus of Philosophy and History.* Edited by Bernard Dauenhauer. Athens: University of Georgia Press, 1987, pp. 20-41. → see A214.a.

A242.   "De filosofie en haar geschiedenis." *Tijdschrift voor Filosofie*
        51 (March 1989): 41- 63.   → see A241.a.

A243.   "Reflections on the Truth of Religion." *Faith and Philosophy* 6
        (July 1989): 260-274.   → see A222.c.

A244.   and William O'Neill. "Social Structures and Structural Ethics."
        *Review of Politics* 51 (Summer 1989): 327-344.
   a.   ▶Also appears in Dutch with slight modifications as "Sociale structuren
        en structurele ethiek." Translated by Sabine Gilleman. *De Uil van
        Minerva* 5 (July 1989): 211-224.   → see A245.
   b.   ▶Also appears in Spanish as "Estructuras sociales y etica estructural."
        *Ideas y Valores* [Bogota, Columbia] 80 (August 1989): 5-12.   → see
        A246.
   c.   ▶Also appears under the authorship of Louis Dupré only with modifications
        in *On Freedom*. Boston University Studies in Philosophy and Religion
        10. Edited by Leroy Rouner. Notre Dame, IN: University of Notre
        Dame Press, 1989, pp. 143-162.   → see A250.

A245.   and William O'Neill as "Sociale structuren en structurele ethiek."
        Translated by Sabine Gilleman. *De Uil van Minerva* 5 (Summer
        1989): 211-224.   → see A244.a.

A246.   "Estructuras sociales y etica estructural." *Ideas y Valores* [Bogota,
        Columbia] 80 (August 1989): 5-12.   → see A244.b.

A247.   "The Glory of the Lord: Hans Urs von Balthasar's Theological
        Aesthetic." *Communio: International Catholic Review* 16 (Fall
        1989): 384-412.
   a.   ▶Also appears in *Hans Urs von Balthasar: His Life and Work*. Edited by
        David Schindler. San Francisco: Communio Books; Ignatius Press,
        1991, pp. 183-206.   → see A263.
   b.   ▶This article includes material from Review of *The Glory of the Lord:
        A Theological Aesthetics*. In *Religion and Literature* 19 (Autumn
        1987): 67-81.   → see B59.
   c.   ▶This article includes material from "Hans Urs von Balthasar's Theology
        of Aesthetic Form." *Theological Studies* 49 (June 1988): 299-318.
        → see A231.

**1990**

A248.   ed. and intro. *Nicholas of Cusa. Special Issue: American Catholic Philosophical Quarterly* 64 (Winter 1990). Washington, D.C.: American Catholic Philosophical Association, Catholic University of America, 1990.   → see A256.   → see A257.

A249.   "Truth In Religion and Truth of Religion." In *Phenomenology of the Truth Proper to Religion.* SUNY Series in Philosophy. Edited by Daniel Guerrière. Albany: State University of New York Press, 1990, pp. 19-42.   → see A222.a.

A250.   "Social Structures and Structural Ethics." In *On Freedom.* Boston University Studies in Philosophy and Religion 10. Edited by Leroy Rouner. Notre Dame, IN: University of Notre Dame Press, 1989, pp. 143-162.   → see A244.c.

A251.   and Jacqueline Mariña. "The Concept of Faith in Philosophy." In *Handbook of Faith.* Edited by James Lee. Birmingham, AL: Religious Education Press, 1990, pp. 47-70.

A252.   "Nature and Grace: Fateful Separation and Attempted Reunion." In *Catholicism and Secularization in America: Essays on Nature, Grace, and Culture.* Edited by David Schindler. Huntington, IN: Our Sunday Visitor; Notre Dame, IN: Communio Books, 1990, pp. 52-73.   → see A223.a.   → see A231.a.   → see C13.

   a.   ▶Also appears in part in *Passage to Modernity.* New Haven, CT: Yale University Press, 170-177, 192-193, 201-202, and 216-218.   → see A274.

A253.   "La teología de la forma estética, de Hans Urs von Balthasar." Translated and condensed by Antonio Bentué. *Selecciones de Teología* [Barcelona] 29 (1990): 67-80.   → see A231.b.

A254.   "Theodicy: The Case for a Theologically Inclusive Model of Philosophy." *Proceedings of the American Catholic Philosophical Association* 64 (1990): 24-39.

a. ▶Also appears in *Prospects for Natural Theology*. Studies in Philosophy and the History of Philosophy 25. Edited by Eugene Long. Washington, D.C.: The Catholic University of America Press, 1992, pp. 221-238. → see A266.

b. ▶Also appears with modifications as "Evil—A Religious Mystery: A Plea for a More Inclusive Model of Theodicy." *Faith and Philosophy* 7 (July 1990): 261-280. → see A255.

A255. "Evil – A Religious Mystery: A Plea for a More Inclusive Model of Theodicy." *Faith and Philosophy* 7 (July 1990): 261-280. → see A254.b.

A256. "Introduction, and the Major Philosophical and Theological Works of Nicholas of Cusa." In *Nicholas of Cusa. Special Issue: American Catholic Philosophical Quarterly* 64 (Winter 1990). Washington, D.C.: American Catholic Philosophical Association, Catholic University of America, 1990, pp. 1-6. → see A248.

A257. "Nature and Grace in Nicholas of Cusa's Mystical Philosophy." *American Catholic Philosophical Quarterly* 64 (Winter 1990): 153-170. → see A248.

a. ▶Compare this with *Passage to Modernity*. New Haven, CT: Yale University Press, 1993, pp. 186- 189. → see A274.

A258. "Transitions and Tensions in Hegel's Treatment of Determinate Religion." *American Catholic Philosophical Quarterly* 64 (Autumn 1990): 429-439.

a. ▶Also appears in *New Perspectives on Hegel's Philosophy of Religion*. Edited by David Kolb. Albany: State University of New York Press, 1992, pp. 81-92. → see A268.

## 1991

A259. *Inny Wymiar*. Translated by Sabina Lewandowska. Cracow: Znak, 1991. → see A77.d.

A260. *De symboliek van het heilige*. Translated by Guido Vanheeswijck. Introduction by Jacques De Visscher. Kampen: Kok Agora; Kapellen: DNB/Pelckmans, 1991. → see A77.e.

For Chapter 1  → see A185.c. For Chapter 3  → see A121.a. Chapters 2, 4, and 5 are from *The Other Dimension,* 1972, Chapters 4, 5 (excluding pp. 229-242), and 6 respectively.

A261. Foreword to *Toward the Death of Man,* by William Kluback. New York: Peter Lang, 1991, vii-ix.

A262. "Ascent and Decline of a Self-Centered Culture." In *Individuality and Cooperative Action.* Edited by Joseph Earley. Washington, D.C.: Georgetown University Press, 1991, pp. 137-147.
   a. ►Compare this with *Passage to Modernity.* New Haven, CT: Yale University Press, 1993.  → see A274.

A263. "The Glory of the Lord." In *Hans Urs von Balthasar.* Edited by David Schindler. San Francisco: Ignatius Press, 1991, pp. 183-206.  → see A247.a.

A264. "Ignatian Humanism and its Mystical Origins." *Communio: International Catholic Review* 18 (Summer 1991): 164-182.
   a. ►Compare this with *Passage to Modernity.* New Haven, CT: Yale University Press, 1993, pp. 224- 226.  → see A274.

A265. "Overgang naar de moderniteit." *De Uil van Minerva* 7 (Summer 1991): 217-227.
   a. ►Also appears in *Academiae Analecta.* Mededelingen van de Koninklijke Academie voor Wetenschappen, Letteren en Schone Kunsten van België. Klasse der Letteren 54 (1992): 41-53.  → see A271.
   b. ►Also appears in *Onder de koepel van het Pantheon: Liber amicorum Jacques Claes.* Kapellen: Pelckmans, 1994, 65-77.  → see A282.
   c. ►Compare this with *Passage to Modernity.* New Haven, CT: Yale University Press, 1993.  → see A274.

**1992**

A266. "Theodicy: The Case for a Theologically Inclusive Model of Philosophy." In *Prospects for Natural Theology.* Studies in Philosophy and the History of Philosophy 25. Edited by Eugene Long. Washington, D.C.: The Catholic University of America Press, 1992, pp. 221-238.  → see A254.a.

A267.   "The Mystical Theology of Cusanus's *De visione Dei.*" In *Eros and Eris: Contributions to a Hermeneutical Phenomenology: Liber amicorum for Adriaan Peperzak.* Phaenomenologica 127. Edited by P. van Tongeren, et al. Dordrecht, Holland: Kluwer Academic Publishers, 1992, pp. 105-117.

   a.   ▶Also appears as "The Mystical Theology of Nicholas of Cusa's *De visione dei.*" In *Nicholas of Cusa on Christ and the Church.* Edited by Gerald Christianson and Thomas Izbicki. Leiden: Brill, 1996, pp. 205-220.   → see A293.

A268.   "Transitions and Tensions in Hegel's Treatment of Determinate Religion." In *New Perspectives on Hegel's Philosophy of Religion.* Edited by David Kolb. Albany: State University of New York Press, 1992, pp. 81-92.   → see A258.a.

A269.   "Ritual: The Divine Play of Time." In *Play, Literature, Religion: Essays in Cultural Intertextuality.* SUNY Series The Margins of Literature. Edited by Virgil Nemoianu and Robert Royal. Albany: State University of New York Press, 1992, pp. 199-212.   → see A197.c.

A270.   "The Joys and Responsibilities of Being a Catholic Teacher." 1992 Marianist Award Lecture. Dayton: The University of Dayton, 1992.

   a.   Also appears in adapted form as "On Being a Christian Teacher of Humanities." *The Christian Century* 109 (April 29, 1992): 452-455.   → see A272.

A271.   "Overgang naar de moderniteit." In *Academiae Analecta.* Mededelingen van de Koninklijke Academie voor Wetenschappen, Letteren en Schone Kunsten van België. Klasse der Letteren 54 (1992): 41-53.   → see A265.a.

A272.   "On Being a Christian Teacher of Humanities." *The Christian Century* 109 (April 29, 1992): 452-455.   → see A270.a.

A273.   "Phenomenology of Religion: Limits and Possibilities." *American Catholic Philosophical Quarterly* 66 (Spring 1992): 175-188.

a.  ▶Compare this with "Philosophy of Religion and Revelation: Autonomous Reflection vs. Theophany." *International Philosophical Quarterly* 4 (December 1964): 499-513.   → see A21.d.

## 1993

A274.  *Passage to Modernity: An Essay in the Hermeneutics of Nature
and Culture.* New Haven, CT: Yale University Press, 1993
→ see A223.b.   → see A252.a   → see A257.a.   → see A262.a.   → see
A264.a.   → see A265.c.

A275.  "Secular Morality and Sacred Obligation." In *Riding Time Like
a River: The Catholic Morality Tradition Since Vatican II.*
Edited by William O'Brien. Washington, D.C.: Georgetown
University Press, 1993, pp. 47-58.

A276.  "La dialettica da Hegel a Marx." In *Dialettica ed ermeneutica.*
Edited by Théodore Geraets. Urbino: Quattroventi, 1993,
pp. 31-54.

A277.  "Jansenius, an Intellectual Biography." Review article of *Jansénius d'Ypres (1584- 1638),* by Jean Orcibal. In *The Journal of
Religion* 73 (January 1993): 75-82.   → see B66.

A278.  "The Common Good and the Open Society." *Review of Politics*
55 (Fall 1993): 687- 712.
a.  ▶Also appears in *Catholic Liberalism: Contributions to American Public
Philosophy.* Cambridge Studies in Religion and American Public
Life. Edited by R. Bruce Douglass and David Hollenbach. New York:
Cambridge University Press, 1994, pp. 172-195.   → see A283.

A279.  "Postmodernity or Late Modernity? Ambiguities in Richard
Rorty's Thought." *Review of Metaphysics* 47 (December 1993):
277-295.
a.  ▶Also appears in Dutch as "Postmoderniteit of laatmoderniteit? Dubbel-
zinnigheden in het denken van Richard Rorty." Translated by J. De
Visscher. In *Richard Rorty: Ironie, politiek en postmodernisme.*
Edited by G. Hottois, M. Van den Bossche, M. Weyembergh.
Antwerp: Hadewijch, 1994, pp. 38-53.   → see A284.

b.   ►Also appears in French as "Postmodernité ou modernité tardive." Translated by M. Weyembergh. In *Richard Rorty: Ambiguïtés et limites du postmodernisme.* Edited by G. Hottois and M. Weyembergh. Paris: J. Vrin, 1994, pp. 39-58.   → see A285.

## 1994

A280.   *Metaphysics and Culture.* The Aquinas Lecture 1994. Milwaukee: Marquette University Press, 1994.

A281.   *Głębsze życie.* Translated by Maria Tarnowska. Cracow: Znak, 1994.
  → see A154.b   → see A179.a.

A282.   "Overgang naar de moderniteit." In *Onder de koepel van het Pantheon: Liber amicorum Jacques Claes.* Kapellen: Pelckmans, 1994, 65-77.   → see A265.b.

A283.   "The Common Good and the Open Society." In *Catholic Liberalism: Contributions to American Public Philosophy.* Cambridge Studies in Religion and American Public Life. Edited by R. Bruce Douglass and David Hollenbach. New York: Cambridge University Press, 1994, pp. 172-195.   → see A278.a.

A284.   "Postmoderniteit of laatmoderniteit? Dubbelzinnigheden in het denken van Richard Rorty." Translated by J. De Visscher. In *Richard Rorty: Ironie, politiek en postmodernisme.* Edited by G. Hottois, M. Van den Bossche, M. Weyembergh. Antwerp: Hadewijch, 1994, pp. 38-53.   → see A279.a.

A285.   "Postmodernité ou modernité tardive." Translated by M. Weyembergh. In *Richard Rorty: Ambiguïtés et limites du postmodernisme.* Edited by G. Hottois and M. Weyembergh. Paris: J. Vrin, 1994, pp. 39-58.   → see A279.b.

A286.   "The Modern Idea of Culture: Its Opposition to Its Classical and Christian Roots." In *Modernity and Religion.* Edited by

Ralph McInerny. Notre Dame, IN: University of Notre Dame Press, 1994, pp. 1-18. → see A194.b.

A287. Introduction to *Letters from Lake Como: Explorations in Technology and the Human Race,* by Romano Guardini. Translated by Geoffrey Bromiley. Grand Rapids: Eerdmans, 1994, pp. xi-xv.

A288. Foreword to *The Unorthodox Hegel,* by Cyril O'Regan. Albany: State University of New York Press, 1994, pp. ix-xi.

A289. "Hegel Reflects on Remembering." *The Owl of Minerva* 25 (Spring 1994): 141-146.

## 1995-1997

A290. *Chong-kye-ae-suh-ui Sang-jing-kwa Shin-hwa.* N. p., 1995. → see A77.f.

A291. "Form and Transformation in the Modern Conception of Humanness." *Proceedings of the American Catholic Philosophical Association* 69 (1995): 47-55.

A292. "Denken over symboliek en cultuur." In *Metabletische Perspectieven.* Festschrift for J. H. van den Berg. Louvain: Acco, 1996.

A293. "The Mystical Theology of Nicholas of Cusa's *De visione dei.*" In *Nicholas of Cusa on Christ and the Church.* Edited by Gerald Christianson and Thomas Izbicki. Leiden: Brill, 1996, pp. 205-220. → see A267.a.

A294. "The Dialectic of Faith and Atheism in the Eighteenth Century." In *Finding God in All Things: Essays in Honor of Michael J. Buckley, S.J.* Edited by Michael J. Himes and Stephen J. Pope. New York: Crossroad, 1996, pp. 38-52.

A295.   "Spiritual Life and the Catholic Intellectual." *CCICA Annual [Catholic Commission on Intellectual and Cultural Affairs]* 15 (1996): 1-10.

A296.   "Hegel and the Enlightenment." *The Owl of Minerva* 28 (1996): 13-26.

A297.   "Cultuur en Metafysica." *Nexus* [Tilburg, The Netherlands] 14 (1996): 77-88.

A298.   "The Case for Jansenism." Review article of *God Owes Us Nothing: A Brief Remark on Pascal's Religion and the Spirit of Jansenism,* by Leszek Kolakowski. In *The Journal of Religion* 76 (October 1996): 607-610.   → see B69.

A299.   *Religious Mystery and Rational Reflection.* Grand Rapids: Eerdmans, [November] 1997.

A300.   and Edith Cardoen, eds. *De weg van de dienaar: Lezen in het Marcusevangelie,* by Luc Geysels. Louvain: Davidsfonds, 1997.

## B.  REVIEWS BY LOUIS DUPRÉ
Complete List to June 1997     IN CHRONOLOGICAL ORDER

(Review articles are cross referenced to section A.)

### 1955-1964

B1.   Review of *Kierkegaard et le catholicisme,* by H. Roos. In *Streven* 8 (June 1955): 278.

B2.   Review of *Sören Kierkegaard,* by Victor Leemans. In *Streven* 10 (October 1956): 90.

B3.   Review of *Briefe,* by Sören Kierkegaard. In *Streven* 10 (October 1956): 95.

B4. Review of *Karl Marx et Friedrich Engels: leur vie et leur oeuvre,* by Auguste Cornu. In *Revue Philosophique de Louvain* 55 (May 1957): 291.

B5. Review of *Der technische Eros: das Wesen der materialistischen Geschichtsauffassng,* by Jakob Hommes. In *Revue Philosophique de Louvain* 55 (May 1957): 292- 295.

B6. "Nieuwe Duitse Kierkegaardliteratuur." *Bijdragen* 18 (1957): 290-298. [Review Article:]
Review of *Die Krankheit zum Tode,* by Sören Kieregaard, pp. 290-292.
Review of *Einübung im Christentum,* by Sören Kierkegaard, p. 292.
Review of *Kierkegaard und der deutsche idealismus,* by Wilhelm Anz, pp. 293-295.
Review of *Sören Kierkegaards Geschichtsphilosophie,* by Sören Holm, pp. 295-297.
Review of *Sören Kierkegaard, Deuter unserer Existenz,* by Anna Paulsen, pp. 297-298.
→ see A6.

B7. Review of *Studi Kierkegaardiani.* In *Bijdragen* 20 (1959): 218-219.

B8. Review of *Dall'essere all'esistente,* by Cornelio Fabro. In *Bijdragen* 20 (1959): 219- 220.

## 1965-1969

B9. "New Publications in Phenomenology." *The New Scholasticism* 40 (April 1966): 199- 216. [Review Article:]
Review of *Phenomenology of Perception,* by Maurice Merleau-Ponty, pp. 199- 200.
Review of *The Phenomenology of Internal Time Consciousness,* by Edmund Husserl, pp. 199-203.
Review of *The Formation of Husserl's Concept of Constitution,* by Robert Sokolowski, pp. 206-212.

Review of *Phenomenology of Language,* by Remy Kwant, pp. 212-213.

Review of *Phenomenology and Atheism,* by William Luijpen, pp. 213-216.

→ see A35.

B10.  "The Problem of a Philosophy of Christianity: A New Study on Henry Duméry." *The Modern Schoolman* 44 (January 1967): 161-168. [Review Article:]

Review of *Philosophie du fait chrétien,* by Henk van Luijk, pp. 161-168.

→ see A42.

B11.  Review of *Phenomenology: Pure and Applied,* edited by Erwin Straus. In *The New Scholasticism* 41 (1967): 130-131.

B12.  Review of *Behaviorism and Phenomenology: Contrasting Bases for Modern Psychology,* edited by Trenton Wann. In *The New Scholasticism* 41 (1967): 418-421.

B13.  Review of *Psychologie Religieuse,* by Antoine Vergote. In *The New Scholasticism* 41 (1967): 547-549.

B14.  Review of *Phenomenology and History,* by John Nota. In *International Philosophical Quarterly* 7 (December 1967): 685-687.

B15.  Review of *The Emergence of Philosophy of Religion,* by James Collins. In *Theological Studies* 29 (March 1968): 102-104.

B16.  Review of *Ideology and Analysis,* by Richard Hinners. In *International Philosophical Quarterly* 8 (September 1968): 474-477.

B17.  Review of *Kierkegaard. The Difficulty of Being Christian,* edited by Jacques Colette, English version by Ralph McInerny and Leo Turcotte. In *Thomist* 33 (July 1969): 600-601.

B18. Review of *Kierkegaard on Christ and Christian Coherence,* by Paul Sponheim. In *Theological Studies* 30 (September 1969): 507-509.

B19. "Themes in Contemporary Philosophy of Religion." *The New Scholasticism* 43 (Fall 1969): 577-601. [Review Article:]
Review of *The God Question and Modern Man,* by Hans Urs von Balthasar, pp. 577-579.
Review of *The Death of God Controversy,* by Thomas Ogletree, pp. 579-580.
Review of *The Credibility of Divine Existence,* by Norman Kemp Smith, pp. 582-583.
Review of *Faith and Speculation,* by Austin Farrer, pp. 583-586.
Review of *The Pragmatic Meaning of the Existence of God,* by Robert Johann, pp. 586-587.
Review of *God and the Permission of Evil,* by Jacques Maritain, pp. 587-590.
Review of *Philosophical Faith and Revelation,* by Karl Jaspers, pp. 590-593.
Review of *On Authority and Revelation,* by Sören Kierkegaard. Translated, introduction, and notes by Walter Lowrie, pp. 593-596.
Review of *The Religious Dimension in Hegel's Thought,* by Emil Fackenheim, pp. 596-598.  → see B24.
Review of *Socratic Memorabilia,* by Johann Hamann. Translated and commentary by James O'Flaherty, pp. 599-601.
→ see A62.

## 1970-1974

B20. Review of *God on Trial: A Brief History of Atheism,* by Georg Siegmund. Translated by E. Briefs. In *Journal of Ecumenical Studies* 7 (1970): 372-373.

B21. Review of *A Christian-Communist Dialogue,* by Roger Garaudy and Quentin Lauer. In *Theological Studies* 31 (March 1970): 215-218.

B22.    Review of *The Alienation of Reason: A History of Positivist Thought,* by Leszek Kolakowski. In *The New Scholasticism* 44 (Spring 1970): 315-316.

B23.    and John Brough. "Recent Books in Phenomenology." *The New Scholasticism* 45 (Winter 1971): 147-156. [Review Article:] Review of *History and Truth,* by Paul Ricoeur, pp. 147-149. Review of *Husserl: An Analysis of his Phenomenology,* by Paul Ricoeur. Translated by Edward Ballard and Lester Embree, pp. 149-152.
Review of *The Foundation of Phenomenology,* by Marvin Farber, pp. 152-154.
→ see A75.

B24.    Review of *The Religious Dimension in Hegel's Thought,* by Emil Fackenheim. In *Hegel-Studien* 6 (1971): 332-337.   → see B19.

B25.    Review of *Man Without God: An Introduction to Unbelief,* by John Reid. In *Theological Studies* 33 (March 1972): 153-155.

B26.    Review of *For Marx* and *Reading Capital,* by Louis Althusser. In *The Commonweal* 95 (December 10, 1971): 260-262. → see B29.   → see B33.

B27.    Review of *On Karl Marx,* by Ernst Bloch. In *Journal of Ecumenical Studies* 9 (Spring 1972): 365-366.

B28.    Review of *Marxism and Philosophy,* by Karl Korsch. In *The American Political Science Review* 66 (December 1972): 1346-1347.   → see B29.   → see B33.

B29.    "Dialectical Philosophy Before and After Marx." *The New Scholasticism* 46 (Autumn 1972): 488-511. [Review Article:] Review of *Introduction to the Reading of Hegel,* by Alexandre Kojève, pp. 488-490.
Review of *L'aliénation dans la "Phénoménologie de l'Esprit" de G. W. F. Hegel,* by Conrad Boey, pp. 491-492.

Review of *Entfremdung,* by Friedrich Müller, pp. 492-493.
Review of *Studies on Marx and Hegel,* by Jean Hyppolite,
pp. 493-494.
Review of *For Marx,* by Louis Althusser, pp. 494-496.
→ see B26.   → see B33.
Review of *Reading Capital,* by Louis Althusser, pp. 496-500.
→ see B26.
Review of *Marxism and Philosophy,* by Karl Korsch, pp. 501-
502.   → see B28.
Review of *The Categories of Dialectical Materialism,* by Guy
Planty-Bonjour, pp. 505-508.
Review of *Buddha, Marx and God,* by Trevor Ling, pp. 508-
509.
→ see A82.

B30.   Review of *Mind: An Essay on Human Feeling.* Vol. 1, by Susanne
Langer. In *The New Scholasticism* 46 (Autumn 1972): 525-
527.

B31.   Review of *Time Invades the Cathedral: Tensions in the School of
Hope,* by Walter Capps. In *Journal of Ecumenical Studies* 10
(1973): 412-413.

B32.   Review of *Language and Belief,* by Jean Ladrière. In *Thomist* 37
(October 1973): 805-806.

B33.   "Recent Literature on Marx and Marxism." *Journal of the History
of Ideas* 35 (October-December 1974): 703-714. [Review
Article:]
Review of *Die Marxsche Theorie,* by Klaus Hartmann, pp. 703-
705.
Review of *The Concept of Nature in Marx,* by Alfred Schmidt,
pp. 705-707.
Review of *Philosophy and Revolution,* by Raya Dunayevskaya,
pp. 707-708.
Review of *L'aliénation dans la "Phénoménologie de l'Esprit"
de G. W. F. Hegel,* by Koenraad Boey, p. 709.

Review of *Entfremdung. Zur anthropologischen Begrundung der Staatstheorie bei Rousseau, Hegel, Marx,* by Friedrich Müller, p. 709.

Review of *Marx's Theory of Alienation,* by Istvan Meszaros, pp. 709-710.

Review of *Alienation,* by Richard Schacht, p. 709.

Review of *Alienation: Marx's Conception of Man in Capitalist Society,* by Bertell Ollman, pp. 710-711.

Review of *From Marx to Hegel,* by George Lichtheim, p. 711.

Review of *Marxism and Philosophy,* by Karl Korsch, pp. 711-712. → see B28.

Review of *History and Class Consciousness,* by George Lukács, p. 712.

Review of *Negative Dialectics,* by Theodor Adorno, pp. 712-713.

Review of *For Marx,* by Louis Althusser, pp. 713-714. → see B26. → see B29.

→ see A104.

## 1975-1979

B34.   Review of *The Idea of God and Human Freedom,* by Wolfhart Pannenberg. In *The Journal of Religion* 55 (January 1975): 156-158.

B35.   Review of *Oppositions of Religious Doctrines: A Study in the Logic of Dialogue among Religions,* by William Christian. In *The New Scholasticism* 49 (Spring 1975): 239-240.

B36.   Review of *Mind: An Essay on Human Feeling.* Vol. 2, by Susanne Langer. In *Journal of the American Academy of Religion* 43 (September 1975): 628.

B37.   Review of *The Concept of Existence in the Concluding Unscientific Postscript,* by Ralph Johnson. In *Journal of the American Academy of Religion* 44 (March 1976): 181.

B38. Review of *Phenomenology and Religion: Structures of the Christian Institution,* by Henry Duméry, trans. Paul Barrett. In *Religious Studies Review* 2 (July 1976): 58.

B39. Review of *Blaise Pascal: The Genius of His Thought,* by Roger Hazelton. In *Religious Studies* 13 (March 1977): 111-112.

B40. Review of *Body as Spirit: The Nature of Religious Feeling,* by Charles Davis. In *Thomist* 41 (July 1977): 441-442.

B41. Review of *Kierkegaard's Pseudonymous Authorship: A Study of Time and the Self,* by Mark Taylor. In *Journal of the American Academy of Religion* 45 (September 1977): 394-395.

B42. Review of *The Self-Embodiment of God,* by Thomas J. J. Altizer. In *The Journal of Religion* 58 (January 1978): 69-70.

B43. Review of *Death and Eternal Life,* by John Hick. In *The Journal of Religion* 58 (April 1978): 217-219.

B44. Review of *Marx's Fate: The Shape of a Life,* by Jerrold Seigel. In *CLIO* 8 (Winter 1979): 285-287.

B45. Review of *The Illusion of Technique: A Search for Meaning in a Technological Civilization,* by William Barrett. In *Commonweal* 106 (June 8, 1979): 343-344.

### 1980-1984

B46. Review of *The Philosophical Foundations of Soviet Aesthetics: Theories and Controversies in the Post-War Years,* by Edward Swiderski. In *Studies in Soviet Thought* 21 (May 1980): 175-179.

B47. Review of *In Pursuit of Wisdom: The Scope of Philosophy,* by Abraham Kaplan. In *The New Scholasticism* 54 (Winter 1980): 115-117.

B48.    Review of *The Cosmological Argument from Plato to Leibniz*, by William Craig. In *The Journal of Religion* 62 (July 1982): 311-312.

B49.    "Some Recent Philosophical Discussions of Religion." *Journal of the History of Ideas* 43 (July-September 1982): 505-518. [Review Article:]
Review of *Dette et désir: Deux axes chrétiens et la dérive pathologique*, by Antoine Vergote, pp. 505-509.
Review of *Reaping the Whirlwind: A Christian Interpretation of History*, by Langdon Gilkey, pp. 509-512.
Review of *Jesus*, and review of *Christ* by Edward Schillebeeckx, pp. 512-517.
Review of *Does God Exist? An Answer for Today*, by Hans Küng, pp. 517- 518.
→ see A168.

B50.    Review of *The Searching Mind: An Introduction to the Philosophy of God*, by Joseph Donceel. In *Religious Studies Review* 9 (January 1983): 52-53.

B51.    "Wij hebben geen sleutel tot Gods cijfers." Review article of *Religion, If There is no God*, by Leszek Kolakowski. *De Standaard* 61 (September 8-9, 1984): Standaard der letteren no. 1687, p. 1.

a.    ▶Also appears in English as Review of *Religion: If There Is No God: On God, the Devil, Sin and Worries of the So-called Philosophy of Religion*, by Leszek Kolakowski. In *The Journal of Religion* 65 (January 1985): 129-131.   → see B53.

B52.    Letter to the Editor, regarding Thomas Sheehan, "The Revolution in the Church." Review of *Eternal Life?*, by Hans Küng. In *New York Review of Books* 31 (November 22, 1984): 56. → see A191.

## 1985-1989

B53.    Review of *Religion: If There Is No God: On God, the Devil, Sin and Worries of the So-called Philosophy of Religion*, by Leszek

Kolakowski. In *The Journal of Religion* 65 (January 1985): 129-131. → see B51.a.

B54. Review of *Rosa Luxemburg, Women's Liberation, and Marx's Philosophy of Revolution*, by Raya Dunayevskaya. In *The Owl of Minerva* 18 (Fall 1986): 77- 79.

B55. Review of *Genèse du materialisme dans les écrits de jeunesse de Karl Marx*, by Jean-Guy Meunier. In *Religious Studies Review* 12 (July-October 1986): 266-267.

B56. Review of *Marxism and Morality*, by Steven Lukes. In *Review of Politics* 49 (Spring 1987): 290-294.

B57. Review of *Lectures on the Philosophy of Religion*, 3 vols., by Georg Wilhelm Friedrich Hegel. New translation by R. Brown, P. Hodgson, J. Stewart. In *Religious Studies Review* 13 (July 1987): 193-197. [Review Essay]. → see A220.

B58. Review of *Marxism and Modernism, An Historical Study of Lukács, Brecht, Benjamin and Adorno*, by Eugene Lunn. In *Studies in Soviet Thought* 34 (October 1987): 195-199.

B59. Review of *The Glory of the Lord: A Theological Aesthetics*, 3 vols., by Hans Urs von Balthasar. Vol. 1 translated by E. L. Merkakis, edited by J. Fessio and J. Riches. Vols. 2 and 3 edited and translation supervised by J. Fessio and J. Riches. In *Religion and Literature* 19 (Autumn 1987): 67-81. → see A247.b.

B60. Review of *The Planetary Man*. Vol. 3, *Let the Future Come*, by Wilfrid Desan. In *Review of Metaphysics* 42 (June 1989): 822-824.

B61. Reviews of *The Spirit of Life: The Holy Spirit in the Life of the Christian*, by Luis Bermejo and *Ignatius Loyola the Mystic*, by Harvey Egan. In *America* 161 (September 30, 1989): 192-195.

**1990-1996**

B62.  Review of *An Interpretation of Religion: Human Responses to the Transcendent,* by John Hick. In *American Catholic Philosophical Quaterly* 65 (Winter 1991): 109-111.

B63.  Review of *Explorations de l'espace théologique: Études de théologie et de philosophie de la religion,* by Antoine Vergote. In *American Catholic Philosophical Quaterly* 65 (Spring 1991): 245-246.

B64.  Review of *The Specter of the Absurd: Sources and Criticisms of Modern Nihilism,* by Donald Crosby. In *Faith and Philosophy* 8 (July 1991): 408-410.

B65.  Review of *The Foundations of Mysticism.* Vol. 1 of *The Presence of God: A History of Western Christian Mysticism,* by Bernard McGinn. In *Thomist* 57 (January 1993): 133-135.

B66.  "Jansenius, an Intellectual Biography." Review article of *Jansénius d'Ypres (1584- 1638),* by Jean Orcibal. In *The Journal of Religion* 73 (January 1993): 75-82.    → see A277.

B67.  Review of *Past Imperfect: French Intellectuals, 1944-1956,* by Tony Judt. In *First Things* 33 (December 1993): 44-48.

B68.  Review of *The Growth of Mysticism,* by Bernard McGinn. In *Thomist* 60 (July 1996): 475-478.

B69.  "The Case for Jansenism." Review article of *God Owes Us Nothing: A Brief Remark on Pascal's Religion and the Spirit of Jansenism,* by Leszek Kolakowski. In *The Journal of Religion* 76 (October 1996): 607-610.    → see A298.

## C. WORKS ON THE THOUGHT OF LOUIS DUPRÉ

C1.  Angelet, Benoit. "Louis Dupré in de Gentse kultuurvereniging [over Marx' kultuurkritiek]." *Kritiek* 8 (1984): 118-122.

C2.   Berry, Donald. "Religion as a Point of View." *Perspectives in Religious Studies* 9 (Fall 1982): 213; 221-222.

C3.   Blanshard, Brand. "Reply to Mr. Dupré['s 'Faith and Reason']." In *The Philosophy of Brand Blanshard*. The Library of Living Philosophers 15. Edited by Paul Schilpp. La Salle, IL: Open Court, 1980, pp. 1002-1014.   → see A147.

C4.   Boers, Hendrikus. "Commentary on Louis Dupré's 'Secular Man and His Religion.' " *Proceedings of the American Catholic Philosophical Association* 42 (1968): 93-96.   → see A54.

C5.   Bouckaert, Luk. *Leren filosoferen. In dialoog met K. Marx, I. Illich, L. Dupré en E. Levinas.* Louvain: Acco, 1981.

C6.   Burrell, David. "A Response (I) to Louis Dupré['s 'Transcendence and Immanence as Theological Categories']." *Catholic Theological Society of America Proceedings* 31 (June 9-12, 1976): 11-14.   → see A120.

C7.   Carr, Anne. "A Response (II) to Louis Dupré['s 'Transcendence and Immanence as Theological Categories']." *Catholic Theological Society of America Proceedings* 31 (June 9-12, 1976): 15-19.   → see A120.

C8.   Casarella, Peter. "On Dupré's *Passage to Modernity*." *Communio (US)* 21 (Fall 1994): 551-561. [Review Article].   → see D224.

C9.   De Visscher, Jacques. "Inleiding: De cultuurkritiek van Louis Dupré." Introduction to *De symboliek van het heilige*. Kampen: Kok Agora; Kapellen: DNB/Pelckmans, 1991, pp. 7-21.

C10.  De Visscher, Jacques. "Vandaag moet de christen het atheïsme in zichzelf onderkennen: Vraaggesprek met de godsdienstfilosoof Louis Dupré." *Kultuurleven* 48 (February 1981): 127-135. [Interview].   → see A158.

C11. Feld, Edward. "Comments on Dupré." *National Institute for Campus Ministries Journal* 7 (Summer 1982): 21-24. → see A167.

C12. Gheisens, Henri. "De Religieuze ervaring volgens Louis Dupré." Licentiaat in de Godsdienstwetenschappen. Thesis. K. U. Leuven, Faculteit der Godgeleerd-heid. Louvain, 1979.

C13. Henrici, Peter. "Response to Louis Dupré." In *Catholicism and Secularization in America: Essays on Nature, Grace, and Culture*. Edited by David Schindler. Huntington, IN: Our Sunday Visitor; Notre Dame, IN: Communio Books, 1990, pp. 74-79. → see A252.

C14. Hill, William. "The God of the Other Dimension." *The New Scholasticism* 50 (Spring 1976): 212-222. [Discussion Article]. → see D76.

C15. Kurtz, Paul. Letter to the Editor regarding Dupré, "The New Humanist Manifesto." *Commonweal* 99 (December 21, 1973): 320-321. → see A92. → see A93.

C16. Levesque, Paul J. *Symbol as the Primary Religious Category in the Thought of Louis Dupré: Foundation for Contemporary Sacramentology*. 2 vols. Ph.D. dissertation. K.U. Leuven, Faculty of Theology. Louvain, 1995.

C17. Levesque, Paul J. "A Symbolical Sacramental Methodology: An Application of the Thought of Louis Dupré." *Questions Liturgiques/Studies in Liturgy* 76 (1995): 161-181.

C18. McCormick, Richard. "Notes on Moral Theology: January-June, 1967." *Theological Studies* 28 (December 1967): 750.
 a. ▶Also appears in *Notes on Moral Theology 1965 through 1980*. Washington, D.C.: University Press of America, 1981, pp. 118, 124.

C19. McCormick, Richard. "Notes on Moral Theology: The Abortion Dossier." *Theological Studies* 35 (June 1974): 351-353.

a. ▶Also appears in *Notes on Moral Theology 1965 through 1980*. Washington, D.C.: University Press of America, 1981, pp. 512-514.

C20. Malone, Nancy. "The Falconer: Comments on Dupré." *National Institute for Campus Ministries Journal* 7 (Summer 1982): 25-31. → see A167.

C21. Milazzo, Alfia. Ph.D. Dissertation. Department of Philosophy, Sacro Cuore University, Milano.

C22. Palmer, Parker. "Who is Absent? Comments on Dupré." *National Institute for Campus Ministries Journal* 7 (Summer 1982): 32-39. → see A167.

C23. Pannenberg, Wolfhart. "A Response to My American Friends." In *The Theology of Wolfhart Pannenberg: Twelve American Critiques, with an Autobiographical Essay and Response*. Minneapolis: Augsburg Publishing House, 1988, pp. 316-317. → see A223.

C24. Prevallet, Elaine. "Comments on Dupré." *National Institute for Campus Ministries Journal* 7 (Summer 1982): 40-48. → see A167.

C25. Quigley, Harold. Letter to the Editor regarding Dupré, "The New Humanist Manifesto." *Commonweal* 99 (December 21, 1973): 319-320. → see A92. → see A93.

C26. Radest, Howard. Letter to the Editor regarding Dupré, "The New Humanist Manifesto." *Commonweal* 99 (December 21, 1973): 318-319. → see A92. → see A93.
   a. ▶Also appears with slight modifications as "Some Comments on Dupré." *Humanist* 34 (January-February 1974): 12. → see A100.

C27. Riordan, P. "Religion as 'Weltanschauung': A Solution to a Problem in the Philosophy of Religion." *Aquinas* 34 (September-December 1991): 519-534.

C28.   Stoneburner, Tony. "Penobscot Observations: Comments on Dupré."
       *National Institute for Campus Ministries Journal* 7 (Summer
       1982): 49-59.   → see A167.

C29.   Swiderski, Edward. "Praxis As Culture: Dupre's Recovery of Marx'
       Project." Review of *Marx's Social Critique of Culture*. In
       *Zeitschrift für philosophische Forschung* 40 (October-December
       1986): 599-606.   → see D179.

C30.   Vandewalle, E. *Van het in-de-wereld-zijn naar ver-inner-lijking.*
       *Existentie en sacraliteit bij Martin Heidegger. Inwendigheid en*
       *transcendentie bij Louis Dupré.* 2 vols. Ph.L. thesis. K.U. Leu-
       ven, Higher Institute of Philosophy. Louvain, 1985. Published
       under the same title in the series Eclectica 15: 67-68. Brus-
       sels: Economische Hogeschool Sint-Aloysius, 1987.

## D.  REVIEWS OF LOUIS DUPRÉ'S BOOKS

*HET VERTREKPUNT DER MARXISTISCHE WIJSBEGEERTE:*
*DE KRITIEK OP HEGELS STAATSRECHT* (1954)

D1.    De Mullewie, M. Review of *Het vertrekpunt der marxistische wijsbe-*
       *geerte.* In *Tijdschrift voor Philosophie* 17 (June 1955): 354-355.

D2.    De Raedemaeker, F. Review of *Het vertrekpunt der marxistische*
       *wijsbegeerte.* In *Streven* 8 (November 1954): 185.

D3.    De Raedemaeker, F. Review of *Het vertrekpunt der marxistische*
       *wijsbegeerte.* In *Bijdragen* 16 (1955): 226-227.

D4.    Decloux, S. Review of *Het vertrekpunt der marxistische wijsbegeer-*
       *te.* In *Nouvelle Revue Théologique* 79 (May 1957): 553-534.

D5.    Grooten, J. Review of *Het vertrekpunt der marxistische wijsbe-*
       *geerte.* In *Vlaams Opvoedkundig Tijdschrift* 34 (July 1954):
       376.

D6. Leemans, Victor. "Spanningen van het economische en het sociale." Review of *Het vertrekpunt der marxistische wijsbegeerte*. In *Tijdschrift voor Philosophie* 18 (June 1956): 277-281.

D7. Van Gestel, C. Review of *Het vertrekpunt der marxistische wijsbegeerte*. In *Kultuurleven* 22 (February/March 1955): 146.

D8. Widart, H. Review of *Het vertrekpunt der marxistische wijsbegeerte*. In *Collectanea Mechliniensia* 40 (January 1955): 115-116.

D9. Wylleman, A. Review of *Het vertrekpunt der marxistische wijsbegeerte*. In *Revue Philosophique de Louvain* 54 (February 1956): 157-161.


*KIERKEGAARDS THEOLOGIE* (1958)
(English 1963, *Kierkegaard as Theologian*)

D10. Notice of *Kierkegaard as Theologian*. In *The Christian Century* 80 (February 27, 1963): 273.

D11. Review of *Kierkegaard as Theologian*. In *The Times Literary Supplement* 63 (June 11, 1964): 517.

D12. Brookfield, C. Review of *Kierkegaard as Theologian*. In *Union Seminary Quarterly Review* 19 (January 1964): 176-178.

D13. Clarke, Jack. Review of *Kierkegaard as Theologian*. In *Library Journal* 88 (January 1, 1963): 105-106.

D14. Demske, James. Review of *Kierkegaard as Theologian*. In *Thought* 39 (Summer 1964): 303-306.

D15. Dru, A. Review of *Kierkegaard as Theologian*. In *Clergy Review* 49 (November 1964): 722-724.

D16. Emge, W. Review of *Kierkegaard as Theologian*. In *Review of Metaphysics* 17 (December 1963): 303.

344 SYMBOLS OF TRANSCENDENCE

D17.  Endres, Benedict. Review of *Kierkegaard as Theologian*. In *Cross and Crown* 15 (Summer 1963): 380.

D18.  Fransen, P. Review of *Kierkegaards Theologie*. In *Bijdragen* 20 (1959): 213-214.

D19.  Gerber, Rudolph. Review of *Kierkegaard as Theologian*. In *America* 108 (May 25, 1963): 775-777.

D20.  Holloway, Maurice. Review of *Kierkegaard as Theologian*. In *The Modern Schoolman* 42 (November 1964 to May 1965): 121-122.

D21.  Holmer, Paul. Review of *Kierkegaard as Theologian*. In *The Journal of Religion* 43 (July 1963): 255-256.

D22.  Kantonen, T. Review of *Kierkegaard as Theologian*. In *Religion in Life* 33 (Winter 1963-1964): 152.

D23.  Lauer, Quentin. Review of *Kierkegaard as Theologian*. In *Theological Studies* 24 (September 1963): 510-512.

D24.  McNassar, John. Review of *Kierkegaard as Theologian*. In *Emmanuel* 70 (February 1964): 89-90.

D25.  Michalson, Carl. Review of *Kierkegaard as Theologian*. In *Thomism Today* 20 (October 1963): 422-424.

D26.  Munster, H. van. Review of *Kierkegaards Theologie*. In *Revue Philosophique de Louvain* 57 (May 1959): 250-251.

D27.  Nota, J. Review of *Kierkegaards Theologie*. In *Streven* 12 (April 1959): 692.

D28.  Santoni, Ronald. Review of *Kierkegaard as Theologian*. In *Philosophy and Phenomenological Research* 25 (December 1964): 301-302.

D29.  Schlitzer, Albert. Review of *Kierkegaard as Theologian*. In *Thought* 39 (June 1964): 303-305.

D30.  Sokolowski, Robert. Review of *Kierkegaard as Theologian*. In *American Ecclesiastical Review* 151 (July-December 1964): 197-198.

D31.  Walgrave, Jan. "Godskennis en Godsdienstfilosofie." Review of *Kierkegaards Theologie*. In *Tijdschrift voor Filosofie* 26 (September 1964): 534-536.

D32.  Willaert, B. Review of *Kierkegaards Theologie*. In *Collationes Brugenses et Gandavenses* 5 (May 1959): 275-276.


*CONTRACEPTION AND CATHOLICS* (1964)

D33.  Review of *Contraception and Catholics*. In *Choice* 1 (February 1965): 564.
  a.  ▶Also appears in *Choice: A Classified Cumulation*. March 1964-February 1974. Vol. 3, *Literature, Performing Arts, Philosophy, Religion*. Totowa, NJ: Rowman and Littlefield, 1976, pp. 964-965.

D34.  Barry, R. Review of *Contraception and Catholics*. In *Perspectives* 9 (November- December 1964): 185.

D35.  Francoeur, Robert. Review of *Contraception and Catholics*. In *Commonweal* 81 (October 16, 1964): 104.

D36.  Gros, Charles. Review of *Contraception and Catholics*. In *Library Journal* 89 (December 1, 1964): 4818-4819.

D37.  Hagerty, John. Review of *Contraception and Catholics*. In *Priest* 21 (May 1965): 429-430.

D38.  Kane, J. Review of *Contraception and Catholics*. In *Ave Maria* 101 (April 10, 1965): 27.

D39.  Lewis, John. Review of *Contraception and Catholics*. In *The Modern Schoolman* 44 (November 1966 to May 1967): 391-395.

D40.  McCormick, Richard. Review of *Contraception and Catholics*. In *America* 111 (November 14, 1964): 628-629.

D41.  Osborne, Harold. Review of *Contraception and Catholics*. In *Journal of Church and State* 7 (Autumn 1965): 473-474.

D42.  Peters, Edward. Review of *Contraception and Catholics*. In *Catholic World* 201 (June 1965): 206-207.

## *THE PHILOSOPHICAL FOUNDATIONS OF MARXISM* (1966)
(Dutch 1970, *De filosofische grondslagen van het marxisme*)

D43.  Review of *The Philosophical Foundations of Marxism*. In *Choice* 3 (October 1966): 663.
   a.  ▶Also appears in *Choice: A Classified Cumulation*. March 1964-February 1974. Vol. 3, *Literature, Performing Arts, Philosophy, Religion*. Totowa, NJ: Rowman and Littlefield, 1976, p. 605.

D44.  Review of *The Philosophical Foundations of Marxism*. In *Science and Society* 31 (Summer 1967): 382.
   a.  ▶Also appears in *Science and Society* 31 (Winter 1967): 126.

D45.  Blakeley, Thomas. Review of *The Philosophical Foundations of Marxism*. In *Thomist* 31 (October 1967): 520-522.

D46.  Collins, James. Review of *The Philosophical Foundations of Marxism*. In *Cross Currents* 17 (Spring 1967): 201.

D47.  De George, Richard. Review of *The Philosophical Foundations of Marxism*. In *The New Scholasticism* 43 (Winter 1969): 178-181.

D48.  Kamenka, Eugene. Review of *The Philosophical Foundations of Marxism*. In *Problems of Communism* 17 (May-June 1968): 49-53.

D49.   Hinners, Richard. Review of *The Philosophical Foundations of Marxism*. In *Theological Studies* 29 (March 1968): 178.

D50.   Lannoy, J. Review of *De filosofische grondslagen van het marxisme*. In *Tijdschrift voor Filosofie* 33 (March 1971): 171-172.

D51.   Lauer, Quentin. Review of *The Philosophical Foundations of Marxism*. In *International Philosophical Quarterly* 8 (December 1968): 636-637.

D52.   Ryerson, Stanley. Review of *The Philosophical Foundations of Marxism*. In *Dialogue* 5 (1967): 643-644.

D53.   Stack, George. Review of *The Philosophical Foundations of Marxism*. In *The Modern Schoolman* 46 (November 1968): 61-63.

D54.   Van Ael, Joris. Review of *De filosofische grondslagen van het marxisme*. In *Collationes Brugenses et Gandavenses* 19 (1973): 140.

*THE OTHER DIMENSION:*
*A SEARCH FOR THE MEANING OF RELIGIOUS ATTITUDES* (1972)
(French 1977, *L'autre dimension*)
(Dutch 1991, *De symboliek van het heilige*)

D55.   Review of *The Other Dimension*. In *Catholic Library World* 44 (November 1972): 232.

D56.   Altizer, Thomas J. J. "Religion Conquering Itself." Review of *The Other Dimension*. In *The Journal of Religion* 54 (January 1974): 86-92.

D57.   Anderson, Tyson. Review of *The Other Dimension*. In *National Catholic Reporter* 8 (May 26, 1972): 15.

D58.   Ayers, Robert. Review of *The Other Dimension*. In *International Journal for Philosophy of Religion* 6 (Fall 1975): 193-197.

D59.   Babolin, Albino. Review of *The Other Dimension*. In *Filosofia* 32 (January 1981): 96.

D60.   Bauer, Dominique. Review of *De symboliek van het heilige*. In *De Uil van Minerva* 9 (Winter 1992/1993): 119-123.

D61.   Burrell, David. Review of *The Other Dimension*. In *Thomist* 38 (April 1974): 377- 378.

D62.   Corrigan, Winifred. Review of *The Other Dimension*. In *The Sign* 51 (July-August 1972): 43-44.

D63.   Cren, P. Review of *L'autre dimension*. In *Lumière* 28 (June-July 1980): 133.

D64.   Dartigues, A. Review of *L'autre dimension*. In *Bulletin de Littérature Ecclésiastique* 81 (July-September 1980): 238-239.

D65.   Donceel, Joseph. Review of *The Other Dimension*. In *International Philosophical Quarterly* 15 (March 1975): 99-109.

D66.   Drane, James. Review of *The Other Dimension*. In *America* 126 (April 15, 1972): 406-407.

D67.   Dubois, Pierre. Review of *The Other Dimension*. In *Revue Philosophique de la France et de L'étranger* 99 (July-September 1974): 340-341.

D68.   Farrelly, M. John. Review of *The Other Dimension*. In *American Ecclesiastical Review* 167 (April 1973): 284-287.

D69.   Febure, Véronique. Review of *L'autre dimension*. In *Bibliographie de la Philosophie* 26 (1979): 340.

D70.   Flew, Antony. Review of *The Other Dimension*. In *Philosophical Books* 14 (January 1973): 5-7.

D71. Fourcade, Jean. Review of *L'autre dimension*. In *La Vie Spirituelle* 60 (May-June 1978): 488-489.

D72. Galot, Jean. Review of *L'autre dimension*. In *Gregorianum* 59 (1978): 415-416.

D73. Garvey, E. Review of *The Other Dimension*. In *Triumph* 8 (February 1973): 32-36.

D74. Gilkey, Langdon. "The Dimensions of Dupré." Review of *The Other Dimension*. In *Commonweal* 97 (October 20, 1972): 63-66.

D75. Heiser, W. Charles. Review of *The Other Dimension*. In *Library Journal* 97 (February 1, 1972): 509.
  a. ▶Also appears in *The Library Journal Book Review 1972*. New York: R. R. Bowker Co., 1973, pp.459-460.

D76. Hill, William. "The God of the Other Dimension." *The New Scholasticism* 50 (Spring 1976): 212-222. [Discussion Article]. → see C14.

D77. Javaux, J. Review of *L'autre dimension*. In *Nouvelle Revue Théologique* 100 (November-December 1978): 924-925.

D78. Long, Eugene. Review of *The Other Dimension*. In *International Journal for Philosophy of Religion* 5 (Fall 1974): 176-180.

D79. Marty, Martin. "Religious Book Week: Critics' Choices." Review of *The Other Dimension*. In *Commonweal* 97 (February 23, 1973): 480.

D80. Marty, Martin. "Religious Book Week: Critics' Choices." Review of *The Other Dimension*. In *Commonweal* 97 (December 8, 1972): 236-237.

D81. Marty, Martin. Review of *The Other Dimension*. In *The Critic* 30 (May 1972): 85.

D82.    McBrien, Richard. "Religious Book Week: Critics' Choices." Review of *The Other Dimension*. In *Commonweal* 97 (February 23, 1973): 479.

D83.    McCormack, John. Review of *The Other Dimension*. In *Thought* 48 (Summer 1973): 311-312.

D84.    Meynell, Hugo. Review of *The Other Dimension*. In *Month* 6 (October 1973): 345- 346.

D85.    Murchland, Bernard. Review of *The Other Dimension*. In *Philosophy and Phenomenological Research* 33 (June 1973): 592-594.

D86.    Nachbahr, Bernard. Review of *The Other Dimension*. In *Theological Studies* 33 (June 1972): 347-349.

D87.    Neufeld, K. Review of *L'autre dimension*. In *Theologie und Philosophie* 53 (1978): 588-589.

D88.    Olivier, P. Review of *L'autre dimension*. In *Recherches de Science Religieuses* 67 (July-September 1979): 472-475.

D89.    Onimus, Jean. "Notes Critiques: *The Other Dimension*. In *Revue de Métaphysique et de Morale* 82 (July-September 1977): 428-429.

D90.    Pinnock, Clark. Review of *The Other Dimension*. In *Christianity Today* 17 (December 8, 1972): 254-255.

D91.    Robert, Jean-Dominique. Review of *L'autre dimension*. In *Laval Théologique et Philosophique* 36 (June 1980): 205-209.
  a.    ▶Also appears in *Revue Philosophique de Louvain* 78 (August 1980): 454-459.

D92.    Robertson, John. Review of *The Other Dimension*. In *Journal of the American Academy of Religion* 44 (September 1976): 579.

D93. Rule, Philip. Review of *The Other Dimension*. In *New Catholic World* 215 (July 1972), 176-177.

D94. Schmitz, Kenneth. "Scrutinizing the Inscrutable." Critical Study of *The Other Dimension*. In *Review of Metaphysics* 27 (December 1973): 346-370.

D95. Shea, William. Review of *The Other Dimension*. In *The Jurist* 34 (Winter/Spring 1974): 236-239.

D96. Stanton, Edward. Review of *The Other Dimension*. In *America* 127 (November 18, 1972): 424.

D97. Tambasco, Anthony. Review of *The Other Dimension*. In *Review for Religious* 31 (November 1972): 1073.

D98. Tracy, David. "The Dialectical Nature of Religion." Review of *The Other Dimension*. In *The Christian Century* 89 (December 6, 1972): 1252-1253.

D99. Vergote, Antoine. Review of *The Other Dimension*. In *Revue Philosophique de Louvain* 73 (May 1975): 427-433.

D100. Walgrave, Jan. Review of *The Other Dimension*. In *Tijdschrift voor Filosofie* 37 (1975): 733-735.

*TRANSCENDENT SELFHOOD:*
*THE LOSS AND REDISCOVERY OF THE INNER LIFE* (1976)
(Revised in Dutch 1981, 1983², *Terugkeer naar innerlijkheid*)

D101. Altizer, Thomas J. J. Review of *Transcendent Selfhood*. In *Religious Studies Review* 3 (July 1977): 184.

D102. Ashbrook, James. Review of *Transcendent Selfhood*. In *Religion in Life* 46 (Autumn 1977): 385-386.

D103. Bertocci, Peter. Review of *Transcendent Selfhood*. In *Religious Studies* 15 (September 1979): 414-417.

D104. Biallas, L. J. Review of *Transcendent Selfhood*. In *Worship* 52 (March 1978): 176- 177.

D105. Burns, Sharon. Review of *Transcendent Selfhood*. In *Theological Studies* 38 (September 1977): 611.

D106. Clarke, W. Norris. Review of *Transcendent Selfhood*. In *International Philosophical Quarterly* 18 (September 1978): 359-361.

D107. Dinan, Stephan. Review of *Transcendent Selfhood*. In *The New Scholasticism* 52 (Summer 1978): 464-466.

D108. Duffy, Stephen. Review of *Transcendent Selfhood*. In *Horizons* 4 (Fall 1977): 271- 272.

D109. Evans, Donald. "New Books in Review: The Shift into Inwardness." Review of *Transcendent Selfhood*. In *Yale Review* 67 (December 1977): 292-296.

D110. Gannon, Edward. Review of *Transcendent Selfhood*. In *Best Sellers* 37 (April 1977): 23.

D111. Green, Patrick. Review of *Transcendent Selfhood*. In *The Christian Century* 94 (November 16, 1977): 1070.

D112. Kelly, James. Review of *Transcendent Selfhood*. In *Commonweal* 104 (February 4, 1977): 94.

D113. Lawler, Michael. Review of *Transcendent Selfhood*. In *Cross and Crown* 29 (September 1977): 297-299.

D114. Long, Eugene. Review of *Transcendent Selfhood*. In *Review of Metaphysics* 32 (September 1978): 133-134.

D115. Marsh, Michael. Review of *Transcendent Selfhood*. In *Thomist* 43 (October 1979): 674-675.

D116. McInerny, Ralph. "Religious Book Week: Critics' Choices." Review of *Transcendent Selfhood*. In *Commonweal* 104 (March 4, 1977): 156.

D117. Moore, William. Review of *Transcendent Selfhood*. In *New Review of Books and Religion* 1 (February 1977): 17.

D118. Morneau, R. Review of *Transcendent Selfhood*. In *Sisters Today* 48 (June-July 1977): 696.

D119. Murchland, Bernard. Review of *Transcendent Selfhood*. In *Philosophy and Phenomenological Research* 39 (September 1978): 147-148.

D120. Parker, Claude. Review of *Transcendent Selfhood*. In *Library Journal* 102 (March 1977): 611.
   a.  ►Also appears in *The Library Journal Book Review 1977*. New York: R. R. Bowker Co., 1978, p. 365.

D121. Peter, Carl. Review of *Transcendent Selfhood*. In *The Journal of Religion* 59 (July 1979): 335-339.

D122. Smith, Newland. Review of *Transcendent Selfhood*. In *Journal of Religion and Health* 17 (July 1978): 217-218.

D123. Trainor, Paul. Review of *Transcendent Selfhood*. In *The Modern Schoolman* 55 (November 1977): 108-109.

D124. Van Doosselaere, Étienne. Review of *Terugkeer naar innerlijkheid*. In *Tijdschrift voor Filosofie* 45 (March 1983): 670.

D125. Review of *Transcendent Selfhood*. In *Kirkus Reviews* 44 (November 1976): 1213.

## A DUBIOUS HERITAGE:
## STUDIES IN THE PHILOSOPHY OF RELIGION AFTER KANT (1977)

D126.   Review of *A Dubious Heritage*. In *Choice* 15 (September 1978): 891.

D127.   Review of *A Dubious Heritage*. In *The Christian Century* 95 (May 17, 1978): 550.

D128.   Babolin, Albino. Review of *A Dubious Heritage*. In *Filosofia* 37 (May-August 1986): 160.

D129.   Begley, John. Review of *A Dubious Heritage*. In *Best Sellers* 38 (April 1978): 92.

D130.   Bonansea, Bernardino. Review of *A Dubious Herigate*. In *Review of Metaphysics* 34 (June 1981): 787-788.

D131.   Boozer, Jack. Review of *A Dubious Heritage*. In *International Journal for Philosophy of Religion* 12 (1981): 127-128.

D132.   Chethimattam, John. Review of *A Dubious Heritage*. In *Journal of Dharma* 2 (June 1977): 339-345.

D133.   Despland, Michel. "Book Notes: *A Dubious Heritage*. In *Religious Studies Review* 5 (January 1979): 71.

D134.   Dinan, Stephen. Review of *A Dubious Heritage*. In *The New Scholasticism* 54 (Autumn 1980): 522-524.

D135.   Kockelmans, Joseph. Review of *A Dubious Heritage*. In *Religious Studies* 15 (September 1979): 411-413.

D136.   Nachbahr, Bernard. Review of *A Dubious Heritage*. In *Thought* 53 (December 1978): 454-456.

D137.   O'Farrell, Frank. Review of *A Dubious Heritage*. In *Gregorianum* 65 (1984): 187-188.

D138. Rose, Mary. Review of *A Dubious Heritage*. In *Horizons* 5 (Fall 1978): 278-279.

D139. Teske, Roland. "Book Reviw: *A Dubious Heritage*. In *The Modern Schoolman* 56 (March 1979): 285-286.

## *THE DEEPER LIFE:*
## *AN INTRODUCTION TO CHRISTIAN MYSTICISM* (1981)

D140. Review of *The Deeper Life*. In *Catholic Library World* 53 (May/June 1982): 422-423.

D141. Review of *The Deeper Life*. In *Catholic Library World* 56 (February 1985): 299.

D142. Review of *The Deeper Life*. In *Choice* 19 (March 1982): 937-938.

D143. Baillie, Hal. Review of *The Deeper Life*. In *Best Sellers* 41 (December 1981): 354.

D144. Christopher, Michael. Review of *The Deeper Life*. In *U.S. Catholic* 47 (January 1982): 50-52.

D145. Collinge, William. Review of *The Deeper Life*. In *Theological Studies* 43 (September 1982): 547-548.

D146. Curtin, Timothy. Review of *The Deeper Life*. In *America* 146 (February 20, 1982): 137.

D147. Hardy, Richard. Review of *The Deeper Life*. In *Eglise et Théologie* 13 (May 1982): 257.

D148. Hinson, E. Glenn Review of *The Deeper Life*. In *Review and Expositor* 79 (Fall 1982): 720.

D149. McPherson, Clair. Review of *The Deeper Life*. In *Library Journal* 107 (January 15, 1982): 183.

D150.    Toolan, David. Review of *The Deeper Life*. In *Religious Studies Review* 10 (April 1984): 160-161.


## *MARX'S SOCIAL CRITIQUE OF CULTURE* (1983)

D151.    Review of *Marx's Social Critique of Culture*. In *Los Angeles Times Book Review* (August 25, 1985): 8.

D152.    Review of *Marx's Social Critique of Culture*. In *Choice* 21 (June 1984): 1478-1479.

D153.    Adamson, Walter. Review of *Marx's Social Critique of Culture*. In *Political Theory* 12 (May 1984): 283-286.

D154.    Allen, Derek. Review of *Marx's Social Critique of Culture*. In *Canadian Philosophical Reviews* 5 (October 1985): 331-333.

D155.    Aman, Kenneth. Review of *Marx's Social Critique of Culture*. In *Man and World* 20 (October 1987): 457-472.

D156.    Blanchette, Oliva. Review of *Marx's Social Critique of Culture*. In *Studies in Soviet Thought* 31 (February 1986): 149-152.

D157.    Bourg, Carroll. Review of *Marx's Social Critique of Culture*. In *Review of Religious Research* 28 (September 1986): 90-92.

D158.    Douglass, R. Bruce. "The 'Spirit of Capitalism' in Marx. In Review of *Marx's Social Critique of Culture*. In *The Review of Politics* 47 (July 1985): 470-473.

D159.    Fitzpatrick, Peter. Review of *Marx's Social Critique of Culture*. In *The Heythrop Journal* 28 (April 1987): 218-219.

D160.    Geoghegan, Vincent. Review of *Marx's Social Critique of Culture*. In *Political Studies* 32 (December 1984): 688-689.

D161. Homann, Frederick. Review of *Marx's Social Critique of Culture*. In *Best Sellers* 43 (January 1984): 383.

D162. Kerlin, Michael. Review of *Marx's Social Critique of Culture*. In *Theological Studies* 45 (September 1984): 587-588.

D163. Kimmerle, H. Review of *Marx's Social Critique of Culture*. In *International Journal for Philosophy of Religion* 16 (1984): 174-175.

D164. Larrain, Jorge. Review of *Marx's Social Critique of Culture*. In *Contemporary Sociology* 14 (November 1985): 780-782.

D165. Lawrence, Fred. Review of *Marx's Social Critique of Culture*. In *Religious Studies Review* 14 (January 1988): 11-14.

D166. McBride, William. Review of *Marx's Social Critique of Culture*. In *The Owl of Minerva* 17 (Spring 1986): 212-214.

D167. McBride, William. Review of *Marxism and Christianity*, by D. Turner and *Marx's Social Critique of Culture*, by L. Dupré. In *Faith and Philosophy* 4 (January 1987): 108-115.

D168. Morgan, James. Review of *Marx's Social Critique of Culture*. In *Review of Metaphysics* 38 (September 1984): 117-118.

D169. O'Malley, Joseph. "The Moral Appeal of Marx's Social Thought." Review Article of *Marx's Social Critique of Culture*. And *Making Sense of Marx*, by John Elster. In *Bulletin of the Hegel Society of Great Britain* 12 (Autumn/Winter 1985): 12-17.

D170. Papa, Edward. Review of *Marx's Social Critique of Culture*. In *Cross Currents* 35 (Summer/Fall 1985): 346-349.

D171. Rehg, William. Review of *Marx's Social Critique of Culture*. In *The Modern Schoolman* 63 (March 1986): 220-222.

D172.   Robertson, Edwin. Review of *Marx's Social Critique of Culture*. In *Theology* 88 (March 1985): 162-164.

D173.   Rockmore, Tom. Review of *Marx's Social Critique of Culture*. In *International Studies in Philosophy* 20 (1988): 73-74.

D174.   Samples, John. Review of *Marx's Social Critique of Culture*. In *Thomist* 53 (April 1989): 346-348.

D175.   Shortland, Michael. Review of *Marx's Social Critique of Culture*. In *Journal of European Studies* 14 (September 1984): 223-224.

D176.   Stafford, William. Review of *Marx's Social Critique of Culture*. In *Literature and History* 11 (Autumn 1985): 305.

D177.   Stillman, Peter. Review of *Marx's Social Critique of Culture*. In *The American Political Science Review* 78 (December 1984): 1184-1185.

D178.   Strain, Charles. Review of *Marx's Social Critique of Culture*. In *Religious Studies Review* 14 (January 1988): 14-16.

D179.   Swiderski, Edward. "Praxis as Culture: Dupré's Recovery of Marx' Project." Review of *Marx's Social Critique of Culture*. In *Zeitschrift für philosophische Forschung* 40 (1986): 599-606.  → see C29.

D180.   Vetö, Miklos. Review of *Marx's Social Critique of Culture*. In *Revue de Métaphysique et de Morale* 92 (January-March 1987): 130-131.

D181.   West, Cornel. Review of *Marx's Social Critique of Culture*. In *The Journal of Religion* 66 (January 1986): 85-86.

D182.   Westphal, Merold. Review of *Marx's Social Critique of Culture*. In *Christian Scholar's Review* 14 (1985): 265-266.

## THE COMMON LIFE: THE ORIGINS OF TRINITARIAN MYSTICISM AND ITS DEVELOPMENT BY JAN RUUSBROEC (1984)

D183. Rolfson, Helen. Review of *The Common Life*. In *Mystics Quarterly* 17 (December 1991): 195-196.

D184. Ludwig, N. Review of *The Common Life*. In *Epiphany* 5 (Winter 1984): 97.

D185. Mary of Jesus, Sr. Review of *The Common Life*. In *Spirituality Today* 37 (Summer 1985): 188-189.

D186. Sullivan-Drury, Maureen. Review of *The Common Life*. In *Best Sellers* 44 (October 1984): 274.


## LIGHT FROM LIGHT: AN ANTHOLOGY OF CHRISTIAN MYSTICISM (1988)

D187. Carabine, Deirdre. Review of *Light from Light*. In *Irish Theological Quarterly* 57 (1991): 248.

D188. Chase, Elise. Review of *Light from Light*. In *Library Journal* 113 (March 1, 1988): 71.

D189. Egan, Keith. Review of *Light from Light*. In *Catholic World* 232 (November/December 1989): 278-279.

D190. Egan, Keith. Review of *Light from Light*. In *Horizons* 16 (Spring 1989): 183-184.

D191. Falardeau, Ernest. Review of *Light from Light*. In *Emmanuel* 95 (April 1989): 180.

D192. Faurot, Jean. Review of *Light from Light*. In *Studia Mystica* 13 (Spring 1990): 68-69.

D193.  Harbert, B. Review of *Light from Light*. In *Priest and People* 3 (March 1989): 117.

D194.  Ivory, Thomas. Review of *Light from Light*. In *Louvain Studies* 15 (1990): 90-91.

D195.  Payne, Steven. Review of *Light from Light*. In *Theological Studies* 50 (September 1989): 613-614.

D196.  Rist, A. Review of *Light from Light*. In *Canadian Catholic Review* 7 (July/August 1989): 266.

D197.  Russell, Kenneth. Review of *Light from Light*. In *Eglise et Théologie* 20 (October 1989): 494.

D198.  Thello, Notto. Review of *Light from Light*. In *Norsk Tidsskrift for Misjon* [Oslo: Universitetsforlaget] 43:3 (1989): 185.

D199.  Wenker, M. Review of *Light from Light*. In *Sisters* 60 (April 1989): 495.

## *CHRISTIAN SPIRITUALITY III: POST-REFORMATION AND MODERN* (1989)

D200.  Review of *Christian Spirituality*. In *Catholic Historical Review* 76 (October 1990): 858.

D201.  Review of *Christian Spirituality*. In *The Christian Century* 107 (March 7, 1990): 260.

D202.  Berry, Donald. Review of *Christian Spirituality*. In *Journal of Ecumenical Studies* 27 (Summer 1990): 595-596.

D203.  Bouyer, Louis. Review of *Christian Spirituality*. In *Catholic Historical Review* 76 (October 1990): 858-861.

D204. Burton-Christie, Douglas. Review of *Christian Spirituality*. In *Horizons* 18 (Fall 1991): 342-343.

D205. Cebollada, Pascual. Review of *Christian Spirituality*. In *Estudios Eclesiásticos* 70 (April-June 1995): 248-250.

D206. Graham, William. Review of *Christian Spirituality*. In *National Catholic Reporter* 28 (March 13, 1992): 18.

D207. Heiser, W. Charles. Review of *Christian Spirituality*. In *Theology Digest* 37 (Fall 1990): 255.

D208. Hinson, E. Glenn. Review of *Christian Spirituality*. In *Review and Expositor* 88 (Winter 1991): 118.

D209. LeFevre, Perry. Review of *Christian Spirituality*. In *Chicago Theological Seminary Register* 80 (Spring 1990): 55.

D210. Lonsdale, David. Review of *Christian Spirituality*. In *Theology* 94 (September/October 1991): 367-368.

D211. Louth, Andrew. Review of *Christian Spirituality*. In *Expository Times* 102 (April 1991): 216.

D212. McGeeney, Robert, Jr. Review of *Christian Spirituality*. In *Military Chaplains' Review* (Spring 1992): 92.

D213. McIntosh, Mark. Review of *Christian Spirituality*. In *Religious Studies Review* 20 (April 1994): 133.

D214. McLeod, Frederick. Review of *Christian Spirituality*. In *Review for Religious* 50 (May/June 1991): 463-465.

D215. Rowold, Henry. Review of *Christian Spirituality*. In *International Review of Mission* 82 (July-October 1993): 412-413.

D216.  Schneiders, Sandra. Review of *Christian Spirituality*. In *Theological Studies* 51 (December 1990): 747-749.

D217.  Sheets, J. Review of *Christian Spirituality*. In *Homiletic & Pastoral Review* 91 (March 1991): 72-73.

D218.  Sheldrake, Philip. Review of *Christian Spirituality*. In *Heythrop Journal* 33 (January 1992): 103-105.

D219.  Wainwright, Geoffrey. Review of *Christian Spirituality*. In *Journal of the American Academy of Religion* 61 (Spring 1993): 140-142.

D220.  Wiseman, James. Review of *Christian Spirituality*. In *Spiritual Life* 36 (Winter 1990): 247-249.

*PASSAGE TO MODERNITY* (1993)

D221.  Notes on Current Books. *Passage to Modernity*. In *Virginia Quarterly Review* 70 (Winter 1994): 14.

D222.  Allen, Diogenes. "The Past Never Ends." Review of *Passage to Modernity*. In *Commonweal* 121 (June 3, 1994): 24-25.

D223.  Byrne, Peter. Review of *Passage to Modernity*. In *Religious Studies* 30 (September 1994): 364-366.

D224.  Casarella, Peter. "On Dupré's *Passage to Modernity*." *Communio (US)* 21 (Fall 1994): 551-561. [Review Article]. → see C8.

D225.  Dannhauser, Werner. Review of *Passage to Modernity*. In *First Things* 50 (February 1995): 45-47.

D226.  De Dijn, Herman. Review of *Passage to Modernity*. In *Tijdschrift voor Filosofie* 56 (September 1994): 552-555.

D227. De Visscher, Jacques. "Archeologie van de moderniteit." Review of *Passage to Modernity*. In *Kultuurleven* 61 (June 1994): 22-25.

D228. Desmond, William. Review of *Passage to Modernity*. In *American Catholic Philosophical Quarterly* 70 (Spring 1996): 298-300.

D229. Galgan, Gerald. Review of *Passage to Modernity*. In *Cross Currents* 44 (Fall 1994): 411-413.

D230. Gallagher, Michael. Review of *Passage to Modernity*. In *America* 172 (February 4, 1995): 22-24.

D231. Gendreau, Bernard. Review of *Passage to Modernity*. In *Review of Metaphysics* 48 (March 1995): 655-657.

D232. Kow, James Paul. Review of *Passage to Modernity*. In *Canadian Philosophical Reviews* 14 (August 1994): 251-254.

D233. Levesque, Paul J. Review of *Passage to Modernity*. In *Louvain Studies* 19 (Spring 1994): 81-83.

D234. Lundin, Roger. Review of *Passage to Modernity*. In *Review of Politics* 57 (Winter 1995): 171-173.

D235. Pambrun, James. Review of *Passage to Modernity*. In *Eglise et Théologie* 25 (1994): 269-276.

D236. Scharlemann, Robert. Review of *Passage to Modernity*. In *Modern Theology* 11 (April 1995): 272-274.

D237. Srajek, Martin. Review of *Passage to Modernity*. In *Journal of the American Academy of Religion* 65 (Spring 1997): 218-221.

D238. Starn, Randolph. Review of *Passage to Modernity*. In *The American Historical Review* 101 (February 1996): 154-155.

D239.  Thiel, John. Review of *Passage to Modernity*. In *Theological Studies* 55 (September 1994): 555-556.

D240.  Valcke, Louis. Review of *Passage to Modernity*. In *Laval Théologique et Philosophique* 51 (October 1995): 671-678.


*METAPHYSICS AND CULTURE* (1994)

D241.  Johnston, Suzie and Leslie Armour. Review of *Metaphysics and Culture*. In *Laval Théologique et Philosophique* 51 (February 1995): 216-218.

D242.  Levesque, Paul J. Review of *Metaphysics and Culture*. In *Review of Metaphysics* 50 (June 1997): 883-884.


## E.  BIOGRAPHICAL SKETCHES OF LOUIS DUPRÉ

E1.  *The American Catholic Who's Who*. Vol. 23, *1980-81*. Edited by Joy Anderson. Washington, D.C.: National Catholic News Service, 1979, p. 218.

E2.  *The Blue Book: Leaders of the English-Speaking World. 1976 ed.* London: St. James Press; New York: St. Martin's Press, 1976; reprint, Detroit: Gale Research Co., 1979, p. 477.

E3.  *Contemporary Authors*. Vols. 9-10. Edited by James Ethridge. Detroit: Gale Research Co., 1964, p. 133.

E4.  *Contemporary Authors. First Revision*. Vols. 9-12. Edited by Clare Kinsman and Mary Ann Tennenhouse. Detroit: Gale Research Co., 1974, p. 253.

E5.  *Contemporary Authors. New Revision Series*. Vol. 3. Edited by Ann Evory. Detroit: Gale Research Co., 1981, pp. 182-183.

E6.  *Contemporary Authors. New Revision Series.* Vol. 18. Edited by Linda Metzger and Deborah Straub. Detroit: Gale Research Col, 1986, p. 135.

E7.  *Contemporary Authors. New Revision Series.* Vol. 39. Edited by Susan Trosky. Detroit: Gale Research Co., 1992, p. 102.

E8.  *Directory of American Scholars 4th ed.* Vol. 4, *Philosophy, Religion & Law.* Edited by Jaques Cattell Press. New York: R. R. Browker Co., 1964, p. 51.

E9.  *Directory of American Scholars 5th ed.* Vol. 4, *Philosophy, Religion & Law.* Edited by Jaques Cattell Press. New York: R. R. Browker Co., 1969, p. 95.

E10.  *Directory of American Scholars 6th ed.* Vol. 4, *Philosophy, Religion & Law.* Edited by Jaques Cattell Press. New York: R. R. Browker Co., 1974, p. 110.

E11.  *Directory of American Scholars 7th ed.* Vol. 4, *Philosophy, Religion & Law.* Edited by Jaques Cattell Press. New York: R. R. Browker Co., 1978, p. 121.

E12.  *Directory of American Scholars 8th ed.* Vol. 4, *Philosophy, Religion & Law.* Edited by Jaques Cattell Press. New York: R. R. Browker Co., 1982, p. 136.

E13.  *The International Authors and Writers Who's Who 9th ed.* Edited by Adrian Gaster. Cambridge, England: International Biographical Centre, 1982, p. 170.

E14.  *The International Authors and Writers Who's Who. 12th ed.* Editorial Director Ernest Kay. Cambridge, England: International Biographical Centre, Melrose Press, Ltd., 1991, p. 234.

E15.  *Who's Who in the South and Southwest. 13th ed. 1973-1974.* St. Louis: Hoffmann Press, 1973, p. 203.

E16.  *Who's Who in America 1978-1979. 40th ed.* Vol. 1. Chicago: Marquis Who's Who Inc., 1978, p. 909.

E17.  *Who's Who in America 1980-1981. 41st ed.* Vol. 1. Chicago: Marquis Who's Who Inc., 1980, p. 942.

E18.  *Who's Who in America 1982-1983. 42nd ed.* Vol. 1. Chicago: Marquis Who's Who Inc., 1982, p. 897.

E19.  *Who's Who in America 1984-1985. 43rd ed.* Vol. 1. Chicago: Marquis Who's Who Inc., 1984, p. 895.

E20.  *Who's Who in America 1986-1987. 44th ed.* Vol. 1. Wilmette, IL: Marquis Who's Who, MacMillian Directory Division, 1986, p. 768.

E21.  *Who's Who in America 1988-1989. 45th ed.* Vol. 1. Wilmette, IL: Marquis Who's Who, MacMillian Directory Division,1988, p. 845.

E22.  *Who's Who in America 1990-1991. 46th ed.* Vol. 1. Wilmette, IL: Marquis Who's Who, MacMillian Directory Division,1990, p. 895.

E23.  *Who's Who in America 1992-1993. 47th ed.* Vol. 1. New Providence, NJ: Marquis Who's Who, A Reed Reference Pub. Co., 1992, p. 933.

E24.  *Who's Who in America 1994. 48th ed.* Vol. 1. New Providence, NJ: Marquis Who's Who, A Reed Reference Pub. Co., 1993, p. 952.

E25.  *Who's Who in America 1995. 49th ed.* Vol. 1. New Providence, NJ: Marquis Who's Who, A Reed Reference Pub. Co., 1994, p. 1016.

E26.  *Who's Who in America 1996. 50th ed.* Vol. 1. New Providence, NJ: Marquis Who's Who, A Reed Reference Pub. Co., 1995, p. 1132.

E27. *Who's Who in America 1997. 51ˢᵗ ed.* Vol. 1. New Providence, NJ: Marquis Who's Who, a division of Reed Elsevier Inc., 1996, p. 1152.

E28. *The Writers Directory 1974-76. 2ⁿᵈ ed.* New York: St. Martin's Press; London: St. James Press, 1973, p. 222.

E29. *The Writers Directory 1976-78 3ʳᵈ ed.* New York: St. Martin's Press; London: St. James Press, 1976, p. 291.

E30. *The Writers Directory 1980-82. 4ᵗʰ ed.* New York: St. Martin's Press, 1979, p. 343.

E31. *The Writers Directory 1982-84. 5ᵗʰ ed.* Detroit: Gale Research Co., 1981, p. 263.

E32. *The Writers Directory 1984-86. 6ᵗʰ ed.* Chicago: St. James Press, 1983, p. 274.

E33. *The Writers Directory 1986-88. 7ᵗʰ ed.* Chicago: St. James Press, 1986, p. 265.

E34. *The Writers Directory 1988-90. 8ᵗʰ ed.* Chicago: St. James Press, 1988, p. 268.

E35. *The Writers Directory 1990-92. 9ᵗʰ ed.* Chicago: St. James Press, 1990, p. 281.

E36. *The Writers Directory 1992-94. 10ᵗʰ ed.* Chicago: St. James Press, 1991, p. 272.

E37. *The Writers Directory. 1994-96. 11ᵗʰ ed.* Detroit: St. James Press, 1994, p. 343.

E38. *The Writers Directory. 1996-98. 12ᵗʰ ed.* Detroit: St. James Press, 1996, p. 416.

# BIBLIOGRAPHY OF ADDITIONAL SOURCES

Alston, William. "Tillich's Conception of a Religious Symbol." In *Religious Experience and Truth: A Symposium*. Edited by Sidney Hook. New York: New York University Press, 1961, pp. 12-26.

Altizer, Thomas J. J. *The Gospel of Christian Atheism*. Philadelphia: Westminster Press, 1966.

Aquinas, Thomas. *Scriptum super libros sententiarum magistri Petri Lombardi*. Edited by R. Mandonnet. Vol. 1. Paris: P. Lethielleux, 1929.

——. *On the Power of God*. Vol. 3. Translated by The English Dominican Fathers. Westminster, MD: Newman Press, 1952.

——. *Summa contra Gentiles*. Translated by Anton Pegis. Vol. 1. Notre Dame, IN: University of Notre Dame Press, 1975.

——. *Summa Theologiae: Latin Text and English Translation*. Translated by Blackfriars. New York: McGraw-Hill; London: Eyre & Spottiswoode, 1964.

Arbuckle, Gerald. "Communicating Through Ritual." *Human Development* 9 (Summer 1988): 21-26.

Aristotle. *Metaphysics*. In *Aristotle*. Vol. 17, *The Metaphysics I, Books I-IX*. The Loeb Classical Library. Edited by T. Page. Translated by Hugh Tredennick. London: William Heinemann; Cambridge: Harvard University Press, 1933.

——. *Nicomachean Ethics*. In *Aristotle*. Vol. 19. The Loeb Classical Library 73. Edited by E. Warmington. Translated by H. Rackham. London: William Heinemann; Cambridge: Harvard University Press, 1934².

——. *Physics*. In *Aristotle: The Physics*. Vol. 1. The Loeb Classical Library. Translated by Philip Wicksteed and Francis Cornford. London: William Heinemann; Cambridge: Harvard University Press, 1957².

Augustine. *Confessions*. Translated by Henry Chadwick. Oxford: Oxford University Press, 1991.

——. *Quaestionum in Heptateuchum libri septem*. In *Corpus Christianorum, Series Latina*. Vol. 33. Edited by I. Fraipoint. Turnhout: Brepols, 1958.

——. *On the Trinity*. In *A Selected Library of the Nicene and Post-Nicene Fathers of the Christian Church*. First Series. Vol. 3. Edited by Philip Schaff. Translated by Arthur Haddan and revised by William Shedd. New York, 1887.

Bellah, Robert. *Beyond Belief: Essays on Religion in a Post-Traditional World*. New York: Harper & Row, 1970.

——. "Transcendence in Contemporary Piety." In *The Religious Situation: 1969*. Edited by Donald Cutler. Boston: Beacon Press, 1969, pp. 896-909; revised version printed in *Transcendence*. Edited by Herbert Richardson and Donald Cutler. Boston: Beacon Press, 1969, pp. 85-97.

Benedict, Ruth. *Patterns of Culture*. New York: Houghton Mifflin, 1934.

Benveniste, Émile. "Le jeu comme structure." *Deucalion* 2 (1947): 161-167.

Berger, Peter. *Facing up to Modernity: Excursions in Society, Politics and Religion*. New York: Basic Books, 1977.

——. *A Rumor of Angels: Modern Society and the Rediscovery of the Supernatural*. Garden City: Doubleday, 1969.

——. *The Sacred Canopy: Elements of a Sociological Theory of Religion*. Garden City, NY: Doubleday, 1967.

Berry, Donald. "Religion as a Point of View." *Perspectives in Religious Studies* 9 (Fall 1982): 209-227, especially 209-227.

Bonaventure. *The Mind's Road to God*. Library of Liberal Arts 32. Translated by George Boas. Indianapolis: Bobbs-Merrill, 1953.

Bouillard, Henri. "La catégorie du sacré dans la science des religions." In *Le sacré: études et recherches*. Actes du XIVᵉ Colloque Organisé par le Centre International d'Études Humanistes et l'Institut d'Études Philosophiques de Rome. Edited by Enrico Castelli. Paris: Aubier, 1974, pp. 42-50.

Braithwaite, R. B. *An Empiricist's View of the Nature of Religion*. Cambridge: Cambridge University Press, 1955.

Bremond, Henri. *A Literary History of Religious Thought in France*. Vol. 1, *Devout Humanism*. Translated by K. Montgomery. New York: Macmillan, 1928.

Brown, Raymond. *The Gospel According to John*. The Anchor Bible 29-29A. 2 vols. Garden City, NY: Doubleday, 1966; London: Geoffrey Chapman, 1971.

—. "Hermeneutics." In *The New Jerome Biblical Commentary*. Edited by Raymond Brown, Joseph Fitzmyer, and Roland Murphy. Englewood Cliffs, NJ: Prentice Hall, 1990, pp. 1146-1165.

Bultmann, Rudolf. *The Gospel of John: A Commentary*. Translated by G. Beasley-Murray. Oxford: Basil Blackwell, 1971.

Cairns, David. *God Up There? A Study in Divine Transcendence*. Philadelphia: Westminster Press; Edinburgh: St. Andrew Press, 1967.

Cajetan, Thomas. *Summa Theologiae cum Commentariis Caietani*. In Thomas Aquinas. *Opera Omnia*. Edited by Pope Leo XIII. Vols. 4-12. Rome: S. C. de Propaganda fide, 1888-1906.

Cassirer, Ernst. *An Essay on Man*. New Haven, CT: Yale University Press, 1944.

—. *Language and Myth*. New York: Dover, 1953.

—. *The Philosophy of Symbolic Forms*. 3 vols. Translated by Ralph Manheim New Haven, CT: Yale University Press, 1953-1957.

—. "Davos Disputation Between Ernst Cassirer and Martin Heidegger [1929]." In Martin Heidegger, *Kant and the Problem of Metaphysics*. Translated by Richard Taft. Bloomington, IN: Indiana University Press, 1990, pp. 171-185.

Cognet, Louis. *Introduction aux mystiques rhéno-flamands*. Paris: Desclée, 1968.

Collins, James. *God in Modern Philosophy*. London: Routledge & Kegan Paul, 1960.

Cox, Harvey. *The Feast of Fools: A Theological Essay on Festivity and Fantasy*. Cambridge: Harvard University Press, 1969.

—. *Religion in the Secular City: Toward a Postmodern Theology*. New York: Simon & Schuster, A Touchstone Book, 1984.

—. *The Secular City*. New York: Macmillan, 1965.

Csikszentmihalyi, Mihaly. *The Evolving Self: A Psychology for the Third Millennium*. New York: Harper Collins, 1993.

Cupitt, Don. *Taking Leave of God*. London: SCM Press; New York: Crossroad, 1980.

Daniel-Rops, Henri. *The Church in the Seventeenth Century*. Translated by J. Buckingham. Vol. 1. Garden City, NY: Doubleday, 1965.

De Pater, Wim. "Analogy, Disclosure, and Narrative Theology." Translated by David Wilken, Pro manuscripto. Louvain: Acco, 1988.

*Decrees of the Ecumenical Councils*. Vol. 2, *Trent-Vatican II*. Edited by Norman Tanner. London: Sheed & Ward; Washington, D.C.: Georgetown University Press, 1990.

Douglas, Mary. *Natural Symbols: Explorations in Cosmology*. New York: Random House, 1971[2].

Dufrenne, Mikel. *Phénoménologie de l'expérience esthétique*. Vol. 2. Paris, 1953.

Duns Scotus, John. *God and Creatures: The Quodlibetal Questions*. Translated by Felix Alluntis and Allan Wolter. Princeton: Princeton University Press, 1975.

Durkheim, Émile. *The Elementary Forms of the Religious Life*. Translated by Joseph Swain. London: Allen & Unwin, 1915.

Edwards, Paul. "Professor Tillich's Confusions." *Mind* 74 (April 1965): 192-214.

Eliade, Mircea. *Images and Symbols: Studies in Religious Symbolism*. Translated by Philip Mairet. New York: Sheed & Ward; London: Harvill Press, 1961.

—. *The Sacred and the Profane: The Nature of Religion*. Translated by Willard Trask. New York: Harcourt, Brace & World, 1959.

Eliot, T. S. *Four Quartets*. New York: Harcourt, Brace, 1944[2].

Erikson, Erik. "The Development of Ritualization." In *The Religious Situation: 1968*. Edited by Donald Cutler. Boston: Beacon Press, 1968, pp. 711- 733.

Evans-Pritchard, E. *Theories of Primitive Religion*. Oxford: Clarendon Press, 1965.

Fackenheim, Emil. *The Religious Dimension in Hegel's Thought*. London: Indiana University Press, 1967; Bloomington: Indiana University Press, 1968.

Farley, Edward. *The Transcendence of God: A Study in Contemporary Philosophical Theology*. Philadelphia: Westminster Press, 1960; London: Epworth Press, 1962.

Ferré, Frederick. *Language, Logic and God*. New York: Harper & Row, 1969.

Feuerbach, Ludwig. *The Essence of Christianity*. Translated by George Eliot. New York: Harper & Row, 1957.

Francis de Sales. *Introduction to the Devout Life*. Translated by Michael Day. Westminster, MD: Newman Press, 1956.

SYMBOLS OF TRANSCENDENCE

—. *Treatise of the Love of God.* Translated by H. Mackey. London: Greenwood Press, 1942.

Fransen, Piet. "Sacraments As Celebrations." *Irish Theological Quarterly* 43 (1976): 151- 170.

Gadamer, Hans-Georg. *Truth and Method.* Translated by Joel Weinsheimer and Donald Marshall. New York: Continuum, 1989².

Gilkey, Langdon. "Can Art Fill the Vacuum?" In *Art, Creativity, and the Sacred: An Anthology in Religion and Art.* Edited by Diane Apostolos-Cappadona. New York: Crossroad, 1984, pp. 187-192.

Greely, Andrew. *Unsecular Man.* New York: Schocken Books, 1972.

Gregory of Nyssa. *Against Eunomius.* In *Nicene and Post-Nicen Fathers.* Second Series. Vol. 5, *Gregory of Nyssa.* Translated by H. Ogle and Henry Wilson. London, 1892.

—. *In Canticum hom.* In *Gregorii Nysseni In Canticum Commentarius.* Gregorii Nysseni Opera 6. Edited by Herman Langerbeck. Leiden: Brill, 1960.

—. *Sermon on the Beatitudes*, 6. In *Gregory of Nyssenus.* Ancient Christian Writers 18. Translated by Hilda Graef. Westminster, MD: Newman, 1954.

—. *On the Soul and the Resurrection.* In *Nicene and Post-Nicene Fathers.* Second Series. Vol. 5, *Gregory of Nyssa.* Translated by Willaim Moore. London, 1892.

Hamann, Johann Georg. *Konxompax.* In *Sämtliche Werke.* Vol. 3, *Sprache, Mysterien, Vernunft 1772-1788.* Edited by Josef Nadler. Vienna: Herder, 1950.

—. *Socratic Memorabilia: A Translation and Commentary.* Translated by James O'Flaerty. Baltimore; Johns Hopkins Press, 1967.

Hamilton, Kenneth. *Revolt Against Heaven: An Enquiry Into Anti-Supernaturalism.* Grand Rapids: Eerdmans, 1965.

Hare, R. M. "Theology and Falsification." In *New Essays in Philosophical Theology.* Edited by Anthony Flew and Alasdair MacIntyre. London: SCM Press, 1955, pp. 99-103.

Hegel, G. W. F. *Hegel's Logic: Part One of the Encyclopaedia of the Philosophical Sciences with the Zusätze.* Translated by William Wallace. Oxford: Clarendon Press, 1873.

—. *Lectures on the Philosophy of Religion*. 3 vols. Edited by Peter Hodgson. Translated by R. Brown, P. Hodgson, J. Stewart. Berkeley: University of California Press, 1984-1987.

—. *The Phenomenology of Spirit*. Translated by A. Miller. Oxford: Clarendon Press, 1977.

Heidegger, Martin. *Being and Time*. Translated by John Macquarrie and Edward Robinson. Oxford: Basil Blackwell; New York: Harper and Row, 1962.

Hepburn, Ronald. "Poetry and Religious Beliefs." In *Metaphysical Beliefs*. Edited by Stephen Toulmin. London: SCM Press, 1957, pp. 75-156.

Herman, Francis. *Histoire doctrinale de l'humanisme chrétien*. 4 vols. Tournai: Casterman, 1947.

Hilary of Poitiers. *Tractatus Mysteriorum*. In *Corpus Scriptorum Ecclesiasticorum Latinorum*. Vol. 65. Edited by Alfred Feder. Vienna: F. Tempsky, 1916, pp. 1-38.

Horkheimer, Max. *The Eclipse of Reason*. New York: Continuum, 1947.

Huizinga, Johan. *Homo Ludens: A Study of the Play Element in Culture*. Translated by R. F. C. Hull. London: Kegan Paul, 1949.

Ignatius of Loyola. *The Spiritual Exercises*. In *Ignatius of Loyola: Spiritual Exercises and Selected Works*. The Classics of Western Spirituality. Translated by George Ganss. New York: Paulist Press, 1991.

James, William. *The Varieties of Religious Experience*. The Gifford Lectures 1901-1902. London: Longman, Green, 1902.

John of the Cross. *The Ascent of Mount Carmel*. In *The Complete Works of St. John of the Cross*. Translated by E. Allison Peers. Vol. 1. Westminster, MD: Newman, 1933.

Jones, Cheslyn. "Mysticism, Human and Divine." In *The Study of Spirituality*. Edited by Cheslyn Jones, Geoffrey Wainwright, and Edward Yarnold. London: SPCK, 1986, pp. 17-24.

Kant, Immanuel. *Critique of Judgment*. Translated by Werner Pluhar. Indianapolis: Hackett, 1987.

—. *Immanuel Kant's Critique of Pure Reason*. Translated by Norman Kemp Smith. London: Macmillan, 1933[2].

Kaufman, Gordon. "On the Meaning of 'God': Transcendence Without Mythology." In *New Theology No. 4*. Edited by Martin Marty and Dean Peerman. New York: Macmillan, 1967, pp. 69-98.

Kierkegaard, Søren. Pseudonym Johannes Climacus. *Concluding Unscientific Postscript to* Philosophical Fragments. Vol. 1, *Text*. Kierkegaard's Writings 12.1. Edited and translated by Howard Hong and Edna Hong. Princeton, NJ: Princeton University Press, 1992.

—. *Søren Kierkegaard's Journals and Papers*. Vol. 3. Edited and translated by Howard Hong and Edna Hong. Bloomington, IN: Indiana University Press.

Knitter, Paul. "Jesus—Buddha—Krishna: Still Present?" *Journal of Ecumenical Studies* 16 (Fall 1979): 651-671.

Langer, Susanne. *Feeling and Form: A Theory of Art Developed From Philosophy in a New Key*. London: Routledge & Kegan Paul, 1953.

—. *Mind: An Essay on Human Feeling*. Vol. 1. Baltimore: Johns Hopkins Press, 1967.

—. *Philosophy in a New Key: A Study in the Symbolism of Reason, Rite, and Art*. Cambridge: Harvard University Press, 1942, 1957[3].

—. *Problems of Art*. New York: Charles Scribner's Sons, 1957.

Leijssen, Lambert. "La contribution de Karl Rahner (1904-1984) au renouvellement de la sacramentaire." *Questions Liturgiques/ Studies in Liturgy* 75 (1994): 84-102.

Lévi-Strauss, Claude. *The Raw and the Cooked*. Introduction to a Science of Mythology 1. Translated by John and Doreen Weightman. London: Jonathan Cape, 1970.

—. *The Savage Mind*. The Nature of Human Society Series. No trans. London: Weidenfeld, 1972[2].

Lonergan, Bernard. *Method in Theology*. New York: Herder & Herder, 1973[2].

Malinowski, Bronislaw. *Magic, Science and Religion*. Doubleday Anchor Books A23. Garden City, NY: Doubleday, 1954.

Mander, Jerry. *In the Absence of the Sacred: The Failure of Technology and the Survival of the Indian Nations*. San Francisco: Sierra Club Books, 1991.

Martin, F. David. *Art and the Religious Experience*. Lewisburg, PA: Bucknell University Press, 1972.

McInerny, Ralph. *The Logic of Analogy*. Notre Dame: University of Notre Dame Press, 1961.

McPherson, Thomas. "Religion as the Inexpressible." In *New Essays in Philosophical Theology*. Edited by Anthony Flew and Alasdair MacIntyre. London: SCM Press, 1955, pp. 131-143.

Mitchell, Leonel. *The Meaning of Ritual*. Wilton, CT: Morehouse-Barlow, 1977.

Moore, Thomas. *Care of the Soul: A Guide for Cultivating Depth and Sacredness in Everyday Life*. New York: Harper Collins, 1992.

*New Revised Standard Version Bible*. New York: Oxford University Press, 1989.

Nietzsche, Friedrich. *The Birth of Tragedy*. Translated by Francis Golffing. Garden City, NY: Doubleday, 1956.

—. *Thus Spoke Zarathustra*. Translated by R. Hollingdale. London: Penguin Books, 1961.

Nisbet, Robert. *The Social Bond*. New York: Knopf, 1970.

Origen. *Commentary on the Song of Songs*. In *Origen: The Song of Songs Commentary and Homilies*. Ancient Christian Writers 26. Translated by R. Lawson. Westminster, MD: The Newman Press, 1957.

—. *First Principles*. In *The Ante-Nicene Fathers*. Edited by Alexander Roberts and James Donaldson. Vol. 4. Edinburgh, 1885.

—. *In Numeros homiliae*. In *Die Griechischen christlichen Schriftsteller*. Vol. 30, *Origenes 7*. Leipzig: Hinrichs'sche Buchhandlung, 1921.

Panikkar, Raimundo. "Man As a Ritual Being." *Chicago Studies* 16 (Spring 1977): 5-28.

Phillips, Dewi. "Faith, Scepticism and Religious Understanding." In *Religion and Understanding*. Edited by Dewi Phillips. Oxford: Basil Blackwell, 1967, pp. 63-79.

Plato. *The Laws*. Book 10. In *Plato: In Twelve Volumes*. Vol. 11, *Laws II, Books VII-XII*. The Loeb Classical Library 192. Edited by E. Warmington. Translated by R. Bury. London: William Heinemann; Cambridge: Harvard University Press, 1926.

Prufer, Thomas. *Recapitulations: Essays in Philosophy*. Studies in Philosophy and the History of Philosophy 26. Washington, D.C.: The Catholic University of America Press, 1993.

Pseudo-Dionysius. *The Divine Names*. In *Pseudo-Dionysius: The Complete Works*. The Classics of Western Spirituality. Translated by Colm Luibheid. New York: Paulist Press, 1987, pp 47-131.

—. *The Mystical Theology*. In *Pseudo-Dionysius: The Complete Works*. The Classics of Western Spirituality. Translated by Colm Luibheid. New York: Paulist Press, 1987, pp. 133-141.

Quasten, Johannes. *Patrology*. 4 vols. Utrecht: Spectrum, 1950.

Rahner, Karl. "Philosophy and Philosophising in Theology." In *Theological Investigations*. Vol. 9, *Writings of 1965-1967 I*. Translated by Graham Harrison. London: Darton, Longman & Todd, 1972, pp. 46-63.

—. "Philosophy and Theology." In *Theological Investigations*. Vol. 6, *Concerning Vatican Council II*. Translated by Karl-H. and Boniface Kruger. London: Darton, Longman & Todd, 1969, pp. 71-81.

—. "The Theology of the Symbol." In *Theological Investigations*. Vol. 4, *More Recent Writings*. Translated by Kevin Smyth. London: Darton, Longman & Todd, 1966, pp. 235-245.

—. "What is a Sacrament." In *Theological Investigations*. Vol. 14, *Ecclesiology, Questions in the Church, The Church in the World*. Translated by David Bourke. London: Darton, Longman & Todd, 1976, pp. 135-148.

—. "The Word and the Eucharist." In *Theological Investigations*. Vol. 4, *More Recent Writings*. Translated by Kevin Smyth. London: Darton, Longman & Todd, 1966, pp. 253-286.

Ramsey, Ian. *Models and Mystery*. The Whidden Lectures 1963. London: Oxford University Press, 1964.

—. *Religious Language: An Empirical Placing of Theological Phrases*. New York: Macmillan; 1957.

—. "Some Further Reflections on Freedom and Immortality." *The Hibbert Journal* 59 (1960-61): 348-355.

Randall, John. *The Role of Knowledge in Western Religion*. Boston: Starr King Press, 1958.

Ricoeur, Paul. *Interpretation Theory*. Forth Worth: Texas Christian University Press, 1976.

Robinson, John A. T. *Honest to God*. Philadelphia: Westminster Press, 1963.

Rorty, Richard. *Essays on Heidegger and Others*. Philosophical Papers 2. Cambridge: Cambridge University Press, 1991.

Rowe, William. *Religious Symbols and God: A Philosophical Study of Tillich's Theology*. Chicago: The University of Chicago Press, 1968.

Schillebeeckx, Edward. *Christ the Sacrament of the Encounter with God.* Translated by Paul Barrett, Mark Schoof, and Laurence Bright. London: Sheed & Ward, 1963.

—. *Church: The Human Story of God.* Translated by John Bowden. London: SCM Press; New York: Crossroad, 1990.

—. *Interim Report on the Books* Jesus *and* Christ. Translated by John Bowden. New York: Crossroad, 1981.

—. *De sacramentele heilseconomie: Theologische bezinning op S. Thomas' sacramentenleer in het licht van de traditie en van de hedendaagse sacramentsproblematiek.* Antwerp-Bilhoven: 't Groeit, 1952.

Schlatter, Adolf. *Der Evangelist Johannes.* Stuttgart: Calwer, 1930.

Schleiermacher, Friedrich. *The Christian Faith.* Translated by H. Mackintosh and J. Stewart. Edinburgh: T. & T. Clark, 1928.

—. *On Religion: Speeches to Its Cultured Despisers.* Translated by John Oman. London: Routledge & Kegan Paul, 1893.

Schnackenburg, Rudolf. *The Gospel According to St. John.* Translated by Kevin Smyth. Vol. 1. New York: Crossroad, 1987.

Smart, J. J. C. "The Existence of God." In *New Essays in Philosophical Theology.* Edited by Anthony Flew and Alasdair MacIntyre. London: SCM Press, 1955, pp. 28-46.

Smith, Jonathan. "The Wobbling Pivot." *The Journal of Religion* 52 (April 1972): 134-149.

Smith, W. Robertson. *Lectures on the Religion of the Semites.* Burnett Lectures 1888-1889. London: Black, 1927[3].

Spiegelberg, Herbert. *The Phenomenological Movement: A Historical Introduction.* Phaenomenologica 5. The Hague: Martinus Nijhoff, 1982[3].

Strauss, Leo. *Natural Right and History.* Chicago: The University of Chicago Press, 1950.

Sylvester of Ferrara. *Summa contra Gentiles cum Commentariis Ferrariensis.* In Thomas Aquinas. *Opera Omnia.* Edited by Pope Leo XIII. Vols. 13-15. Rome: Riccardi Garroni, 1918-1930.

Tillich, Paul. "The Religious Symbol." Translated by James Adams with Ernst Fraenkel. *The Journal of Liberal Religion* 2 (Summer 1940): 13-33. Reprint in *Symbolism in Religion and Literature.* Edited by Rollo May. New York: George Braziller, 1960, pp. 75-98. Also reprint in *Religious Experience and Truth: A Symposium.* Edited by Sidney Hook. New York: New York University Press, 1961, pp. 301-321.

—. *Systematic Theology*. 3 vols. Chicago: The University of Chicago Press, 1951- 1963.

Tomas, Vincent. "Aesthetic Vision." In *Aesthetics and the Philosophy of Criticism*. Edited by Marvin Levich. New York: Randam House, 1963.

Tracy, David. *Blessed Rage for Order: The New Pluralism in Theology*. New York: Seabury Press, 1975.

Turner, Victor. *Dramas, Fields and Metaphors: Symbolic Action in Human Society*. Ithaca: Cornell University Press, 1974.

Underhill, Evelyn. *Mysticism*. London: Methuen, 1930[12].

Urs von Balthasar, Hans. *The Glory of the Lord: A Theological Aesthetics*. 7 vols. Edited by Joseph Fessio and John Riches. Translated by Erasmo Leiva-Merikakis. Edinburgh: T. & T. Clark; San Francisco: Ignatius Press, 1982-1991.

van Buren, Paul. *The Secular Meaning of the Gospel*. London: SCM Press, 1963.

Van der Leeuw, Gerardus. *Religion in Essence and Manifestation: A Study in Phenomen ology*. Translated by J. Turner. London: Allen & Unwin, 1938. Reprinted in two vols., with additions of the second German edition by Hans Penner, New York: Harper & Row, 1963.

—. *Sacred and Profane Beauty: The Holy in Art*. Translated by David Green. New York: Holt, Rinehart & Winston, 1963.

Van Roo, William. *Man the Symbolizer*. Analecta Gregoriana 222. Rome: Gregorian University Press, 1981.

—. "Symbol According to Cassirer and Langer— I." *Gregorianum* 53 (1972): 487- 530.

—. "Symbol According to Cassirer and Langer— II-III." *Gregorianum* 53 (1972): 654-668.

van Ruusbroec, Jan. *The Sparkling Stone*. English and Latin translation with Middle Dutch original. In *Corpus Christianorum, Continuatio Mediaevalis*. Vol. 110. Edited by G. de Baere, Th. Mertens and H. Noë. Introduction by Th. Mertens and P. Mommaers. Translated by A. Lefevere. Turnhout: Brepols; Tielt: Lannoo, 1991.

—. *The Spiritual Espousals*. English and Latin translation with Middle Dutch original. In *Corpus Christianorum, Continuatio Mediaevalis*. Vol. 103. Edited by J. Alaerts. Introduction by P. Mommaers. Translated by H. Rolfson. Turnhout: Brepolis; Tielt: Lannoo, 1988.

Vander Kerken, Libert. "De religieuze beleving als voorstelling." *Tijdschrift voor Philosophie* 34 (March 1972): 3-24.

Vergote, Antoine. "Secularized Man and Christian Rite." *Louvain Studies* 2 (Fall 1968): 141-157.

—. "Symbolic Gestures and Actions in the Liturgy." Translated by Barbara Wall, in *Concilium.* Vol. 2/7, *Worship of Christian Man Today.* Edited by Herman Schmidt. London: Burns & Oates, 1971, pp. 40-52.

Vroom, Hendrik. *Religions and the Truth: Philosophical Reflections and Perspective.* Translated by J. Rebel. Grand Rapids, MI: Eerdmans, 1989.

Watson, Burton. "Introduction." In *Hsün Tzu: Basic Writings.* Translated by Burton Watson. New York: Columbia University Press, 1963, pp. 1-14.

William of St. Thierry. *The Golden Epistle: A Letter to the Brethren at Mont Dieu.* Cistercian Fathers Series 12. Translated by Theodore Berkeley. Kalamazoo, MI: Cistercian Publications, 1980.

# INDEX OF NAMES

Hilary of Poitiers, 117
Horkheimer, M., 208n
Huizinga, J., 140-142
Ignatius of Loyola, 188, 250-253, 256, 257, 258n
James, W., 4, 13
John of the Cross, 18, 25n, 50, 258n, 262
Jones, C., 13n
Kant, I., 31-33, 61-64, 69, 91, 92, 122, 209, 215
Kaufman, G., 245, 246
Kierkegaard, S., 31, 107-110, 112, 137, 280
Knitter, P., 136-138
Lamberts, J., xvii
Langer, S., 31, 60, 61, 63n, 64n, 70-76, 85, 90, 95, 97, 122, 184, 279
Leijssen, L., xvii, 98n
Lévi-Strauss, C., 132, 143, 175
Lonergan, B., 50n
McInerny, R., 106
MacIntyre, A., 100n, 217
McPherson, T., 99, 100
Malinowski, B., 133n
Mander, J., 241n
Martin, F. D., 158n
Merrigan, T., xvii
Mitchell, L., 230n
Moore, T., 262n
Nietzsche, F., 129, 130n, 215-218, 224
Nisbet, R., 247n
Ockham, W., 200, 212
Origen, 20-22, 117
Panikkar, R., 126
Pascal, B., 244
Phillips, D., 4
Plato, 65, 80, 88, 134, 180, 192, 208
Prufer, T., 191n

Pseudo-Dionysius, 22, 23, 262
Quasten, J., 21n
Rahner, K., 20n, 30n, 50n, 98, 151, 153
Ramsey, I., 110-112
Randall, J., 102n, 217
Ricoeur, P., 60
Robinson, J., 244, 245
Rorty, R., 215, 217
Rowe, W., 122n
Schillebeeckx, E., 147, 150, 265, 266
Schlatter, A., 19n
Schleiermacher, F., 1, 31-37, 41n, 45, 158, 184, 279
Schnackenburg, R., 18n
Smart, J. J. C., 99, 100
Smith, J., 176n
Spiegelberg, H., 52n, 53n
Strauss, L., 132, 143, 175, 191n, 217
Sylvester of Ferrara, 201n
Tillich, P., 114, 120-122
Tomas, V., 155, 156
Tracy, D., 37n, 47n
Turner, V., 8n, 230n, 231n
Underhill, E., 18n, 28n, 29
Urs von Balthasar, H., 17n, 89, 154, 280
van Buren, P., 6, 242, 243, 244n, 247
Van der Leeuw, G., 8n, 53, 54n, 55n, 143, 161n, 163, 166n, 169
Van Roo, W., 63n, 64n
van Ruusbroec, J., 11, 18n, 22, 26, 28, 29, 60, 258n
Vander Kerken, L., 41n
Vergote, A., 49n, 125-127, 263n
Voegelin, E., 217
Vroom, H., 48n
Watson, B., 128n
William of St. Thierry, 28, 139

PRINTED ON PERMANENT PAPER • IMPRIME SUR PAPIER PERMANENT • GEDRUKT OP DUURZAAM PAPIER - ISO 9706

ORIENTALISTE, KLEIN DALENSTRAAT 42, B-3020 HERENT